The Nanyang Revolution

In this innovative reading, the development of the Malayan Communist Party (MCP) is explored in the context of an emerging nationalism in Southeast Asia, the interplay of overseas Chinese networks and the Comintern. Based on extensive new archival material, Anna Belogurova shows how the MCP was shaped by the historical contingencies of anti-imperialism in Southeast Asia, long-term Chinese migration trends, networks, identity, and the organizational practices of the Comintern. This is the story of how a group of left-leaning Chinese migrant intellectuals engaged with global forces to create a relevant and lasting Malayan national identity, providing fresh international perspectives on the history of Malaysia, Chinese communism, the Cold War, and decolonization.

Anna Belogurova is a research fellow at the Institute for China Studies, the Free University of Berlin.

T0384592

The Nanyang Revolution

The Comintern and Chinese Networks in Southeast Asia, 1890–1957

Anna Belogurova

Free University of Berlin

CAMBRIDGE
UNIVERSITY PRESS

CAMBRIDGE
UNIVERSITY PRESS

University Printing House, Cambridge CB2 8BS, United Kingdom

One Liberty Plaza, 20th Floor, New York, NY 10006, USA

477 Williamstown Road, Port Melbourne, VIC 3207, Australia

314-321, 3rd Floor, Plot 3, Splendor Forum, Jasola District Centre, New Delhi - 110025, India

103 Penang Road, #05-06/07, Visioncrest Commercial, Singapore 238467

Cambridge University Press is part of the University of Cambridge.

It furthers the University's mission by disseminating knowledge in the pursuit of education, learning and research at the highest international levels of excellence.

www.cambridge.org
Information on this title: www.cambridge.org/9781108458184
DOI: 10.1017/9781108635059

First published 2019
First paperback edition 2022

A catalogue record for this publication is available from the British Library

Library of Congress Cataloging in Publication data
Names: Belogurova, A. E. (Anna Eduardovna), author.
Title: The Nanyang revolution : the Comintern and Chinese networks in Southeast Asia, 1890–1957 / Anna Eduardovna Belogurova.
Description: Cambridge ; New York : Cambridge University Press, 2018. | Includes bibliographical references.
Identifiers: LCCN 2019004120 | ISBN 9781108471657
Subjects: LCSH: Malayan Communist Party – History. | Communist International – History. | Malaysia – Politics and government – 20th century. | Communism – Malaysia – History. | Chinese – Malaysia – History – 20th century. | China – Relations – Malaysia. | Malaysia – Relations – China. | China – Politics and government – 1912–1949.
Classification: LCC JQ1062.A98 M3627 2018 | DDC 959.5/03–dc23
LC record available at https://lccn.loc.gov/2019004120

ISBN 978-1-108-47165-7 Hardback
ISBN 978-1-108-45818-4 Paperback

Contents

Figures and Tables

Acknowledgments

I have accumulated many debts of gratitude while working on this project. It would not have been completed without the help and encouragement of many people, first and foremost my PhD advisor at the University of British Columbia (UBC), Timothy Cheek, as well as my dissertation committee members, Glen Peterson and John Roosa. I also owe much to the late Ivan Avakumovic.

This project has been shaped by the intellectual atmosphere at UBC and within the field of China studies in British Columbia in general, and by conversations with my teachers and peers: Timothy Brook, Abidin Kusno, Diana Lary, Hyung Gu Lynn, Paul Rae, Paul Evans, Alison Bailey, Steven Lee, Daniel Overmyer, Carla Nappi, Jeffrey Byrne, Jessica Main, Craig Smith, Alex Ong, Huang Xin, Li Hua, Jack Hayes, Tim Sedo, David Luesink, Jamie Sedgwick, Victor Zatsepine, Desmond Cheung, Malcolm Thomson, Frederik Vermote, Dominic Yang, Colin Green, Tom Peotto, and the late Susan Hicks, as well as Jeremy Brown at Simon Fraser University and Chen Zhongping at the University of Victoria.

This project would also not have been possible without access to sources in archives and libraries. My gratitude goes to Konstantin Markovich Tertitskii, Moscow State University, for introducing me to the Russian State Archive of Sociopolitical History (RGASPI), and to those who helped me there: Valeriy Nikolaevich Shepelev, Svetlana Markovna Rozental, Larisa Ivanovna Reshetilo, Yuriy Petrovich Ivanov, Valentina Nikolaevna Shechilina, Iuri Tikhonovich Tutochkin, and Irina Nikolaevna Selezneva. My heartfelt thanks go to Liu Jing and Eleanor Yuen at the UBC Asian Library, who warmly provided support with Chinese sources over the years, as well as to UBC's interlibrary loan department. I also extend my thanks for guidance and help in accessing sources to Lin Hsiao-ting at the Hoover Archives, Paul Rae and Yeap Chong Leng at the National University of Singapore, Luo Biming at the Wang Gung Wu Library at Nanyang Technological University, Eiji Kuge at Harvard–Yenching Library, Zhang Changhong at the library of the

Southeast Asia Research Centre at Xiamen University, and Li Li at the Xiamen Overseas Chinese Museum.

I have been fortunate to have had encouragement and important feedback from Wen-hsin Yeh, Klaus Mühlhahn, Dominic Sachsenmaier, Bryna Goodman, Liu Hong, John Fitzgerald, Xu Jilin, Shen Zhihua, Joseph Tse-hei Lee, Josh Fogel, David Ownby, Verena Blechinger-Talcott, Hans van de Ven, John Mccole. Barbara Andaya Watson, and Stephen Anthony Smith, as well as Leslie James and Elisabeth Leake who not only took an interest in my project but also helped me to articulate my ideas and to convey them legibly. I am indebted to Brooks Jessup for his intellectual generosity.

I am grateful to those who listened to my ideas and read my texts at the Kruzhok of Russian and Asian History at Ludwig Maximilian University, namely Tatiana Linkhoeva, Andreas Renner, and Sören Urbansky; at the East Asian Colloquium at Brown University, especially Cynthia Brokaw, Rebecca Nedostup, Tamara Chin, Kerry Smith, and Wang Lingzhen; in the UBC China Studies Group, Global and Transregional Studies Platform at the University of Göttingen in 2017, especially Fan Xin and Lou Apolinario Antolihao. I also thank Alex Cook at the Institute of East Asian Studies at UC Berkeley in 2012; Leslie James and Elisabeth Leake, Susan Pennybacker, Arne Odd Westad, and Martin Thomas at the conference "Negotiating Independence: New directions in the History of Decolonization and the Cold War" at Trinity College, Cambridge; and Richard Chu, William McCarthy, and other co-panelists and the audience at the Philippine history panel at the annual meeting of the Association for Asian Studies conference in Washington, DC, in 2013. At Nanyang Technological University, I must thank Ong Weichong, Joey Long, the late Mr. S. R. Nathan, Leo Suryadinata, and Wang Zhenping. I also thank Wang Gungwu, Leon Comber, C. C. Chin, and Geoff Wade, as well as Huang Jianli and Portia Reyes at the National University of Singapore, and Mario I. Miclat and Alma Miclat in Manila in 2013. I thank my students at the University of Oregon and Brown University, who were often the first to hear some of the ideas that went into this book and helped me refine them with their questions.

My thanks for support of my research in Fujian and Singapore in December 2010 to Jiang Yihua at Fudan University; Wang Rigeng, Chen Zhiping, Chen Yande, Zhao Haili, and Shi Xueling at Xiamen University; Teng Phee Tan in Singapore; and He Qicai. My special thanks go also to Hong Buren at the Xiamen City Library and to party historian Chen Fang in Zhangzhou, who kindly shared his insights and recollections with me, as well as to Zhang Kan at Xiamen University and Li Xuehua at the Fujian Provincial Centre of Overseas Connections

(Fujian sheng haiwai jiaoliu xiehui) for their help on my Fuzhou research. Lin Xiaoyu and the late Ling Hanmei both kindly shared their thoughts and recollections. I would also like to thank Ms. Ling's son, Chen Yuesheng, for providing materials about his mother.

Song Hong and Yu Zhansui helped me decipher some handwritten materials. Maria Petrucci, Matthias von dem Knesebeck, and Sanjia Stroeh helped me with Japanese and some German translation and Liu Tianhan and Feng Xinyue identified some terms in Chinese. I am indebted to Julia Stützer and especially to Katrin Gengenbach and Andrea Dünschede for their support at the Free University of Berlin; Matt Fennessy at the Global and Transregional Studies Platform, the University of Göttingen; Tatiana Balanda and Margarita Ponomarenko in Moscow; and Talia Leduc. I am indebted to Deborah Rudolf for her help with the Chinese romanization and bibliography. I am grateful to Keila Diehl and Katherine Chouta for their encouragement and to Nancy Hearst for her editorial help during book production.

I thank the participants at the workshop "Beyond the Sinosphere: Modalities of Interwar Globalization: Internationalism and Indigenization among East Asian Marxists, Christians, and Buddhists, 1919–1945," hosted by the Free University of Berlin's Graduate School of East Asian Studies in Hanover, Germany, and generously funded by the Volkswagen Foundation in July 2016, for the conversation that refined my understanding of the interwar global moment. I am also grateful to Oleksa Drachewych, Ian McKay, and other participants at the workshop "Transnational Leftism: The Comintern and the National, Colonial and Racial Questions" at the L. R. Wilson Institute for Canadian History, McMaster University, September 2017, and to Yuexin Rachel Lin and other organizers and participants of the workshop "The Asian Arc of the Russian Revolution: Setting the East Ablaze?" at Yale–NUS College in November 2017 for productive discussions. The suggestions of the three anonymous reviewers and those of Lucy Rhymer at Cambridge University Press improved the book tremendously.

Work on this manuscript was supported by a POINT postdoctoral fellowship, funded by the German Excellence Initiative and the Marie Curie Program of the European Commission in 2015–2017 at the Free University of Berlin, and a postdoctoral fellowship at Nanyang Technological University, Singapore, in 2012–2013, as well as by the Global Summer Semester Residency at the Global and Transregional Studies Platform at the University of Göttingen, supported by the Social Science Research Council's InterAsia Program in 2017. Funding from the following sources made it possible for me to complete my dissertation research: the Chiang Ching-kuo Foundation, the UBC

Graduate Fellowship, the UBC Department of History Travel Fellowship, and a research grant from Timothy Cheek. I gratefully acknowledge the Institute for China Studies, Free University of Berlin, for funding the book production costs.

It is only with all of this support and with the help and encouragement of my mother, Tamara Grigorievna Remizova, and my brother, Arseny Eduardovich Belogurov, that I was able to complete this book. I dedicate this book to them and to my late father, Eduard Alekseevich Belogurov.

Note on Transliteration

All Chinese proper names are spelled using pinyin romanization with the exception of proper names which are commonly used in English in a different Romanization, i.e., Chiang Kai-shek, Canton. Names of individuals are spelled in Pinyin if the characters are known. When it was impossible to identify a person's name in Chinese characters, I used the English Romanization of their names found in the original text. For the place names that were Romanized from Mandarin or a Chinese dialect pronunciation that I was unable to identify, I used the Romanization that I found in the original English-language text and italicized it. As a rule, I provided Chinese characters only for the personal names which are commonly not available in English-language studies of the MCP. The original English language of the documents has been minimally corrected for better flow and easier understanding.

Terms and Abbreviations

AAIL	All-American Anti-Imperialist League
AEBUS	Anti-Enemy Backing-Up Society
AIL	Anti-Imperialist League(s)
ASCWPRA	Alliance for the Support of the Chinese Workers and Peasants Revolution in America
CC	Central Committee
CCP	Chinese Communist Party
CI	Communist International
CO	Colonial Office Records
CP	Communist Party
CPPI	Communist Party of the Philippine Islands
CPUSA	Communist Party of the United States of America
CYL	Communist Youth League
DEI	Dutch East Indies
ECCI	Executive Committee of the Third Communist International (the Comintern)
FEB	Far Eastern Bureau of the Comintern
FESLAI	Far Eastern Secretariat of the League Against Imperialism
GMD	Chinese Nationalist Party, Guomindang
huaqiao	Chinese overseas
ICP	Indochinese Communist Party
KMM	Kesatuan Melayu Muda (Young Malay Union)
KPD	Kommunistische Partei Deutschlands
KUTV	Kommunisticheskii universitet trudiashchikhsia Vostoka (Communist University of the Toilers of the East)
LAI	League Against Imperialism
MCA	Malayan Chinese Association
MCP	Malayan Communist Party
MFLU	Malayan Federation of Labor Unions
minzu	"nation," "nationality," "people," "national"

Minzu Guoji	"International of Nationalities"
MPAJA	Malayan Peoples' Anti-Japanese Army
MRCA	"Monthly Review of Chinese Affairs"
Nanyang	The areas of Chinese migration that roughly correspond to the contemporary English-language definition of Southeast Asia
NARA	National Archives and Records Administration
NEI	Netherlands (Dutch) East Indies
NGLU	Nanyang General Labor Union
NIANKP	Nauchno-issledovatel'skaia assotsiatsiia po izucheniiu natsional'no-kolonial'nykh problem (Academic Research Association for the Study of National-Colonial Questions)
NKVD	People's Commissariat for Internal Affairs
NPC	Nanyang Provisional Committee of the CCP
PKI	Partai Komunis Indonesia (Communist Party of Indonesia)
PPTUS	Pan-Pacific Trade Union Secretariat of the Red International of Trade Unions (Tikhookeanskii secretariat Profinterna)
PTI	Partai Tionghoa Indonesia (Chinese Party of Indonesia)
RGASPI	Rossiiskii gosudarstvennyi arkhiv sotsial'no-politicheskoi istorii (Russian State Archive of Sociopolitical History)
SCP	Siamese Communist Party
SIRD	Strategic Information Research Department
SMP	Shanghai Municipal Police
UMNO	United Malays National Organization
USSR	Union of Soviet Socialist Republics

Part I

Revolution in the Nanyang

1   Prologue
A Durian for Sun Yatsen

The world of Chinese migrant communists in Malaya is a window into interwar Chinese communist networks, which formed as Chinese communists in the Nanyang (南洋), the historical region of Chinese migration, the South Seas, spanning from Vietnam and the Philippines down to Indonesia and across the Malay Peninsula to Siam, founded communist cells and brought their compatriots to their adopted homes for employment. These networks were often built onto existing Chinese networks, and, in addition to being empowered by the Comintern, they were used by the Chinese Communist Party (CCP) and the Chinese Nationalist Party, the Guomindang (GMD), during the second united front period in the 1930s and 1940s, including for the recruitment of Eighth Route Army fighters in communist guerrilla areas in mainland China.[1] These networks also became launching pads for anti-Japanese guerrilla forces during the war in Malaya. Many members of these networks maintained connections with both the GMD and the communists in the Nanyang, as both parties continued to make a Chinese Revolution there, that is, a struggle for the political rights of the Chinese overseas, which had started in the time of Sun Yatsen. These Chinese intellectuals, mostly school teachers and journalists and editors, set for themselves the task of civilizing both the local Chinese, by making them more "Chinese" in terms of language and culture, and the locals, by liberating them from British imperialism together with the Chinese, whose economic and political rights were jeopardized by British policies.

In that world, the torn relationship between Chinese overseas, China, and their adopted motherland, as well as the longing to become local while preserving a unique form of Chineseness, is represented by the metaphor of the durian, a Southeast Asian fruit with a strong smell. In Chinese, the word for "durian" (榴 莲, *liulian*) is a homophone of the word for "to linger" (流连). A taste for durian foretold that a Chinese

---

[1] Lai, H. Mark, *Chinese American Transnational Politics* (Urbana, IL: University of Illinois Press, 2010), p. 104.

person who had come to the Nanyang was destined to stay. In 1928, Chinese writer Xu Jie (许杰), dispatched by the Central Committee of the GMD to work for the GMD newspaper *A Paper for the Benefit of the Public* (*Yiqunbao*) in Kuala Lumpur, imagined the smelly durian as a symbol of the stink of the Nanyang's capitalist society and the money-oriented mentality of Chinese hawkers.[2] Thus, in the story of Zheng He, a Chinese Muslim explorer of Southeast Asia, the durian tree was said to have grown from a latrine. Publication of Xu Jie's essay ridiculing Chinese migrants' attachment to the durian was not allowed, and since Xu was not willing to sell out his ideals, as he explained, after struggling for one year, he decided to leave the stinky world of the Nanyang. But where, he asked, would he go to leave the world of capitalism?[3] Around the same time, in 1932 the Singapore-born founder of Sun Yatsen's Revolutionary Alliance, Zhang Yongfu, moved to China. In his recollection, Sun could not stand the durian either.[4]

Regardless of Sun's taste for the durian in reality, Zhang's reminiscence was intended to demonstrate Sun's loyalty to China at a time when the GMD promoted the identification of overseas Chinese (*huaqiao* 华桥) with China. It was during this epoch that the Malayan Communist Party (Malaiya gongchandang) (MCP), consisting of former GMD and CCP members aiming to promote the Chinese Revolution, also attempted to mediate between the Chinese community and the local environments, and to indigenize by using the communist language of anticolonial liberation and by recruiting non-Chinese members into Chinese organizations. Amid the confusion of sojourning between China and the Nanyang, Chinese communists in Malaya organized themselves in ways both familiar, as Chinese organizations among sojourners had for centuries, and novel, as Bolshevik revolutionary parties. The result was a hybrid product of the interwar global moment, a mix of old and new, shaped by misunderstandings, miscommunications, and contingencies.

<hr/>

[2] Ching Fatt Yong, *Origins of Malayan Communism* (Singapore: South Sea Society, 1991), p. 43.
[3] Xu Jie, "Liulian [Durian]," in Xu Jie, *Yezi yu liulian: Zhongguo xiandai xiaopin jingdian* [*Coconut and Durian: Little Souvenirs of Contemporary China*] (Shijiazhuang: Hebei jiaoyu chubanshe, 1994), pp. 39–46.
[4] During the war, Zhang held high positions in Wang Jingwei's government and was imprisoned by the GMD for two years. He was not forgiven by old friends when he returned to Singapore in 1949 and so he moved to Hong Kong, where he lived in seclusion until his death in 1957. Liu Changping and Li Ke, *Fengyu Wanqingyuan: Buying wangque de Xinhai geming xunchen Zhang Yongfu* [*Trials and Hardships of Wangqing Garden: Meritorious Official of the Xinhai Revolution Zhang Yongfu Should Not Be Forgotten*] (Beijing: Zhongguo wenshi chubanshe, 2011), pp. 239–240; Zhang Yongfu, *Nanyang yu chuangli Minguo* [*Nanyang and the Establishment of the Republic*] (Shanghai: Zhonghua shuju, 1933), p. 99.

Although the MCP was a predominantly Chinese overseas organization, it was rooted in the regional historical experience of Southeast Asian forms of organization in response to a shared set of challenges that came with colonialism. Similar to 1920s' Java, we can see in Malaya that a new sense of agency was expressed in languages and forms that were novel at the time, "but at the same time based on the old ones," such as newspapers, rallies, strikes, parties, and ideologies.[5] Similar to leftist Chinese immigrant intellectuals in Malaya, journalists in Java assumed new roles aside from being editors, writers, and commentators on readers' letters: they talked at rallies and negotiated between the authorities and members of the political parties.[6] Similar to the MCP's translation of national categories, a transformation of the national consciousness, *pergerakan*, was a process of translation and appropriation that "allowed people to say in new forms and languages what they had been unable to say."[7] Similar to *pergerakan*, which involved the rise of Indonesian nationalism and the imagery of a free world in pan-Islamic and pan-communist terms, the MCP imagined its nation as part of a world liberated from colonialism.

In response to imperialism, across maritime Southeast Asia new ideas of nationalism and radicalism were grafted onto existing concepts and organizational forms, which shaped the hybridization of anti-imperialist and labor organizations. Independence ideas were translated through the religious appeal and social relevance of a Christian narrative among Philippine peasants into the early 1900s; the historical relationship between the middle-class leadership, landownership, the Catholic Church, and the revolutionary societies such as Katipunan, secret societies akin to Freemasonry, and early labor organizations[8] resulted in the active participation of secret society members in the communist party. Javanese Muslims joined forces with the Partai Komunis Indonesia (PKI) because communism offered the best way of practicing Islam.[9] The worlds of Christianity, Islam, communism, and nationalism intersected. It was the Comintern's Bolshevization that was to remedy such hybridity and, common to the communist parties of the 1930s, the divide between elite communists and labor movements and the party and "the masses." Bolshevization also involved the adaptation of policies to local conditions, that is, indigenization.

---

[5] Takashi Shiraishi, *An Age in Motion: Popular Radicalism in Java, 1912–1926* (Ithaca, NY: Cornell University Press, 1990), pp. xiii–xiv.

[6] Ibid., p. 59.

[7] Ibid., pp. 339–340.

[8] Ken Fuller, *Forcing the Pace: The Partido Komunista ng Pilipinas: From the Founding to the Armed Struggle* (Diliman, Quezon City: University of the Philippines Press, 2007), pp. 10–11; Reynaldo Clemeña Ileto, *Pasyon and revolution: Popular movements in the Philippines, 1840–1910* (Quezon City: Ateneo de Manila University Press, 1979).

[9] Shiraishi, *An Age in Motion*, pp. 244, 249.

The MCP's history and the discourse of its Malayan nation were an illustration of the global connections of the interwar period and the products of the prevailing global trends of internationalization and indigenization, comparable with those of other international organizations such as Protestant missions and Buddhist organizations.[10] In this ideological moment, to borrow from Cheek,[11] all three movements, although offering conflicting visions of modernity, had structural similarities and embraced nationalism. Thus, nationalism did not contradict internationalism. In the MCP and in the Philippines and Indonesia, the movement for independence was intertwined with globalist thinking in the form of Comintern internationalism, the pan-Asianism of Sun Yatsen, Christianity, Islam, and anarchism.[12]

In the context of the interwar internationalist moment,[13] while the 1917 Revolution transformed the Russian empire into what Terry Martin has called the "affirmative empire" of Soviet nationalities,[14] the internationalist Comintern acted through the only recognized "national" communist parties in the colonies to support and create nationalism. As the Comintern sought to break the world imperialist system through its "weakest link" in pursuit of a world proletarian revolution, in the context of societies with significant immigrant populations, the Comintern's variant of internationalism created or built on existing discourses of multiethnic nations, similar to the Soviet republics.[15]

While the roles that the Comintern and Chinese communist organizations in Malaya played in indigenous nationalism were unique among Chinese communist organizations overseas, similarly, in the Dutch East Indies the first to use the marker "Indonesia" were communists.[16] Also,

---

[10] Don A. Pittman, *Toward a Modern Chinese Buddhism: Taixu's Reforms* (Honolulu, HI: University of Hawaii Press, 2001); Dana L. Robert, "First Globalization? The Internationalization of the Protestant Missionary Movement between the World Wars," in Ogbu Kalu and Alaine Low, eds., *Interpreting Contemporary Christianity: Global Processes and Local Identities* (Grand Rapids, MI: William B. Eerdmans Publishing Company, 2008), pp. 93–130.

[11] Timothy Cheek, *The Intellectual in Modern Chinese History* (Cambridge: Cambridge University Press, 2015).

[12] For the role of transnational anarchism, see Benedict Richard O'Gorman Anderson, *Under Three Flags: Anarchism and the Anti-Colonial Imagination* (London; New York, NY: Verso, 2005).

[13] Erez Manela, *The Wilsonian Moment: Self-Determination and the International Origins of Anticolonial Nationalism* (Oxford: Oxford University Press, 2007).

[14] Terry Martin, *The Affirmative Action Empire: Nations and Nationalism in the Soviet Union, 1923–1939* (Ithaca, NY: Cornell University Press, 2017).

[15] Francine Hirsch, *Empire of Nations: Ethnographic Knowledge and the Making of the Soviet Union* (Ithaca, NY: Cornell University Press, 2005).

[16] Norman G. Owen, ed., *The Emergence of Modern Southeast Asia: A New History* (Honolulu, HI: University of Hawaii Press, 2005), p. 298.

Austrian communists were key in the shaping of nationalist discourses in a previously nonexistent nation.[17] At the same time, in the interwar global moment and internationalist zeitgeist,[18] the lack of contradiction between nationalism and internationalism in the MCP, as expressed in the Comintern's promotion both of nations through the establishment of national parties and of a world revolution, fit the GMD and CCP's aspiration for a world of equal nations. Through this discourse and the organization of a "national" party through an internationalist alliance of various ethnic groups, the MCP became both nationalist and internationalist. Thus, Malaya, similar to cosmopolitan China, in the words of Hung-Yok Ip, became an "internationalist nation."[19] Comintern internationalism helped to ground the "ungrounded empire" of Chinese networks in Malaya.[20]

The MCP was one node in the international network of the 1920s and 1930s, throughout which we can see the operation of the global interwar networks of Chinese communists, of the Comintern, and of transnational anti-imperialism. Similarly, according to Michele Louro, when Nehru participated in the League Against Imperialism (1927), he viewed nationalism and internationalism as not mutually exclusive, and his distinction between nationalism and internationalism, India and the world, was blurred.[21] Through the workings of this interwar globalization and the conjuncture of nationalism and internationalism in Chinese networks due to the nature of Chinese migration, which prompted overseas Chinese to be embedded in both sending and receiving environments and nationalism, the MCP's nation under Chinese leadership in a multiethnic community illustrates the Chinese role in nationalism in Southeast Asia.

***

To explain the relationships among Southeast Asia, China, and the goals of a communist revolution in the 1930s, apart from a consideration of

---

[17] I am grateful to Felix Wemheuer for this point and for the reference. Robert Menasse, *Das war Österreich: Gesammelte Essays zum Land ohne Eigenschaften* (Frankfurt am Main: Suhrkamp, 2005), pp. 60–61.
[18] Daniel Laqua, *Internationalism Reconfigured: Transnational Ideas and Movements between the World Wars* (London: I. B. Tauris, 2011).
[19] Hung-Yok Ip, "Cosmopolitanism and the Ideal Image of Nation in Communist Revolutionary Culture," in Kai-wing Chow, Kevin M. Doak, and Poshek Fu, eds., *Constructing Nationhood in Modern East Asia* (Ann Arbor, MI: University of Michigan Press), pp. 215–246.
[20] To borrow from Aihwa Ong and Donald Nonini, *Ungrounded Empires: The Cultural Politics of Modern Chinese Transnationalism* (London: Routledge, 1997).
[21] Michele Louro, "India and the League Against Imperialism: A Special 'Blend' of Nationalism and Internationalism," in Ali Raza, Franziska Roy, and Benjamin Zachariah, eds., *The Internationalist Moment: South Asia, Worlds, and World Views 1917–39* (New Delhi: SAGE Publications India, 2014), pp. 22–55, esp. p. 43.

indigenous communist movements in Southeast Asia, we must consider the connections among three sides: the overseas Chinese, the *huaqiao*, shaped by the policies of their host governments; the Third Communist International or Comintern, run out of Moscow, with the Far Eastern Bureau (FEB) regional office in Shanghai; and China itself, including Sun Yatsen, GMD revolutionaries, and Chinese communists. Comintern networks were merely an added layer of a global network of Chinese sojourning communities in which Soviet ideology and, above all, nationalist Chinese communism were secondary to the survival behavior of the *huaqiao* community. This community was larger than families and smaller than the state, although it was trying to become the state in and of itself, and it promoted the anticolonial revolution in the region of the Nanyang. We see in what follows, as well, how these communities operated over long distances, and we gain insights into their organizational and justificatory structures.

Yet the earliest communist envoys in British Malaya were Sneevliet, Darsono, Semaun, and Baars, a group of Dutch and Indonesians from the Dutch East Indies who passed through Singapore in 1921–1922 on their way to and from Shanghai, Moscow, or Holland,[22] as well as Bao Huiseng, a founding member of the CCP who worked in Malaya in 1922. Tan Malaka's activity in 1924 in Singapore cooperating with Chinese and supported by the Comintern notwithstanding, after the defeat of the uprising in Java in 1926–1927, many PKI refugees, such as Alimin, Musso, Winanta, Subakat, and Jamaluddin Tamin, among others, fled through Singapore.[23] The paths of Indonesian and Chinese communists thus ran parallel in Malaya. Despite a small number of Malays in the MCP during the 1930s, the MCP was unable to solve what has usually been seen as its main problem, that is, its Chinese orientation. The party was unable to attract any significant non-Chinese membership, yet the party genuinely identified with Malaya.

Philip Kuhn's conception of Chinese overseas as having a need to be doubly rooted in China and in their local environments helps make sense of the MCP's dual nationalism.[24] In MCP texts, this is expressed in the multiple meanings of the word *minzu* as "nation," "nationality," "people," and "national." The concept of *minzu* moved between different meanings

[22] Cheah Boon Kheng, *From PKI to the Comintern, 1924–1941: The Apprenticeship of the Malayan Communist Party. Selected Documents and Discussion* (Ithaca, NY: Southeast Asia Program, Cornell University, 1992), p. 7.
[23] Ibid., pp. 9, 10.
[24] Philip A. Kuhn, "Why China Historians Should Study the Chinese Diaspora, and Vice-Versa," Liu Kuang-ching Lecture, 2004, University of California, Davis, *Journal of Chinese Overseas* 2(2) (2006), pp. 163–172.

for different audiences at different times, and even between different meanings for the same audience at different times. However, this process of slippage in meaning is not the same as a misunderstanding. I show that the variant meanings of *minzu* were consistent and coherent within specific discursive domains. Similarly, Comintern ideas of "national" parties helped Chinese communists in Malaya secure their place in the Malayan nation, which the British government promoted at the time despite not granting Chinese immigrants political rights. The British government rather promoted one "Malayan" identity, which would be based on the common language, Malay or English, and a "love for the land."[25]

These circumstances were channeled through a translation slippage of the word *minzu*. In the following decade, in the ranges of different meanings employed by different actors in the revolution in the Nanyang, this notion of "nation" literally sojourned between Malaya and China in MCP discourse. As "sojourning" better describes this process, it does not imply the negative connotation that was associated with Chinese immigrants at the time, as sojourners who were not really present in a new place and were always outsiders in some fashion. However, scholarship on overseas Chinese has shown that "sojourning Chinese" contradicted this perception in their historical experience. Sojourning Chinese were emphatically part of their host societies. In the same fashion, the sojourning concept for *minzu* was both changed by and rooted in the discursive worlds it entered. This book maps this movement over time and through contemporary documents and demonstrates the actual mechanics and ways in which Chinese immigrant communists imagined the "nation."[26] The enduring meaning and flexibility of the concept of *minzu*, which can be found only in the details, did not only reflect the historical change but also played a role that shaped history. Those details are a key part of my story.

The MCP's story is a history of the conjuncture of words, concepts, and changed social experiences. Chinese in Shanghai and Singapore used Russian directives in English based on their often global experience in the late 1920s. Perched in their different environments, they assigned significantly different meanings to these borrowed words and concepts. The mechanism for this was twofold, conceptual and social. When speakers of different languages interpreted authoritative texts or generated their own

[25] "United Malaya," *Malaya Tribune*, December 26, 1933, p. 3.
[26] For the MCP's "national" outlook, see Sze-Chieh Ng, "Silenced Revolutionaries: Challenging the Received View of Malaya's Revolutionary Past" (MA Thesis, Arizona State University, 2011), p. 21; C. C. Chin, "The Revolutionary Programmes and Their Effect on the Struggle of the Malayan Communist Party," in Karl Hack and C. C. Chin, eds., *Dialogues with Chin Peng: New Light on the Malayan Communist Party* (Singapore: National University of Singapore Press, 2004), pp. 260–278.

texts using the conceptual training available to them, a key word's pragmatic definition (the change in the meaning of a key word reflected in its
actual use) conjoined with the changed social experience of text writers
and text readers to produce different meanings for the same words. I build
on Koselleck's *Begriffsgeschichte* (history of concepts) to map the social
history of these meanings in the language.[27]

Malayan Chinese communists' adoption of the ideas of Comintern
internationalism and of a national party was similar to the Hakka ethno-
cultural group's adoption of Christianity in Guangxi Province in the mid-
nineteenth century, as they too had to assert their interests vis-à-vis the
local population. In both cases, novel concepts and language effectively
represented a change in the social experience of the local population. At the
same time, as Kuhn has stressed, imported concepts and language (which,
by the twentieth century, often came in the form of an integrated ideology)
are not simply adapted to a new locality but also bring their own internal
logic to the new environment. Thus, the novelty of an imported ideology (if
it finds social efficacy) is twofold: it offers new ways to perceive and address
the changed social reality, and it injects some new intentions and reasoning
into a locality.[28] The case of the MCP's Malayan nationalism offers
a concrete look at the workings of ideological borrowing.

Minzu was a key word, one of the "significant, indicative words" that
conveyed "strong feelings or important ideas" at the time, and despite
nominal continuity in its general meaning, changes in its definition across
cultural contexts were "radically different or radically variable, yet sometimes hardly noticed." Raymond Williams tells us that these meanings are
not confined to language but extend to "the users of language and to the
objects and relationships" about which language speaks, and those "exist,
indeed primarily, in material and historical ways."[29]

Language, central to the MCP story, defined how a nation was imagined and what a nation was to become. Slippages in meaning thus
underlined the role of language in forming the basis for historical change
and national consciousness. Yet language divisions impeded the MCP in

[27] Reinhart Koselleck, "*Begriffsgeschichte* and Social History," in *Futures Past: On the
Semantics of Historical Time* (Cambridge, MA: MIT Press, 1985), pp. 73–91. I also
draw on the methodology from Timothy Cheek, "The Names of Rectification: Notes
on the Conceptual Domains of CCP Ideology in the Yan'an Rectification Movement,"
Indiana East Asian Working Paper Series on Language and Politics in Modern China, no. 7,
East Asian Studies Center, Indiana University, January 1996.

[28] Philip A. Kuhn, "Origins of the Taiping Vision: Cross-Cultural Dimensions of a Chinese
Rebellion," *Comparative Studies in Society and History* 19(3) (July 1977), pp. 350–366.
I thank Timothy Cheek for this point.

[29] Raymond Williams, *Keywords: A Vocabulary of Culture and Society* (London: Fontana,
1983), pp. 9, 13, 15, 20.

its goal to become the (multi)national party of Malaya even while facil-
itating communication in transnational networks. The MCP's "nation" is
yet another example of the strategic use of Bolshevik language by various
actors in the 1920–1930s and an example of how language formulations
effected policies in the world of the Chinese Communist Party.[30] As
minzu was translated between different languages and semantic fields,
as in the case of comparable strategic adoption, where political power
(real or symbolic) underpins the choice of meaning in "translingual
practices,"[31] ultimately, the consequences of the "semantic hybridity"
of translated concepts across cultures and intersecting ideological and
political fields[32] were unintended. Marshall Sahlins's concept of the
structure of conjuncture, that is, meanings, accidents, and causal forces
that shape conditions whose interactions in particular times and spaces
seal the fates of whole societies,[33] is instructive to explain the case of the
MCP's Malayan nation, as during the same time period comparable
ambiguities and fluidity in the meaning of the terms "country," "ethnicity," and "people" can be found in the contexts of Indonesia,[34] Japan,[35]
and the Harlem Renaissance movement.[36]

The MCP's Malayan nation was one among other concepts of national
belonging, as the Malayan community was multicultural and various
actors experimented with ways to imagine a nation for those who lived
in the Malayan peninsula in sultanates under British domination. For
Malay-speaking Muslims, Indians who spoke South Asian languages, and
those speaking the dialects of South China but writing in Mandarin,
English, as the official language of the British government was the

---

[30] Michael Schoenhals, *Doing Things with Words in Chinese Politics: Five Studies* (Berkeley, CA: Institute of East Asian Studies, University of California, 1992); Stephen Kotkin, *Magnetic Mountain: Stalinism as a Civilization* (Berkeley, CA: University of California Press, 1997).
[31] Lydia He Liu, *Translingual Practice: Literature, National Culture, and Translated Modernity: China, 1900–1937* (Stanford, CA: Stanford University Press, 1995).
[32] Kai-wing Chow, "Narrating Nation, Race, and National Culture: Imagining the Hanzu Identity in Modern China," in Chow, Doak, and Fu, eds., *Constructing Nationhood in Modern East Asia* (Ann Arbor, MI: University of Michigan Press, 2001), pp. 47–84, esp. p. 48.
[33] Marshall Sahlins, *Historical Metaphors and Mythical Realities: Structure in the Early History of the Sandwich Islands Kingdom* (Ann Arbor, MI: University of Michigan Press, 1981). My thanks to James Wilkerson for introducing me to Sahlins's work.
[34] Leo Suryadinata, *Peranakan Chinese Politics in Java, 1917–42* (Singapore: Singapore University Press, 1981). See more in Chapter 4.
[35] Kevin M. Doak, "Narrating China, Ordering East Asia: The Discourse on Nation and Ethnicity in Imperial Japan," in Chow, Doak, and Fu, eds., *Constructing Nationhood in Modern East Asia*, pp. 85–116.
[36] Anthony Dawahare, *Nationalism, Marxism, and African American Literature between the Wars: A New Pandora's Box* (Jackson, MI: University Press of Mississippi, 2002), p. 62.

medium of communication. How does one imagine a community if the community speaks three or more languages? Thus, it should not surprise us that the residents of British Malaya sought ways of imagining an inclusive community other than the single-language print capitalism described by Benedict Anderson, which, however, the British government successfully employed to imbue the idea of a Malayan nation in Chinese immigrants as well as a sense of common identity through Malay-language newspapers among Malays in the early 1930s.[37] Malay concepts of national belonging, such as *bangsa*, excluded immigrants, who in 1921 comprised half the population of British Malaya. Thus, these concepts could not appeal to the Chinese, who themselves comprised more than one-third of the population. Other imaginations that were comparable to national belonging and collective living in the Malay Peninsula, such as an Islamic community (*umat*) excluding non-Muslims, as a sultan-centered loyalty (*kerajaan*), and as a British Malayan nation, did not accommodate the political rights of a large immigrant population.[38] The MCP's Malayan nation was to awaken as a proletarian multiethnic nation, similar to China as imagined by the Chinese communists,[39] run by an alliance of three communist parties representing the three largest communities of British Malaya, Chinese, Malay, and Indian, as the "national" Malayan Communist Party. However, the MCP is best understood as a "hybrid organization" with roots in older forms of Chinese associational life as well as in more novel forms and idioms of Bolshevization rather than as a mere pawn of the Comintern.[40]

The heterogeneous origins of the Malayan national concept highlight the ambiguities of nationalism and help us to understand why this concept is still being debated today. After World War II, a form of territory-based civic nationalism among Chinese immigrants, which was invented

---

[37] Benedict Anderson, *Imagined Communities: Reflections on the Origin and Spread of Nationalism*. Revised Edition. (London; New York, NY: Verso, 1991), p. 43; Ariffin Omar, *Bangsa Melayu: Malay Concepts of Democracy and Community, 1945–1950* (Kuala Lumpur; New York, NY: Oxford University Press, 1993), p. 18.

[38] Anthony Milner, *The Invention of Politics in Colonial Malaya: Contesting Nationalism and the Expansion of the Public Sphere* (Cambridge: Cambridge University Press, 1994), pp. 282–283.

[39] John Fitzgerald, *Awakening China: Politics, Culture, and Class in the Nationalist Revolution* (Stanford, CA: Stanford University Press, 1998).

[40] For other parties' agency in their relations with the Comintern, see Matthew Worley, ed., *In Search of Revolution: International Communist Parties in the Third Period* (London: I. B. Tauris, 2004); Kevin McDermott and Jeremy Agnew, *The Comintern: A History of International Communism* (Houndmills: Macmillan, 1996); Tim Rees and Andrew Thorpe, eds., *International Communism and the Communist International, 1919–1943* (Manchester: Manchester University Press, 1998).

by the intelligentsia (similar to the nationalism in Eastern Europe, Africa, Latin America, Southeast Asia, China, India, and even North America) in the 1930s and incorporated immigrant bourgeoisie into the nation, prevailed over the primordial ethnic (or perennial)[41] Malay concept of national belonging based on language, rights to land, or loyalty to a sultan, and over the concepts of the larger communities of Islam and Greater Indonesia. More continuities and similarities exist between MCP attitudes, those of the GMD, and those of the postwar Malayan Chinese Association (MCA) with the incorporation of Chinese into the independent body politic of Malaya.

As in the majority of modern nation-states, several forms of nationalism, as defined by Anthony D. Smith, can be distinguished in the MCP's Malayan nation as can elements of all three types of nationhood: as a bureaucratic incorporation, as a vernacular mobilization by the intelligentsia, and as plural nations built by settlers in North America and Australia.[42] Malaya is thus an example of a constructed Southeast Asian nation where, as in other places in Asia, Africa, and Latin America, colonialism was a primary source of nationalism.[43] Similar to other nationalist movements, the MCP sought political power.[44] An imported concept, the MCP's Malayan nation was an exemplary "derivative discourse" based on colonial borders and concepts.[45]

As to the central question in studies of nationalism, which is, according to Hobsbawm, the criteria for nationhood, the MCP's Malayan nation offers a complex answer.[46] It was invented, not as a tradition,[47] but rather as part of a novel national vision embedded in the interwar internationalist zeitgeist and in the British colonial discourse of the Malayan nation and Malayanization (a preferential policy, protection, and promotion of the Malay language) – that is, through state-sponsored top-down nationalism, as described by Ernest Gellner.[48] It

---

[41] For the categorization of nationalism, see Anthony D. Smith, *Nationalism and Modernism: A Critical Survey of Recent Theories of Nations and Nationalism* (London: Routledge, 1998), pp. 55–56, 223–226, 194. For the Southeast Asian context, see Clifford Geertz, *The Interpretation of Cultures* (London: Fontana, 1973).
[42] Smith, *Nationalism and Modernism*, pp. 212, 193–194.
[43] See Nicholas Tarling, *Nationalism in Southeast Asia: If the People Are with Us* (London: Routledge, 2004); Smith, *Nationalism and Modernism*, p. 70.
[44] John Breuilly, *Nationalism and the State* (Chicago, IL: University of Chicago Press, 1994).
[45] Partha Chatterjee, *Nationalist Thought and the Colonial World: A Derivative Discourse* (London: Zed Books, 1986).
[46] Eric J. Hobsbawm, *Nations and Nationalism since 1780: Programme, Myth, Reality* (Cambridge: Cambridge University Press, 2012), p. 5.
[47] Eric Hobsbawm and Terence Ranger, eds., *The Invention of Tradition* (Cambridge: Cambridge University Press, 1983), introduction, pp.11–14.
[48] Ernest Gellner, *Nations and Nationalism* (Oxford: Blackwell Publishing, 2006).

was imagined by the Chinese émigré intellectuals for the Chinese community, similar to Anderson's Latin American creoles, the contested pioneers of nationalism,[49] and indigenous Malays considered themselves to be excluded from the category of "Malayans."[50] Chinese communists borrowed concepts and models from the Comintern, specifically concerning national parties and the principle of separate ethnic organizations among communists in the labor and communist movements in the United States. Those two models fit the local context because they allowed communists to imagine the nation promoted by the British government in a different way, one in which Chinese would have equal rights. Ultimately, the MCP's Malayan nation was the beginning of the postwar phase of nationalism in Southeast Asia, described by Anderson as a response to global imperialism, led by bilingual intelligentsia and based on the distilled experience of European and American models.[51]

The MCP was shaped by unintended consequences and by the historical contingencies of anti-imperialism in Southeast Asia, Chinese long-term migration trends, network connections, identity and localization, organizational behavior originating in South China, Soviet and GMD geostrategic visions, and the organizational practices of the Comintern and the international communist movement. The efforts by the GMD, the CCP, and the Comintern in the making of a world revolution overlapped in Southeast Asia, and an independent "national" Malayan communist organization was established as the Chinese communists in Malaya sought the Comintern's international legitimacy and finances (Chapter 2). Combined with a growing need for Chinese immigrants to adopt a Malayan identity and to create a distinct Nanyang Chineseness, this resulted in the MCP's adoption of the discourse of an independent Malayan nation led by communists and including Chinese immigrants (Chapter 3). The MCP's discourse and activities show its hybrid – and torn – nature. The MCP tried to act in the traditional role of Chinese associations as a broker between the Chinese and the British government and, at the same time, it campaigned for the overthrow of governments in Malaya and China (Chapter 4). A comparison with the Chinese immigrant organizations' relation to local nationalism in the American Philippines and the Dutch East Indies demonstrates that the policies of the colonial governments toward the Chinese immigrants and the nuances of their identity shaped the involvement of the Chinese immigrants in the indigenous

---

[49] For a survey of the critique of Anderson's idea, see, for instance, Nicola Miller, "Latin America: State-Building and Nationalism," in John Breuilly, ed., *The Oxford Handbook of the History of Nationalism* (Oxford: Oxford University Press, 2013), pp. 388–391.
[50] Omar, *Bangsa Melayu*, p. 113.
[51] Anderson, *Imagined Communities*, ch. 7.

national project. Another unintended result of the MCP's interaction with the Comintern and of their overlapping interests in the mobilization of locally born Chinese was the strengthening of Chinese communist networks in Southeast Asia (Chapter 5). The GMD's nationalist education policies in overseas Chinese schools were responsible for the rising popularity of communist ideas in Malaya (Chapter 6). Chinese communists in Malaya succeeded because of their dual Chinese and Malayan nationalism and in spite of, not because of, their propaganda. Xu Jie's durian story captures the main problem in the relationship between the MCP and the Chinese community, that is, the tensions between the business orientation of the community and the MCP's radicalism, which was disastrous for its following by the beginning of the war (Chapter 7). Yet the experience of the Japanese occupation was crucial in shaping the Chinese community's identification with the territory of sovereign Malaya.

This book is based on a collection of materials produced by the MCP and collected by the Comintern, now archived in Moscow at the Rosskiiskii gosudarstvennyi arkhiv sotsial'no-politicheskoi istorii (Russian State Archive of Sociopolitical History) (RGASPI) and covering 1928–1935 and 1939–1941; MCP members' memoirs from local literary and historical materials (*wenshi ziliao*), Chinese- and English-language periodicals from China and British Malaya, British Colonial and Foreign Office records that contain analytical reports and translations of MCP documents (which scholars sometimes regard as a "state perspective" and not as genuine MCP sources[52]) as well as translations of press clippings from China; the materials of the Shanghai Municipal Police (SMP), including those at the National Archives and Records Administration (Washington, DC), as well as the GMD collection at the Hoover Archives. Because reports in Comintern correspondence are mostly signed by the Central Committee of the MCP, and only a few letters are signed by individuals, it is impossible, with rare exceptions, to attribute ideas and policies to certain individuals. This shortcoming thus migrated to this book, in which I have to refer to the Central Committee of the MCP (CC MCP) or, even worse, to the MCP or the Communist Youth League (CYL) as monolithic actors. Moreover, due to the inconsistent Romanization of different Chinese dialects as well as the large number of aliases that communists used, in many cases the Chinese characters for the names of people in Comintern sources cannot be determined.

***

[52] Personal communication with C. C. Chin in Singapore in December 2010. A similar view of police sources on the MCP is taken by Cheah, *From PKI to the Comintern*, pp. 5–6.

In admission of my own commitments, I must state that I was born and raised in the Soviet Union. I had to join the Oktiabriata (Little Octobrist) and Young Pioneer organizations, but by the time I reached the age at which I would have joined the Komsomol (Communist Youth League), it was no longer mandatory. In school, we had to memorize the resolutions of party meetings in history classes. In university, my textbooks on the history of the "Ancient East" had quotes from Marx, Engels, and Lenin. When the Comintern was preparing to give 50,000 gold dollars for work in Malaya, my late grandmother, Anna Fedorovna Remizova, lived through famine in the Volga region in 1930–1932 and recalled how, as a child, she would go to the fields to look for edible plants. When I see requests for money in the letters from the Malayan communists to the Comintern, I think of my grandmother and of her father, who was arrested by the People's Commissariat for Internal Affairs (Narodnyi Komissariat Vnutrennikh Del) (NKVD) for hiding a Bible. All this, no doubt, translates into the detachment, even cynicism, with which I approach MCP texts.

I also believe, however, that my attention to the practical aspects of the relationship between the Comintern and the MCP is not unreasonable. As I show in this book, the MCP consciously manipulated rhetorical and organizational tools designed for mobilization while its members asked the Comintern for money. The members of the MCP were practical, even if they dreamed of a soviet federation of Malayan states in which they would form the government. Aspirations to make one's way to power with weapons, even in the name of the "masses," can hardly be called idealism. Nonetheless, my job as a historian is first to understand and explain how things came to pass. Judgment must await future research.

2 The Global World of Chinese Networks in the 1920s

The Chinese Revolution and the Liberation of the Oppressed *Minzu*

"So we want to know where internationalism [*shijiezhuyi*] comes from? It comes from nationalism."[1]

From Global Trade to Global Emancipation: The Chinese Revolution in Moscow, Tokyo, Berlin, San Francisco, and Singapore

By the second half of the nineteenth century, Chinese migration had become a globalizing force of its own. The abolition of the transatlantic slave trade had created a demand for Chinese labor, and the opening of Chinese ports after the Opium Wars facilitated coolie trade to the Americas. Population crises and new opportunities across the globe, including the gold rush and the demand for indentured labor on plantations, pushed the Chinese from South China, who had a tradition of searching for opportunities overseas, to leave China for the British, Dutch, and Spanish colonies in the Americas and Southeast Asia, including sovereign Siam. Although the number of migrants is difficult to estimate because of inconclusive data, the 14.7 million departures from Xiamen, Shantou, and Hong Kong in 1869–1939 give an idea of the scale of the migration.[2]

---

[1] Sun Zhongshan [Sun Yatsen], "Sanminzhuyi [Three People's Principles," in *Minzuzhuyi* [*Nationalism*], lecture 4, February 17, 1924, in *Sun Zhongshan quanji* [*Collected Works of Sun Yatsen*], 11 vols. (Beijing: Zhonghua shuju, 1986), vol. 9, pp. 220–231, esp. p. 226. In the English translation, *shijiezhuyi* is translated as "cosmopolitanism": "We must understand that cosmopolitanism grows out of nationalism." *The Three Principles of the People, San Min Chu I. By Dr. Sun Yat-Sen. With Two Supplementary Chapters by Chiang Kai-shek. Translated into English by Frank W. Price. Abridged and edited by the Commission for the Compilation of the History of the Kuomintang* (Taipei: China Publishing Company, 1960), pp. 21–27, esp. p. 25.

[2] Philip A. Kuhn, *Chinese among Others: Emigration in Modern Times* (Lanham, MD: Rowman & Littlefield Publishers, 2008), pp. 114, 150; Kaoru Sugihara, "Patterns of Chinese Emigration to Southeast Asia, 1869–1939," in Kaoru Sugihara, ed., *Japan, China, and the Growth of the Asian International Economy, 1850–1949* (Oxford: Oxford University Press, 2005), pp. 244–274.

Although localized centuries-old communities of Chinese were politically second class to the Europeans, they were involved in administration and helped govern the colonies. They "borrowed" the Dutch and British empires in Southeast Asia and were essential middlemen for the functioning of those empires.[3] Chinese merchants had been rising to the position of rulers in the indigenous polities of today's mainland Southeast Asia since the early second millennium. In Dutch and then British colonies, the Chinese had functioned as tax collectors, and they thrived on revenue farms until the late nineteenth century, particularly through the opium trade.[4] Yet European discriminatory policies toward the alien migrant Chinese and toward the circulation of nationalist ideas made acquisition of a local identity desirable for the Chinese. In the second half of the nineteenth century in the Philippines, in addition to helping to form the basis of the Manila-centered Hispanicized culture, which led people to identify as "Philippine" versus "non-Philippine" after the American takeover, Chinese mestizos were seen as potential challengers to Spanish rule because of their strong economic status as landholders. Indeed, Chinese mestizos played an important role in the Philippine Revolution of 1896–1898, even if they did not identify as Chinese.[5]

In the meantime, emerging Chinese nationalism inside China resonated with and was amplified by the discriminatory policies of the colonial governments in overseas communities in Southeast Asia and in North American settler colonies. Despite the resentment of the Chinese overseas toward the Qing government for its inability to defend its subjects from the discriminatory policies of European colonial governments, they embraced Qing re-Sinicization efforts. From the establishment of Qing diplomatic representation and modern Chinese schools with Mandarin as the medium of instruction to the granting of patrilineal Chinese nationality beginning in 1909, the Chinese overseas sought to assert their Chinese and indigenous identities at the same time.

The Chinese nationalism of the early twentieth century is inseparable from the history of world anticolonial movements. The anticolonial struggles of Cuba and the Philippines, the Boer Wars, and the Asian migrant campaigns for rights in southern Africa, where the Chinese entered into an alliance with Indian migrants led by none other than

[3] Kuhn, *Chinese among Others*, p. 58.
[4] Craig A. Lockard, "Chinese Migration and Settlement in Southeast Asia before 1850: Making Fields from the Sea," *History Compass* 11(9) (2013), pp. 765–781; Kuhn, *Chinese among Others*, pp. 75, 184.
[5] Edgar Wickberg, "The Chinese Mestizo in Philippine History," *Journal of Southeast Asian History* 5(1) (1964), pp. 62–100.

Gandhi[6] not only provided a stimulus for the development of Chinese nationalism but also set an organizational precedent for anti-imperialist leagues, which would become the mode of twentieth-century international anticolonial organizations and have been referred to as the precursors of the 1955 Bandung Conference.[7] The earliest one, the American Anti-Imperialist League (1898–1920), was established in the United States to protest the annexation of the Philippines and Cuba, whereas the beginnings of anti-imperialist leagues in East Asia were found in pan-Asian societies in the early 1900s in Japan and Shanghai. The goals of Chinese nationalism at the turn of the century included both the solution of China's problems and the making of a world of independent nations. Liu Shipei, a member of the Indo-Chinese Asian Solidarity Society (Yazhou heqinghui) in Tokyo (1907), pointed out the importance of the solidarity of the "weak peoples" (*ruozhong*) of Asia in the confrontation between China and Asia and the imperialism of Japan and the West.[8]

In these new networks of the transnational Save the Emperor Society (Baohuanghui) in the early 1900s and of the GMD and the CCP in the 1920s, preexisting ideas and aspirations for an interconnected just world were linked to new ideas of national identity and of a world communist revolution. These ideas were transported to diasporic networks, where long-held Chinese migrant ideas about the need for assimilation into local societies and policies of re-Sinicization were at work. Given the history of Chinese ideas about global interconnections, expressed in ancient concepts such as *Tianxia*, "All under Heaven," and *Datong*, "Great Unity," the pan-Asian ethos of the Chinese Revolution, and Sun Yatsen's own discussions of internationalism (*shijiezhuyi*) stemming from nationalism, and the convergence of nationalism and internationalism in the May Fourth Movement, is not surprising.[9]

---

[6] Melanie Yap and Dianne Leong Man, *Colour, Confusion, and Concessions: The History of the Chinese in South Africa* (Hong Kong: Hong Kong University Press, 1996), pp. 138–168.

[7] Rebecca E. Karl, *Staging the World: Chinese Nationalism at the Turn of the Twentieth Century* (Durham, NC: Duke University Press, 2002); Fredrik Petersson, "'We Are Neither Visionaries Nor Utopian Dreamers': Willi Münzenberg, the League Against Imperialism, and the Comintern, 1925–1933" (PhD dissertation, Åbo Akademi University, 2013), pp. 1–2.

[8] Fred H. Harrington, "The Anti-Imperialist Movement in the United States, 1898–1900," *Mississippi Valley Historical Review* 22(2) (1935), pp. 211–230; Karl, *Staging the World*, pp. 113–114, 169–173.

[9] Sun, "Minzuzhuyi [Nationalism]," p. 226; Xu Jilin, "Wusi: Shijiezhuyi de aiguo yundong [May 4th: Cosmopolitan Patriotic Movement]," *Zhishi fenzi luncong* [*Compendia of Intellectual Debates*] 9 (2010); Fitzgerald, *Awakening China*, p. 347.

The first Comintern agent in Asia was Dutchman Henricus Sneevliet, who founded the first communist party in Asia, the Partai Komunis Indonesia (PKI), in 1920 and modeled cooperation between the CCP and the GMD after cooperation between Indonesian communists and Islamic nationalists. He critically reflected that many GMD members linked Chinese traditional philosophy with socialist ideas.[10] For instance, the Datong party originated from the New Asia Alliance (Xin Ya tongmengdang) established by Chinese and Koreans in 1915 in Japan. The Comintern affirmed that the vision of "human equality and international harmony" and the anti-imperialist aspirations of Korean and Chinese members of the Datong party who sought Comintern support in founding the Korean and Chinese communist parties in 1920–1921 were socialist and were on the way to "becoming communist."[11] However, members of the Datong party were unsuccessful in founding a Comintern-supported Chinese communist party because they lacked the reputation and organizational skills of Chen Duxiu and Li Dazhao. Also, as was often the case in the world of slow and unreliable 1920s transportation, they were late for the Third Comintern congress in June 1921 and could not join the group of official representatives of China who would establish the CCP the following month in the presence of Sneevliet.[12] The Datong party did not become the communist party of China, but these ideas permeated the world of Chinese communism, especially as the global expansion of Chinese organizations facilitated their further development.

In 1924, Sun Yatsen postulated in his lectures on nationalism that only if China returned to its historical policy of "helping the weak" (ji ruo fu qing) and opposing the strong and allied itself with the polities in the former Chinese sphere of influence, which had been lost to European colonial encroachment, would China be able to rise to power again.[13] New ideas of Asian unity in juxtaposition to the West and traditional ideas of China's role as a benevolent patron in the region, which Sun Yatsen called the kingly way (wangdao) as opposed to the hegemonic

---

[10] Henk Sneevliet, "The Revolutionary-Nationalist Movement in South China," in *Die Kommunistische Internationale*, September 13, 1922, in Tony Saich, *The Origins of the First United Front in China: The Role of Sneevliet (Alias Maring)* (Leiden: Brill Academic Publishers, 1991), pp. 748–757, esp. p. 751.

[11] Wu Jianjie, "Cong da Yazhouzhuyi zouxiang shijie datongzhuyi: Lilun Sun Zhongshan de guojizhuyi sixiang [From Pan-Asianism to World Great Harmony: Sun Yatsen's Internationalism]," *Jindai shi yanjiu [Studies in Modern History]* 3 (1997), pp. 183–198; Ishikawa Yoshihiro, *The Formation of the Chinese Communist Party*, tr. Joshua Fogel (New York, NY: Columbia University Press, 2012), pp. 131–132, ch. 2.

[12] Ishikawa, *The Formation of the Chinese Communist Party*, pp. 141–142.

[13] Sun, "Minzuzhuyi [Nationalism]," p. 253.

ways of Western powers (*badao*),[14] were channeled into new anticolonial liberation ideologies and institutionalized in communist networks. Sun's ideas evolved from China's geopolitics and were shaped by anti-colonial wars in the Philippines, Africa, and Cuba and by Lenin's 1918 discourse on the oppressed peoples and Bolshevik foreign policy as well as by the failure of the Versailles Treaty to solve the colonial question.

Sun Yatsen imagined the way to China's revival as a world power was through an alliance with Japan or with the oppressed nations of Asia. Together with Mongolia, India, Afghanistan, Persia, Burma, and Annam, China would form a federation, a Great State of the East (Dongfang daguo). In 1924, Sun Yatsen defined pan-Asianism as "the question of what suffering Asian nations should do in order to resist the powerful nations of Europe – in other words, the great question focused on the elimination of injustices towards oppressed peoples."[15] Sun's "oppressed nations" were not only former Chinese vassals, friendly neighbors, and decolonized countries in the Americas but also Soviet Russia and post-Versailles Germany. The second anti-imperialist league, the League Against Imperialism (LAI), established with Comintern funding, began as the Hands-Off China Society created by Workers International Relief, based in Berlin.

Germany had a special place in Sun's vision. In 1923, Sun harbored the idea of a three-country alliance wherein the Soviet Union would provide ideology and Germany would provide military technology and advisors to China. Sun planned that once China had restored its position as a powerful nation, it would help Germany restore its position, which had been undermined by the Versailles Treaty.[16] The German branch of the CCP (Lü De zhibu), established in 1922, became the Chinese-language faction of the Kommunistische Partei Deutschlands (KPD) (Degong Zhongguo yuyanzu) in 1927, one of the leaders of

---

[14] Sun, "Dui Shenhu shanghui yisuo deng tuanti de yanshuo [Address to the Chamber of Commerce and Other Organizations in Kobe]," November 28, 1924, in *Sun Zhongshan quanji* [*Collected Works of Sun Yat-sen*], vol. 11, pp. 401–409.

[15] Duan Yunzhang, *Zhongshan xiansheng de shijieguan* [*The Worldview of Mr. Sun Yatsen*] (Taibei: Xiuwei zixun keji, 2009), p. 168; Sun, "Minzuzhuyi [Nationalism]," pp. 193, 200, 253, 304, 409.

[16] Fei Lu (Roland Felber), "Jiezhu xinde dang'an ziliao chongxin tantao Sun Zhongshan zai ershi niandai chu (1922–1923) yu Su E guanxi yiji dui De taidu de wenti [Regarding Sun Yatsen's Views on Relations with the Soviet Union (1922–1923) and His Attitudes toward Germany Based on New Archival Materials]," in *Sun Wen yu huaqiao: Jinian Sun Zhongshan danchen 130 zhounian guoji xueshu taolunhui lunwenji* [*Sun Yatsen and Chinese Overseas: The Proceedings of the Academic International Conference Commemorating the 130th Anniversary of the Birth of Sun Yatsen*] (Kobe: Caituan faren Sun Zhongshan jinianhui, 1997), pp. 57–69.

which was Liao Chengzhi, a celebrated leader of the international
Chinese seamen organization and the son of assassinated GMD leader
Liao Zhongkai.[17]
Germany did not have a large Chinese labor community, but German
communists treated Chinese students as China's national voice. In
response to the German branch of the CCP's protest letter regarding
Reuters's report that the May Thirtieth Movement in China was yet
another expression of Chinese xenophobia and another Boxer Uprising,
newspapers published a retraction the following day and arrested
Chinese students, participating in KPD-organized rallies against
British imperialism and in support of China, received police apologies
and were let go. Among them were Liao Huanxing, the future secretary
of the LAI's international secretariat and a Comintern cadre in Berlin
who had been dispatched originally by the British GMD to establish
a branch there, and the future leader of the People's Liberation Army,
Zhu De.[18]
In 1927, at the Brussels inaugural congress of the LAI, a world congress
of nationalist organizations, one-fifth of all representatives came from the
GMD.[19] Initially, the GMD Central Committee decided to appoint Hu
Hanmin, who had just returned from his Moscow trip during which he
had advocated for GMD membership in the Comintern independently of
the CCP, as the GMD's representative to the first LAI congress. Liao, as
Hu's assistant, was to go in his place if Hu could not make it. In the
meantime, in 1923 Liao started to work as a referent for the Varga Bureau
in Berlin, the information office of the Comintern for Western Europe.
He acted as a self-appointed representative of all worker parties of China

---

[17] Liao Huanxing, "Zhongguo gongchandang lü Ou zongzhibu, 1953 [The European
Branch of the Chinese Communist Party, 1953]," in Zhongguo shehui kexueyuan
xiandaishi yanjiushi, Zhongguo geming bowuguan dangshi yanjiushi, eds., *Zhongguo
xiandai geming shi ziliao congkan. "Yi Da" qianhou. Zhongguo gongchandang di yi ci daibiao
dahui qianhou ziliao xuanbian [Series of Materials on Chinese Modern Revolutionary History.
Around the Time of the First Congress: A Selection of Materials,* vol. 2] (Beijing: Renmin
chubanshe, 1980), pp. 502–510.

[18] Liu Lüsen, "Zhongcheng jianyi de gongchandang ren: Geming xianqu Liao Huanxing
tongzhi zhuanlüe [Loyal and Persistent CCP Member: A Biography of the Revolutionary
Avant-Garde Comrade Liao Huanxing]," in Zhonggong Hengnan xianwei dangshi
lianluo zhidaozu Zhonggong Hengnan xianwei dangshi bangongshi, ed., *Yidai yingjie
xin minzhuzhuyi geming shiqi Zhonggong Hengnan dangshi renwu [An Era of Heroes: Party
Members during Hengnan's Revolutionary Period of New Democracy]* (1996), pp. 3–11; Liu
Lüsen, "Zhongcheng jianyi de gongchandang ren Liao Huanxing [Loyal and Persistent
CCP Member Liao Huanxing]," *Hunan dangshi yuekan [Hunan Party History Monthly]*
11 (1988), pp. 20–22.

[19] Hans   Piazza,   "Anti-Imperialist   League   and   the   Chinese   Revolution,"   in
Mechthild   Leutner,   Roland   Felber,   Mikhail   L.   Titarenko,   and
Alexander M. Grigoriev, eds., *The Chinese Revolution in the 1920s: Between Triumph and
Disaster* (London: Routledge, 2002), pp. 166–176.

at the Brussels congress,[20] at which he quoted Sun Yatsen's plea that the GMD unite with the oppressed classes of the West and with the oppressed nations of the world to oppose oppressors and imperialists.[21] The LAI congress in 1927 devoted special attention to China. It is not difficult to see how the Chinese discourse on an alliance of oppressed peoples would be attractive among some circles in Germany, given Sun Yatsen's support of the German cause. The KPD election campaign in competition with the Nazis against the peace at Versailles in the early 1930s, which was allegedly initiated by Stalin,[22] reflected the mood of postwar Germany. A GMD cadre reported the following in 1929 about the situation in Germany to the GMD Central Committee:

After the Great War, Germany was repressed by the Versailles Treaty and dared not offend other nations. Thus, their foreign policy is very prudent. Furthermore, the Sino–German unequal treaties were abolished long ago. Recently, attempting to gain our country's markets in order to compete with other countries, they have mostly expressed sympathy with our nationalist movements (the Germans call themselves an oppressed nation, so they want very much to ally with weak and small nations in order to rise again). [Their sympathy] does not really come from the heart, but temporarily they do not constitute a big obstacle to our country either ... The KPD previously had positive feelings toward us and were enthusiastic in aiding us.[23]

Although the GMD cadre had reservations about the colonialist impulses lying behind Kaiser Wilhelm's ambitions in Asia as a motivation for the KPD to aid the Chinese Revolution, it is clear from the letter that the GMD's own motivation in its alliance with the KPD was strategic. Despite antipathy to foreigners among working-class

[20] Li Yuzhen, "Fighting for the Leadership of the Chinese Revolution: KMT Delegates' Three Visits to Moscow," *Journal of Modern Chinese History* 7(2) (2013), pp. 218–239; Liao's response to the criticism of the KPD Chinese language group, February 4, 1929, "An die I.K.K." RGASPI 495/225/1043, pp. 31–37, esp. pp. 32, 34.

[21] Liao Huanxing, "Zhongguo renmin zhengqu ziyou de douzheng: Guomindang zhongyang changwu weiyuanhui daibiao de jiangyan [The Righteous Struggle of the Chinese People: Speech by the Representative of the Standing Committee of the GMD]," in Zhonggong Hengnan xianwei dangshi ziliao zhengji bangongshi, ed., *Zhonggong Hengnan difang shi: Xin minzhuzhuyi geming shiqi [The History of the CCP in Hengnan County: The Revolutionary Period of New Democracy]* (Beijing: Zhonggong dang-shi chubanshe, 1995), pp. 142–145.

[22] Gregor Benton, *Chinese Migrants and Internationalism* (London: Routledge, 2007), pp. 32, 35–36.

[23] The report of the Chinese Nationalist Party [Guomindang], French General Branch Report on European Party Affairs to the Third National Congress (March 1929), in Marilyn Levine, *The Found Generation: Chinese Communists in Europe during the Twenties* (Seattle, WA: University of Washington Press, 1993) pp. 122–153, esp. pp. 149–150. Original Source: Service de liaison des originaires des territoires français d'outre-mer (SLOTFOM) VIII, 6.

supporters of the KPD and the KPD's own use of China in its domestic
political struggle,[24] KPD leaders extended a warm welcome to arriving
Chinese communists and students.[25] In the soul searching of post-
Versailles Germany, there was an intellectual fascination with China as
a model of a nation that had changed dramatically and rapidly through
revolution.[26]

In the meantime, in Canton in 1925 Liao Zhongkai and Vietnamese
leader Ho Chi Minh established an anti-imperialist league (AIL)[27] consisting of Vietnamese ("Annamites"), Koreans, Indians, and Javanese.
This organization became the breeding ground for the key Vietnamese
Marxist organization, the Association of Vietnamese Revolutionary
Youth (Thanh Niên).[28] In 1927, the Union of the Oppressed Peoples
of the East (Dongfang bei yapo minzu lianhehui) began to operate in
Hankou and Shanghai, drawing membership from migrants of the same
countries.[29] Vietnamese sources suggest that the GMD established
the Shanghai AIL to wrest the leadership of the Asian communists from
the Comintern.[30] Whether or not this is true, GMD attempts to join the
Comintern in 1923–1927, promoted by Hu Hanmin among others, were
pragmatic, aiming to realize the party's vision of a world revolution.[31] Hu
hoped to convert the Comintern into a global organization as an
"International of Nationalities" (minzu guoji), alluding in the name to
the "Third [Communist] International" (Disan guoji [gongchandang]),
the Comintern, and with the GMD playing the leading role. Hu put this
as follows:

[24] Joachim Krüger, "Die KPD und China," in Mechthild Leutner, ed., Rethinking China in the 1950s (1921–1927) (Münster: LIT Verlag, 2000), pp. 107–116.
[25] Liao left the LAI and his Berlin post for Moscow after the conflict with Münzenberg in 1928. Joachim Krüger, "A Regular China Voice from Berlin to Moscow: The China-Information of Liao Huanxin, 1924–1927," in Leutner, Felber, Titarenko, and Grigoriev, eds., The Chinese Revolution in the 1920s; Petersson, "We Are Neither Visionaries Nor Utopian Dreamers," p. 199.
[26] Li Weijia, "Otherness in Solidarity: Collaboration between Chinese and German Left-Wing Activists in the Weimar Republic," in Qinna Shen and Martin Rosenstock, eds., Beyond Alterity: German Encounters with Modern East Asia (New York, NY: Berghahn Books, 2014), pp. 73–93.
[27] To distinguish the numerous anti-imperialist leagues founded across Asia autonomously from the League Against Imperialism in Brussels, the acronyms AIL will be used for the former and LAI will be used for the latter throughout the text.
[28] Sophie Quinn-Judge, Ho Chi Minh: The Missing Years, 1919–1941 (Berkeley, CA: University of California Press, 2003), pp. 83–84.
[29] "Dongfang bei yapo minzu lianhehui shang zhongzhihui cheng [A letter from the Union of the Oppressed Peoples of the East to the Central Committee of the GMD]," July 23, 1927, File 7625.1, Hankou dang'an, reel 64, Hoover Archives.
[30] Quinn-Judge, Ho Chi Minh, p. 167.
[31] Li, "Fighting for the Leadership."

In the days when Zong Li [Sun Yatsen] was alive, I contend that he proposed to organize a *minzu guoji* [International of Nationalities][32] so that we, the Guomindang, could lead the international national revolutionary movement [*lingdao guoji de minzu geming yundong*] ourselves; when I went to Russia [in 1926] and suggested that the Guomindang become a Comintern member directly, I wanted the Guomindang to independently join the Comintern, acquire [independent] status, and not be subjected to communist control and secret dealings. So the idea to organize a *minzu guoji* and the idea to join the Comintern were consistent with each other and were in the same spirit ... Frankly, my proposal to join the Comintern was because I hoped to organize a *minzu guoji*.[33]

In the geopolitical imagination of China's two anti-imperialist parties, the CCP and the GMD, both organizationally structured after a Bolshevik party and striving for a one-party dictatorship, the restoration of China's power in its former imperial borders held an important place. Just as the Bolsheviks drew on tsarist imperial borderland policies, the CCP inherited the imperial borderland policies of the Qing dynasty as well as GMD internationalism, aspiring to liberate together the Chinese and indigenous peoples, in addition to appropriating Comintern internationalism.[34] In 1928, a CCP program prepared by Hungarian Eugen Varga, a renowned Soviet economist and the head of the Information-Statistical Institution of the Executive Committee of the Communist International (ECCI) in Berlin, included the restitution of the territories "seized by imperialists," such as "Formosa, Indochina, Manchuria, etc.," along with the abolition of the unequal treaties and the return of the concessions.[35] Varga's information on China was provided by Liao Huanxing.[36]

---

[32] David P. Barrett translates this as "Nationalist International" in "Marxism, the Communist Party, and the Soviet Union: Three Critiques by Hu Hanmin," *Chinese Studies in History* 14(2) (1980–1981), pp. 47–73.

[33] Hu Hanmin, "Minzu guoji yu disan guoji [International of Nationalities and the Third (Communist) International]," in Cuncui xueshe, ed., *Hu Hanmin shiji ziliao huiji, di si ce* [*Hu Hanmin's Works*, vol. 4] (Xianggang: Dadong tushu gongsi, 1980), pp. 1395–1401, esp. pp. 1400–1401.

[34] Vera Tolz, *Russia's Own Orient: The Politics of Identity and Oriental Studies in the Late Imperial and Soviet Periods* (Oxford: Oxford University Press, 2011), pp. 134–167; Joseph Esherick, "How the Qing Became China," in Joseph Esherick, Hasan Kayali, and Eric van Young, eds., *Empire to Nation: Historical Perspectives on the Making of the Modern World* (Lanham, MD: Rowman & Littlefield Publishers, 2006), pp. 229–259.

[35] "Draft Program of the CCP, April 1928," in Titarenko, Mikhail L. and Mechthild Leutner, eds., *VKP(b), Komintern i Kitai. Dokumenty. T.III. VKP(b), Komintern i sovets-koe dvizhenie v Kitae, 1927–1931* [*CPSU (Bolshevik), the Comintern, and China. Documents. Volume 3. CPSU (Bolshevik), the Comintern, and the Soviet Movement in China, 1927–1931*] (Moscow: AO Buklet, 1999), pp. 364–371.

[36] Krüger, "A Regular China Voice from Berlin to Moscow."

At the same time, the GMD was developing its overseas organizations and was promoting the anti-British cause among overseas Chinese. As a result of the Comintern policy of cooperation between the two parties, many CCP members had dual CCP and GMD membership. At the second national convention of the GMD in Canton in 1926, delegates from Malaya, Java, Burma, Siam, and Indochina planned the establishment of the Overseas Chinese Communist Division. Their goal was unity of the Chinese in the Nanyang and propaganda of emancipation among the "small weak races" (i.e., the indigenous peoples).[37] In 1926–1927, the GMD organized classes for overseas Chinese (*huaqiao xuexiban*) propaganda cadres who were to lead the overseas Chinese movement (*huaqiao yundong*) in Malaya.[38]

During the interwar period, various international organizations, such as those of Protestant missionaries and Buddhists, which offered different visions of modernity, had structural similarities. They embraced internationalism and indigenization (involving locals in the organizations to put down roots in local chapters) as their modi operandi.[39] By the 1930s, these well-established trends could also be seen in the promotion of the Chinese Revolution by the Comintern and by the GMD and the CCP. These two parties' overseas branches were hybrids of Chinese overseas organizations and political parties and had the need to localize so as to fit in better with local society.[40] As the Comintern sought to expand its organization, promoting global solidarity of the working class and world revolution, it also adopted indigenization strategies.

The Comintern, Nationalism, and Southeast Asia

The internationalism of the Comintern in the 1920s was one of many expressions of internationalism by transnational organizations in the interwar world, and it channeled the regional and national aspirations of

---

[37] British Colonial Office Records (CO), "Monthly Bulletin of Political Intelligence" (MBPI), January 1926, p. 1, CO 273/534, in *Records of the Colonial Office, Commonwealth and Foreign and Commonwealth Offices, Empire Marketing Board, and Related Bodies Relating to the Administration of Britain's Colonies* (Kew, Surrey: National Archives, 2009).

[38] Li Yinghui, *Huaqiao zhengce yu haiwai minzuzhuyi (1912–1949)* [*Overseas Chinese Policy and Overseas Chinese Nationalism (1912–1949)*] (Taibei: Guoshiguan, 1997), p. 491.

[39] Robert, "First Globalization?"; Pittman, *Toward a Modern Chinese Buddhism*.

[40] Kuhn, "Why China Historians Should Study the Chinese Diaspora"; Li Minghuan, *Dangdai haiwai huaren shetuan yanjiu* [*Contemporary Associations of Overseas Chinese*] ([Xiamen]: Xiamen daxue chubanshe, 1995), and John Fitzgerald, *Big White Lie: Chinese Australians in White Australia* (Sydney, NSW: University of New South Wales Press, 2007) approach the GMD as a Chinese association.

anticolonial movements. Following the Bolsheviks' international isolation of 1919, the Second Comintern Congress promoted nationalities and the colonial question in 1920. At the same time, various groups of Asian immigrants in Soviet Russia made efforts to advance the communist movement in Asia. Prior to the establishment of the Comintern office in China, the union of Chinese laborers in Russia established its own bureau of Chinese communists within the Russian communist party, the Bolsheviks, in 1920 and petitioned the Soviet government to send representatives to China. Chinese and Korean communists also approached the Comintern with suggestions to organize Comintern-supported parties. Contingency and luck were often decisive factors through which organizations became national communist parties. Thus, the initiatives of the members of the bureau of Chinese communists within the Russian communist party, who referred to themselves as the Chinese Communist Party, to organize their branches in Shanghai and Tianjin would have been approved by the Comintern in December 1920, if not for the death of the head of the party, Liu Qian.[41]

Ideas of national liberation were intertwined with pan-regional concepts. In 1923, Indonesian communist leader Tan Malaka envisioned a federation of Eastern communists.[42] In 1924, members of the French Communist Party's Union Intercoloniale African, Lamine Senghor, and Ho Chi Minh established the Ligue de Défense de la Race Nègre. In 1927, they attended the inaugural congress of the LAI in Brussels. In the 1920s, the Comintern's support of the African cause by proposing to create a belt of black states within the United States, South Africa, Brazil, and Cuba in the manner of the invention of new nations in the Union of Soviet Socialist Republics (USSR) as soviet republics channeled African diasporic intellectuals' pan-Africanism.[43] The idea of an indigenous nation-state, like Wilson's self-determination slogans of a few years earlier, held great appeal in the colonized world.[44]

Tan Malaka, a proponent of a pan-Asian communist network, and Sneevliet, defining his mission as to bring Marxist prophecies to China

[41] Ishikawa, *The Formation of the Chinese Communist Party*, pp. 83–84, 137–139.
[42] "Guiding Principles in the Colonial Question, by Tan Malaka," 1923, RGASPI 495/154/700/23–5.
[43] Brent Hayes Edwards, *The Practice of Diaspora: Literature, Translation, and the Rise of Black Internationalism* (Cambridge, MA: Harvard University Press, 2003), p. 29; Piazza, "Anti-Imperialist League"; Marc Gallicchio, *The African American Encounter with Japan and China: Black Internationalism in Asia, 1895–1945* (Chapel Hill, NC: University of North Carolina Press, 2000), p. 68; Marc Becker, "Mariátegui, the Comintern, and the Indigenous Question in Latin America," *Science & Society* 70(4) (October 2006), pp. 450–479; Hirsch, *Empire of Nations*.
[44] Manela, *The Wilsonian Moment*.

and to connect the Chinese movement with the international network, shaped the Comintern's approach in the region. The Comintern sent Sneevliet to Shanghai in March 1921 to study the "movement in different countries in the Far East" so as to establish an office there. Sneevliet was impressed by the labor movement in South China and proposed connecting the movements in the Philippines, Indochina, and the Dutch East Indies with British India because of their similarities.[45] The Eastern Department of the ECCI was responsible for deciding the "guiding line" in the Malay Archipelago. This line was based on Sneevliet's proposal to ECCI representative Tan Malaka, who had the task of building connections between the anti-imperialist movement in Indonesia and "all countries of the East," especially with the "national liberation movement in China," by building their organizations in the Malay Archipelago, Indochina, Siam, and Singapore.[46] Singapore was intended to be the platform to bring together the communist movements of China and Indonesia, including the movements of the overseas Chinese.[47] In 1923, with the rise of radicalism in Java, the most populous Indonesian island of the Dutch East Indies, Moscow started to strategize with regard to the Dutch East Indies. For the Comintern, the Malay Archipelago was an important strategic position between the Pacific and Indian Oceans, "near the most populated countries of the globe – China and India."[48]

Sun Yatsen's alliance with the Soviet Union in 1923 and his ideas of anti-British pan-Asian unity matched Soviet plans for an alliance in the Far East.[49] Sneevliet's and Malaka's visions fit the international needs of the Soviet state. In 1923, in order to subvert the influence of British imperialism in China and Singapore, the Comintern planned to establish

---

[45] "Report of Comrade H. Maring to the Executive," July 11, 1922, in Saich, *The Origins of the First United Front in China*, pp. 305–323, esp. p. 307; Saich, "Introduction," The Origins of the First United Front in China, pp. 3, 91.

[46] Maring, "Instruktsia upolnomochennomu vostochnogo otdela ispolkoma Kominterna po rabote v Indonesii [Instructions for the Representative of the Eastern Department of the ECCI on Work in Indonesia]," undated, but judging from the referenced fourth Comintern congress, it must be 1922–1923. RGASPI 495/154/700/18–20. This is a Russian translation of "Instruktion an den Bevollmächtigten des Ost-Ressorts (Abteilung) der Exekutive der Komintern für die Arbeit in Indonesien [Instructions to the Representative of the East Department (Division) of the Executive of the Comintern on Activities in Indonesia]," drafted by Henk Sneevliet. Undated. Henk Sneevliet Papers, inv. no. 349, accessed on August 2, 2012, at the International Institute of Social History, Amsterdam, www.iisg.nl/collections/sneevliet/life-4.php.

[47] Hassan [Tan Malaka], Letter, July 7, 1924, RGASPI 534/4/106/1–2.

[48] Popov, "Gollandskaia Indiia [Dutch East Indies]," December 17, 1923, RGASPI 495/214/700/32–36.

[49] Boris Nicolaevsky, "Russia, Japan, and the Pan-Asiatic Movement to 1925," *Far Eastern Quarterly* 8(3) (1949), pp. 259–295.

the "most important element of the anti-imperial struggle," an organization of transport workers linking South China, the Malay Archipelago (Java and Sumatra), Indochina, Singapore, and Siam in order to stimulate a national revolutionary movement "in the deep interior of international imperialism on the Pacific coast and islands." Propaganda in native languages (newspapers) would be launched from some port in the Pacific to develop a "national revolutionary movement." Tan Malaka, posing as "a journalist from a national bourgeois paper so that he could legalize himself and as a nationalist could do a lecture tour against imperialism," would be dispatched to establish communist cells in Java, Singapore, Bangkok, Hong Kong, Canton, and Shanghai. On the basis of information supplied via this communication channel through Vladivostok to Moscow, the Eastern secretariat would provide a guiding line to printing offices in Singapore and Hong Kong.[50]

In 1924, Tan Malaka reported from his grand Asian tour, sponsored by the Comintern, that in Singapore, a Comrade L. had sufficiently established a school of 100 students and had made connections among plantations and "town workers." Echoing Sneevliet, Malaka suggested that Singapore offered a chance to work not only in Malaya but also in India because it was "not very far" and because of the large number of Indian migrant workers in Singapore.[51] To promote a united front between the Chinese and Javanese, Tan Malaka had a plan to establish with "Comrade Tan" a Java–China special committee in Canton to study Chinese conditions in Java and to work among the "politically and economically important Chinese population." Consisting of one member each from Hong Kong, Canton, and Java (including Malaka himself), this committee, which was established in June 1924 but was short lived, would build connections with the Javanese party and design policy for the Sino–Java Committee in Java. A graduate of the Whampoa Military Academy was to leave for Java to work as a teacher.[52] In Singapore, however, Malaka found that Chinese and Indians were more responsive to communist ideas than were the local Indonesian and Malay

---

[50] Grigorii Voitinskii, the Head of the Eastern Secretariat, "Spravka [A Note]," 1923, RGASPI 495/154/700 /8, 8ob.

[51] Tan Malaka's letter from Canton to Heller, signed by his alias, "Hassan," July 7, 1924, RGASPI 534/4/106/1–2. Original English text. L. N. Heller (1875–?) was the head of the Eastern Department of the Profintern in 1922–1930. Titarenko and Leutner, *Komintern i Kitai [Comintern and China]*, vol. 3, p. 1526.

[52] Tan Malaka's letter, July 7, 1924. Tan Malaka only cited *Encyclopaedie van Nederlandsch-Inndië*. 2nd edn. (Gravenhage: Martinus Nijhoff, 1917–1939), without providing his own account of the events regarding the Canton bureau. Tan Malaka, *From Jail to Jail*. Translated and introduced by Helen Jarvis (Athens, OH: Ohio University Center for International Studies, 1991), vol. 1, pp. 103–106, 109–115, 245n18.

communities.[53] In response to Malaka's request, experienced organizer Fu Daqing and a Hainanese labor organizer were dispatched to Singapore to organize Hainanese plantation laborers, among whom Cantonese-speaking Comrade L. was useless.[54] During a visit in 1925, PKI leader Alimin Prawirodirdjo, who did not speak Chinese, was reportedly able to recruit only Chinese and Indian laborers, yet the number of Indonesian communists did increase there when many fled to Singapore following the suppression of the 1926–1927 PKI uprising.[55]

Aside from two Profintern "agents" who published a newspaper in Singapore in 1924,[56] a number of members of the Nanyang CCP organization studied in Moscow in the 1920s. These included Han Guoxiang; Yang Shanji, head of the Communist Youth League (CYL) in 1926 and the secretary of the Nanyang Provisional Committee (NPC) in 1928 (see Figure 2.1); Chen Yannian, son of Chen Duxiu;[57] and Xu Tianbing, a member of the older generation of the Revolution of 1911.[58] Fu Daqing, a member of the Guangdong Provincial Committee and the head of the NPC's propaganda department, studied in Moscow in 1922–1924. He also participated in the Nanchang and Guangzhou uprisings as well as in Lenin's funeral, and he was Borodin's interpreter at the same time that Ho Chi Minh was Borodin's secretary.[59] The NPC received either CCP or Comintern money occasionally. Once, after the fall of 1929, Fu Daqing's subsidy saved the editorial board of the *Nanyang Worker* from starving for four days.[60]

[53] Cheah, *From PKI to the Comintern*, p. 9.
[54] Tan Malaka's letter, July 7, 1924; Gene Z. Hanrahan, *The Communist Struggle in Malaya*. With an introduction by Victor Purcell (New York, NY: Institute of Pacific Relations, 1954), p. 9; "Monthly Review of Chinese Affairs" (MRCA), December 1931, p. 6, CO 273/572.
[55] Ruth Thomas McVey, *The Rise of Indonesian Communism* (Ithaca, NY: Cornell University Press, 1965), p. 231; Santos [Alimin], "Brief Description of My Activities in the Past," January 10, 1939; Alimin, untitled, undated, RGASPI 495/214/3/123–124, 161–165.
[56] Tan Malaka's letter from Canton, September 16, 1924, RGASPI 534/ 4/106/9.
[57] Yong, *Origins of Malayan Communism*, pp. 50–51, 68.
[58] Zhu Yihui, "Xu Tianbing," *Hainan mingren zhuanlüe (xia)* [*Biographical Dictionary of Famous Hainanese. Second Part*] (Guangzhou: Guangdong lüyou chubanshe, 1995), pp. 143–146.
[59] "Proverochniy list studenta, Fedorov (Fu Tagin) [Student's Registration Card (Fu Tagin)]," RGASPI 495/225/793/5. Fang Chuan and Zhang Yi, eds., *Zhongguo xiandai mingren zhenwen yishi* [*Stories of Famous People in Modern China*] (Beijing: Zhongguo huaqiao chubanshe, 1989), pp. 393–394; Zhonghua renmin gongheguo minzhengbu, ed., *Zhonghua zhuming lieshi di ershisan juan* [*Famous Martyrs of China*, vol. 23] (Beijing: Zhongyang wenxian chubanshe, 2002), pp. 560–562.
[60] Then sixteen-year-old Xie Fei, a native of Wenchang County in Hainan and the future first wife of Liu Shaoqi, was a Nanyang Provisional Committee CCP member from June 1929 to February 1932. Xie Fei, "Huiyi Zhongguo gongchandang Nanyang linshi weiyuanhui de gongzuo, 1929–1930 [Remembering the Work of the Nanyang Provisional Committee, 1929–1930]," in *Geming huiyilu: Zengkan 1* [*Revolutionary*

Figure 2.1 Yang Shanji, 1924.
Born in Hainan, head of the Communist Youth League (CYL) in 1926
and secretary of the Nanyang Provisional Committee in 1928 during his
studies at the University of the Toilers of the East in 1924.[61] Published
with permission of the RGASPI.

The defeat of the communist uprising in the Dutch East Indies in 1926
shaped the Comintern's approach to Singapore and Malaya. They were to
be the basis from which to resurrect the Indonesian party and to build an
intra-Asian network. At the same time, the Chinese Communist Party also
started as a multicentered movement and expanded globally in the late
1920s.[62]

Reminiscences: Expanded edition 1] (Beijing: Renmin chubanshe, 1983), pp. 159–169, esp.
   p. 166.
[61] Komarov's Personal File (Yang Shanji), RGASPI 495/225/652.
[62] Hans van de Ven, *From Friend to Comrade: The Founding of the Chinese Communist Party,
   1920–1927* (Berkeley, CA: University of California Press, 1991); Ishikawa, *The Formation
   of the Chinese Communist Party.*

The Global World of the Chinese Revolutionaries

Since the turn of the twentieth century, the ideas and organizational modes of Chinese networks had traveled across the world. Workers returning from the United States to China brought with them the modes of unionizing and striking, which they then used in Hong Kong and China in Sun Yatsen's organization.[63] In the 1920s, the founding members of the CCP and the first generation of GMD envoys of re-Sinicization were dispatched around the world. Dong Chuping (董锄平), alias Dong Fangcheng (董方诚), visited Cuba in 1925, as well as a Philippine university together with Bao Huiseng, who had previously worked in Malaya in 1922.[64] The newspaper *Datongbao* was first published by the Chinese workers' union in Soviet Russia in 1918 and commissioned by the Soviet government to propagate the Russian Revolution and Marxism among Chinese workers, but the title was chosen in a way that would attract Chinese readers. After the Chinese laborers who published *Datongbao* in Russia returned to China, they established the Datong society,[65] the newspaper of which was also published in the Philippines.[66]

The activities of the LAI were closely intertwined with the activities of the Chinese revolutionaries. For example, the first Chinese communist organization in the United States was established after contact with the LAI network. A member of the American communist party, Ji Chaoding, alias C. T. Chi, represented the Students' Society for the Advancement of

---

[63] Lai, *Chinese American Transnational Politics*, p. 57.

[64] Gao Zinong, "Zhongguo gongchan qingnian tuan Feiliebin tebie difang gongzuo baogao [Work Report of the Philippine Special Local Committee of the Chinese Communist Youth League]," June 1–December 7, 1928, RGASPI 495/66/7/137–169; Bai Dao, "Dong Chuping: Wode geming yinluren [Dong Chuping: My Revolutionary Fellow Traveler]," in *Bai Dao wenji di qi ji* [*Collected Works of Bai Dao*, vol. 7] (Beijing: Zhongguo xiju chubanshe, 2002), pp. 549–569; Peng Zhandong, "Cong aiguo qiaoling Peng Zemin zhandou yisheng kan huaqiao huaren zai Zhongguo geming lichengzhong de tuchu gongxian [The Life of Patriotic Overseas Chinese Peng Zemin as an Example of the Contributions of the Overseas Chinese to the Chinese Revolution]," *Qiaowu huigu* [*Overseas Chinese Reminiscences*, vol. 2] (Beijing: Guowuyuan qiaowu bangongshi, 2006). Online version accessed on March 17, 2019: http://qwgzyj.gqb.gov.cn/qwhg/129/64 .shtml; Yong, *Origins of Malayan Communism*, p. 43.

[65] Xue Xiantian, "Guanyu lü E huagong lianhehui jiguanbao Datongbao [On *Datongbao*, the Newspaper of the Union of Chinese Workers in Russia]," *Jindai shi yanjiu* [*Studies in Modern History*] 3 (1991); Gao Jinshan, "Lü E huagong zai Makesezhuyi chuanbozhong de tezhu zuoyong [The Role of Chinese Laborers in Russia in Marxist Propaganda]," *Dangshi bocai* [*CCP History*] 11 (2004), cited in Zhang Weibo, "Datong lixiang yu Zhonggong chuangjian [The Idea of Datong and the Establishment of the CCP]," in Zhonggong yida huizhi jinianguan, ed., *Zhongguo gongchandang chuangjian shi yanjiu* [*Studies on the Founding of the CCP*] (Shanghai: Renmin chubanshe, 2012), pp. 42–54, esp. p. 52.

[66] Gao Zinong, "Zhongguo gongchan qingnian tuan Feiliebin tebie difang gongzuo baogao [Work Report of the Philippine Special Local Committee of the Chinese Communist Youth League]," p. 141.

Sun Yatsenism in America and the American Anti-Imperialist League at the Brussels World Anti-Imperialist Congress as well as at the International Congress of Oppressed Peoples in 1927. Upon returning, he, Shi Huang, and Xu Yongyin[67] established a Chinese-language faction (Meigongdang zhongyang fushu Zhongguoju)[68] under the anti-imperialist committee of the American party.[69] After breaking with the GMD in 1927, the Chinese faction planned to take over the anti-imperialist activities of leftist GMD organizations in the United States, Canada, Cuba, and Mexico through branches of the Alliance for the Support of the Chinese Workers and Peasants Revolution in America (ASCWPRA) across the United States and in Havana. A revolutionary tradition of Chinese participation in the Cuban national independence struggle dated back to the Cuban war of independence, and local Cuban leaders such as Jose Marti had included the Chinese in internationalist solidarity and in the pan-American vision.[70] As Chinese communists borrowed the regional imagination of the Monroe Doctrine, their goals were to promote cooperation of Chinese and American workers and pro-China policies, such as the abolition of the unequal treaties as well as the interests of Chinese immigrants.[71]

Chinese revolutionary networks helped staff regional Comintern organizations in the Americas through connections between the Chinese faction and party members in Cuba, the Philippines, Canada, Chile, Mexico, and Peru.[72] The All-American Anti-Imperialist League (AAAIL) was reestablished by the Workers Party of America with Comintern authorization in 1925, but in 1927 it existed only on paper.[73] The All-American Alliance of Chinese Anti-Imperialists (est. 1928) consisted of Asian immigrants and established the Oriental branch of the American Anti-Imperialist League in 1929.[74] That same year, the

---

[67] Liao Huanxing, "Zhongguo gongchandang lü Ou zongzhibu, 1953 [European Branch of the Chinese Communist Party, 1953]"; Lai, *Chinese American Transnational Politics*, p. 65.

[68] Wang Ming's letter to the Chinese faction of the Communist Party of the United States of America (CPUSA), undated, RGASPI 515/1/4117/30.

[69] "Report of the Bureau of the Chinese Fraction, Translation from Chinese," August 5, 1928, RGASPI 515/1/1451/41–48.

[70] Benton, *Chinese Migrants and Internationalism*, pp. 37–47; "Guba huaqiao ying jiaji geming huodong [Cuban Chinese Must Intensify Revolutionary Activities]," *Xianfengbao* [*The Chinese Vanguard*] (107), November 15, 1933.

[71] "Report of the Bureau of the Chinese Fraction. Translation from Chinese," August 5, 1928.

[72] Letter to the Chinese Faction of the CPUSA, April 4, 1933, RGASPI 515/1/4117/31–38ob.

[73] Petersson, "We Are Neither Visionaries Nor Utopian Dreamers," pp. 70, 175.

[74] Josephine Fowler, *Japanese and Chinese Immigrant Activists Organizing in American and International Communist Movements, 1919–1933* (New Brunswick, NJ: Rutgers University Press, 2007), pp. 145–147.

ASCWPRA participated in the second anti-imperialist world congress in Frankfurt and joined the LAI.[75] A Chinese cadre on the Comintern – likely Wang Ming, who was the Moscow liaison for the Chinese section of the CPUSA[76] – suggested that the Chinese faction should become the center of *huaqiao* work in the Americas by recruiting avant-garde members of the AIL into the party and establishing local CCP cells. The Chinese faction was to help the parties in the Americas in organizing the *huaqiao* but was not to build local parties in Mexico or Canada. The Chinese faction acted as a liaison between the Comintern and the CCP, as this Chinese Comintern cadre asked the Chinese faction to forward to Moscow or Paris the materials from the CCP.[77] Chinese communists in Europe sent Comintern publications to Chinese communists in the United States, who in turn sent copies of *The Chinese Vanguard* (*Xianfengbao*) to Europe and to the LAI and to party propaganda to Malaya. Additionally, Chinese students such as Un Hong Siu, sponsor of the MCP, translated party publications into Chinese, as discussed in Chapter 6.[78]

By 1928, Comintern activities aiming to bring workers to power internationally had ended in defeat in Europe and Asia alike. While in 1924 the Comintern had attributed this failure to the stabilization of world capitalism, at its Sixth Congress in 1928 the Comintern announced the beginning of a new Third Period of the "class against class" struggle.[79] The Comintern no longer encouraged legal methods through parliaments and the press as a strategy for communist parties, and cooperation with moderate labor movements and social democrats was banned. Instead, the Comintern started to establish communist parties in the colonies as

[75] Lai, *Chinese American Transnational Politics*, p. 73.
[76] Gao Hua, *Hong taiyang shi zenyang shengqide: Yan'an zhengfeng yundong de lailong qumai* [*How the Red Sun Rose: The Yan'an Rectification Movement*] (Xianggang: Zhongwen daxue chubanshe, 2011), p. 101.
[77] "Pismo v kitaiskoe buro KP SSha s predlozheniami po voprosu o rabote sredi kitaiskikh emigrantov [A Letter to the Chinese Faction of the CPUSA: With Suggestions Regarding the Work among Chinese Migrants]," RGASPI 515/1/3181/19–23. It was likely written sometime after July 10, 1933, for the letter mentions the "Extraordinary National Conference" held in New York, July 7–10, 1933. The Communist Party of America (1919–1946). Party History. Accessed August 31, 2015. www.marxists.org/history/usa/eam/cpa/communistparty.html.
[78] Zhang Bao, "Er, sanshi niandai zai Meiguo de Zhongguo gongchandang ren [CCP Members in America in the 1920s and the 1930s]," in *Guoji gongyun shi yanjiu ziliao* [*Research Materials on the History of the International Communist Movement*] 4 (1982), pp. 150–161.
[79] Alexander Vatlin and Stephen A. Smith, "The Comintern," in Stephen A. Smith, ed., *The Oxford Handbook of the History of Communism* (Oxford: Oxford University Press, 2014), pp. 187–194.

a way of undermining European imperialism through its "weakest link."[80] Such a shift would have come as no surprise given the successful launch of the anti-imperialist league project, for even if its results were modest at best, the scope of its ambitions was captivating.

Old Networks, New Ideas: The Nanyang Organization

Because of the demand for labor after World War I in the colonies and because of easy travel, the Nanyang was a popular destination for "progressive Chinese and revolutionaries" (*Zhongguo de jinbu de renshi he gemingzhe*).[81] In 1921–1925, journalists and teachers, GMD and often CCP members, spread the ideas of the May Fourth Movement and found employment with Chinese schools and newspapers in the Nanyang. Various organizations, including the GMD, the Guangdong CCP and CYL, the All-China General Labor Union, the Shanghai Student Federation, and the Kheng Ngai Revolutionary Alliance (Qiongya geming tongzhi datongmeng), sent envoys to promote both the ideas of the Chinese Revolution and anti-British sentiments among the overseas Chinese.[82] The head of the Overseas Bureau of the GMD in China, older Tongmenghui member Peng Zemin, dispatched cadres to organize local student unions, labor unions, and GMD branches in the Nanyang Chinese Union of Public Societies (Nanyang huaqiao ge gongtuan lianhehui) so as to promote the anti-British cause.[83] Such propaganda was especially relevant in the aftermath of the so-called May Thirtieth Incident, during which several student participants in the protests against Japanese business owners were killed by the police of the International Settlement in Shanghai, and which led to worldwide growth of CCP membership.

In 1925, All-China General Labor Union cadres in Singapore established worker night schools and unions among seamen and servants in foreigners' houses – who, in the English version of the document, were given the dramatic title of "foreign affairs workers" (*waiwu*, 外务).[84] In

[80] *Shestoi kongress Kominterna: Stenograficheskii otchet*. Vyp. 4, *Revoliutsionnoe dvizhenie v kolonial'nykh i polukolonial'nykh stranakh* [*The Sixth Comintern Congress: Stenographic Report*, vol. 4: *Revolutionary Movement in Colonial and Semi-Colonial Countries*] (Moscow; Leningrad: 1929), p. 24.

[81] Xie Fei, "Huiyi Zhongguo gongchandang Nanyang linshi weiyuanhui de gongzuo, 1929–1930 [Remembering the Work of the Nanyang Provisional Committee, 1929–1930]."

[82] Yong, *Origins of Malayan Communism*, pp. 65, 69; "The Minutes of the Third Representative Conference of Nanyang," April 23, 1930, RGASPI 514/1/634/93–158, esp. p. 110.

[83] Yong, *Origins of Malayan Communism*, p. 51.

[84] "Report on the Labour Movement," in "Minutes of the Third Representative Conference of Nanyang," pp. 110–112; Huang Muhan, "Worker Movement in Federated Malay States," March 5, 1931, RGASPI 495/62/9/1–4.

1926, more than 300 students and workers in Singapore were involved with the communists.[85] The Nanyang regional committee of the CCP (Zhongguo gongchandang Nanyang qubu weiyuanhui), covering British Malaya and the Dutch East Indies, and the CYL of about 300 members were formed in Malaya in 1926, but their organizational relationship with the CCP was ambiguous.[86] Hainanese trade guilds were the first to display communist sentiments in the 1920s when labor unions took shape, and Hainanese dominated unions of rubber tappers, domestic servants, shoemakers, carpenters, seamen, and mechanics.[87] The driving forces behind communist organizations in Malaya were Hainanese members of the leftist GMD, who were teachers at night schools (known as the Main School), although they did not have permanent headquarters. They instead organized student unions and spread propaganda and Chinese nationalism among workers' unions. Acting within their Nanyang jurisdiction, they discussed the failed uprising in the Dutch East Indies at their meetings.[88] In 1927, the founder of the CYL, Pan Yunbo (潘云波), attended the Pan-Pacific Trade Union Conference in Hankou where he likely learned the ideas of communist organizations around the world, including the model of separate ethnic organizations in the United States.[89]

After the CCP's defeat in China in April 1927 at the hands of the Guomindang, especially after the Canton uprising, many CCP members fled to the Nanyang. The majority of refugee communists settled in Malaya because it was easier to establish party cells and labor unions there, where the Chinese were sympathetic to the Chinese Revolution and more "relatively progressive" (bijiao jinbu) than in places where the GMD was strong, similar to Siam. Others went to Indochina and to Palembang in Sumatra.[90] In 1928, the Nanyang CCP was renamed the Nanyang Provisional Committee of the CCP (Zhongguo gongchandang Nanyang linshi weiyuanhui), reflecting the fact that the committee's relationship with the CCP was being established because of the CCP's destruction after April 1927.[91]

The jurisdiction of the committee was as ambiguous as the boundaries of the Nanyang itself, which included all of mainland and maritime

[85] Huang Muhan, "Worker Movement in Federated Malay States."
[86] Yong, Origins of Malayan Communism, p. 69; Zhou Nanjing, Shijie huaqiao huaren cidian [Dictionary of the Overseas Chinese] (Beijing: Beijing daxue chubanshe, 1993), p. 560.
[87] Heng Pek Koon, Chinese Politics in Malaysia: A History of the Malaysian Chinese Association (Singapore; New York, NY: Oxford University Press, 1988), p. 25.
[88] Yong, Origins of Malayan Communism, pp. 73–74.
[89] Pan Yunbo is discussed in more detail in Chapter 6.
[90] Xie Fei, "Huiyi Zhongguo gongchandang Nanyang linshi weiyuanhui de gongzuo, 1929–1930 [Remembering the Work of the Nanyang Provisional Committee, 1929–1930]."
[91] Yong, Origins of Malayan Communism, p. 72.

Southeast Asia.[92] The predominantly Hainanese organization consisted of the members of the Nanyang General Labor Union (NGLU), the night schools, and the Nanyang CYL. The committee consisted of thirteen persons, mainly Hainanese, including a five-member standing committee.[93] The committee was to direct local committees (*diwei*) in Singapore, Penang, Malacca, Johor, Kuala Lumpur, Seremban, Ipoh, Sungai Lembing, Riau in the Netherlands East Indies (NEI), Selangor, Negeri Sembilan, Terengganu, Kelantan, Palembang (Sumatra), and Siam, with subcommittees for labor, propaganda, the armed forces, women, finance, and relief.[94] In October 1928, the party had 600 members.[95]

In 1929, the NPC included secretaries Zhang Chengxiang (张成祥) and Xu Tianbing (徐天炳), also known as Wu Qing (吴青); Chen Sanhua (陈三华); Fu Daqing (傅达庆), head of the propaganda department; and Wei Zhongzhou (魏忠洲), head of the secretariat. The editorial board of *Nanyang Worker* (*Nanyang gongrenbao*), with the exception of Zhang Chengxiang, lived in the secretariat's office and posed as a *huaqiao* family. The Chinese and English publications of *Nanyang Worker* were in demand; its distribution increased from several hundred copies to 2,000. Although there was one comrade from Siam, as well as A-Fu, a sixteen-year-old who spoke fluent Malay and was indispensable for party operations, the NPC focused on China. At party meetings, which were held once or twice a month or every other month, the NPC held theoretical discussions about Marxism-Leninism and the crisis of capitalism as well as the reasons for the failure of the Chinese Revolution. It also handled routine questions about party fees, the recruitment of new members, the establishment of a revolutionary mass organization, patriotic propaganda, and international education among overseas Chinese, and complained about the low cultural level of workers in night schools.[96]

---

[92] Ibid., p. 92; "Obshchee polozhenie profdvizheniia v Nan'iane [General Conditions of the Labor Movements in the Nanyang]," April 21, 1931, RGASPI 495/62/9/9–14. In Russian, "Nanyang" was translated as "South Islands" and "the Islands in the Pacific Ocean." See "Doklad o polozhenii na ostrovakh Tikhogo okeana [Report about the Conditions in the Islands of the Pacific Ocean]," December 28, 1929, RGASPI 495/66/13/67.

[93] "Doklad o polozhenii na ostrovakh Tikhogo okeana [Report about the Conditions in the Islands of the Pacific Ocean]," p. 94. For the backgrounds of the committee members, see Yong, *Origins of Malayan Communism*, pp. 90–99, 101.

[94] Report by the Secretary of Chinese Affairs, "Kuo Min Tang and Other Societies in Malaya, January–March 1928," April 27, 1928, pp. 1–7, esp. p. 3, CO 273/542.

[95] "Minutes of the Third Representative Conference of Nanyang," p. 130.

[96] Xie Fei, "Huiyi Zhongguo gongchandang Nanyang linshi weiyuanhui de gongzuo, 1929–1930 [Remembering the Work of the Nanyang Provisional Committee, 1929–1930]."

Singaporean leaders paid rare visits to the Malay states and had little influence there.[97] Front organizations of the NPC were the NGLU, the AIL, the CYL, and the Nanyang General Seamen Union, all of which had overlapping leaderships. The NPC leaders were often arrested and deported by the British authorities, especially after bombings during a shoemakers' strike and assassination attempts on visiting GMD officials in 1928, when one of the bomb throwers was found to be in possession of communist literature. Although the strike was preceded by the formation of a shoemakers' union as an affiliate of the NGLU, and the NPC was assumed to have been behind the strike, the MCP in its later correspondence with the Comintern blamed the bombings on the "masses."[98] Thus, the NPC's role remained uncertain. The NPC also piggybacked on the anti-Japanese boycott and the campaign organized by the Chinese community to commemorate the GMD's retreat from Ji'nan, known as the Ji'nan Incident.[99] In 1928, the *Straits Times* reported that the communists had "good organization, clever leaders, and the will to progress."[100]

As we have seen, the CCP's local organization in Malaya was shaped by the historical trends of Chinese migration and the political forces in China as well as by the interwar global and Southeast Asian communist connections. The need of Chinese organizations to indigenize so as to fit in better with local society matched the need for the localization of Comintern operations.

World Revolution, Chinese Revolution: Indigenization and Internationalization

Since the emergence of Chinese nationalism in the late nineteenth century, Chinese community organizations had been concerned with bringing in and representing not only Chinese. The MCP's impulse to involve non-Chinese in its activities paralleled the impulses not only of newly emerging Chinese organizations like the GMD but also of organizations with longer histories, such as temples. In 1893, the leader of the Chinese community in Kuala Lumpur, *Kapitan Cina* (Chinese Captain) Yap Ah Loy, founded a temple dedicated to the previous

---

[97] "Societies Opposed to Kuo Min Tang," in "The Report by the Secretary of Chinese Affairs on Kuo Min Tang up till June 30th 1927," p. 147, CO 273/542/52010.
[98] CC MCP, "From Malaya. To the FEB [Far Eastern Bureau of the Comintern]," February 7, 1931, RGASPI 495/62/10/2–3. For more details on the shoemakers' strike, see Yong, *Origins of Malayan Communism*, pp. 113–118.
[99] See Chapter 7.
[100] "Communism in Malaya: Present Positions," *Straits Times*, November 16, 1928, p. 11.

Kapitan, and the processions of the temple included Indians and Japanese along with headmen of Chinese subethnic groups. Yap Ah Loy sought to portray himself as representing not only the Chinese but the wider community as well.[101]

During the 1920s, the GMD further put into practice its earlier Asianist ideas of the liberation of the oppressed peoples. Since 1927, efforts by Chinese political organizations to embed themselves in their host environments had been evident in the left-wing GMD and in the CCP's Nanyang Provisional Committee, as both had called for local non-Chinese in British Malaya, that is, Malays, Javanese, and Tamils,[102] to be involved in a united movement for liberation from colonial oppression.[103] During the commemorative demonstration on the anniversary of Sun Yatsen's death on March 12, 1927, which resulted in clashes with the police, known as the Kreta Ayer Incident, the GMD issued pamphlets promoting the common interests of the "weak nationals" of the Nanyang and overseas Chinese in their goal to achieve self-determination and to end the discrimination against Chinese.[104] The leftist GMD, which was strong in Singapore, controlling twenty-one of twenty-nine branches (the Main School),[105] proclaimed that its goal was "the emancipation of the [Chinese] race."[106] The Comintern's plan to infiltrate Southeast Asia through indigenization, using local agents and propaganda in native languages, was likewise central to the CCP's expansion into the Nanyang. In July 1928, the NPC had already decided to start a "national" movement to attract Malays and Indians to the Chinese party organization. It also set a goal of unifying all nationalities and seeking the Comintern's guidance and leadership.[107]

---

[101] Sharon A. Carstens, "Chinese Culture and Policy in Nineteenth-Century Malaya: The Case of Yap Ah Loy," in David Ownby and Mary Somers Heidhues, eds., *"Secret Societies" Reconsidered: Perspectives on the Social History of Modern South China and Southeast Asia* (Armonk, NY: M. E. Sharpe, 1993), pp. 120–153, esp. p. 142.

[102] MBPI, May 1927, CO 273/535/ C28030, p. 4.

[103] Yong, *Origins of Malayan Communism*, pp. 78, 160; "Resoliutsia priniataia posle obsledovaniia raboty vremennogo komiteta v 1929 [Resolution Adopted after Investigation of the Work of the (Nanyang) Provisional Committee in 1929]," RGASPI 495/62/1/ 23–27, esp. 23.

[104] "Message to the Overseas Chinese in Respect of the Second Anniversary of the Death of Sun Chung San [Sun Yatsen]," CO 273/538.

[105] Quinn-Judge, *Ho Chi Minh*, p. 134.

[106] "Purport of the General Registration of Tang Members of China Kuo Min Tang," September 22, 1928, pp. 1–3, CO 273/542/ 52010/28.

[107] Vremennyi komitet malaiskogo arkhipelaga [Nanyang Provisional Committee], "V tsentral'nyi komitet. Otchet Malaiskogo Komiteta profsoiuzov [To the Central Committee. The Report of the Soviet of Trade Unions of the Malay Archipelago]," July 19 and August 22, 1928, RGASPI 495/62/1/1–17, esp. 2, 3.

The CCP's aim of involving non-Chinese in its organization is reflected in the writings of Li Lisan, who by 1928 was the head of the Guangdong Provincial Committee and the de facto CCP leader. He had experience working in France among Chinese laborers, and his charismatic leadership and ability to adapt to different local cultural contexts had resulted in the CCP's first successful labor mobilization in 1922 in the Anyuan coal mines.[108] Li Lisan criticized the Nanyang communists in his January 1, 1929, diary entry for "making a Chinese Revolution." This "Chinese Revolution" referred specifically to anti-Japanese propaganda and boycotts, to the campaign for democratic freedoms and improved labor conditions, and to protests against British attempts to control Chinese education in Malaya.[109] Li Lisan promoted the establishment of a CCP organization independent of the GMD. Criticizing the GMD policy of promoting "patriotism" in Chinese communities, Li instead advocated a Nanyang Revolution that would mark the beginning of a "national" movement:

The Party's Nanyang branch has been established for three years; the number of comrades has increased greatly. However, there has been a fundamentally erroneous idea from the beginning, i.e., to "make a Chinese Revolution" in the Nanyang. Although, certainly, to make a "Chinese Revolution" in the Nanyang is a joke, it has deep historical roots. Was not the Nanyang the "cradle" of the Guomindang? This is because the Chinese in the Nanyang were brutally oppressed by imperialism; for this reason they thought, "This is because China is too weak, and cannot protect Chinese immigrants." That is why Chinese in the Nanyang have a very strong patriotic mentality [*aiguo guannian*]. This patriotic mentality is the source of making a Chinese Revolution in the Nanyang. Now our party must completely rectify this mentality; it must promote the following idea among the broad masses: "In order to achieve the liberation of the Chinese people in the Nanyang, the Nanyang Revolution must succeed, and for this reason we must go back to making the Nanyang revolutionary movement." This will put the Nanyang Revolution on the right track and will be the correct starting point for the Nanyang party line.[110]

The same words were included in a draft resolution of the Central Committee (CC) of the CCP to the Nanyang Provisional Committee entitled "the revolutionary movements and policies of our party in the

[108] Ren Guixiang and Zhao Hongying, eds., *Huaqiao huaren yu guogong guanxi* [*Chinese Overseas and CCP–GMD Relations*] (Wuhan: Wuhan chubanshe, 1999), p. 80; Elizabeth J. Perry, *Anyuan: Mining China's Revolutionary Tradition* (Berkeley, CA: University of California Press, 2012), pp. 85–86, 148.

[109] Vremennyi komitet malaiskogo arkhipelaga [Nanyang Provisional Committee], "V tsentral'nyi komitet. Otchet Malaiskogo Komiteta profsoiuzov [To the Central Committee. The Report of the Soviet of Trade Unions of the Malay Archipelago]."

[110] Zhonggong zhongyang dangshi yanjiushi diyi yanjiubu, ed., *Li Lisan bai nian dancheng jinianji* [*Commemoration on the 100th Anniversary of Li Lisan's Birth: Collection of Writings*] (Beijing: Zhonggong zhongyang dangshi chubanshe, 1999), "1 January 1929," pp. 68–69.

Nanyang." The directive set the goals of the Nanyang Revolution as national independence from the British and Dutch governments, an alliance of "Nanyang nationalities," and a Nanyang republic. The central point of the directive was that a Nanyang communist party consisting exclusively of Chinese promoting a Chinese Revolution indicated a need to adapt the communist strategy to the local context, as policies developed in the labor and anti-imperialist movements in China were applied in the Nanyang without consideration of local conditions. Those conditions included the Nanyang's colonial status, the "many nationalities" living there, and its more developed industry.[111] Although the idea that the Nanyang Revolution depended on the success of the revolution in China was also criticized, Li Lisan's directive still tasked the Chinese with emancipation of the Nanyang and emphasized that Chinese and locals could not achieve colonial liberation separately. Written in English, this letter makes his opinion clear:

We should further impress these slogans and conception deeply upon the minds of the Chinese to remove their wrong ideas as to look down on other nations [i.e., ethnic groups] and then the real unity can be obtained ... But it is known that Chinese there did oppress Malay people, because the latter are poor and backward in civilisation. So it is the fundamental task of our party to tighten the relationship of all the oppressed nations and to make the Malay people understand that in order to release them from the yoke of the imperialists, the unity of the oppressed is absolutely necessary. If the Chinese want to claim for emancipation, it is possible only when all the oppressed nations are released. It is absolutely impossible to release any single nation separately ... Thus, the principal task of our party is first of all to make all the oppressed unite and strive for the goal of national emancipation.[112]

The directive echoes two central points that were discussed at the Comintern congress in Moscow. Specifically, these were the Chinese Revolution as a frame of reference and the need for each party's policy to be based on local conditions,[113] that is, the policy of indigenization of the communist movement. These points were also echoed in statements by leaders of other communist parties, such as the Taiwanese Communist Party and the Philippine Communist Party, in 1928–1930.[114]

[111] CCP CC, "A Letter from the Central Committee of the CCP to the Nanyang Provisional Committee. A Draft Resolution of the Central Committee of the Chinese Communist Party on the Revolutionary Movements and Policies of Our Party in the Nanyang," January 22, 1929, RGASPI 514/1/532/8–13, pp. 13, 8–9.
[112] Ibid., p. 10.
[113] Stenograficheskii otchet VI kongressa Kominterna [Stenographic Report of the Sixth Congress of the Comintern] (Leningrad: Gosudarstvennoe izdatel'stvo, 1929), vypusk 5 [issue 5], p. 143, vypusk 4 [issue 4], p. 414.
[114] Konstantin Tertitskii and Anna Belogurova, Taiwanskoe kommunisticheskoe dvizhenie i Komintern. Issledovanie. Dokumenty (1924–1932) [The Taiwanese Communist Movement and the Comintern: A Study. Documents. 1924–1932)] (Moscow: Vostok-Zapad, 2005), p. 95; Gao Zinong, "Zhongguo gongchan qingnian tuan Feiliebin tebie difang gongzuo

Li Lisan's suggestions reflected what was happening in the Comintern. In 1928, he participated in the Sixth Congress of the CCP (June 18 to July 11) and in the Sixth Congress of the Comintern (July 17 to September 1) in Moscow. The CCP's Sixth Congress elected a new leadership aligned closely with the Comintern, announced the goal of organizing soviets, and supported guerrilla warfare.[115] According to two sources, the reorganization of the Nanyang communist organization in 1928 into the NPC took place at the Sixth Congress of the CCP.[116] However, the Nanyang communists' views on the Nanyang Revolution were independent of the Comintern's. Moreover, Li Lisan (and others) referred to this letter to the Nanyang communists as a draft for discussion only, as they considered the problems of the Nanyang "complicated." Although they also submitted this draft directive to the Comintern for approval, Li Lisan asserted that even prior to that, the Nanyang communists were to follow the draft resolution.[117] In doing so, the CCP was making a gesture toward the Comintern and also redirecting responsibility to the Comintern.

According to available documentary evidence, it was the CCP that first suggested the organization of a Nanyang party under Comintern leadership: "The party in the Nanyang should make preparations to establish an independent party of the Nanyang, directly instructed by the Third International." Moreover, it stated, "suggestions should be submitted to the Third International to call their attention to the work of the Nanyang because it would occupy a very important position during the looming World War, and to ask them to convene a meeting of the parties of various nations to discuss the work of the Nanyang."[118] (In the Comintern's analysis, the coming war would resolve contradictions among the imperialist powers that persisted after the First World War.) The CC thus redirected the Nanyang communists to the Comintern and Profintern to obtain the resources necessary to implement these suggestions.[119]

An ECCI letter written in October 1930, after the MCP had been formally established, confirms the local initiative for the establishment

baogao [Work Report of the Philippine Special Local Committee of the Chinese Communist Youth League]."
[115] Tony Saich, "The Chinese Communist Party during the Era of the Comintern (1919–1943)," unpublished manuscript.
[116] Xie Fei, "Huiyi Zhongguo gongchandang Nanyang linshi weiyuanhui de gongzuo, 1929–1930 [Remembering the Work of the Nanyang Provisional Committee, 1929–1930]." p. 161; "Hu Zhiming de shehuizhuyi sixiang [The Socialist Thought of Ho Chi Minh]," in He Baoyi, *Shijie shehuizhuyi sixiang tongjian* [*World Socialist Thought*] (Beijing: Renmin chubanshe, 1996), p. 492.
[117] CC CCP, "A Letter from the Central Committee of the CCP to the Nanyang Provisional Committee," 1929.
[118] Ibid., p. 10.
[119] Ibid.

of the MCP and calls the newly established party "nothing more than a Singapore organization of the CCP that recently decided to separate into an independent communist party of the Malay states." The ECCI letter continued: "It is a very serious step forward, as it is absolutely clear that it is necessary to establish an independent communist party of the Malay states which will include the proletariat of all nationalities who inhabit them and which will be capable of organizing and leading a united struggle of the toiling masses of Malaya."[120] However, in its letter to the British communist party, the MCP emphasized that the Nanyang communists followed the "advice of the 'Bureau' in reorganizing themselves into an independent communist party of Malaya," apparently stressing its international credentials.[121]

However, far from expressing an intention to undermine the CCP's position in Southeast Asia,[122] in 1928 the Comintern also considered establishing a CCP overseas center "near China (Singapore, Manila, etc.)," where Central Committee members could carry out their work unrecognized, unlike the situation in Shanghai, where they were known to the now hostile GMD.[123] After the establishment of the MCP, the Comintern echoed Li Lisan in criticizing the MCP for "mechanistically grafting the methods and slogans of the Chinese movement in Malaya."[124] The Comintern's recommendations and Li Lisan's directive to stop focusing on the Chinese Revolution both aimed to promote the indigenization of the revolution, that is, a united front with the non-Chinese.[125] Similar to the migrant structure of the communist movement and of society at large, the MCP's vision of a multiethnic party organization was likely influenced by the American communist movement. Li Lisan suggested that the Pan-Pacific Trade Union Secretariat could help the MCP

[120] Executive Committee of the Communist International (ECCI), "Malaiskoe pis'mo [Malayan Letter]," Letter to the FEB, October 23, 1930, RGASPI 495/62/2/1,2.
[121] MCP, "To the English Komparty [sic], London," June 1, 1930, RGASPI 495/62/6/1–1ob.
[122] Cheah, *From PKI to the Comintern*; Yong, *Origins of Malayan Communism*, pp. 131–134; Rene H. Onraet, *Singapore: A Police Background* (London: Dorothy Crisp, 1947), p. 109; Quinn-Judge, *Ho Chi Minh*, p. 168. One exception to this view is Charles B. McLane, *Soviet Strategies in Southeast Asia* (Princeton, NJ: Princeton University Press, 1966), pp. 202–203.
[123] "Pis'mo A. E. Albrekhta I. A Piatnitskomu [The Letter of A. E. Albreht to I. A. Piatnitskii]," May 1, 1928, in Titarenko and Leutner, *Komintern i Kitai [Comintern and China]*, vol. 3, pp. 381–384. A. E. Albrekht was the representative of the Comintern's International Liaison Department (*Otdel Mezhdunarodnykh Sviazei*) (OMS) in China. Iosif (Osip) A. Piatnitskii was a member of the ECCI presidium. For their biographical information, see Titarenko and Leutner, *Komintern i Kitai [Comintern and China]*, vol. 3, pp. 1514, 1557–1558.
[124] ECCI Letter to the FEB, October 23, 1930.
[125] Ibid.

"in building a stable foundation" for the trade union movement in the Nanyang, which should first be organized among separate ethnic groups and then be united into one trade union.[126] The head of the Pan-Pacific Trade Union Secretariat (est. 1927 in Hankou) was American communist Earl Browder, whose organizational ideas originated in the American multiethnic context. Moreover, the Comintern promoted the same policy of indigenization in Malaya as in the United States, where Americanization was a response to pressures by American communists, as immigrant sections in the CPUSA were the largest.[127] Much as Li Lisan had appealed to the Nanyang communists, the Chinese Comintern cadre from Moscow reminded Chinese communists in the United States that they had to pay attention to local conditions in those countries where they established chapters of the AAAIL, but at the same time they should not forget to conduct revolutionary work among Chinese migrants in the United States.[128] In the Chinese communist networks enhanced by the Comintern, policies were generally built on locally based approaches and applied elsewhere as well.

This was possible with the globally mobile Chinese communists. The translator of Li Lisan's letter, lacking knowledge of the South Seas, mistranslated "Zhaowa" (Java) as "Cuba" and "Senmeilan" (Sembilan) as "Ceylon." One of few translators available since Tan Malaka's desperate search for one in 1924,[129] the translator was likely Stanford student Shi Huang, who was dispatched to Cuba and Canada in 1929 by the Chinese faction of the CPUSA to build an Oriental branch of the American Anti-Imperialist League on the Pacific coast among local communists. After visiting Cuba, Shi went to Moscow to study and he returned to China in 1930 to work as a translator for the Central Committee of the Chinese Communist Party, though he perished in a GMD jail in 1934.[130]

By 1930, while the two trends of the interwar global moment, internationalism and indigenization, were manifested in the transnational organization of the Chinese Revolution, the importance of the Chinese Revolution as a harbinger of global changes perceived as the world revolution originally advocated by the Comintern, had become integral to the

[126] CC CCP, "A Letter from the Central Committee of the CCP to the Nanyang Provisional Committee," 1929.
[127] Jacob A. Zumoff, *The Communist International and US Communism, 1919–1929* (Leiden; Boston, MA: Brill, 2014), p. 15, ch. 5.
[128] Letter to the Chinese Faction of CPUSA, April 4, 1933.
[129] Tan Malaka's letter, October 1924, RGASPI 534/4/106/19–22, esp. 20.
[130] Fowler, *Japanese and Chinese Immigrant Activists*, pp. 145–146; Hu Xianzhang, ed., *Ziqiang buxi houde zaiwu: Qinghua jingshen xunli* [*Self-Discipline and Social Commitment Are Tsinghua Spirit*] (Beijing: Qinghua daxue chubanshe, 2010), pp. 124–127; CC CCP, "A Letter from the Central Committee of the CCP to the Nanyang Provisional Committee," 1929.

platforms of both the CCP and the GMD. In the words of Hu Hanmin, "Our Chinese nation is truly so large that our national revolution must obtain international assistance and establish international contacts. Of course, the responsibilities that we, the Chinese people, ought to bear will be heavy ones indeed. To the smaller and weaker nations we should offer support in order to strengthen the forces of revolution and secure the foundation for revolution."[131] Li Lisan considered China to be the site of the most acute conflicts of interest (*protivorechie*) among the imperialist powers, where the prospect of a communist revolution seemed most likely. Li Lisan therefore argued, "[i]ncreasing international propaganda for the Chinese Revolution among the international proletariat and regarding the defense of the Chinese Revolution as the most serious task of the Chinese Communist Party."[132] Li Lisan continued Hu Hanmin's earlier attempts to use the Comintern for the benefit of the Chinese Revolution and to promote Chinese nationalism. On April 17, 1930, one week before the MCP's founding, he suggested establishing a new, more efficient Far Eastern Bureau (FEB) of the Comintern, which had been reestablished in late 1928 in Shanghai. In communications with the Eastern secretariat of the Comintern in Moscow, he specifically demanded that organizational activities among foreign sailors, while carried out by "foreign comrades from England, France, Japan, India, [and] Indochina," should remain under CCP leadership.[133] Despite Li Lisan's exile to Moscow for his devastating policy of doomed uprisings, which nearly destroyed the CCP, he was involved in a number of important Comintern projects, working in the mid-1930s in the Xinjiang border region.[134] Li Lisan also took part in drafting policies for the MCP.

Conclusion

The proximity of British Malaya to the Dutch East Indies, a place of great interest to the Comintern as well as the homeland of one of the visionaries of early communism in Indonesia, Tan Malaka, on the one hand, and a historically large Chinese community in British Malaya, on the other, shaped the birth of communism in the British colony.

---

[131] Hu Hanmin, "Minzu guoji yu disan guoji [International of Nationalities and the Third (Communist) International]."

[132] "Pismo Li Lisania Zhou Enlaiu i Tsiui Tsiubo [Li Lisan's Letter to Zhou Enlai and Qu Qiubo (Qu Qiubai)]," April 17, 1930, in Titarenko and Leutner, *Komintern i Kitai* [*Comintern and China*], vol. 3, pp. 865–868.

[133] Ibid.

[134] Elizaveta Kishkina (Li Sha), *Iz Rossii v Kitai – put' dlinoiu v sto let* [*From Russia to China: One Hundred Years' Journey*] (Moscow: Izdatel'skii proekt, 2014), p. 100.

Globalizing forces brought about a new political imagination and new forms of activism in Asia. Pan-Asianism, anticolonialism, and indigenous nationalist projects shaped the two Chinese political parties overseas, the GMD and the CCP. Traditional Chinese universalist ideas and organizational patterns of Chinese migration, as well as discrimination against Chinese migrants, resonated with the interwar internationalist moment and with Sun Yatsen's idea of allying with the oppressed for the sake of China's revival. As we see in Chapter 6, Sun's ideas permeated school curricula both in China and in overseas communities and thus channeled the Chinese migrant revolutionaries' struggle for equal rights where they intended to settle in their search for employment and livelihood. The Comintern's goal of liberating the colonies offered an internationalist legitimization for those revolutionaries. Chinese communists argued that in the Philippines, in Cuba, and around the world, Chinese communists could help the revolutions of local residents (*juliudi de minzu geming*) along with the revolution in China[135] and that a world revolution and national liberation of the colonies would be beneficial for China's national interests and for the "soviet" (*suweiai*) revolution.[136]

Chinese communists borrowed existing imperial imaginations and institutions to develop their own networks and to improve the livelihood of their compatriots and revive China as well as to build a better world of justice and equality. The result was hybrid organizations of anti-imperialist leagues based on the American imagination of the Monroe Doctrine and on the global Comintern vision. They took responsibility for the movement in the Americas based on *huaqiao* organizations, as it was in the Nanyang, where its policy matched China's patterns of historical patronage in Southeast Asia, as discussed in Chapter 5. In this global quest for China's revival, Chinese migrants found partners among those whom Sun Yatsen described as the "oppressed nations." Among Germans, discriminated Chinese workers in the United States, native

[135] Gao Zinong, "Zhongguo gongchan qingnian tuan Feiliebin tebie difang gongzuo baogao [Work Report of the Philippine Special Local Committee of the Chinese Communist Youth League]"; Xu Yongying, "Zhongguo Guomindang yu Guba geming [The Chinese GMD and the Cuban Revolution]," *The Chinese Vanguard* (105), October 15, 1933.
[136] Han Han (possibly Chen Hanxing), "Lun zai huaqiao gongzuo zhong zhixing geming luxian [Regarding the Revolutionary Line in Working among Chinese Overseas]," *The Chinese Vanguard*, March 15, 1934, p. 3. The phrase "China's soviet revolution" (*Zhongguo suweiai geming*) migrated to the CCP texts from the Comintern's discourse, which promoted the "soviet movement" (*sovetskoe dvizhenie*) in China. It referred to the specific mode of government by *soviets*. A *soviet* ("council" in Russian) was a governing organization made up of the "toiling masses" during the Russian Revolution of 1917. Thus, the phrase "China's soviet revolution" describes the aspired revolutionary government led by the communist party.

workers in the American colonies, and native Filipinos and Malays, who were oppressed by their colonizers, the label of being an "oppressed nation" reflected their subjugated status vis-à-vis the winners at Versailles.

In these overlapping networks of Chinese migrants and the Comintern, organizational modes circulated across the globe. The internationalization of the idea of the Chinese Revolution and the indigenization of two Chinese overseas organizations, the CCP and the GMD, manifested a feature of interwar global connectedness in conjunction with a continuous need for Chinese organizations to localize. Worldwide economic nationalism as a reaction to the Great Depression led scholars to proclaim "the end of globalization,"[137] yet, as we see in what follows, a new localized chapter of a global organization had been established by 1930 in the Nanyang. The era was one of those "global moments" that, in the context of "developing a global consciousness in diverse social contexts," contributed to the integration and overlap of distinct discursive communities on local, national, and regional levels.[138]

The discourse of the Nanyang Revolution as an indigenized revolution and the concern with the CCP directive being inappropriate for local conditions demonstrated a conjuncture of the Comintern's indigenization and the indigenization of the Chinese organizations, the GMD and the CCP.[139] These cast a fresh light on the ways in which both MCP nationalism and the Comintern's ideas about indigenization were used for mobilization purposes. Moreover, these indigenization trends coincided with the quest for local identity and subculture among *huaqiao* intellectuals in British Malaya.

[137] Harold James, *The End of Globalization: Lessons from the Great Depression* (Cambridge, MA: Harvard University Press, 2001).
[138] Sebastian Conrad and Dominic Sachsenmaier, "Introduction: Competing Visions of World Order: Global Moments and Movements, 1880s–1930s," in Sebastian Conrad and Dominic Sachsenmaier, eds., *Competing Visions of World Order: Global Moments and Movements, 1880s–1930s* (New York, NY: Palgrave Macmillan, 2007), pp. 1–25, esp. p. 15.
[139] The trope of central missives being inappropriate for local conditions echoes the fears of scholarly officials that bureaucracy could substitute written texts for living "practical" experience. Alexander Woodside, *Lost Modernities: China, Vietnam, Korea, and the Hazards of World History*. Edwin O. Reischauer Lecture. (Cambridge, MA: Harvard University Press, 2006), pp. 20–21.

3 The Nanyang Revolution and the Malayan Nation, 1929–1930

Nations, Migrants, Words

Background

In Southeast Asia, indigenous nationalists adopted the Western concept of nation-states. The nation-states there had also been shaped by the geopolitical limits of colonial and precolonial polities as well as by the colonial concepts of boundaries and colonial ethnic policies.[1] During the late nineteenth and early twentieth centuries, the exclusion and xenophobia generated by increasing Chinese migration to Southeast Asia and the Pacific region fostered the nationalism of the host countries and helped strengthen the idea of territorial borders.[2] British Malaya was not an exception. While the idea of a Malayan nation was first promoted by the British government, immigrants did not have political rights in that nation.

British Malaya came under colonial control between 1874 and 1919. A mass migration of Chinese laborers to the Malay Peninsula began after Britain imposed its rule in the western Malay states in 1874 to pacify feuds among Chinese tin mine owners.[3] These owners benefited from the British takeover,[4] but violence by Chinese secret societies led to a British ban on such organizations beginning in 1890, including on the GMD in Malaya (1925) and in Singapore (1930). Noncompliant Straits Settlement Chinese community leaders were deported, Chinese were denied their Chinese political rights as "aliens," and re-Sinicization through Chinese-language education and the press of the Chinese

---

[1] Thongchai Winichakul, *Siam Mapped: A History of the Geo-Body of a Nation* (Honolulu, HI: University of Hawaii Press, 1994); David Henley, "Ethnogeographic Integration and Exclusion in Anticolonial Nationalism: Indonesia and Indochina," *Comparative Studies in Society and History* 37(2) (1995), pp. 286–324; Christopher E. Goscha, *Going Indochinese: Contesting Concepts of Space and Place in French Indochina* (Copenhagen: Nordic Institute of Asian Studies, 2012).

[2] Sebastian Conrad and Klaus Mühlhahn, "Global Mobility and Nationalism: Chinese Migration and the Re-territorialization of Belonging, 1880–1910," in Conrad and Sachsenmaier, eds., *Competing Visions of World Order*, pp. 181–212.

[3] Kuhn, *Chinese among Others*, pp. 160–161.

[4] Ibid., p. 182.

government was restricted.[5] In contrast, the British recruited Malays into lower administrative ranks, protected Malay land rights, and preserved Malay peasant customs.[6] The Chinese in Malaya viewed such actions as oppressive, and leaders of commercial, clan, and regional associations therefore promoted Chinese political rights. The Chinese dominated the cities of the Malay Peninsula and comprised the majority of the population in most of the states. According to the 1921 census, nearly half of the Malayan population, around 3,358,000 people, was Indian (14.2 percent) or Chinese (35 percent), and in 1931, the shares increased to 16 percent and 39 percent, respectively.[7] At this time, 65 percent of Chinese in Malaya worked in tin mines, small rubber holdings, and farms, while 75 percent of Indians worked on European rubber estates.[8]

Malays felt "left behind" in their world during the colonial period, invaded by foreign capital, goods, and labor, and they were alarmed by the rise in Chinese immigration.[9] Toynbee famously wrote in 1931 that Malaya was destined to become "a Chinese province by peaceful penetration."[10] In these circumstances, debates took place regarding the creation of a Malay nation based on race, descent, and land rights (*bangsa Melayu*). Newspapers promoted the spirit of Malay unification and the erosion of boundaries dividing the Malay community, and Malay intellectuals talked about the crisis of Malay Muslim society and promoted "the values of rationalism and egalitarianism."[11] In the 1930s, Malay newspapers were filled with articles discussing service to the *bangsa* (nation). *Warta Bangsa*, the first issue of which was published in 1930, declared that its goal was to "raise up" the Malay race. The *bangsa* excluded non-Malays, though it was not based on Islam. To counter the rise of pan-Islamic sentiments, the British government supported the cultivation of a Malay identity on which the creation of a *bangsa*

---

[5] Ching Fatt Yong and R. B. McKenna, *The Kuomintang Movement in British Malaya, 1912–1949* (Singapore: Singapore University Press, 1990), pp. 47, 137, 141; Wang Gungwu, "The Limits of Nanyang Chinese Nationalism, 1912–1937," in Charles D. Cowan and Oliver W. Wolters, eds., *Southeast Asian History and Historiography* (Ithaca, NY: Cornell University Press, 1976), pp. 405–423.

[6] William Roff, *The Origins of Malay Nationalism* (New Haven, CT: Yale University Press, 1967), pp. 118, 122.

[7] Cheah Boon Kheng, *Red Star over Malaya: Resistance and Social Conflict during and after the Japanese Occupation of Malaya, 1941–1946* (Singapore: Singapore University Press, 1983), p. 3; Roff, *Origins of Malay Nationalism*, p. 208.

[8] Yeo Kim Wah, *The Politics of Decentralization: Colonial Controversy in Malaya, 1920–1929* (Kuala Lumpur: Oxford University Press, 1982), pp. 33–35.

[9] Anthony Milner, *The Malays* (Malden, MA; Oxford: Wiley-Blackwell, 2008), pp. 110–111.

[10] Ibid., p. 227.

[11] Milner, *Invention of Politics in Colonial Malaya*, pp. 270, 290.

community was contingent.[12] Originally, the Malay sense of identity evolved around *kerajaan*, a community oriented toward a royal ruler, the *raja*. After World War I, the issue of descent came to the forefront, as Malays refused to recognize the right of the Peranakan Chinese, Indians, and Arabs to serve as representatives on the Legislative Councils of the Malay States and of the Straits Settlements in light of the economic gap between Malays and non-Malays. At the same time, Malays were reluctant to participate in politics because of the disapproval of the Malay elite and the British authorities. In 1931, a comment by Penang Chinese leader Lim Cheng Yan that the Chinese community had become inseparable from Malaya sparked a debate in the Malay press, which created a sense of solidarity in the Malay community. The Malay press discussed *bangsa Melayu* and argued against the historical legitimacy of the term *Malaya*.[13] For many Malays, the term *Malayan* invoked the threat of immigrant domination.[14]

As a consequence of the Great Depression in Malaya, the world's foremost producer of tin and rubber, both the new wave of poor Chinese migrants who had no citizenship rights in the colony and the more affluent locally born Chinese were hit hard. Not only did the economic depression and British protectionist policies undermine Chinese economic power in Malaya but the British government also introduced legislation limiting Chinese migration. For immigrants, it became crucial to become a part of the "Malayan nation" promoted by the British government and to have the legal status of locals in order to gain political and landowning rights as well as to decrease the risk of deportation.

The Founding of the MCP

An independent Nanyang party was formed in 1930 through the initiative of the Nanyang Provisional Committee of the Chinese Communist Party (CCP) in Singapore, which became the core of the newly established MCP.[15] The Comintern policy of creating national parties and fostering a world revolution based on local conditions[16] was related to several

---

[12] Ibid., pp. 272–273.
[13] Omar, *Bangsa Melayu*, pp. 1, 14–19.
[14] Yamamoto Hiroyuki, Anthony Milner, Midori Kawashima, and Kazuhiko Arai, eds., *Bangsa and Umma: Development of People-Grouping Concepts in Islamized Southeast Asia* (Kyoto: Kyoto University Press, 2011); Anthony Reid, "Melayu as a Source of Diverse Modern Identities," in Timothy Barnard, ed., *Contesting Malayness: Malay Identity across Boundaries* (Singapore: Singapore University Press, 2004), pp. 1–24.
[15] Letter of the ECCI to the FEB, October 23, 1930; Hanrahan, *The Communist Struggle in Malaya*, pp. 38–39.
[16] FEB, "To the Malayan Comrades," December 17, 1930, RGASPI 495/62/12/1–2ob.

factors: the indigenization trend in the CCP, a growing tendency for
Malayan Chinese to see advantages in identifying with Malaya, and
a sense among Chinese intellectuals of an identity independent of China.
Chinese communists in Singapore and Malaya hoped that the establishment of the MCP would help expand their organizational network,
saying, "[t]he CP of [the] Malaya Peninsula can help the organization in
those districts where the communist party has not been formed."[17] Since
the work of Nanyang Chinese organizations was insufficiently active for
the organization of a new party, in consultation with the CC CCP in
Guangdong, Chinese communists decided to first reestablish party organizations and then to revive party work. Because of this decision and
because of arrests, their conference was delayed for more than a year.
However, twenty individuals eventually attended the third conference of
the Nanyang party, the MCP founding conference, from April 22 to 23,
1930. Eleven of these individuals were arrested on April 29, including the
secretary of the party, the secretary of the labor union, and a member of
the Central Committee.[18]

Two Comintern envoys, Fu Daqing and Ho Chi Minh, the head of the
Comintern's office in Hong Kong in 1930 – who was also possibly
the head of the Southern Bureau of the CCP with jurisdiction over the
Nanyang – presided over the conference.[19] Among other founders were
Li Guangyuan (黎光远), Wu Qing (吴清), Secretary Wei Zongzhou (魏宗
周),[20] Lin Qingchong (林庆充), Wang Yuebo (王月波), Chen Shaochang
(陈绍昌), Pang Qinchang, and Lee Chay-heng. The standing committee
of MCP members included Wu Qing, Fu Daqing, and Li Guangyuan. All
were predominantly Hainanese and in their twenties.[21] Also in atten-
dance was a CYL representative from Siam.[22] Famous writer Ai Wu,

[17] "Resolutions Adopted at the Third Congress of the Malaya Party," 1930, RGASPI 495/
62/3/1–10.
[18] "Minutes of the Third Representative Conference of Nanyang," p. 109; "Protokol der.3.
Delegierten Konferenz von Nanyang (Malayische) [Protocol of the Third Representative
Conference of the Nanyang Party (Malayan)]," undated, but likely 1930, RGASPI 514/
1/634/86–92; MCP, "To the English Komparty." The existing MCP historiography has
conflicting dates for the MCP's establishment. See Hack and Chin, eds., *Dialogues with
Chin Peng*, pp. 61–62. There are also conflicting accounts of the place. According to Fujio
Hara and Yong, the MCP was established either in Sembilan, Kuala Pilah, or in Johor,
Buloh Kesap. Fujio Hara, "Di'erci shijie dazhan qiande Malaiya gongchandang [The
MCP before the Second World War]," *Nanyang ziliao yicong* [*Compendia of Nanyang
Materials*] 160(4) (2005), pp. 56–70, esp. p. 57; Yong, *Origins of Malayan Communism*,
pp. 128–129. Nowhere in the MCP documents collected by the Comintern was the place
of the MCP's establishment mentioned.
[19] Quinn-Judge, *Ho Chi Minh*, p. 162.
[20] Likely, the same individual as Wei Zhongzhou. See Chapter 2.
[21] Yong, *Origins of Malayan Communism*, pp. 72, 98, 130, 134–141.
[22] "Minutes of the Third Representative Conference of Nanyang," pp. 137–140.

who had joined a communist cell in Burma in 1928, missed the meeting because the ship on which he was traveling was placed under quarantine.[23]

The establishment of the MCP was under double supervision, that of both "the central committee and K," likely "Kvok" (Nguyen Ai Quoc, or Ho Chi Minh) or the Comintern, who decided the political line in the Nanyang. The representative of the Far Eastern Bureau (FEB), that is, Ho Chi Minh, chaired the conference.[24] Ho was concerned about the CCP's domination in mainland Southeast Asia over Vietnamese communist networks and sought to balance this out with the Comintern's authority. He had decided to establish his Indochinese party under Comintern jurisdiction a month earlier so as to exclude the influence of the CCP's Singapore branch, which by 1930 was attempting to lead communist organizations in Annam (central Vietnam), Indochina, and Siam on behalf of the Comintern. Then, possibly to counter the influence of the Vietnamese, the NPC decided to hold a reorganization meeting as soon as possible, without waiting for NPC inspector "Comrade Li"[25] to return from Siam and Indochina, citing that it was running out of money, apparently hoping for Comintern subsidies. Once the MCP had been established, Ho proposed a joint three- to five-member committee of the CCP, the Annamese party, and the Comintern's FEB in order to foster cooperation between the Yunnan and Tonkin sections, Hong Kong and Annam, and the Annamese working in China. Despite Ho formally proposing cooperation among the Vietnamese, the CCP, and the Comintern, his suggestions ran contrary to Li Lisan's proposal to keep Indochinese seamen in China under the guidance of the CCP (see Chapter 2). Ho was worried that the Chinese communists in "the secretariat of Nanyang" considered the Philippines, Indochina, Siam, Malaya, and the Dutch East Indies to be under their leadership. Ho, however, did not hesitate to instruct the MCP to build independent parties in Siam, Borneo, and Sumatra at the MCP's founding meeting. Six weeks prior to this meeting, as the FEB was planning "the conference of [the] communist organization of Malaya," Ho approached the FEB in Shanghai with some suggestions regarding future strategies. As a result, the Comintern decided to dispatch Ho to Singapore together with Moscow-trained

[23] Fan Quan, "Ji Ai Wu yige kule yibeizi, xiele yibeizi de zuojia [Remembering Ai Wu: A Bitter Life, a Writer of the Lifetime]," in Fan Quan, *Wenhai xiaoyan* [*The Smoke of the Sea of Literature*] (Ha'erbin: Heilongjiang renmin chubanshe, 1998), pp. 68–91.
[24] "Protokol der.3. Delegierten Konferenz von Nanyang (Malayische) [Protocol of the Third Representative Conference of the Nanyang Party (Malayan)]," p. 86.
[25] There are two possible candidates for this "Comrade Li" in the Nanyang party: Li Qingxin (李启新) or Li Guangyuan (黎光远).

Chinese representative Fu Daqing, who had been involved in communist organizations in Malaya since the mid-1920s.[26] Ideas about Vietnamese and Chinese responsibility for the emancipation of the peoples of Southeast Asia can be traced to regional imaginations, not unlike the inter-polity relations of the tributary system of dynastic times. With the influence of social Darwinist ideas, these nostalgic visions were enhanced with new force. Further reinforcement for these ideas came in the form of Comintern-promoted internationalism. Ho Chi Minh, who was familiar with the problem of embedding a predominantly Hainanese communist organization in Siam in the 1920s,[27] reprimanded the Chinese communists for not learning Malay. Like the Chinese, Vietnamese communists also sought to indigenize their revolution, and Ho presented himself as a role model, as he had learned French and English while working as a migrant laborer in London.[28]

The MCP's Malayan Nation (Post-1930)

Like the CCP, the newborn MCP emerged as a text-focused party that spent much time producing, interpreting, and disseminating written material and that was aptly described by the British as a "paper movement." From October to November 1931, for example, police in Singapore seized a total of 4,716 copies of various documents.[29] The MCP's efforts to become "international" were based on Comintern texts as a means of communication and of bonding with non-Chinese. In this multilingual community, there were clear slippages in meaning between different languages. The mechanism for these slippages was twofold, conceptual and social. As speakers of different languages interpreted authoritative texts and key words using the conceptual training available to them, a key word's pragmatic definition (the change in the meaning of

---

[26] Quinn-Judge, *Ho Chi Minh*, pp. 156–157; Ho Chi Minh, "Malay," November 18, 1930, RGASPI 534/3 /549/25–27. Ho's authorship is established based on the content of the report; Christopher E. Goscha, *Thailand and the Southeast Asian Networks of the Vietnamese Revolution, 1885–1954* (Richmond: Curzon Press, 1999), pp. 76–113; "Protokol der.3. Delegierten Konferenz von Nanyang (Malayische) [Protocol of the Third Representative Conference of the Nanyang Party (Malayan)]," p. 87; "Minutes of the Third Representative Conference of Nanyang," pp. 134, 144–146; "The FEB Letter to the ECCI," March 3, 1930, in Titarenko and Leutner, *Komintern i Kitai* [*Comintern and China*], vol. 3, pp. 821–823.

[27] Goscha, *Thailand and the Southeast Asian Networks of the Vietnamese Revolution*, p. 89.

[28] "Minutes of the Third Representative Conference of Nanyang," p. 145.

[29] Hans J. van de Ven, "The Emergence of the Text-Centered Party," in Tony Saich and Hans J. van de Ven, eds., *New Perspectives on the Chinese Communist Revolution* (Armonk, NY: M. E. Sharpe, 1995), pp. 5–32; Hanrahan, *The Communist Struggle in Malaya*, p. 9; MRCA, December 1931, pp. 31–32, 55; MRCA, October 1931, pp. 44–45, CO 273/572.

a key word reflected in its actual use) joined with the changed social experience of the text's writers and readers to produce different meanings for the same words. I take inspiration from Koselleck's *Begriffsgeschichte* to connect conceptual history and social history.[30]

Shifts in the meaning of one particular key word, *minzu*, came in conjunction with the changed social experience of Chinese migrant identification with Malaya and created the basis for the MCP's formulation of its idea of a form of Malayan nationalism inclusive of immigrants. The genealogy of the word *minzu*, used to connote the Comintern concept of "national," can be traced to Sun Yatsen's use of both *minzu* and *guojia* (country) as translations of the English word *nation* when referring to China. Both the GMD and the CCP used *minzu* in this dual meaning as "nation" and "nationality." Multiple meanings of *minzu* as "ethnic," "people," "nation," and "nationality" are reflected in a CCP statement from 1929: "The national problem of the Nanyang – the nations [*minzu*] in the Nanyang are very complex."[31] In MCP discourse, a Chinese term meaning "nation," "nationality," "race," "ethnic group," and "national," *minzu*, came to mean "Malayan nation."[32] These multiple meanings resulted in a semantic slippage when the Comintern embarked on establishing a Malayan national party in a country that only existed in relation to the British colonial concept of Malaya, meaning the Malay Peninsula. Point seventeen of the twenty-one requirements for official acceptance as a Comintern section stated that an applicant party should be named a "party of a country" (*partiia etoi strany*).[33] By adding the attribute "Malayan" to "nation" (i.e., *minzu*), the Comintern reinforced the concept of a Malayan country that was territorially based on British Malaya.

---

[30] Koselleck, "*Begriffsgeschichte* and Social History," pp. 73–91.

[31] Tan Liok Ee, "The Rhetoric of Bangsa and Minzu: Community and Nation in Tension, the Malay Peninsula, 1900–1955," Working Paper (Clayton, Australia: Centre of Southeast Asian Studies, Monash University, 1988), pp. 27–28; CC CCP, "A Letter from the Central Committee of the CCP to the Nanyang Provisional Committee," p. 10.

[32] In the English-language discourse of the day, *minzu* pointed to race. However, because the English-language MCP documents do not use the word *race*, nor is the relevant Chinese word, *zhongzu*, used to any significant extent, I do not analyze this meaning of *minzu*. One of the few uses of the word *race* in MCP texts is as follows: "We are not animals and we want to preserve our races." "An Open Letter from the C. C. of the C. P. of Malay to the Working Class of Malay," November 7, 1930, RGASPI 495/62/6/ 1a–4. For the ambiguity and negotiation of the meaning of *minzu* in other contexts in the twentieth-century Chinese world, see James Leibold, "Searching for Han: Early Twentieth-Century Narratives of Chinese Origins and Development," in Thomas Mullaney, ed., *Critical Han Studies: The History Representation and Identity of China's Majority* (Berkeley, CA: University of California Press, 2012), pp. 210–233.

[33] *21 uslovie priema v Komintern* [*Twenty-One Conditions for Acceptance into the Comintern*]. 2nd edn. Introduction by O. Piatnitskii, (Izdatel'stvo TsK VKP(b), 1934).

The Chinese communists in the Nanyang, however, imagined another national Malayan party, a federation of communist parties organized along ethnic lines. There were several reasons for that. For one, as discussed in the previous chapter, this was likely based on the model that originated in the multiethnic context of the United States. The CCP understood the word *minzu* to mean "people," probably also because the communist cells in mainland Southeast Asia were organized according to ethnicity, differentiating, for instance, Chinese from Vietnamese.[34] Since 1927, the predominately Chinese party's base had presented a problem for the "relationship between the revolutionary parties of the other peoples" and was hard to solve without organizing parties of "various peoples" separately.[35] Another possible factor was the reality of ethnic division within industries, which impacted the makeup of trade unions.[36]

Since 1929, the CCP had intended to unify Chinese ethnic cells across the Nanyang into one party.[37] In 1930, to solve the problem of the party's focus on Chinese communities, the MCP members-to-be suggested "[establishing] a nucleus among each people [i.e., ethnic community], in order to establish an independent party of each people."[38] In other words, the Nanyang communists interpreted the Comintern's principle of national parties as being based on ethnic groups. The MCP's political resolution in English stated the following:

In view of the mistake that the system of [the] Malay party belongs to [the] Chinese party, some members insist to organise an unity party embracing all people in Malaya. This organisational line is also contradictory to the organisational principle of [an] international party, for the unit of organisation is people. Each native people should organise a national party … To organise a unity party consisting of various peoples is incorrect.[39]

This statement was incompatible with the Comintern's policy of having one communist party per country. Over this paragraph, a Comintern cadre wrote *Sovershenno neverno* ("Absolutely wrong"). Elsewhere, the FEB noted that "[t]he idea of creating several Communist parties based on the [different] nationalities in Malaya must be energetically

---

[34] Goscha, *Thailand and the Southeast Asian Networks of the Vietnamese Revolution*, pp. 76–113.
[35] "Minutes of the Third Representative Conference of Nanyang," pp. 116–118.
[36] N. A. K. [Nguyen Ai Quoc, alias Ho Chi Minh], "Economic Conditions in Malay, Letter from Singapore," June 10, 1930, RGASPI 495/62/8/4–6.
[37] CC CCP, "A Letter from the Central Committee of the CCP to the Nanyang Provisional Committee," p. 12.
[38] "Resolutions Adopted at the Third Congress of the Malaya Party," p. 8.
[39] Ibid., p. 4.

combated"; in the Malayan state, there was to be only one party, which would include "workers of all nationalities."[40]

In CCP documents from 1928–1929, the term *Malaya* was not used, and there was thus no correlation with "national."[41] However, starting with the MCP's founding conference minutes, the terms *Malaya party* and *Nanyang party* were used interchangeably and had the meaning of "national party." The goal of the MCP's revolution was to achieve "a united front of the oppressed peoples" and to organize "the Democratic Republic by free union among the various people of [the] Nanyang," a concept that, in the same paragraph, was termed the "Democratic Republics of the Malay States."[42] The idea of a soviet federation made sense in Malaya – and in the Nanyang – with its multiple *minzu*, which, for the Comintern, translated into the Russian *natsionalnost'* (nationality).[43] Following the Comintern's directives, the MCP now conceived of the Malayan nation as encompassing all Malayan ethnic groups in the fashion of the multiethnic Soviet federation. Thus, the Comintern gave Chinese communists in the Nanyang the discursive tools to imagine Malaya, consisting at the time of several sultanates under British dominion, as a nation-state.

As a result of different understandings of the word *minzu* by the CCP and the Comintern, a communist organization that was built according to people became the basis of a countrywide communist party of a nonexistent nation. With the equating of the ethnic Chinese party with the national Malayan party, the Chinese communists were to lead Malaya's oppressed peoples to colonial liberation and nationhood on behalf of the Malayan nation and the Malayan Revolution. It was this slippage that made Malaya a territorialized nation and a country in MCP discourse, since, like the Comintern, the MCP used *national* to refer to the jurisdictional space of the party, so "national" meant "Malayan." Before the establishment of the MCP, the Chinese communists imagined the place where they were, the Nanyang and the Malayan Peninsula, as a place inhabited by different ethnic groups (*minzu*). By promoting a national (i.e., Malayan) party and a Malayan Revolution, the Comintern conformed to the nascent idea of a national Malayan identity among Chinese immigrant communists and their jurisdiction over both the Nanyang and Malaya.

---

[40] FEB, "To the Malayan Comrades," December 17, 1930.
[41] Vremennyi komitet malaiskogo arkhipelaga [Nanyang Provisional Committee], "V tsentral'nyi komitet. Otchet Malaiskogo Komiteta profsoiuzov [To the Central Committee. The Report of the Soviet of Trade Unions of the Malay Archipelago]."
[42] "Minutes of the Third Representative Conference of Nanyang," pp. 118–119.
[43] "Resoliutsia priniataia posle obsledovania raboty vremennogo komiteta v 1929 [Resolution Adopted after Investigation of the Work of the (Nanyang) Provisional Committee in 1929]."

The boundaries between the Malayan party and the Nanyang party remained ambiguous. From 1928, the twentieth plenum of the CCP Central Executive Committee in Guangdong, in accordance with the Comintern line, decided to transform the special committees of Siam, Annam, Burma, and the Indian islands into the Siam Committee, the Annam Committee, and the Communist Party of the Nanyang Peoples.[44] In 1928, the NPC plenum decided that the communists had to start a "national movement" in the Nanyang so as to attract Malays and Indians to the Chinese party organization and to accept the Comintern's leadership.[45] The party of the Nanyang was to become independent when the parties of various nations in the Nanyang were united into a general organization.[46] Since 1929, the CCP had planned that the "Communist Party of the Nanyang Nationalities" (Kommunisticheskaia partiia nan'ianskikh narodnostei) would include the larger territory of the Indian islands, meaning the Malay Archipelago, Burma, and the Annam and Siam committees.[47]

At the MCP's founding conference, the Nanyang party was to be renamed the Nanyang Various Peoples Communists' Joint Secretariat as a transitional organization for "the communist party in the various oppressed peoples of [the] Nanyang" and would include a Malay communist party or a "Communist Committee of [the] Malay Peninsula."[48] Comintern documents before 1930 also demonstrate that the Nanyang was termed alternatively as the Malay Archipelago, the Malay states, or Indonesia.[49] As early as 1918, *Nanyang* had been translated into English as "Malaysia" by the first "area studies" institution in China, at Ji'nan University, and Comintern translators also translated *Nanyang* as "Malaya."[50] The Comintern confirmed this conception of the Nanyang

[44] "Otchet o polozhenii v Nan'iane [Report about the Situation in Nanyang]," January 1930, RGASPI 514/1/632/7–28, esp. 16.

[45] Vremennyi komitet malaiskogo arkhipelaga [Nanyang Provisional Committee], "V tsentral'nyi komitet. Otchet Malaiskogo profsoiuzov [To the Central Committee. The Report of the Soviet of Trade Unions of the Malay Archipelago]," pp. 2, 3.

[46] CC CCP, "A Letter from the Central Committee of the CCP to the Nanyang Provisional Committee," p. 12.

[47] "Otchet o polozhenii v Nan'iane [Report about the Situation in Nanyang]," p. 16.

[48] "Minutes of the Third Representative Conference of Nanyang," p. 120.

[49] Vremennyi komitet malaiskogo arkhipelaga [Nanyang Provisional Committee], "V tsentral'nyi komitet. Otchet Malaiskogo Komiteta profsoiuzov [To the Central Committee. The Report of the Soviet of Trade Unions of the Malay Archipelago]"; FEB, "To the Malayan Comrades," December 17, 1930.

[50] "Zhongguo yu Nanyang. China and Malaysia" [Bulletin of Ji'nan University] 1 (1918) in Meng Liqun, ed., *Nanyang shiliao xubian* [*Continuation of the Compilation of Nanyang Historical Materials*], vol. 1 (Beijing: Guojia tushuguan chubanshe, 2010), p. 1; "List of Circulars Issued by the C. C. of the C. P. of Malaysia," 1933–1934, RGASPI 495/62/24/46–47.

as a Malay region by assigning responsibility for movements in Indonesia, Siam, and Burma to the MCP in 1934.[51]

In these uncertain boundaries of the Nanyang, populated by various peoples, we recognize the pattern of Sun Yatsen's idea of a Chinese nation comprising multiple peoples. In 1912, in his inaugural address as provisional president of the Republic of China, Sun Yatsen spoke of the future republic as uniting all territories of the former Qing empire and all five ethnicities (*zu*) – Manchu, Han, Mongol, Hui, and Tibetan – in one nation (*yiren*), which would be the "unity of the nation."[52] The similarity of the multiethnic conditions in Malaya and in the Chinese empire, now a republic, in both of which the Chinese were the dominant *minzu*, rendered the application of the Comintern's principle of internationalism logical.

In 1930, the MCP, which primarily consisted of CCP members, subsequently changed its idea of a national party in accordance with the Comintern idea of an ethnically inclusive party in order to acquire Comintern recognition and funding. However, because of the MCP's inability to involve non-Chinese in the organization, the de facto ethnic mode of organization of workers and nationalist movements continued throughout the 1930s. The founding conference, as in 1929, thus criticized the party for its continuing failure to indigenize, accusing it of not understanding "the revolutionary task in Nanyang"[53] and of not adapting "to the practical life of Malaya."[54] The Nanyang comrades recognized that Malay natives should participate in the revolution in the Nanyang, but because of a lack of money and cadres, this recognition did not go further than discussions about the tactics of the party, educational classes, and the establishment of party publications.[55] The party did not adapt to Malay conditions because it consisted of Chinese immigrants and because of the "patriotism of Chinese toiling masses in Malaya," as well as a lack of investigation into the conditions in Malaya and a lack of special instructions from the CC CCP to the "Malay party." The way to fix this, the MCP imagined, was by establishing organizations consisting of members of different nationalities.[56] The

---

[51] FEB, "Pismo Ts.K.Malaiskoi K.P. o VII kongresse i.t.d [Letter to the CC MCP about the 7th Congress of the Comintern, etc.]," June 1, 1934, RGASPI 495/62/22/13–13ob.

[52] Sun Zhongshan, "Linshi da zongtong xunyanshu [The Proclamation of the Provisional President]," in *Sun Zhongshan quanji* [*Collected Works of Sun Yatsen*], vol. 2 (Beijing: Zhonggua shuju, 1981), cited in Joseph Esherick, "How the Qing Became China," in Joseph Esherick, Hasan Kayalı, and Eric van Young, eds., *Empire to Nation: Historical Perspectives on the Making of the Modern World* (Lanham, MD: Rowman & Littlefield Publishers, 2006), pp. 229–259, esp. p. 245.

[53] "Minutes of the Third Representative Conference of Nanyang," pp. 130–131.

[54] Ibid., pp. 130, 136–137.

[55] Ibid., pp. 133–134.

[56] "Resolutions Adopted at the Third Congress of the Malaya Party," pp. 3, 8.

indigenization of the MCP, which had been previously promoted by the GMD and the CCP in 1929, was now also promoted by the Comintern. The MCP's indigenization ran through the rhetoric of internationalism and world revolution. The MCP thus promoted the liberation of Malaya through a Malayan Revolution, which would contribute to the world revolution: "Comrades! The III congress [the founding meeting] has entrusted us with the full responsibility for the revolutionary movement of the Malay Peninsula. We must organize the Malayan proletariat and poor peasantry into a new army of the world revolution for the emancipation of all oppressed peoples of [the] Malay [P]eninsula."[57]

Indigenizing the Chinese Revolution through the Malayan Nation, Advancing Malay Civilization through the Chinese Revolution

In 1930 the Comintern promoted the mobilization of Malaya's three major ethnic communities through the MCP, calling for support for the Chinese and Indian Revolutions and "the liberation of Malaya."[58] Malaya was a unique place to promote slogans of support for the Chinese and Indian Revolutions that would also benefit the Malayan and world revolutions, since in 1931 Indians and Chinese comprised such a sizable proportion of Malaya's population. In the MCP texts, this translated into the "emancipation of the oppressed Malay nationalities" (*Malai bei yapo de minzu jiefang*) or the "the people of Malaya" (*Malai de renmin*), who consisted of "complex nationalities" (*fuza de minzu*).[59] The MCP argued that it had to organize Malay and Indian workers to address the low political awareness of the Chinese masses (*qunzhong de zhengzhi shuiping jiaodi*), which manifested itself in an immigrant mentality (*yimin de xinli*). In the Darwinian world of revolution, the establishment of a workers and peasants' state (*gongnong de guojia*) would bring liberation to the Malayan nation (*Malai minzu duli*) or "the people of Malaya" (*Malai de minzhong*), rendered in English translation as "Malaya." It would also help overcome economic backwardness and

---

[57] CC MCP, "Notice Issued by the C. C. of the Communist Party of the Malay States Relating to the Conclusion of the III Delegate Congress of the Nanyang Communist Party," May 1, 1930, RGASPI 495/62/3/11–25, esp. 25.
[58] FEB, "To the Malayan Comrades," December 17, 1930.
[59] "Zhongyang tonggao di si hao. Guanyu Yingguo muqian de zhengzhi qingxing yu women de gongzuo [Central Committee Circular no. 4. On Contemporary British Politics and Our Work]," August 10, 1930, RGASPI 495/62/13/31–32; "Gongren ying zuo shenme shiqing [What Workers Should Do]," November 15, 1930, RGASPI 495/62/23/84–93.

would bring the Malay "civilization"[60] to a higher stage of development (*xiang zhao geng gao de wenming fazhan*).[61]

For the MCP, colonial emancipation meant "civilizational progress": "The British often say in Malaya that peoples of the East are of the second sort [*xiadeng de dongxi*], regardless of whether they are educated elites or not, and they do so because otherwise the peoples of the East will stand up, work on their own country [*jiajin ziji guojia de gongzuo*], and overcome imperialist domination, and their civilization will advance [*wenming jinbu*]."[62] Propaganda rhetorically defending the Soviet Union, which had been "economically and culturally backward" but in ten years had surpassed any "so-called civilized country," made sense because it offered a model of civilizational breakthrough.[63]

Internationalism was intrinsic to indigenization through these discourses of aid to the Chinese and Indian Revolutions for the sake of the Malayan Revolution and ultimately the world revolution. Because Malaya's production depended on a labor influx from these two countries, revolutions in China and India became the first conditions for the emancipation of the Malay nation (*Malai minzu jiefang*), the MCP argued. To help the Indian and Chinese Revolutions and to expand the movement in Malaya, the MCP needed to organize Chinese and Indian workers. The revolution in India was important because it would help to spread revolution in other British colonies and to bring down British imperialism.[64] The Comintern

---

[60] "Civilization" (*wenming*) here is used interchangeably with "culture," as the comment on the Soviet Union in the next paragraph demonstrates, and it does not refer to a particular Malay civilization as an entity. For a similar interchangeable usage of *wenming* and *wenhua* in discussions on the relative benevolence of the Chinese civilization over the European colonial one, attracting other peoples for assimilation and thus bearing the responsibility to emancipate the oppressed, see "Zhongguo duiyu shijie de shiming [China's Responsibility to the World]," in Lü Simian, *Gaoji zhongxueyong benguoshi. Er ce [The History of Our Country for Middle School. Second Part]* (1935), pp. 254–258, Wang Gung Wu Library, Chinese Heritage Centre, Nanyang Technological University.

[61] "Zhongyang tonggao di qi hao. Yuanzhu Zhongguo Yindu geming yu muqian gongzuo de zhuanbian [Central Committee Circular no. 7. Aid to Chinese and Indian Revolutions and the Changes in Our Current Work]," September 15, 1930, RGASPI 495/62/13/36–38; "What Workers Should Do," 1930, p. 86; "What Workers Should Stand For," November 11, 1930, RGASPI 495/62/5/9–20, esp. 10.

[62] Singapore City Committee of the MCP, "Shijie wuchan jieji geming lingxiu Liening tongzhi qushi di qi zhounian jinian [Commemorating the Seventh Anniversary of the Death of the Leader of the World Proletarian Revolution Comrade Lenin]," January 21, 1931, RGASPI 495/62/5/26.

[63] "The Present Situation in Malaya and the Task of the CPM (Draft Letter)," July 10, 1931, RGASPI 495/62/17/27–53, esp. 32; the C. C. of the C. P. of Malay, "Central Circular no. 9. The Commemoration of the October Revolution and the Preparation for the Solidarity Strike," October 3, 1930, RGASPI 495/62/13/40–44.

[64] "Zhongyang tonggao di si hao. Guanyu Yingguo muqian de zhengzhi qingxing yu women de gongzuo [Central Committee Circular no. 4. On Contemporary British Politics and Our Work]"; "Zhongyang tonggao di qi hao. Yuanzhu Zhongguo Yindu geming yu

thus provided a new international justification for the internationalism of the Chinese Revolution of Sun Yatsen by merging Chinese nationalism and Asianism together in the MCP's Malayan nationalism. The Comintern responded to MCP initiatives[65] with a directive to promote these two revolutions. In the earliest such document, dated December 1930, the Comintern recommended that the MCP promote support for the Chinese and Indian Revolutions among their respective ethnic communities and use different slogans in each. The rationale was that the emancipation of Malaya would help the emancipation of China and India, which would be beneficial for the Malayan Revolution. This attitude also provided a rhetorical tool to attract members of the Chinese community and, most important, on behalf of and to the benefit of the national liberation of Malaya. For instance, the Comintern suggested that among the Chinese population, the slogan that the emancipation of Malaya would help the emancipation of China had to be used, as the same imperialists who oppressed China also oppressed Malaya. The same was promoted among Hindu workers regarding Indian emancipation: "You must tell the native workers that the emancipation of Malaya can be put into practice only through the united front of all toiling masses of the Malay state regardless of nationalities."[66] The FEB suggested that the MCP explain to the native Malay workers that they should fight not for the lowering of wages among Chinese and Indian workers to their level but for the opposite.[67]

As had Li Lisan in the past, the Comintern criticized the MCP, saying it was a group of Chinese immigrants who were living "by the interests of the Chinese movement" and who were "separated from the life of the indigenous strata of toiling Malays" and Malaya-born "indigenous Chinese" because of their "attempt to mechanistically graft the methods and some slogans of the Chinese movement in Malaya."[68] The Comintern felt that the MCP was still "more of a CCP organization . . . working among the Chinese workers who fled from China, rather than an independent party of Malaya States."[69] The ECCI considered the MCP to be "the Singapore group" and recommended that the FEB connect with it and "establish leadership over its activity, and try to convert it and use it for the establishment of the communist party of the Malay

muqian gongzuo de zhuanbian [Central Committee Circular no. 7. Aid to Chinese and Indian Revolutions and the Changes in Our Current Work]."
[65] The C. C. of the C. P. of Malay, "Central Circular no. 2. Preparation for the Mass Demonstration on 'Aug. 1st' the International Red Day," June 18, 1930, RGASPI 495/62/13/18–22a.
[66] FEB, "To the Malayan Comrades," December 17, 1930.
[67] Ibid.
[68] ECCI Letter to the FEB, October 23, 1930.
[69] FEB, "To the Malayan Comrades," December 17, 1930.

archipelago, including Malay, Indian, and Chinese (including indigenous) workers," who would be able to lead the revolutionary movement of Malaya. The FEB was to help the MCP prepare Chinese, Malay, and Indian cadres, who would be able to organize an independent MCP and who "would help the communist movement in Indonesia to form."[70]

Moreover, the Comintern pointed out, "[t]he proletarian movement in Singapore can play a huge role in the agitation and organization of the countries that surround it." The FEB continued, "[i]t is necessary to create an organizational network through the whole country of Malaya states. You already have an organizational basis in the Chinese communist group. Now it is necessary without delay to make every effort that these Chinese communists no longer exist like a group of Chinese emigrants, living with their minds and hearts solely upon events in China and mechanically reproducing all such [phenomena] in the Malaya states." The Comintern refused to recognize the established MCP as the Malayan communist party and suggested that the "communist party in the Malaya States" should be established on the basis of the preliminary committee that the Nanyang communists had established in April 1930.[71]

The Comintern's vision echoed the same method of indigenization of immigrant communist networks that Ho Chi Minh had promoted in Indochina and that the GMD had advocated in Malaya. This indigenization was rooted in the civilizing aspirations of immigrant communists in Southeast Asia. The revolution offered a way of localizing the Chinese communist organization in Malayan society, as the MCP was eager to build a cross-ethnic alliance. When the party distributed its pamphlets during the celebration of a communist festival in "Hindus" and "Malayan" languages, it reported that "the native masses seemed very pleased" to have revolutionaries among themselves as well, while the Chinese were also pleased that Malays and Indians "[were] with them now."[72] However, despite aloof slogans and an emphasis on non-Chinese membership numbers, it was obvious that non-Chinese membership was negligible.

Malays in the MCP

Although membership at the founding conference was reported as 1,500 as well as 5,000 labor union members, the party had only 1,130

[70] ECCI Letter to the FEB, October 23, 1930.
[71] Ironically, the authors of this Comintern letter, apparently unaware of Li Lisan's promotion of a Nanyang Revolution, labeled the proponents of the China-leaning policy in the MCP as leftist and influenced by Li Lisan and Chen Duxiu. Ibid.
[72] "Report from Malay," 1931, RGASPI 495/62/11/27–29.

party members (including five Malays) and more than 4,250 members of communist-influenced red trade unions in October 1930. The conference itself included only one Malay and one representative from the Netherlands East Indies.[73] However, the term *Malay* may be deceptive, for by April 1, 1930, of six Malays arrested because of their association with the Chinese communists, five (Ahmed Baiki bin Suile, Ali Majid, Jamal Ud Din, Emat, alias Abdul Hamid, and Haji Mohamed bin Hashim) came from Sumatra, Sulawesi, and Java, and it is likely that the sixth, Salleh Bin Sapi, did as well.[74] Despite its alleged goals, the MCP was still said to be exclusively Chinese (apart from one Indian) and appeared to have "no plan to involve non-Chinese other than vulgar conversation and politeness," because of difficulties with their different "language and custom."[75] The discrepancy in the documents sent to the Comintern, which report an MCP membership of 10 percent "Malaysians and Indians," may have been because the CC in Singapore relied on reports from local cells, which were often intercepted and therefore irregular. Some MCP envoys claimed that they themselves did not have sufficient knowledge of party membership to make accurate reports.[76] Furthermore, when the CC and other local organizations sent envoys to Shanghai in 1930 as MCP representatives in hopes of gaining Comintern funding and recognition of autonomy,[77] there was a clear benefit to show growing recruitment of non-Chinese, which had been a condition stipulated by the Comintern. It is evident, however, that these estimates were exaggerated, since other sources (see Table 3.1) show no improvement.

Obviously, those few Malays were not very visible in the MCP, since in 1931 Comintern envoy Ducroux discovered that in the MCP,

---

[73] "Minutes of the Third Representative Conference of Nanyang," pp. 130, 136–137; "Protokol der.3. Delegierten Konferenz von Nanyang (Malayische) [Protocol of the Third Representative Conference of the Nanyang Party (Malayan)]" "Resolutions Adopted at the Third Congress of the Malaya Party," p. 4; "Informatsiia o Malaiskikh Shtatakh [Information about the Malay States]," October 3, 1930, RGASPI 495/62/7/2–4.

[74] "A Report Showing the Connection between Chinese and Non-Chinese Concerned in Communist Activities in Malaya," April 1, 1930, CO273/561/72074, cited in Cheah, *From PKI to the Comintern*, pp. 53–56.

[75] Ho Chi Minh, "Malay"; "Report from Malay"; "To the C. C. of the Chinese Party and the Comintern," sometime in 1930, RGASPI 495/62/11/1–4; "Informatsiia o Malaiskikh Shtatakh [Information about the Malay States]."

[76] "To the C. C. of the Chinese Party and the Comintern," p. 3; Wang Yung Hai, "To the Far Eastern Bureau," December 28, 1930, RGASPI 495/62/6/17–21.

[77] The FEB's Letter to Ducroux, May 20, 1931, RGASPI 495/62/2/6–7.

Table 3.1 *Non-Chinese members in communist organizations in Malaya*

	MCP	Red labor unions
1930	5 Indians Malays: 2 members and 1 candidate, possibly including a former PKI member, Subajio; 1 CC member and 5 CC candidates	300 Indians and Malays (at least 30 Malays and 220 Indians)
March 1931	Total: 1,220	Indians: 350 Malays: 30, as well as 72 Javanese Total: 5,830
September 1931		1,220 Indians and Malays Total: 8,175
December 1931	Indians: 28 Malays: 17, as well as 1 Javanese	Indians: 180 Malays: at least 700 In Singapore, 10 percent Malays, Tamils, and Javanese, 9 Javanese and 57 Indians "under influence"[78]

there was "no single Malay or Indian, but Indians were in the Malaya trade unions."[79] Overall, there were more non-Chinese in the AIL.[80] However, the MCP had no language skills and asked the Comintern for the help of the Javanese and Indian parties, who could send Chinese, Indians, or Javanese from the Kommunisticheskii universitet trudiashchikhsia Vostoka (KUTV), and of Comintern cadres

---

[78] Because of secrecy considerations, MCP communications rarely mention names. Undated report, probably 1931, RGASPI 495/62/7/9–8; "Declaration of Subajio," June 21, 1930, RGASPI 495/154/752/37–38; MCP's Letter to Ho Chi Minh and Ho Chi Minh's Letter to the Comintern, November–December 1930, RGASPI 495/62/6/5–7; "Report from Malay"; Huang Muhan, "Worker Movement in Federated Malay States"; "A Report from 12 September 1931 from Malaya about the Labour Union to CC MCP," MRCA, December 1931, pp. 41, 44, CO 273/572.

[79] Letter from the FEB to the "Center" regarding Malaya, Indonesia, and India, June 10, 1931, Shanghai Municipal Police Files (SMP), 1929–1945 (Wilmington, DE: Scholarly Resources, 1989) D2510/49–50.

[80] Khoo Kay Kim, "The Beginnings of Political Extremism in Malaya, 1915–1935" (PhD dissertation: University of Malaysia, 1973), pp. 127–128, 312–318, 356; McLane, *Soviet Strategies in Southeast Asia*, pp. 131–136; Yong in Hack and Chin, eds., *Dialogues with Chin Peng*, pp. 72, 238.

who knew different languages to help recruit Indians and Malays into communist organizations.[81]

The MCP's difficulties in engaging Malays were not surprising, given the typically condescending attitudes that perpetuated European nineteenth-century stereotypes.[82] An MCP report stated that: "All aborigines are lazy. Though they have fertile land, they do not persevere to till it but spend their fatal time in sexual abuses, idleness and superstition."[83] Ho Chi Minh, in his report, described the MCP's arrogance eloquently:

Chauvinism and provincialism: They thought that being Chinese, they must work only for China, and only with the Chinese. They looked upon the natives as inferior and unnecessary people. There were no contacts, no relations between the Chinese members and the native masses. The consequences of that exclusiveness are that when they need the cooperation of the natives they find no one or find only mediocre elements.[84]

For example, the MCP decided that the Malay and Hindu comrades had an "infantile education" and therefore could not be trusted with the press to publish Malay- and "Hindu"-language propaganda.[85] Some party members in Selangor, Singapore, and Malacca "[sabotaged] the work on the grounds that Indian and Malayan workers were too backward and [were] not receptive to revolutionary ideas."[86] However, the CC MCP in 1930 was critical of such attitudes toward Malays and insisted that though Malays were not revolutionary because of the current British policy of harmonization, they still needed to be dragged out of their present economic condition and their civilizational level had to be raised: "A Malay workers and peasants' state can only be established by Malayan workers and peasants."[87] Malay intellectuals, in the view of the MCP, lacked nationalism and collaborated with the British government, which destroyed their "conception of independence and emancipation."[88]

Member of the MCP, artist and musician Zhang Xia (张霞) also described Malays as lazy and as having low cultural levels (*landuo, wenhua shuiping you di*) in contrast to the industrious, intelligent, and patient

---

[81] The MCP's Letter to Ho Chi Minh, December 18, 1930, RGASPI 495/62/6/5–7; "Informatsiia o Malaiskikh Shtatakh [Information about the Malay States]."

[82] Milner, *Invention of Politics in Colonial Malaya*, ch. 3, esp. p. 64.

[83] "To the C. C. of the Chinese Party and the Comintern," p. 2.

[84] Ho Chi Minh, "Malay," p. 25.

[85] "Report from Malay."

[86] "Resolution on the Labour Movement Passed by the C. C. of the C. P. of Malaysia on March 24, 1934 (Abridged Translation)," RGASPI 495/62/23/46–49.

[87] "Zhongyang tonggao di qi hao. Yuanzhu Zhongguo Yindu geming yu muqian gongzuo de zhuanbian [Central Committee Circular no. 7. Aid to Chinese and Indian Revolutions and the Changes in Our Current Work]," p. 38.

[88] "Minutes of the Third Representative Conference of Nanyang," p. 114.

(*qinlao, naiku, congying*) Chinese.[89] The *Weekly Herald* (*Xingqi daobao*), in a 1935 article about the British colonization of Malaya, reported that the British and the Malays had different cultural levels (*wenhua chengdu buyi*) and that the Malayan national movement (*minzu yundong*) comprised Chinese. The article included a cartoon of "drunken and stupefied" colonial people sleeping in the middle of the day, which illustrates the Nanjing GMD government's outlook on the "oppressed" peoples of the Nanyang, an outlook the MCP shared.[90]

Indonesian communists continued to attempt to organize Malays in the Malayan Peninsula in 1928–1930, mostly unsuccessfully, but Alimin and Musso allegedly organized a Malay section of the AIL and built connections with Indonesians and Malays studying in Cairo. In Lenggeng in Negeri Sembilan, there was a Sumatran Islamic reformist movement, Kaum Muda, which was connected with the communists in Indonesia.[91] Indonesian Comintern agents were also unsuccessful in recruiting Malays into the MCP. Similarly, a group of Chinese sent by the Nanyang party to Indonesia in 1930 failed to generate links to the PKI. Fearing arrest in Singapore, PKI leader Alimin went to Shanghai in 1931, where he worked among Malay and Javanese seamen until arrests decimated the local Comintern bureau in June 1931. It was hoped that Tan Malaka, whom the Comintern discovered in Shanghai, where he had been in hiding since 1927, would be an effective organizer, but he was arrested en route in Hong Kong.[92] In Malaya itself, the MCP had no connection with the short-lived Belia Malaya (Young Malaya) (1930–1931), established by Malay student teachers at Sultan Idris Training College, including Ibrahim Yaacob, inspired by the idea of unity with Indonesia in a greater *Malaysia Raya* (but since 1926 they had contacts with Alimin and Sutan Djenain, a member of the CC MCP and of the

[89] Zhang Xia, "Xianyou xian lü Ma huaqiao yu geming huodong [Immigrants from Xianyou County in Malaya and Revolutionary Activities]," in Zhongguo renmin zhengzhi xieshang huiyi Fujian sheng Xianyou xian weiyuanhui, ed., *Xianyou wenshi ziliao di er ji* [*Literary and Historical Materials of Xianyou County*, vol. 2] (1984), pp. 34–39.
[90] "Guoji lunping duxuan: Yingguo tongzhi Malaiya zhi zhengce ji qi minzu yundong (jielu Nanyang yanjiu) [Selected International Review Readings: The Policy of British Colonization of Malaya and Its National Movement (Excerpts from Nanyang Studies)]," *Weekly Herald* (*Xingqi daobao*), no. 7 (1935), p. 5.
[91] Cheah, *From PKI to the Comintern*, pp. 9–11.
[92] "Minutes of the Third Representative Conference of Nanyang," pp. 144–146; Alimin, Letters, April 23, September 29, 1930, RGASPI 495/214/752/40–41, 86; Santos [Alimin], "Brief Description," 1939; Santos [Alimin], Untitled, undated; Santos, "Svedeniia o Malake [Information about Malaka]," June 7, 1939, RGASPI 495/214/3/35–37; Musso, "Situatsiia v Indonesii posle vosstaniia [The Situation in Indonesia after the Uprising]," September 22, 1930, RGASPI 495/214/752/53–76.

Malayan Racial Emancipation League, respectively).[93] This apparent gap in communication is significant, given that in 1937 Yaacob and his Young Malay Union (Kesatuan Melayu Muda) (KMM) were credited with creating the discourse of an inclusive multiethnic Malayan nation.[94]

In 1934, when the Comintern requested that the MCP send Malays to Moscow for training, the MCP responded that it was difficult to persuade the five Malay comrades (*Ma ji*) they had found in Melaka and Selangor to leave their families even for one week. One comrade in Singapore was sufficiently qualified to conduct propaganda among Malays (*Malai minzu gongzuo de zhongxin*): "The long-term education of Malay comrades [*Malaiya ji tongzhi*] is very needed. However, they do not want to come to us; we can only go to the locality and teach there and after, perhaps, can gather a training group of Malay comrades." A lack of help from local organizations was also blamed for the lack of Malay involvement (in Sembilan), and many MCP members considered efforts in this direction to be futile.[95]

However, with overall MCP membership in decline by 1934 due to arrests, one letter mentions only seven Malays (although it does not state whether this refers to all Malays in the party, which had a total membership of 588).[96] The total union membership of 6,035 included 518 Malays and 52 Indians.[97] Malay membership in the Singapore CYL increased from 3 in 1932 to 20 in 1934 (with 411 Chinese). During 1932, the number of Indians in the Singapore labor union fell from 120 to 20 and the number of Malays from 50 to 20 (total membership of 3,000).[98] Since 1931, the MCP had printed propaganda material in Malay, and in 1934, Indonesian communists provided language help, although they were concerned with the independence of Indonesia rather than Malaya.[99] Amir

[93] Roff, *Origins of Malay Nationalism*, pp. 224–225, 255; Cheah, *From PKI to the Comintern*, p. 21.
[94] Tan Liok Ee, "The Rhetoric of Bangsa and Minzu."
[95] Guo Guang, "Magong laixin san hao [A Letter from the MCP no. 3]," March 24, 1934, RGASPI 495/62/22/1–7, esp. 5.
[96] "Magong laijian. Malaiya de qingshi yu dang de renwu [A Document Received from the MCP. The Situation in Malaya and the Tasks of the Party]," August 25, 1934, RGASPI 495/62/27/1–5; Guo Guang, "Magong laixin san hao [A Letter from the MCP no. 3]."
[97] "Report of Labour Federation of Malaya no. 1 to the Profintern," March 25, 1934, RGASPI 495/62/24/13–16ob.
[98] MRCA, October 1932, p. 37, CO 273/580; "Magong zhongyang laijian. Zhengge tuan de zuzhi gaikuang [A Document Received from the CC MCP. The Organizational Situation in the CYL]," August 25, 1934, RGASPI 495/62/27/7.
[99] MRCA, December 1931, pp. 31–48, CO 273/572; Straits Settlement Police Special Branch, "Review of Communism in Malaya during 1934," December 31, 1934, *Political Intelligence Journal*, pp. 2, 3, CO 273/616. For an example of Malay-language propaganda by the MCP, see CC MCP, "Surat yang terbuka kepada saudara-saudara kita Melayu

Hamzah Siregar left Singapore for Java in 1934 and was arrested there; an MCP inspector, a Christian Batak named Djoeliman Siregar, was arrested during his tour of Negeri Sembilan and Malacca. A Salim sent a report on Selangor to the CC MCP in 1937.[100] Despite having founded the Malayan Racial Emancipation League in 1936, headed by a committee with two Tamils and two Malays, the MCP remained almost entirely Chinese, also likely because of Malay anti-immigrant stances.[101]

"The Future of the Nanyang Revolution"

The history of the Chinese words for "assimilation into local society" (*tonghua*) and "allegiance to China" (*guihua*) provides insight into the MCP's understanding of how non-Chinese peoples could be involved in the party. As China expanded territorially before the twentieth century, these terms had come to denote the assimilation of non-Han peoples in the borderlands (*tonghua*) and foreigners into Chinese culture (*guihua*); however, there was no word for the reverse process. Although Chinese communities in the Nanyang had been characterized by social adaptation (and a certain loss of their Chineseness), increased migration in the nineteenth and early twentieth centuries had encouraged a process of re-Sinicization by the Chinese state that only encountered barriers when Chinese migration was restricted after 1929.[102] The Nanjing GMD state's vocabulary of assimilation reflected its acknowledgment of the foreignness of overseas Chinese, who were being re-Sinicized (*guihua*) to prevent their assimilation into the local culture (*tonghua*).[103]

Closer links with China, however, also led to tensions between descendants of earlier Chinese migrants who had married local women and had developed more connections with local society. In the face of increased Malay activism, some locally born Chinese leaders, like English-educated Tan Cheng Lock (1883–1960), even began to speak of the "*Malayan*

---

dan Indian [An Open Letter to Our Malay and Indian Brothers]," 1934, RGASPI 495/62/22/14–17.
[100] Cheah, *From PKI to the Comintern*, pp. 19–20.
[101] "Supplement no. 1 of 1937 to the Straits Settlements Police Special Branch, *Political Intelligence Journal*, Review of Communist Activities in Malaya, 1936," pp. 3, 4; "Straits Settlements Police Special Branch Report for the Year 1936," p. 7, CO 273/630.
[102] Zhao Gang, *The Qing Opening to the Ocean: Chinese Maritime Policies, 1684–1757* (Honolulu, HI: University of Hawaii Press, 2013), pp. 4–5, 188–190; Kuhn, *Chinese among Others*, pp. 250–282.
[103] Wang Gungwu, "*Tonghua, Guihua,* and History of the Overseas Chinese," in Ng Lun Ngai-ha and Chang Chak Yan, eds., *Liangci shijie dazhan qijian zai Yazhou zhi haiwai huaren* [*Overseas Chinese in Asia between the Two World Wars*] (Hong Kong: Chinese University of Hong Kong, 1989), pp. 11–23.

spirit and consciousness" (emphasis added).[104] Tan was a prominent Malaya-born Chinese businessman and politician, the head of the Straits Chinese British Association in Malacca from 1928 to 1935. There are parallels between his and the MCP's activity and discourse. He promoted Malaya's self-government in 1926 as well as Chinese participation in the Legislative Councils of the Federated Malay States and of the Straits Settlements.[105]

However, for other Chinese the restrictions on Chinese immigration as a result of the depression and the dramatic increase of Malaya's locally born Chinese population, from 20.9 percent in 1921 to 29.9 percent in 1931, increased anxiety about the Chineseness of locally born Chinese.[106] Many teachers from Chinese-language schools and writers for Chinese-language newspapers, as well as intellectuals prominent in the MCP, were also GMD members.[107] One example was Xu Jie, the author of the durian story. He was appointed by the CC GMD as an editor of *Yiqunbao* in Kuala Lumpur in 1928–1929. Xu Jie maintained connections with local communists who shared news with him. In addition to founding *New Rise Literature* (*Xinxing wenyi*, 新兴文艺), which was a disguised form of the proletarian revolutionary literature movement, he was involved in local literary movements and with local writers, and he also promoted the concept of "more purely indigenous literature," Malayan Chinese literature (*Ma hua wenxue*), and the idea of a Nanyang "local color" (*Nanyang secai*). This was a response to the condescending attitude toward a local "imitation" of Chinese culture expressed by the first generation of educated migrant Chinese. These local Chinese writers were creating a Nanyang *huaqiao* culture while also asserting their difference from China. The reorientation toward a Nanyang (local) color was an attempt to redefine the place of Chinese emigrants in Chinese culture, not, as Kenley puts it, "to become indigenous."[108] Along with the

[104] Tan Cheng Lock, "Extract from Mr. Tan Cheng Lock's Speech at the Meeting of the Legislative Council Held on 1st November 1926," in C. Q. Lee, ed., *Malayan Problems from the Chinese Point of View* (Singapore: Tannsco, 1947), pp. 88–93, esp. p. 90.

[105] Kennedy Gordon Tregonning, "Tan Cheng Lock: A Malayan Nationalist," *Journal of Southeast Asian Studies* 10(1) (1979), pp. 25–76; Heng, *Chinese Politics in Malaysia*, p. 27.

[106] Kanagaratnam Jeya Ratnam, *Communalism and the Political Process in Malaya* (Kuala Lumpur: University of Malaya Press, 1965), p. 9; Wang, "The Limits of Nanyang Chinese Nationalism."

[107] Yōji Akashi, "The Nanyang Chinese Anti-Japanese Boycott Movement, 1908–1928: A Study of Nanyang Chinese Nationalism" (Kuala Lumpur: Department of History, University of Malaya, 1968), pp. 69–96, esp. p. 77; Ching Fatt Yong, "An Overview of the Malayan Communist Movement to 1942," in Hack and Chin, eds., *Dialogues with Chin Peng*, pp. 247–251.

[108] Ke Pingping as related by Xu Jie, *Kanke daolu shang de zuji* [*Road Full of Misfortunes*] (Shanghai: Huadong shifan daxue chubanshe, 1997), pp. 149–151, 171–217;

dissatisfaction of the local Chinese with the *huaqiao* education program that came from the central government in Nanjing and did not take their needs into account, this literary trend can also be viewed as a manifestation of the adaptation efforts by the immigrant Chinese in Malaya. There were complaints that Mandarin teachers who came from China did not want to learn about Malaya. It was hoped that with time locally born teachers would come to teach Mandarin in the schools.[109]

According to Kenley, the rise of aspirations for local Chineseness among Chinese intellectuals and their desire to liberate Malaya's "native" peoples from the British government were the consequences of the increased influence of communist political immigrants from China after 1928.[110] Moreover, Chinese intellectuals' aspirations for a Nanyang *huaqiao* culture resonated with the CCP's impulse, expressed in Li Lisan's letter, to make a Nanyang – not a Chinese – revolution in the Nanyang and with the establishment of a local communist party. This was also encouraged by the Comintern, which ultimately offered an opportunity to put these aspirations into practice. This is illustrated in a story by Xu Jie, a follower of a "nativist" group (*xiangtupai*), who relied on true stories (which he also mentions in his memoir) as the basis for fiction.[111]

Xu Jie published a story at the same time in January 1929[112] when the Chinese communists in Malaya received Li Lisan's letter. This story contains a discussion of the Nanyang Revolution, echoing Li Lisan's directive and the reports of the Nanyang communists to the CCP and the Comintern. Xu's discussion of a Nanyang Revolution likely reflected discussions among Kuala Lumpur communists with whom he was in contact. Xu Jie viewed the revolution in the Nanyang as different from the revolution in China. Whereas in China the revolution was confined to a limited territory because of undeveloped infrastructure, in the Nanyang it would not be easy to stir up a revolution (presumably due to relatively good living conditions), but developed transport and infrastructure would make it easier to coordinate a revolution once it arose. Thus, infrastructure would help not only to crush the revolution but also to

David Kenley, *New Culture in a New World: The May Fourth Movement and the Chinese Diaspora in Singapore (1919–1932)* (London: Routledge, 2003), pp. 157–176, 180–181, n. 50.

[109] Li Yinghui, *Huaqiao zhengce yu haiwai minzuzhuyi (1912–1949)* [*The Origin of Overseas Chinese Nationalism (1912–1949)*], p. 476; Ta Chen, *Emigrant Communities in South China: A Study of Overseas Migration and Its Influence on Standards of Living and Social Change* (New York, NY: Secretariat, Institute of Pacific Relations, 1940), p. 277.

[110] Kenley, *New Culture in a New World*, p. 153.

[111] Ke Pingping as related by Xue Jie, *Kanke daolu shang de zuji* [*Road Full of Misfortunes*], pp. 171, 173, 208.

[112] Ibid., pp. 170–177.

conduct it more effectively. Moreover, capitalism in the Nanyang, while fulfilling its own tasks, at the same time contributed to the success of the world revolution. As Xu Jie's analysis of the Nanyang conditions suggests, the Nanyang's prosperity struck the Chinese because of its contrast with China.[113] The CC CCP letter written by Li Lisan mentioned the same issues and presented the Nanyang as a place of highly developed industries and hence as the center of the labor movement in the Pacific and the center of communication. The Nanyang CYL also debated with the CCP about the nature of the Nanyang Revolution.[114]

Xu's idea that young locally born Chinese would become leaders of the liberation of the oppressed peoples of the Nanyang if they knew the Chinese language was an expression of the GMD's global vision as well as the goal of cultivating an identification with China among overseas Chinese. In another short story, Xu wrote:

At the bookstore I saw that youngster, Ai Lian ... He had a touch of melancholy. I thought, this is that specific expression that the oppressed peoples of the colonies have. In a flash, I also recalled the eyes of that [Indian] man, and the yellow scraggy eyes of that Malay, and also recalled those two flashing bayonets. Ai Lian furtively read Chinese books; he especially liked to read books on social sciences ... At that time, our eyes met. Again, like last time on the road, he smiled slightly at me. I also nodded but did not say a word. "You, promising youth, when you train yourself, strengthen yourself, you will become the center of the Nanyang Revolution!"[115]

Xu's point – that the hope of the Nanyang Revolution, who would liberate their oppressed fellow countrymen, including Malays and Indians, would be young locally born Chinese who maintained a Chinese identity – provides a rare insight into the intersection of the

[113] Xu Jie, "Yelin de bieshu [Mansion in the Coconut Grove]," and "Liang ge qingnian [Two Youths]," in Xu Jie, *Yezi yu liulian: Zhongguo xiandai xiaopin jingdian* [*Coconut and Durian: Little Souvenirs of Contemporary China*], pp. 18–33, 34–48.
[114] CC CCP, "A Letter from the Central Committee of the CCP to the Nanyang Provisional Committee," p. 13. Ke Pingping as related by Xue Jie, *Kanke daolu shang de zuji* [*Road Full of Misfortunes*], p. 171. The CYL disagreed with the CC CCP's definition of the formulation of the essence of the revolution in the Nanyang, where an anticapitalist national revolution (*fan zibenzhuyi de minzu geming*) was required. The Nanyang CYL decided that *xing* (性) in *fan zibenzhuyi xing de minzu geming*, which was decided by the CCP to be the nature of the Nanyang Revolution, was to be erased. The essences of the Chinese and Siamese Revolutions were similar because of similar conditions in both countries, which were both semi-colonies. "Dui dang jueyi Nanyang geming xingzhi de yijian [Suggestions Regarding the Party Decision on the Nature of the Nanyang Revolution]," in the CC of the Nanyang CYL, "Nanyang gongzuo baogao [Nanyang Work Report]," 1928, RGASPI 533/10/1818/4–16, p. 16.
[115] Xu Jie, "Liang ge qingnian [Two Youths]," p. 48.

discourses of the Comintern, Malayan Chinese immigrant intellectuals, the GMD, the CCP, and the English-language public sphere in British Malaya. It also demonstrates the changes in conceptual and social aspects of the discursive community of Chinese revolutionaries.

Xu Jie wanted to include the locally born Chinese in the Nanyang Revolution so that they could fulfill the mission of emancipating "weak nations" through their Chinese identity and Chinese language, which ensured that they were not "slaves" who spoke Malay and English, the language of the colonial regime. The CYL had similar concerns.[116] In fact, the two locally born Chinese in Kuala Lumpur, students of a Methodist English school, who figured in Xu's short story were recruited by the local CYL after they published pieces in *Yiqunbao*.[117] Thus the Nanyang communist organizations started to recruit locally born Chinese who would soon become active in the liberation of Malaya and its oppressed peoples and who would also be in demand by the Comintern, as we see in Chapter 5.

The Chinese identity of the locally born thus translated into their participation in the indigenous revolutionary and nationalist project. The Chinese in another revolutionary project in the Nanyang, the Philippine party, despite its similarities with the Malayan party, did not embrace indigenous nationalism. Here, the Chinese identity of the locally born Chinese also played an important role.

Chineseness: The Philippines

As in Malaya, the first communist organization established in the Philippines was a CCP chapter. There, as among other Chinese overseas communities, the popularity of communist parties grew after the March Eighteenth Massacre (1926), when a demonstration protesting Japanese pressure in the Dagu port was suppressed by the North China (Beiyang) government, and after the May Thirtieth Movement.[118] The CCP sent Lin Xingqiu (林星秋) to establish a CCP cell in the Philippines in 1926.[119] The Special Philippine Branch (Feilübin tebie zhibu) in Manila (est. 1927) consisted of five communist cells of three people. One student cell was at the University of the Philippines, which intended

---

[116] Nanyang gongzuo baogao [Nanyang Work Report], p. 5; Xu Jie, "Liang ge qingnian [Two Youths]."
[117] Ke Pingping as related by Xue Jie, *Kanke daolu shang de zuji* [*Road Full of Misfortunes*], pp. 173–175.
[118] Gao Zinong, "Zhongguo gongchan qingnian tuan Feiliebin tebie difang gongzuo baogao [Work Report of the Philippine Special Local Committee of the Chinese Communist Youth League]."
[119] Ibid.

to recruit Filipinos; one was at the Philippine Chinese middle school (*Feiqiao zhongxue*); one was at a night school; and two were in the GMD, consisting of workers and shop employees. Shop employees were the majority of party members (twenty-three) as well as primary school students and women outside of Manila.

Altogether, there were thirty "pure" party members (*danchun dangyuan*). There was also a cell of three people in Suzugun (Japan) and two in Cebu.[120] In 1927, 300 shop employees established the Association of Chinese Migrant Workers (Fei huaqiao laodong xiehui).[121] In 1928, drawing on the report of Gao Zinong (高子农), alias Meditsinskii (Medical), a Fujianese member of the Chinese CYL sent by the CCP to study in Moscow,[122] the Comintern planned to establish a communist party in the Philippines.[123] Like the Chinese communists in Malaya, Gao promoted political rights for Chinese immigrants in the Philippines and viewed the Nanyang as a location of strategic commercial and military ports, and as a market.[124]

The Philippine party was a chapter of the Chinese transnational communist network. Shared characteristics with the Malaya organization included the popularity of anarchist ideas,[125] study societies and night schools as hotbeds of Marxist ideas, student and shop employee membership, a connection gap between student leaders and workers, and a workers' preference for traditional ways of self-organizing ("yellow" unions, as the communists called them) over radical red unions.[126] As in Malaya, Chinese laborers were reluctant to become involved in local politics or with non-Chinese (*yizu*), and even with Chinese outside their native place or surname associations (*tongxinghui*). They were beyond the reach of revolutionary propaganda, as they were illiterate, participated in brotherhoods and friendship associations (*xiongdihui and youyishe*), and were afraid to protest against their Chinese bosses (see Chapter 4). The GMD had more appeal among "capitalists," students, and women's organizations. Chinese

[120] Ibid., esp. p. 166.
[121] Ibid.
[122] Gao Zinong's letter to Xiang Zhongfa, June 1, 1928, RGASPI 495/66/7/134–135; Gao Zinong, "Zhongguo gongchan qingnian tuan Feiliebin tebie difang gongzuo baogao [Work Report of the Philippine Special Local Committee of the Chinese Communist Youth League]."
[123] V. Demar, "Vopros o sozdanii sektsii kommunisticheskogo Internatsionala na filippinskikh ostrovakh [Regarding the Establishment of the Comintern Section in the Philippine Islands]," April 17, 1928, RGASPI 495/66/5/1-4.
[124] Gao Zinong, "Zhongguo gongchan qingnian tuan Feiliebin tebie difang gongzuo baogao [Work Report of the Philippine Special Local Committee of the Chinese Communist Youth League]," pp. 145 ob., 156.
[125] Lai, *Chinese American Transnational Politics*, p. 53.
[126] Gao Zinong, "Zhongguo gongchan qingnian tuan Feiliebin tebie difang gongzuo baogao [Work Report of the Philippine Special Local Committee of the Chinese Communist Youth League]," p. 141.

communists were also on a mission to liberate the masses of low political and cultural levels (*zhengzhi sixiang* [*wenhua*] *di*), affected by a colonial education, and were happy to report progress among students at Philippine University, formerly "the most backward in the East."[127] The Comintern approach to Philippine national emancipation was, similar to its approach in Malaya, by a united front of the Philippine population, under the leadership of the communist party, to bring together "the proletariat, the peasantry, the urban poor, and the revolutionary students – the Moros, mountain tribes, and Chinese toilers, as well as the Christian Filipinos."[128] The Comintern also promoted unity between Chinese immigrants and Filipino labor movements and campaigned against the deportation of Chinese workers in the Philippines and internationalist support for the Chinese Rrevolution.[129] As it had done in Malaya, the Comintern promoted solidarity with the Chinese and Indian Revolutions and contacts with the revolutionary movements in China, Indonesia, Malaya, and the United States.[130] Why did the Chinese communists in the Philippines not come up with the discourse of a multiethnic Philippine nation despite similarities with the party in Malaya, the long-term presence of a large number of ethnic Chinese, and rule by colonial authorities to overthrow? For one, unlike in Malaya, the Comintern promoted the "equality of all minorities, regardless of race or creed, and their absolute right to self-determination – including complete separation."[131] Also, the Comintern policy of naming one communist party per host country shaped the organizational forms of Chinese communist organizations in different settings. Where there was already a Comintern-endorsed communist party, Chinese communists joined as a Chinese-language faction, similar to that in Germany and the United States.[132] In the historical area of Chinese emigration in the Nanyang, where Chinese communists were the earliest communists, and in Malaya

[127] Ibid., pp. 141, 157–159.
[128] Eastern Secretariat of ECCI, "Letter regarding tasks of the CPPI," December 14, 1931, RGASPI 495/66/16/1–5, esp. 3.
[129] ECCI, "Draft Letter Regarding the Situation in the Philippines and Tasks of the CPPI," October 10, 1931, RGASPI 495/66/16/187–208; "Draft Resolution on the Revolutionary Trade Union Movement in the Philippines," August 16, 1931, RGASPI 495/66/23/59–67, esp. 67.
[130] Tim Ryan, "The Present Situation in the Philippines and the Immediate Tasks of the Communist Party," February 17, 1931, RGASPI 496/66/23/1–24, esp. 22–23.
[131] Eastern Secretariat of the ECCI, "Draft Letter to C. P. of the Philippines," July 22, 1931, RGASPI 495/66/16/65–91, esp. 81.
[132] In the United States the Chinese communists in 1927 wanted to call themselves the Chinese communist party, but the executive secretary of the CPUSA, Ruthenberg, did not permit them to do so, suggesting they should be called the Chinese faction of the American party. Fowler, *Japanese and Chinese Immigrant Activists*, p. 125.

and the Philippines, they established national parties. The Philippine party consisting of Chinese migrants had no CCP organizational identity. In contrast to the Nanyang Communist Party, which was responsible for the regional revolution in the Nanyang, the chapter of the Chinese Communist Party in the Philippines was already known as the Philippine Communist Party (Feilübin gongchandang) in 1928 and was organizationally autonomous from the CCP.[133] The Comintern established the Communist Party of the Philippine Islands (CPPI) on November 7, 1930, and one year later the Comintern was still pushing the party to connect with the CCP.[134]

In the Philippines, communists were not the only ones promoting independence, unlike in Malaya. Moreover, Chinese mestizos were already considered a part of the Philippine nation and there was an insufficient number of new Chinese immigrants whose rights the party would promote. There was no sense of an intergenerational Chinese identity to bridge the two groups in the late 1920s and early 1930s, despite the continuity of Chinese mestizos' participation in the Philippine liberation movement, from Jose Rizal to the anti-Japanese resistance during World War II.[135] As a matter of fact, in 1928 Gao Zinong did not even see Rizal as Chinese. On the contrary, because he was celebrated by the American government as an anti-Spanish Philippine hero, Rizal was considered to be an ally of the "American imperialists."[136] There was a lack of shared Chinese identity between Chinese immigrants like Gao and locally born Chinese mestizos, who instead shared a Christian identity with the locals.[137]

As a consequence of Spanish policies regarding the "Filipinization" of Chinese mestizos, by the end of the nineteenth century mestizo culture had become part and parcel of Filipino culture and, after the American takeover, of the discourse of the Philippine "nation" that the American government took up in an effort to coopt nationalist demands. Because of the leadership of Chinese mestizos in the Philippine Revolution, it has been argued that Chinese mestizos laid a foundation for the independent Philippine nation.[138]

---

[133] Gao Zinong, "Zhongguo gongchan qingnian tuan Feiliebin tebie difang gongzuo baogao [Work Report of the Philippine Special Local Committee of the Chinese Communist Youth League]."

[134] Profintern, "Direktivy po rabote na Fillippinakh [Directive for Work in the Philippines]." The document is undated, but since the previous document in the file is dated 1931, this document is possibly from 1931 as well. RGASPI 534/6/148/162–163.

[135] Shubert S. C. Liao, ed., *Chinese Participation in Philippine Culture and Economy* (Manila: Bookman, 1964).

[136] Gao Zinong, "Zhongguo gongchan qingnian tuan Feiliebin tebie difang gongzuo baogao [Work Report of the Philippine Special Local Committee of the Chinese Communist Youth League]."

[137] Ibid.

[138] Wickberg, "The Chinese Mestizo in Philippine History," pp. 95–96. The Philippine National Assembly was established in 1907, and in 1916, the date of eventual

American policies also favored Chinese mestizos' self-identification as Filipino. Not only culturally, Chinese mestizos had already formed a part of the Filipino identity in the late nineteenth century.[139] Unlike Malaya, the Philippines already existed as a nation-state, albeit not an independent one, and former Chinese mestizos, now called Filipinos, were part of the Philippine people.[140] Gao said the Americans had curtailed the national movement (*minzu yundong*) through assimilation and manipulation of the nonhomogeneous attitudes of various Philippine nationalities toward independence (*Fei ge minzu dui duli yundong de yijian bu yizhi*), promoting the idea of the Philippines as part of the confederation of the United States (*Meiguo lianbang*).[141]

American exclusion laws had barred the immigration of Chinese laborers to the Philippines, so the communist party lacked the potential constituency of immigrant Chinese who had to become local so as to improve their lot. Unlike their counterparts in British Malaya, by the second half of the nineteenth century Chinese mestizos in the Philippines already owned large landholdings. Moreover, they were able to improve their economic position after the American takeover. In contrast, during the same period in British Malaya, the economic position of locally born Chinese deteriorated.[142] In absolute numbers in 1903–1939, the Chinese population in the Philippines grew from 41,035 to 117,487, which was negligible to the 2 million Chinese immigrants in Malaya. Moreover, unlike in Malaya, beginning in 1935, a Chinese person born in China could – albeit with many conditions that included property ownership – naturalize as Filipino.[143]

Finally, in 1930, there were only twenty-five Chinese Communist Party members and sixty-two Filipinos, including one Chinese member of the Politburo. At the party's founding conference, there was one

---

decolonization was set for 1946. Richard T. Chu, *Chinese and Chinese Mestizos of Manila: Family, Identity and Culture, 1860s–1930s* (Leiden: Brill, 2010), pp. 321–325, 277–278.

[139] The reasons included American simplification of the earlier Spanish designation of Philippine residents as either Filipino or non-Filipino, economic competition with Chinese immigrants, the weakness of China, and a caution not to identify with Chinese mestizo leadership in the Philippine Revolution, which was feared by the American government. Wickberg, "The Chinese Mestizo in Philippine History."

[140] Gao Zinong, "Zhongguo gongchan qingnian tuan Feiliebin tebie difang gongzuo baogao [Work Report of the Philippine Special Local Committee of the Chinese CommunistYouth League]."

[141] Ibid., p. 157.

[142] Wickberg, "The Chinese Mestizo in Philippine History."

[143] However, as a consequence of the rise of Chinese nationalism, many Chinese born in the Philippines chose Chinese citizenship rather than naturalization as Filipinos. In the 1920s, anti-Chinese sentiments increased due to the economic problems of the time, as did Chinese nationalism, which was propagated in Chinese schools by the GMD. Chu, *Chinese and Chinese Mestizos of Manila*, pp. 288–298, 316, 327–329.

Chinese delegate, although Chinese trade unions were the most active in the Philippines.[144] To summarize, by the early 1930s the absence of a discourse of a multiethnic nation among the Chinese communists in the Philippines could be explained by a lack of Chinese members in the communist party, a comparatively low number of Chinese laborers in the Philippines, the relative economic affluence of the local Chinese mestizos, and, possibly, conflicting Comintern ideas about national unity and the self-determination of minorities. In addition, the local Chinese had already became "Filipino" and had become a part of the indigenous nation of the Philippines.

Conclusion

The Comintern exported from Europe not only revolution but also the idea of the nation-state. In British Malaya, this export was facilitated by the Chinese immigrant community that needed to gain political rights that no other existing discourse of national belonging could provide. By 1930, Comintern insistence on the founding of national parties based on separate countries, as well as the British fostering of a Malayan nation, led the MCP to become an early adopter of the multiethnic Malayan state.

The case of *minzu* is an example of how different understandings of a single word had far-reaching consequences. The term *national* communicated different meanings to partners in revolution who did not fully understand one another. The shift in the meaning of *minzu* was produced by the interaction of three realms: the Malayan, the Chinese, and the international, including the Comintern in Moscow and communist organizations in the United States. The crossing of languages, groups, intellectual worlds, and how they perceived and reasoned with shared authoritative texts to address their problems shaped conceptual categories and discourses. The altered meaning of the word *minzu* reconciled the "Malayan nation" with Chinese nationalism for the members of the MCP.

To involve non-Chinese in a Chinese revolutionary organization, promoted by both the CCP and the GMD, was the MCP's survival strategy, which we can call indigenization, though the organization was to remain rooted in China by advocating for the rights of the Chinese and by promoting a Chinese identity among locally born Chinese. What Kuhn calls the "embeddedness" of the Chinese community in local society was

[144] "Report on the Philippines," January 1, 1931, RGASPI 495/ 66/ 2/48–62, esp. pp. 48–49, 53.

to be achieved through Chinese leadership in the joint liberation of oppressed local peoples and resident Chinese. The Comintern's emphasis on the importance of colonial revolutions in the fall of empires in the form of local, that is, Malayan, nationalism offered a perfect solution for the need to be connected to both ends of migration among the Chinese living in colonies overseas. This was through dual nationalism, Chinese and indigenous.[145] As in other transnational identities that provided the basis for the "pan" movements – Slavic, Islamic, and African – that had emerged during the nineteenth century, interwar internationalism also became significant as a vehicle for national identities because it provided an international legitimization for national sovereignty.[146]

By encouraging a Malayan Revolution, the Comintern stimulated the nationalization of the revolution in Malaya as opposed to a revolution led by international or expatriate forces. However, though the Chinese communists sought to create a non-Chinese revolution, they continued to perceive the Nanyang in terms of China's regional imagination, where China was the leader.

In this context, the newly formed MCP understood the Comintern's communist internationalism and support for the Chinese Revolution as referring to the defense of Chinese interests and the liberation of oppressed nations along the lines of Sun Yatsen's ideas about China's political alliance. For Chinese communists located in Singapore and Malaya, the evolving discourse matched the indigenizing need of Chinese organizations, which was also promoted by the Nanjing GMD. Chinese nationalism grafted onto Comintern internationalism became Malayan nation–based nationalism, locally relevant and internationally progressive. This allowed the MCP to secure an unoccupied niche necessary for localization – the niche of the liberators of Malaya.

In another place in Southeast Asia with a long history of Chinese patronage, settlement, and localization, the Philippines, the spread of the Western idea of the nation-state and the patterns of Chinese migration and localization also shaped the formation of an indigenous nation by the end of the nineteenth century with a strong role of the local Chinese.[147] Yet, as the discourse of a soon-to-be-independent Philippine nation had been embraced by the American government,

---

[145] See Kuhn, "Why China Historians Should Study the Chinese Diaspora."

[146] Cemil Aydin, *The Politics of Anti-Westernism in Asia: Visions of World Order in Pan-Islamic and Pan-Asian Thought* (New York, NY: Columbia University Press, 2007), pp. 4, 201–203.

[147] Wickberg, "The Chinese Mestizo in Philippine History." Political leadership is still a common approach of Chinese indigenization in the Philippines. See Teresita Ang See, "Integration, Indigenization, Hybridization and Localization of the Ethnic Chinese Minority in the Philippines," in Leo Suryadinata, ed., *Migration, Indigenization and*

Chinese communists could not claim a niche as liberators of the Philippines from colonialism, for that niche was already occupied.[148] As such, the Comintern's brand of internationalism was redundant for Chinese localization in the Philippines. In this story of international forces and regional imaginations, the Chinese identity of migrant Chinese was an important factor determining whether they would engage in indigenous nationalism.

Comparable concerns about political rights in Western colonies in Southeast Asia shaped Chinese political participation in indigenous nationalist projects and their identities vis-à-vis the local population. Different colonial policies shaped the configuration of ideas of ethnic, civic, and national belonging in the Malay realm. Writing in the late 1940s, Tan Malaka, who, together with Alimin,[149] in 1925 prepared the first manifesto of a communist party in the Philippines, attributed the participation of mestizos in the Philippine Revolution to the common religion, Christianity, but called them "indigenous Indonesians" and stressed the continuity between the Philippine Revolution and the Indonesian communist movement.[150] Tan Malaka embraced the idea of *Indonesia Raya*, Greater Indonesia, which in precolonial times included the Philippines, Malaya, and Indonesia;[151] Ibrahim Yaacob was also a proponent of Greater Malay Unity (*Melayu Raya*), which he based on *bangsa* (common descent), thus excluding non-Malays.[152]

Despite differences resulting from the position of Malays as the dominant group in Malaya and Malay concepts of national belonging in East Sumatra and Malaya, Malaya and the Dutch East Indies saw parallels in the development of the concepts of national belonging, the place of communists in that development, and Chinese participation in its gestation during the same time period. In Malaya and East Sumatra, with similar political cultures centered on the institution of a sultanate (*kerajaan*) and analogous colonial policies undermining the authority of sultans, and a high proportion (more than 50 percent) of immigrant Chinese, which spurred similar resentment among the Malays, Malays saw the idea of Indonesia as undermining their rights to land. In Malaya in

Interaction: Chinese Overseas and Globalization (Singapore: Chinese Heritage Centre, World Scientific Publishing, 2011), pp. 231–252.

[148] According to Kuhn, the Chinese migrant community had to find an unoccupied niche in the economy in order to survive. Kuhn, *Chinese among Others*, p. 48.

[149] "Santos" [Alimin], "Tovarishcham Kuusinenu i Manuil'skomu [To Kuusinen and Manuilsky]," January 6, 1936, RGASPI 495/16/8/22–27.

[150] Tan Malaka, *From Jail to Jail*, vol. 1, pp. 162, 117–120.

[151] Ramon Guillermo, "Andres Bonifacio: Proletarian Hero of the Philippines and Indonesia," *Inter-Asia Cultural Studies* 18(3) (2017), pp. 338–346.

[152] Omar, *Bangsa Melayu*, p. 11.

the 1920s, sultans called for restoration of their power and even in 1940, at the Malay congress, participants were unwilling to link the descent-based *bangsa* to *kebangsaan* (nationalist and independence) goals in defining the Malay identity.[153]

In the Dutch East Indies, where by the early 1920s the term *Indonesia* was accepted and used among nationalist organizations,[154] the communist PKI was the first to adopt "Indonesia" in its name, as the Comintern promoted the concept of "one party, one country." In 1927, the Perserikatan Tionghwa Indonesia (Union of Chinese of Indonesia) was founded by the *Peranakan* Chinese, and in 1928, a conference of social groups in Batavia adopted the goal of one nation, one homeland, one language. The Dutch also promoted Malay, or Bahasa Indonesia, as a unifying language, and in the following year, Sukarno organized the Partai Nasional Indonesia, the Nationalist Party of Indonesia.[155]

Comparable discussions of concepts of national belonging among the MCP and among the Chinese in Indonesia stemmed from the Chinese community movement for political and landownership rights. The relationship with local nationalism among Chinese communities in the Malay realm was shaped by a reaction to colonial policies in Southeast Asia and the Comintern's promotion of national parties and Chinese participation in those parties. All these also shaped the parties' organizational hybridity.

---

[153] Ibid., pp. 5, 9, 11, 20–21, 24–25.
[154] Robert Edward Elson, *The Idea of Indonesia: A History* (Cambridge: Cambridge University Press, 2008), p. 44.
[155] Owen, *The Emergence of Modern Southeast Asia*, pp. 298–299.

Part II

The Comintern, the MCP, and Chinese
Networks, 1930–1935

4   The MCP as a Hybrid Communist Party
Structure, Discourse, and Activity, 1930–1934

As outlined in the introduction to this volume, the MCP was shaped by responses to the common challenges of global imperialism in Southeast Asia. Aside from the organizational and ideological hybridity the MCP inherited from its Chinese and CCP origins, it also shared characteristics with other communist parties in Asia. One was the dire straits in which most of the parties of the time found themselves, as political suppression and the elite origins of early communism had resulted in low membership among outlawed and suppressed parties in the early 1930s,[1] such as the Chinese, Indonesian, Japanese, Taiwanese, Korean, and Vietnamese parties. Additionally, a gap appeared between the party and the labor movements, as in many of these places an industrial proletariat was not commonly found. Winning over the masses as the precondition to a communist rise to power had been the main theme among small communist parties of the Third International since the Third Comintern Congress in 1921.[2] Gaps between the party and the masses were common not only in other Asian contexts; to begin with, the Leninist Bolshevik Party's very mission was to imbue revolutionary and class consciousness into the masses and to lead them.

In many contexts, Soviet communism appealed to the nationalist elites in Asia, especially to intellectuals, because of its anticolonial stance. In all contexts, party founders were intellectuals, and the policy of Bolshevization aimed to make small communist parties in Asia into mass parties and to connect them to labor movements that originated in older forms of trade associations and mutual help societies. Unique in the region, the Philippine Communist Party was not dominated by intellectuals before 1938 and had no ambition to accept Marxist orthodoxy. Instead, middle-class leadership was installed in the labor movement in

---

[1] See Stephen A. Smith, "Introduction: Towards a Global History of Communism," and Tim Rees, "1936," in Smith, ed., *The Oxford Handbook of the History of Communism*, pp. 1–36, 187–194, respectively.

[2] John Riddell, *To the Masses: Proceedings of the Third Congress of the Communist International, 1921* (Leiden: Brill, 2015).

the Philippines in order to provide legitimacy in the eyes of the public when the labor party sought political participation.[3] American communist Harrison George, while contemplating the future of the Philippine communist movement, saw possible allies in the so-called secret societies, akin to the Katipunan society, which had been crucial in the Philippine independence war of the late nineteenth century, and in the Freemasons, who opposed the Catholic Church owning land.[4] Indeed, in the CPPI in 1930, the "majority of the present party membership [were] members of either Masonic Lodges or Secret Societies." Politburo member Antonio de Ora was a deputy master of a Masonic temple, and one of the CPPI's founders, Crisanto Evangelista, was a member of the executive board of the "Sons of the People Society," that is, the Katipunan.[5]

Communist movements in the Philippines, Indonesia, and Malaya grew from different organizational contexts, which shaped their trajectories, their various configurations of legal and illegal activities, and their engagement with non-radical political movements. The MCP's unique configuration stemmed from the fact that the party had the function of a legal Chinese organization but its goal was to overthrow the British colonial government. In the Philippines, the Dutch East Indies, and British Malaya, where the emerging concepts of Malay and Chinese national belonging overlapped, a comparison of the balance between legal and illegal communist activities among leftist organizations, active to different extents but all banned, sheds light on Chinese political participation in the region and the integration of Chinese into indigenous polities.

The Southeast Asian Chinese community in Malaya – where earlier special rules had allowed Chinese businesses and organizations to develop unhindered by the bureaucracies and ideologies of the Qing empire and its successor Chinese nation-state[6] – once again became a frontier enclave of Chinese migration, where Chinese communists could organize safe from the depredations of Chinese warlord armies and especially from Chiang Kai-Shek's GMD back in China proper and could respond to the opportunity for international legitimacy and cash provided by the Comintern. The MCP took up an organizational form that was explicitly revolutionary – and shaped by interwar global connections but part of the Comintern world – yet this form was deeply local.

<hr />

[3] Fuller, *Forcing the Pace*, pp. 16–17, 57, 60, 61.
[4] "Report by Comrade Harrison George on the Philippine Islands," October 17, 1927, RGASPI 495/66/4/1–14.
[5] "Report on the Philippines," January 1, 1931, RGASPI 495/66/24/48–62, esp. 60. De Ora was killed in a car accident in January 1931. McLane, *Soviet Strategies in Southeast Asia*, pp. 166–167.
[6] Kuhn, "Why China Historians Should Study the Chinese Diaspora."

Membership and Constituency: The Party and the Masses

Origins and Organizational Structure

The MCP was an organization of Chinese. The MCP's dual nationalism, discourse, organizational structure, and activities reveal that it was a hybrid of a Chinese overseas organization and a communist party. The majority of its membership was comprised of Chinese migrants from Guangdong, Fujian, and Hainan who were not from the industrial proletariat but were shop and restaurant employees, servants in the homes of foreigners, rubber tappers, and handicraftsmen. In one key aspect the MCP acted in ways that call to mind Chinese overseas associations, and like those associations, the MCP promoted Chinese political rights and attempted to represent the interests of the Chinese vis-à-vis the British colonial state. Its ultimate goal, however, was to foment a revolution in China and Malaya and to install soviet governments in both places under a communist leadership, a vision of a revolution that increasingly stemmed from Comintern correspondence. The party continued to attempt to bring in non-Chinese members and to engage in a cross-community alliance for Malayan liberation. Like other Chinese organizations, the MCP was affected by the economic downturn caused by the Great Depression, and it both campaigned against British anti-Chinese policies and desperately embraced the policy of Malayanization.

The MCP was a synthesis of the organizational habits and expectations of the actors involved and the new ideas, opportunities, resources, and constraints of the international communist movement embodied by Comintern support. Similar to other new kinds of Chinese organizations, such as chambers of commerce, the MCP had an organizational basis in native place associations, but it also united people from different places of origin in nationalist movements both inside and outside of China.[7] In the MCP, the mode of bonding through native place ties was not exclusive. The MCP's organization, genealogy, and mutual aid functions also resembled those of brotherhood associations, including secret societies and religious associations.

Like the CCP, the secret societies of imperial South China were imported to Southeast Asia after they had been suppressed in China. For example, members of the Tiandihui – the Heaven and Earth Society – who were suppressed after the rebellion of 1787–1788,[8] fled to the Nanyang from South China and engaged in robbery, local religion, and rebellion as they

[7] Kuhn, *Chinese among Others*, p. 264.
[8] David Ownby, "Introduction: Secret Societies Reconsidered," and Dian Murray, "Migration, Protection, and Racketeering: The Spread of the Tiandihui within China,"

adapted to the new environment. Like the Tiandihui, the MCP functioned as a poor man's *huiguan* (regional lodge) for peddler merchants and seasonal laborers from different places of origin,[9] and like the secret societies, the MCP organized mutual aid societies,[10] which were akin to guilds and urban associations and flourished in contexts where the Confucian state and elites were absent or weak. They assumed rudimentary political functions in frontier environments, not necessarily rebelling against the state but sometimes becoming predatory.[11] Similarly, MCP member Zhang Xia, an Esperantist and art teacher in Fujian, participated in the CCP kidnapping of the son of a landlord in order to seek ransom money for party activities, was exposed to the GMD, and had to escape to Malaya after his students stole two mimeograph machines from their school to print communist and anti–New Life movement propaganda. As in secret societies and other Chinese mutual aid organizations – but also as in communist organizations – the funds of the Malayan Federation of Labour Unions and the MCP were derived from members' contributions.[12] Like brotherhood associations, which built new communities and enterprises to supplement those that had been weakened, the MCP was built on the basis of the banned and emasculated GMD.[13]

Native place bonds had structured migrant labor forces in Chinese cities since the eighteenth century.[14] In an age of increased migration both inside and outside of China, native place lodges, or *huiguan*, became key organizations providing services and protection for migrants. Native place bonds also became the organizational foundation for the spread of new ideas. From the 1910s, Shanghainese native place associations played a crucial role in the mobilization of the nationalist movement.[15]

---

both in Ownby and Heidhues, eds., *"Secret Societies" Reconsidered*, pp. 3–33, esp. p. 20 and pp. 177–189, respectively.

[9] Murray, "Migration, Protection and Racketeering," p. 179; Ownby, "Chinese Hui and the Early Modern Social Order: Evidence from Eighteenth-Century Southeast China," in Ownby and Heidhues, *"Secret Societies" Reconsidered*, pp. 34–67, esp. p. 54.

[10] "Otchet o polozhenii v Nan'iane [Report about the Situation in Nanyang]," p. 25.

[11] Ownby, "Introduction," pp. 15–17.

[12] Zhang Xia, "Xianyou xiandai zhongxue de geming huoguang [The Revolutionary Fire of the Modern Middle Schools in Xianyou County]," in Zhongguo renmin zhengzhi xieshang huiyi Fujian sheng Putian shi weiyuanhui wenshi ziliao yanjiu weiyuanhui, ed., *Putian shi wenshi ziliao di yi ji [Literary and Historical Materials of the City of Putian, vol. 1]* (1985), pp. 43–48; Huang Muhan, "Worker Movement in Federated Malay States"; "Otchet o polozhenii v Nan'iane [Report about the Situation in Nanyang]," p. 28; Ownby, "Introduction," p. 18.

[13] Ownby, "Introduction," p. 21.

[14] Kuhn, *Chinese among Others*, p. 45.

[15] Bryna Goodman, "The Locality as Microcosm of the Nation? Native Place Networks and Early Urban Nationalism in China," *Modern China* 21(4) (1995), pp. 387–419.

Early Marxist societies in urban China also used native place ties. In the aftermath of the May Fourth Movement, Shanghai's *Weekend Review*, launched by Sun Yatsen and run by the GMD, was built on co-provincial ties and "functioned to sustain the uprooted [Marxist] provincials in the big city."[16] Some members of those study societies, *xue hui*, became the founders of the Chinese Communist Party.[17] Communist labor unions were organized along native place ties in Shanghai and Beijing.[18]

The MCP embraced Malayan nationalism because it helped the MCP to indigenize as a Chinese organization by claiming leadership over the emerging Malayan nation. The Chinese communists in Malaya used means that were socially available to them to think about a problem and to organize a response in a specific time and place; these were native place associations. Similar to other Chinese organizations in Malaya,[19] the MCP and other communist-influenced organizations, such as trade unions, the Anti-imperialist League (AIL), and the Communist Youth League (CYL), organized according to their dialects and native place ties. These ties culminated in conflicts between the Hainanese and Hakka factions of the party leadership in 1932 and 1936.[20] Additionally, British authorities pitted different ethnic groups against one another.[21] The lack of cadres who knew English or Malay limited the MCP's potential constituency to the Chinese, and the members of labor organizations and the party were mostly Hainanese.[22] The Nanyang General Labor Union (Nanyang geye zonggonghui) (NGLU) established in 1926, was an amalgamation of various Hainanese offshoots of older mutual aid societies,[23] and Hainanese had dominated the CYL, the CCP, labor unions, and the GMD since 1926.[24] Different dialects were the main obstacle in propaganda work among laborers.[25] Reportedly, they had no connections to the organizations of Malays and Indians.[26] In the spring of 1928, the NGLU of 4,000 members had a majority comprised of servants in foreign households, and 98 percent

---

[16] Yeh Wen-hsin, *Provincial Passages: Culture, Space, and the Origins of Chinese Communism* (Berkeley, CA: University of California Press, 1996), p. 200.

[17] Ibid., pp. 201–205. See also van de Ven, *From Friend to Comrade.*

[18] Elizabeth J. Perry, *Shanghai on Strike: The Politics of Chinese Labor* (Stanford, CA: Stanford University Press, 1993); Joseph Esherick, *Ancestral Leaves: A Family Journey through Chinese History* (Berkeley, CA: University of California Press, 2011), p. 173.

[19] Yen Ching-Hwang, "Early Chinese Clan Organizations in Singapore and Malaya, 1819–1911," *Journal of Southeast Asian Studies* 12(1) (March 1981), pp. 62–91, esp. p. 69.

[20] Yong, *Origins of Malayan Communism*, pp. 168–169.

[21] "To the C. C. of the Chinese Party and the Comintern."

[22] "Report from Malay," p. 28.

[23] Yong, *Origins of Malayan Communism*, p. 69.

[24] Ibid., chs. 4 and 5.

[25] Huang Muhan, "Worker Movement in Federated Malay States."

[26] Ho Chi Minh, "Malay."

of all members were from *Tin-chao* in Guangdong.[27] The Hainanese, a small dialect group, thus organized themselves for "communal and security reasons" into communist-influenced organizations.[28] Ho Chi Minh provided an ample description of native place ties within the MCP:

Owing to the difference of dialects, there exists even a pronounced provincialism between the members. The Fokienese likes to work only with his Fokienese comrade, to listen only to Fokienese speakers, to recruit only Fokienese friends, etc. In a discussion, the Fokienese generally side with the Fokienese and the Hainanese with their own "countrymen."[29]

In 1930, most party members were seamen, workers on rubber plantations, tin miners, and "builders," though the party also had a "small number of intellectuals" such as teachers and "independents" (such as restaurant keepers).[30] Overall, 70 percent of the party members in leading organs at various levels were workers. There were five local committees and four special subdistrict committees. Six out of ten Chinese party members were Hainanese, who made up 20 to 25 percent of the overall Cantonese population (60 percent).[31] The labor union had 5,342 members, including 1,000 seamen. Of the membership, 35 percent were industrial workers, 40 percent were rubber tree cutters, 5 percent were "foreign affairs" workers, 5 percent were shop employees, and 14 percent had other professions.[32]

[27] Huang Muhan, "Worker Movement in Federated Malay States."
[28] Yong, *Origins of Malayan Communism*, pp. 141–144. For more on the revolutionary activities of the Hainanese, see Jeremy A. Murray, *China's Lonely Revolution: The Local Communist Movement of Hainan Island, 1926–1956* (Albany, NY: State University of New York Press, 2017).
[29] Ho Chi Minh, "Malay," p. 25.
[30] Ibid. For example, *Chiayinpa* (possibly Kangar) had twenty-three comrades, 70 percent of them "gum cutters," 20 percent *falang* makers (珐琅, Cloisonné, metalwork decorated with enamel), and 10 percent shop employees. *Pasen* had six comrades who were "small dealers and foreign workers" (i.e., servants in foreigners' homes). In all of Kuala Lumpur district, there were fourteen nuclei and 108 comrades. In Penang, where party work was said to be the most developed, intellectuals (predominantly teachers) were the most active and constituted 30 percent of the members, while 20 percent were rubber and small traders, 40 percent were seamen, and 10 percent had other professions. Altogether, there were seventy members, all Chinese. Seventy percent of them were Cantonese. Sembilan had 150 party members, mostly rubber workers. In Ipoh (*Japo*), there were 120 members, 5 percent of whom were teachers. Kuching (*Futsing*), in Borneo, had sixty comrades. "Minutes of the Third Representative Conference of Nanyang," pp. 93–104.
[31] "To the C. C. of the Chinese Party and the Comintern."
[32] "Report on the Labour Movement," in "Minutes of the Third Representative Conference of Nanyang," pp. 110–112. However, according to another report, of the total 5,830 members, 1,500 were seamen, 1,630 were workers in the rubber industry, 860 were foreigners' household servants, and the rest were shop employees (300), tree cutters (220), and members of other industries. Huang Muhan, "Worker Movement in Federated Malay States."

Moreover, despite having the structure of a communist party, some features of the MCP organization were reminiscent of those of Chinese associations of the time. For one, the Nanjing GMD promoted an organizational structure of committees specific to the GMD in the regional lodges. Moreover, *huiguan* in the 1920s and the 1930s in Singapore also became politicized and were transformed from mutual aid organizations to organizations articulating the interests of the Chinese community. *Huiguan* thus became sites for popular mobilization. Clan associations in Malaya had a three-tier structure comparable to that of the MCP: a standing committee, a management committee, and rank-and-file members, who democratically elected the management committee.[33] There was also a secretary.

Similar to Chinese associations structured as two-level organizations in the twentieth century in the United States, Mexico, and Hong Kong,[34] the MCP experienced a disconnect, literal and figurative, between its upper ranks (*shangji*), or the Central Committee (CC), and its "lower ranks" (*xiaji*), that is, members and leaders of local party branches as well as among comrades within branches (*zhibu*). The upper ranks were urged to adequately understand the living conditions and lead the work of the lower ranks.[35] On the other hand, the MCP experienced a disconnect with larger constituencies (i.e., "the masses"), both Chinese and non-Chinese comrades in the party and the trade unions.[36]

Not only did this disconnect resemble historical weaknesses in China's managerial patterns, since weak communication between high and low

---

[33] Yen Ching-hwang, *A Social History of the Chinese in Singapore and Malaya, 1800–1911* (Singapore; New York, NY: Oxford University Press, 1986), p. 79; Wing Chung Ng, "Urban Chinese Social Organization: Some Unexplored Aspects in Huiguan Development in Singapore, 1900–1941," *Modern Asian Studies* 26(3) (July 1992), pp. 469–494, esp. p. 485.

[34] The Chaozhou *huiguan* in Hong Kong in the 1970s had an upper- and lower-level structure. The former was a tightly knit network of chambers of commerce, industry/trade-based associations, and large native place associations dominated by medium to large entrepreneurs. The latter was a loose network of neighborhood and surname organizations whose leaders were typically small business owners, while the members were working-class men. Susanne Yuk Ping Choi, "Association Divided, Association United: The Social Organization of Chaozhou and Fujian Migrants in Hong Kong," in Kuah-Pearce Khun Eng and Evelyn Hu-Dehart, eds., *Voluntary Organizations in the Chinese Diaspora* (Hong Kong: Hong Kong University Press, 2006), pp. 121–140, esp. pp. 128–129.

[35] Dangtuan zhongyang [CC of the MCP and CYL], "Magong lianzi tonggao di ba hao: Guanyu yanmi dangtuan de zuzhi wenti [Circular no. 8 of the MCP Regarding the Organization of the Secret Work of the Party and CYL]," August 15, 1933, RGASPI 495/62/20/29–30; "Dangwu wenti jueyian [Resolution on Party Work]," in "Malaiya gongchandang di yi ci kuodahui jueyian [The Resolutions of the First Enlarged Congress of the MCP]," April 5, 1933, RGASPI 495/62/21/1–21, esp. 9–13; "Resolutions Adopted at the Third Congress of the Malaya Party," p. 8.

[36] "Resolution on the Labour Movement," March 24, 1934; "Decisions of the C. C. of the Malayan Party on the Intensification of the Labour Movement Passed on 20 March 1934," RGASPI 495/62/23/57–59ob.

bureaucratic ranks was a concern in all East Asian mandarinates,[37] it was also the result of the MCP's problems as a communist party that, like many other parties in the region, had no connection with the "masses." This structural similarity partly explains the content and language of the MCP's self-criticism: its frame of reference was that of a Chinese association, but one that was increasingly inflected by Bolshevik language over the course of the 1930s. The MCP saw the problem as follows: many local party branches imagined that building an upper organization (*shangceng jiguan de*) was enough for party activity without engaging the masses and building the organization at the lower (*fadong xiaji dangbu*) and practical (*shiji*) levels. Such was the Union to Aid the Chinese Soviet Revolution (Yuanzhu Zhongguo suweiai geming datongmeng), the campaign of which is discussed in Chapter 7. Above all, it is likely that in some cases the lack of a connection was a euphemism for the absence of a lower grade, that is, the absence of the "masses" altogether.[38]

A look at the map of the communist organization in 1928 helps us understand the two-level disconnect within the party. The MCP was a four-tier organization with cells and branches in grassroots, district, state, and municipal organizations, as well as with a central committee of eleven members.[39] As we can see, the leadership was much more numerous than it was in local lower-level cells. The distance from the upper- to the lower-level comrades was more than the number of cells at the grassroots level, as shown in Table 4.1.

Thus, MCP members' leadership in labor unions conformed both to communist party tactics in labor organizing and to the two tiers, leaders and members, of Chinese associations. Following the Comintern's policy of communists working within legal (usually labor) parties to convert their members to illegal communist parties, MCP and CYL leaders were building front organizations – including the Anti-Imperialist League, the Red Aid Society, and trade unions – and during the 1930s they increasingly attempted to penetrate Chinese associations (*shetuan*) to recruit members in various strata of the population.[40]

---

[37] Woodside, *Lost Modernities*, p. 5.
[38] "Magong zhongyang tongzhi. Zenyang qu jinxing yu fazhan yuanzhu Zhongguo suweiai geming yundong de gongzuo jueyi [CC MCP Circular. The Resolution on How to Carry Out and Develop Aid to the Soviet Revolutionary Movement in China]," December 24, 1933, RGASPI 495/62/20/34–37; "To the C. C. of the Chinese Party and the Comintern."
[39] Yong, *Origins of Malayan Communism*, pp. 152–153.
[40] "Magong zhongyang guanyu Liening tongzhi shishi dishi zhounian jinian yu Libokeneixi Lusenbao er tongzhi bei sha dishi zhounian jinian de gongzuo jueding [CC MCP Work Resolution Regarding the Fifteenth Anniversary of Liebknecht and Luxembourg's Death and the Tenth Anniversary of Lenin's Death]," December 26, 1933, RGASPI 495/62/20/38–40.

Table 4.1 *The organizational structure of the Nanyang Provisional Committee in 1928*[41]

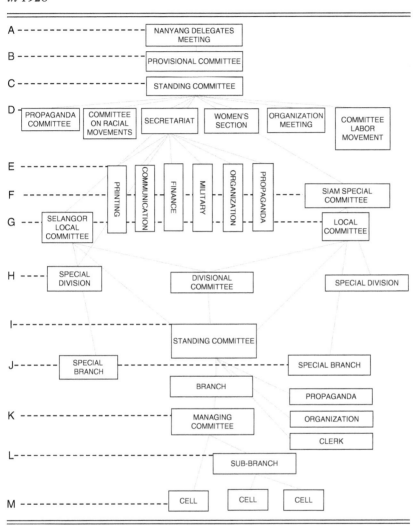

Structural reasons accounted for a lack of cohesion among different levels of cadres in the party. Similar to Chinese overseas associations,

[41] Ibid., p. 93. Original Source: Foreign Office Records 371/13243, F 3518/154/61, MBPI, no. 63, August 1928, Supplement to the MBPI Singapore, August 31, 1928, Appendix A.

MCP members lacked a sense of formal organizational hierarchy and lines of authority. The subordination of the party branches and the need to accept the center's resolutions were new to members.[42] Circulars for party leaders explained that they had to attend nucleus meetings where they would explain to the workers the significance of organizing a general solidarity strike on the anniversary of the October Revolution.[43]

In addition, the lack of regular transport connections upset communications among different levels of the CCP organizations, such as the Guangdong CC CCP, the Nanyang Provisional Committee (located in Singapore), and the local branches, both before and after the founding of the MCP. Sometimes there was no way to deliver literature to local cells.[44] Police interception of mail and a lack of funds in 1928 also affected communications between the provisional committee and lower-level leadership organs of the CYL, as the CYL could not afford to buy postage stamps to mail circulars.[45] Inspection trips were expensive and rare,[46] and very little inspection work was done due to a lack of cadres and finances. Incomplete reports from the Nanyang party were thus blamed for the inadequate directives from the CC CCP.[47] For instance, to get from Bangkok to Singapore, one had to pay a tax of $100, with an additional $100 for a second-class ticket. This amount was equal to one month of earnings by the CC MCP in 1930.[48]

One such investigator united cells in the East Indies and conveyed decisions and instructions for lower party organizations from upper party organs. He investigated the real conditions of lower party organizations, which would confirm whether recommendations from superiors fit local conditions and would solve local disputes.[49] The MCP even argued that "[t]he party has not done an investigation of the conditions of life in Malayan society, so the character of the Malayan Revolution has not been confirmed."[50] Investigation campaigns were a common practice in the world of the Guangdong provincial committee, such as in Hong Kong,

[42] "Minutes of the Third Representative Conference of Nanyang," p. 10; "Magong zhong-yang gei Ma Yin ji tongzhi de yifen gongkaixin [CC MCP Open Letter to Malay and Indian Comrades]," August 8, 1933, RGASPI 495/62/20/21–24.
[43] "Central Circular no. 9," 1930.
[44] "Otchet o polozhenii v Nan'iane [Report about the Situation in Nanyang]," p. 14.
[45] Nanyang gongzuo baogao [Nanyang Work Report], 1929, RGASPI 533/10/1818/55–68, p. 67.
[46] "Otchet o polozhenii v Nan'iane [Report about the Situation in Nanyang], [Report about the Situation in Nanyang]." p. 27.
[47] "Minutes of the Third Representative Conference of Nanyang," pp. 108–109.
[48] Letter from "King" in Bangkok to "Fong" in Singapore, March 4, 1936, SMP, D7376; "Informatsiia o Malaiskikh Shtatakh [Information about the Malay States]."
[49] "Otchet o polozhenii v Nan'iane [Report about the Situation in Nanyang]," p. 14.
[50] "Minutes of the Third Representative Conference of Nanyang," pp. 128–129.

and the investigator in that case was Taiwanese party member and Comintern cadre Weng Zesheng.[51] Scholars such as Kuhn would see the CCP's extension of bureaucratic practices to control the entire population as an example of the increasing penetration of the state into society in twentieth-century China.[52]

The MCP was affected by the economic depression in the same way as were the regional lodges. *Huiguan* were declining in the early 1930s, and their members were unable to pay their dues. In 1931, the MCP could not collect subscriptions, and headquarters were struggling to make ends meet.[53] Yet with all its similarities with brotherhood associations, unlike them the MCP was an elite organization, disconnected from the "masses" also because of different paths of employment migration. Party member and artist Zhang Xia described those migrants who joined the party as having a higher cultural level (*wenhua shuiping gao*). There was a spatial disconnect, as the potential party leaders, teachers, and journalists from Xianyou County in Fujian who had joined the party, and the party "masses," laborers also from Xianyou County, almost none of whom joined the party, ended up in different places of the Malay Archipelago and the Malay Peninsula when they migrated to the South Seas.[54] In this sense of cultural superiority, we see what Ip has referred to as the Chinese intellectuals' sense of elitism based on their self-perception as the most progressive and modern elements. This became the justification for Chinese communists to lead the emancipation movement.[55]

The MCP was not unique in positioning the party as the agent of modernity. In the early 1920s, both the GMD and the CCP felt a responsibility for civilizing and awakening the uneducated and politically backward general public and described their parties' key roles as community organizers.[56] Truly a hybrid, however, similar to Chinese associations, the MCP leadership was divorced from its own membership, and like many other communist parties in Asia at the time, including the CCP, the MCP could involve neither its stated target population – the proletariat of Malaya – nor the "broader masses" of Malaya – its larger social

---

[51] He Chi, *Weng Zesheng zhuan* [*A Biography of Weng Zesheng*] (Taibei: Haixia xueshu, 2005), p. 230.

[52] Philip A. Kuhn, *Origins of the Modern Chinese State* (Stanford, CA: Stanford University Press, 2002).

[53] Wing-chung Vincent Ng, "Huiguan: Regional Institutions in the Development of Overseas Chinese Nationalism in Singapore, 1912–41" (MA dissertation, University of Hong Kong, 1987); MRCA, December 1931, p. 43 CO 273/572.

[54] Zhang Xia, "Xianyou xian lü Ma huaqiao yu geming huodong [Immigrants from Xianyou County in Malaya and Revolutionary Activities]," p. 38.

[55] Hung-Yok Ip, *Intellectuals in Revolutionary China: Heroes, Leaders and Sophisticates* (London: Routledge Curzon, 2005).

[56] Fitzgerald, *Awakening China*, p. 174; van de Ven, *From Friend to Comrade*, p. 52.

constituency of local people (Malay, Indian, and Chinese) – in its activities and organization.[57]

In the meantime, the Comintern promoted Bolshevization, which entailed the establishment of party organizations in the factories of the main industries, railway station cities, ports, and Singapore military bases; the organization of movements among peasants, women, youth, and the unemployed;[58] the centralized organization of party and trade unions; and the implementation of tactics described as promoting a multiethnic united front.[59] The Comintern targeted different "parts of the population" with propaganda of different slogans,[60] and the goal of this adaptation and indigenization, along with the involvement of non-Chinese, was the creation of a mass party. The MCP was to "pay special attention to the difference in nationality, language, and customs in order to organize the masses of the toilers."[61] This Comintern-demanded Bolshevization would be carried out through regular party meetings to "discuss questions of local character" and to "determine resultant concrete tasks along organizational and agitational lines."[62] All these fit with the MCP's indigenization impulse as an organization of Chinese migrants, but how was the party to appeal to the targets of this civilizing project?

The Masses

The MCP viewed the Chinese community as follows. Among the Singapore Chinese, 10 percent were "lackeys of imperialists," 10 percent were students, 20 percent were merchants, and 60 percent were "toiling masses and liberal businessmen."[63] The MCP targeted an audience that was busy with "physical games, Christian doctrines and remnants of theories in China."[64] To be sure, one of the theories or "-isms" that held the masses under its sway was "afraidism" (*haipazhuyi*).[65] The MCP's radicalism scared away the workers, and the party was portrayed as "standing outside shouting radical slogans."[66] In 1930 and 1931, the

---

[57] "Report from Malay."
[58] This is reflected in "Magong laijian. Malaiya de qingshi yu dang de renwu [A Document Received from the MCP. The Situation in Malaya and the Tasks of the Party]," August 25, 1934.
[59] FEB, "To the Malayan Comrades," December 17, 1930.
[60] Ibid.
[61] Ibid.
[62] Ibid.
[63] "To the C. C. of the Chinese Party and the Comintern."
[64] Ibid.
[65] "Dangwu wenti jueyian [Resolution on Party Work]," p. 9.
[66] "Resolution on the Labour Movement," March 24, 1934; "Zhigong yundong jueyian [Resolution on the Labour Movement]," in "Malai gongchandang di yi ci kuoda hui

party lost "over half" of its cadres and about 90 percent of its labor union cadres to arrests and deportations.[67] The MCP thought that open propaganda in newspapers, in pamphlets, and on wall posters would eliminate the fears and suspicions of the workers. As the masses in Malaya lacked revolutionary experience and had a "backward cultural level," they would have been more attracted to a "small" struggle focusing on immediate demands.[68] Instead, the MCP used slogans from CCP and Comintern programs rather than slogans originating from the masses, such as those from the soldiers' movement, made up of mostly Malays. However, apart from "stimulating their national consciousness," the MCP did plan to recruit in soldiers' clubs and committees (*shibing julebu, shibing weiyuanhui*) and to attract them with slogans of standing against forced participation in the war, demanding improvements in the quality of food, gaining permission to wear civilian (*suibian*) clothing after service, standing up against officers' beatings, and earning the right to marry without officers' approval.[69]

In 1933–1934, the MCP attributed its failure to attract the masses, in the language of Comintern circulars, to the influence of reformism and to the party's "mechanistic" leadership. The party and the CYL were condescending to the masses, whose daily life conditions they did not know. With the exception of Singapore, the party did not talk to Malays about world and Malayan politics.[70] The MCP stated that the "quality of party and CYL members was not higher, and in practical work was even lower than that of the revolutionary masses."[71] Ho Chi Minh, as always, hit the nail on the head:

GENERAL LEVEL: they are devoted, but inexperienced. They want to do things, but do not know how to do them. Owing to the lack of training and of education materials, their doctrinal and political knowledge is generally low; thus

jueyian [The Resolutions of the First Enlarged Congress of the MCP]," April 1933, RGASPI 495/62/21/1–21, esp. 14–17, esp. 15.

[67] Huang Muhan, "Worker Movement in Federated Malay States."

[68] "Central Circular no. 5. The General Lesson of the Demonstration on Aug. First," August 17, 1930, RGASPI 495/62/13/33–35; "Resolutions Adopted at the Third Congress of the Malaya Party."

[69] "Dangwu wenti jueyian [Resolution on Party Work]," p. 9; CC MCP, "An Address to the Oppressed Peoples of Malaya," August 10, 1933, RGASPI 495/62/20/25–28; "Resolutions Adopted at the Third Congress of the Malaya Party," p. 10; "Shibing yundong jueyian [Resolution on the Soldiers' Movement]," in "Malai gongchandang di yi ci kuoda hui jueyian [The Resolutions of the First Enlarged Congress of the MCP]," August 1934, RGASPI 495/62/21/1–21, esp. 20–21.

[70] "Resolution on the Labour Movement," March 24, 1934; "Malaiya qingshi fenxi yu dang de renwu. Jieshou Zhonggong zhongyang wu yue ershisan laixin de jueyi [The Analysis of the Situation in Malaya and the Tasks of the Party. Accepting the CC CCP Resolution from the CC CCP Letter Dated May 23]," September 5, 1933, RGASPI 495/62/21/31–48.

[71] "Decisions of the C. C. of the Malayan Party on the Intensification of the Labour Movement Passed on 20 March 1934."

their daily work is backward … Nuclei are being formed, but the members in charge of them [do] not know how to organise the meeting, what to do or to say during the meeting, and how to keep the nuclei working.[72]

The self-critical verdict was harsh: the MCP could not become the "revolutionary vanguard," that is, it failed to perform the main functions of the party.[73] The party's image was that of a tail of the backward masses.[74] Even as the majority of the party were workers, many those were former intellectuals who could not find appropriate jobs and made a living doing manual jobs like rubber tree cutting.[75] In 1930, six out of nine CC members were workers,[76] but during the rallies and in the labor unions, where party members appointed leaders based on personal connections (*ganqing*) and "bureaucracy," the leadership did not represent "the worker masses" because they did not understand what the workers suffered.[77] The party also neglected trade union work.[78] A report stated: "All they can do is 'sing some revolutionary songs' with the workers."[79]

The workers themselves were not drawn to the unions. The party even had to explain the significance of economic slogans, such as demands for wage increases and unemployment relief as well as the need for solidarity among workers.[80] In 1933, the party claimed to have the support of "free professional workers" (*ziyou zhiye gongren*), likely self-employed.[81] Although in 1930 the MCP had reported its main membership as being in the "rubber tree gardens," in 1933 the MCP stated that the party and the CYL were unable to penetrate rubber plantations and tin mines.[82] The MCP's serious

---

[72] Ho Chi Minh, "Malay," p. 25.

[73] Ibid.

[74] "Minutes of the Third Representative Conference of Nanyang," p. 132.

[75] Xie Fei, "Huiyi Zhongguo gongchandang Nanyang linshi weiyuanhui de gongzuo, 1929–1930 [Remembering the Work of the Nanyang Provisional Committee, 1929–1930]"; Zhang Xia, "Xianyou xian lü Ma huaqiao yu geming huodong [Immigrants from Xianyou County in Malaya and Revolutionary Activities]," pp. 34–39.

[76] Ho Chi Minh, "Malay," p. 25.

[77] "Central Circular no. 9," 1930; "Resolutions Adopted at the Third Congress of the Malaya Party," p. 9.

[78] "Decisions of the C. C. of the Malayan Party on the Intensification of the Labour Movement Passed on 20 March 1934," esp. 58.

[79] "Report from Malay," p. 29.

[80] "Central Circular no. 2." "The C.C. of the C.P. of Malay," "Central Circular no. 2. Preparation for the mass demonstration on 'Aug.1st.', the International Red Day," June 18, 1930, RGASPI 495/62/18–22a.

[81] "Magong zhongyang tonggao di sijiu hao. Guoji qingnianjie de gongzuo jueyi [CC MCP Circular no. 49. Resolution Regarding the International Youth Day]," July 31, 1933, RGASPI 495/62/20/15–20, esp. 17.

[82] "To the C. C. of the Chinese Party and the Comintern"; "Magong zhongyang tonggao di sijiu hao. Guoji qingnianjie de gongzuo jueyi [CC MCP Circular no. 49. Resolution Regarding the International Youth Day]"; "Malaiya qingshi fenxi yu dang de renwu [The Analysis of the Situation in Malaya and the Tasks of the Party]," September 5, 1933.

rivals in machine companies, railways, rubber plantations, and tin mines were labor contract system unions and the social democratic party. The MCP also described the workers' class consciousness as "very indistinct."[83] The most developed red union organizations were among the "tin mines, gum works, and seamen," which produced a majority of the unemployed.[84]

However, the MCP was not able to lead spontaneous strikes with economic demands during the period of unemployment resulting from the Great Depression, although there was a successful strike in Kuala Lumpur Railway in 1934.[85] The MCP explained to the Comintern, bitterly criticizing unorganized violence, that it was the masses who had engaged in unorganized mass action and terrorism, not the party.[86] The MCP even tried to force workers to go on strike, which made the masses "hate" the party. As a result, the "masses" did not consider the red unions organized by the party to be their own organizations.[87] The MCP arranged drills to seize power in order to test the strength of the party in fomenting a world revolution, but it overestimated the masses' support. For this failure, the MCP labeled the masses "unconscious."[88] The MCP's relations with the masses were reminiscent of the efforts of earlier Chinese elites to educate common people in Confucian precepts. These attempts led to a pessimism among the educated, whereas common people subverted the Confucian teachings with heterodox ideas and degraded the status of the gentry.[89] The MCP's internationalist propaganda, which connected Malaya's situation with the world situation on International Red Day, August 1, 1929, left the workers indifferent.[90] Ho Chi Minh reported that "[v]ery few could explain why there would be a second imperialist war or why they must defend the USSR, and although they know the names of Marx and Lenin, they do not know their teachings."[91]

Comintern indigenization directives did make sense in this way, and the MCP figured that instead of preoccupying itself with the world situation, the party should be grounded in the situation in Malaya and in the workers' daily demands.[92] The party would explain the general strike and the celebration of the October Revolution in a simple and clear way

---

[83] "Resolutions Adopted at the Third Congress of the Malaya Party."
[84] "To the C. C. of the Chinese Party and the Comintern"; "Report from Malay."
[85] Yong, *Origins of Malayan Communism*, p. 174.
[86] This was criticized in the letter, FEB, "To the Malayan Comrades," December 17, 1930, p. 1; CC MCP, "From Malaya. To the FEB," February 7, 1931.
[87] "Resolutions Adopted at the Third Congress of the Malaya Party"; "To the C. C. of the Chinese Party and the Comintern," p. 4.
[88] Ibid., "Central Circular no. 3," July 15, 1930, RGASPI 495/62/13/23–25.
[89] Kai-Wing Chow, *Ethics, Classics and Lineage Discourse* (Stanford, CA: Stanford University Press, 1994), p. 226.
[90] "Central Circular no. 2."
[91] Ho Chi Minh, "Malay," p. 25.
[92] Ibid.

instead of "[writing] essays, groaning and [persuading] the masses to tolerate" it.[93] However, MCP members did write essays in literary supplements (*fuzhang*) about communist ideas, which were potentially understandable only to an educated audience, such as Chinese students, who often were fellow newspaper writers, like the protagonists in Xu Jie's stories.[94] During the MCP founding conference, *Lat Pao*'s (*Lebao*) literary supplement published an article by Yi Hong (衣虹), "Xinxing wenxue de xingshi wenti" (On the question of the form of the new literature), discussing how art forms are determined by the forces of social production.[95] In order to raise the masses' political level through education, the MCP launched literacy movements in trade unions.[96] However, being in possession of a newspaper exposed one to accusations of belonging to the MCP. Moreover, Nanyang communists reported that oral propaganda was the only reliable propaganda in the Nanyang, as "comrades" did not like the newspapers because they were printed poorly and were difficult to read.[97]

Similar to the case of the CCP in China, MCP propaganda was successful when it used familiar cultural techniques – "cultural positioning," as Perry has termed it – to translate foreign communism to the "masses" of youth, soldiers, women, and "workers and peasants."[98] The MCP used the language of charity, which was familiar to the Chinese community, to promote the Red Aid organization in Singapore, the goal of which was to help the unemployed and bankrupt. The MCP pamphlet stated that: "The Red Aid organization will give revolutionaries sympathy, regardless of what party they belong to, their class or place, their age or gender. Or, in other words, the Mutual Aid Society is a benevolent society that focuses on humanitarianism" (*hujihui jiu shi zhu zhang ren dao zhuyi de cishan tuanti*).[99] Workers enthusiastically donated to the organization,[100] because providing financial help (*jiji*) to friends and relatives was essential to staying in Malaya when the British government was deporting unemployed migrants.[101]

---

[93] "Central Circular no. 9," 1930; "Central Circular no. 2."
[94] "Central Circular no. 2."
[95] *Lat Pao*, April 24, 1930, p. 25. For more about *fuzhang* and leftist publishing in Singapore Chinese newspapers, see Kenley, *New Culture in a New World*.
[96] "Central Circular no. 2."
[97] "Doklad o polozhenii na ostrovakh Tikhogo Okeana [Report about the Conditions on the Pacific Islands]," undated, likely 1927–1928, RGASPI 495/66/13/67–78, esp. 77.
[98] Perry, *Anyuan*, p. 14.
[99] "Malai huji zonghui Xingzhou Dapo qu di yi zhi fenhui chengli xuanyan [The Declaration of the Founding of the Dapo District Branch of Singapore of the Red Aid Society of Malaya]," September 25, 1930, RGASPI 495/62/5/6–a.
[100] "Otchet o polozhenii v Nan'iane [Report about the Situation in Nanyang], [Report about the Situation in Nanyang]." p. 25.
[101] Zhang Xia, "Xianyou xian lü Ma huaqiao yu geming huodong [Immigrants from Xianyou County in Malaya and Revolutionary Activities]," pp. 34–39.

As Li Lisan's insurrection policy gained momentum in 1930, condemned by the Comintern along with anarchist "individual terror,"[102] the MCP linked communist uprisings with the traditional aspiration for freedom, likely tapping into the legacy of earlier anarchist and Malay peasant revolts: "As to armed insurrection, it is a special bequeath from the ancestors to fight against oppressors. Three years ago [1927], was there not an armed revolt of peasants in Trengganu? Now, we need only to explain to them the scientific sense of insurrection, and lead them in the political direction."[103]

Goal and Activities of the MCP: Adaptation and Political Representation of Chinese Migrants

The goals of the MCP's activities were expressed in increasingly Bolshevik language, but they were similar to those of voluntary Chinese overseas organizations. The MCP and the GMD aimed to mediate between Chinese migrants and the British state.[104] The MCP was established and started its activities at the same time that the British banned the GMD in Singapore in 1930, a ban that ran against the interests of British–GMD negotiations about extraterritoriality. One of the most outspoken critics of this ban was Hu Hanmin, whom some among the British authorities viewed as the most powerful man in the Nanjing government. Infuriated by British policy in Malaya, Hu called for an end to Western oppression in China. It was in 1930 that he published his piece about the *minzu guoji*. Although the Malayan GMD organization was banned, individual membership in the Chinese GMD was negotiated, and the GMD continued its activities in Malaya.[105] Thus, the MCP, the first organization to promote the identification of Chinese with Malaya, was left the exclusive niche of a Malayan Chinese organization throughout the

[102] FEB, "To the Malayan Comrades," December 17, 1930.
[103] "Report from Malay," p. 28ob. A reader wrote "1927" next to this paragraph.
[104] For example, in Hong Kong the traditional role of voluntary associations was to be the point of contact and to serve as power brokers between the colonial administration and the migrants. Zhou Min and Rebecca Y. Kim, "Paradox of Ethnicization and Assimilation: The Development of Ethnic Organizations in the Chinese Immigrant Community in the United States," in Kuah-Pearce and Hu-Dehart, eds., *Voluntary Organizations in the Chinese Diaspora*, pp. 231–252, esp. p. 244. Also see Li Minghuan, Dangdai haiwai huaren shetuan yanjiu [Contemporary Associations of Overseas Chinese], p. 18; Shi Cangjin, *Malaixiya huaren shetuan yanjiu* (*A Study of Chinese Associations in Malaysia*) (Beijing: Zhongguo huaqiao chubanshe, 2005).
[105] The extraterritorial treaty was formalized in 1932 but was never ratified. Western powers continued to enjoy extraterritorial rights until the 1940s. Yong and McKenna, *The Kuomintang Movement in British Malaya*, pp. 154, 161, 171.

1930s,[106] speaking for the rights of Chinese as both a Chinese and a
Malayan organization and moreover striving to gain non-Chinese membership, at least in its discourse. "The Chinese residents in this land have
to wake up," the MCP cried out, as the British plotted to "[displace] the
Chinese with the aborigines."[107]

The "democratic" appearance of the British colonial state in Malaya
empowered Chinese communists to protest the exclusion of Chinese as
aliens from the political life of the British colony. The petty bourgeoisie
(*xiao zichan jieji* intellectuals, and the foreign proletariat (*waiqiao wuchan
jieji*) were disadvantaged, as they did not have economic and political
freedoms.[108] In 1928, the Nanyang committee pointed out the hard lives
of workers on rubber plantations and in foreign enterprises, shop employees, hawkers, and *rikshas*, as well as the radicalization of hawkers, members of the intelligentsia, and merchants.[109] The lack of equal rights for
immigrants pushed MCP members to adopt Bolshevik language in order
to express the disenfranchisement of the Chinese community metaphori-
cally in the language of class contradiction.

The MCP's desire for a "democratic movement" was in line with the
demand for democratic freedoms as part of the CCP's united front program
in the early 1930s.[110] It also made sense to the Chinese communists who
had fled from Chiang Kai-shek's persecution and had moved to Malaya in
search of employment. They had found themselves in a situation similar to
that of political radicals in safe refuges, such as the treaty ports in China and
Hong Kong.[111] The MCP members planned to explain to the "masses" the

[106] K. Vilkov, A. Ziuzin, and Dashevskii, "Spravka o rabote sredi kitaiskikh emigrantov v
Malae. Sostavlena na osnove materialov 1939–1940 g.g.) [Note about the Work among
Chinese Immigrants Compiled from the Materials Dated 1939–1940]," February 4,
1942, RGASPI 495/62/30/10a–54, 17 (henceforth "Spravka o rabote"); Stephen Mun
Yoon Leong, "Sources, Agencies and Manifestations of Overseas Chinese Nationalism
in Malaya, 1937–1941" (PhD dissertation, UCLA, 1976), p. 819.
[107] "To the C. C. of the Chinese Party and the Comintern."
[108] "Magong lianzi tonggao di yi hao. Dangtuan zhongyang guanyu waiqiao dengji lüli yu
women de gongzuo de jueyi [MCP Central Circular no. 1. Resolution of the CC of the
MCP and CYL Regarding the Alien Registration Ordinance]," October 12, 1932,
RGASPI 495/62/20/1–6.
[109] "Doklad soveta professional'nykh soiuzov Malaiskogo arkhipelaga o profsoiuznom
dvizhenii [Report of the Labour Union of Malay Archipelago]," October 8, 1928,
RGASPI 495/62/1–22, esp. 21–22; "Otchet o polozhenii v Nan'iane [Report about
the Situation in Nanyang], [Report about the Situation in Nanyang]." p. 13.
[110] Titarenko, Mikhail L. and Mechthild Leutner, eds., *VKP(b), Komintern I Kitai.
Dokumenty. T. IV. VKP(b), Komintern i sovetskoe dvizhenie s Kitae, 1931–1937 [CPSU
(Bolshevik), the Comintern, and China. Documents. Volume 4. CPSU (Bolshevik), the
Comintern, and the Soviet Movement in China, 1931–1937]* (Moscow: ROSSPEN,
2003), "Introduction," pp. 25–62, esp. p. 34.
[111] Michael Share, *Where Empires Collided: Russian and Soviet Relations with Hong Kong,
Taiwan, and Macao* (Hong Kong: Chinese University Press, 2007), p. 91.

"legality" of the communist movement.[112] However, Bolshevik language contradicted the MCP's aim of mediating for the Chinese community as Chinese associations did, for the Chinese community preferred legal methods for promoting their rights in the early 1930s, such as through political councils. While the MCP campaigned for the freedoms of assembly, speech, the press, education, immigration into Malaya, strike, and belief, it promoted anti-British attitudes by building on anti-Japanese moods and the slogans of campaigns for the rights of Chinese, such as freedom of business and education, the chief concern of Chinese associations. Yet the MCP's ultimate goal remained seizing power and establishing the Workers and Peasants' Republic of Malaya.[113]

The MCP had to compete with other Chinese labor organizations, such as the secret societies (*sihuidang*),[114] for the allegiance of workers, and it used its traditional channels and methods of regulating labor conflicts. For example, the Malayan Federation of Labor Unions (MFLU) petitioned the Chinese protectorate for redress of grievances.[115] An MCP rival among workers was the Three Star Society (Sanxing dang), which the MCP called an "organization of rascals."[116] In Johor, communists adapting to local conditions even advocated for a labor–capital alliance similar to traditional guilds, which united employers and employees in their ranks and which had supported the GMD in the 1920s.[117] This situation was common in other Chinese communist organizations overseas. Similarly, the Chinese faction in San Francisco, consisting of seven students, among whom only two spoke the language of the majority of Chinese migrants in the United States, Cantonese,[118] promoted an anti-Japanese boycott and, riding the wave of anti-GMD sentiment, unsuccessfully competed with "Chinese Freemasons" (*Zhigongdang*) and royalists (*Baohuanghui*).[119]

---

[112] "Central Circular no. 1. The Conclusion of the Third Delegate Conference of the C. P. of Malay," May 1, 1930, RGASPI 495/ 62/13/1–17, esp. 16–17.

[113] CC CCP, "A Letter from the Central Committee of the CCP to the Nanyang Provisional Committee," p. 10; CC MCP, "An Address to the Oppressed Peoples of Malaya."

[114] Chen Zhenchun, "Xinjiapo binggan gongchang gongren de douzheng [Struggle of the Workers at a Cookie Factory in Singapore]," in Zhongguo renmin zhengzhi xieshang huiyi Guangdong sheng weiyuanhui wenshi ziliao yanjiu weiyuanhui, ed., *Guangdong wenshi ziliao di wushisi ji* [*Literary and Historical Materials of Guangdong*, vol. 54] (Guangzhou: Guangdong renmin chubanshe, 1988), pp. 155–161.

[115] MRCA, December 1931, p. 43, CO 273/572.

[116] "Decisions of the C. C. of the Malayan Party on the Intensification of the Labour Movement Passed on 20 March 1934."

[117] "Resolution on the Labour Movement," March 24, 1934; Heng, *Chinese Politics in Malaysia*, p. 25.

[118] "May First Manifesto of the Chinese Faction of the Workers (Communist) Party of America," undated, late 1920s, RGASPI 515/1/1451/53–58; Letter to Comrade Gomez, December 29, 1927, RGASPI 515/1/1111/26.

[119] Memorandum, undated, RGASPI 515/1/4117/42–59.

In 1930–1934, the MFLU criticized the following issues: isolation from the masses and right opportunism, passiveness, putschism, a lack of preparation, an inability to seize leadership during a struggle, and abandoning work among young workers, the unemployed, women, and yellow and "rascal" organizations (i.e., secret societies and triads) because those "could not participate in the revolution," as well as a lack of factory and unemployed committees.[120] The top leadership of the red labor union was bureaucratic and too general, and it lacked control and education, and neglected secret work. Such issues as "different and complicated peoples, languages, customs and habits," arrests, and a lack of experienced cadres and funds – which the MFLU requested from the Profintern – were not properly dealt with.[121]

In 1934, of the 6,000 workers in the MFLU, more than 90 percent were Chinese. There were forty women, fewer than 10 percent of whom were industrial workers and more than 70 percent of whom were agricultural workers. The local party committees either had a "disdainful" attitude toward the labor movement or simply paid lip service to the work.[122] Despite attempts to organize strikes, rallies in schools, and performances, the MCP had limited involvement in the labor unrest of the early 1930s.[123] The MCP's most common activity was organizing commemorative demonstrations on a long list of revolutionary occasions. These included the anniversary of the October Revolution, Labor Day, the establishment of the Paris Commune, the death dates of Lenin and of Rosa Luxembourg, International Day of the Unemployed (August 1), International Communist Youth Day (September 7), the anniversary of the Canton Uprising of 1927, and Anti-Christian Propaganda Day (December 25), as well as China's national commemorations, such as the dates of the Ji'nan Incident and the Double Ten Festival.[124]

As the British police noticed in their role as an ever-vigilant chronicler of the MCP, MCP reports dealt mostly with self-criticisms and plans for the future.[125] The party planned to attract new members by organizing a

---

[120] "Report of Labour Federation of Malaya no. 1 to the Profintern," March 25, 1934.
[121] Ibid.
[122] "Resolution on the Labour Movement," March 24, 1934.
[123] Tai Yuen, *Labour Unrest in Malaya, 1934–1941: The Rise of the Workers Movement* (Kuala Lumpur: Institute of Postgraduate Studies and Research, University of Malaya, 2000); "Magong zhongyang gongzuo jueding [CC MCP Work Resolution Regarding the Fifteenth Anniversary of Liebknecht and Luxembourg's Death and the Tenth Anniversary of Lenin's Death]."
[124] Various documents in the MCP collection from the years 1928–1934 illustrate this point, and MRCA, December 1930, pp. 54–56, MRCA, "March 1931," p. 38, "January 1931," p. 13, CO 273/571.
[125] Report by the Secretary of Chinese Affairs, "Kuo Min Tang and Other Societies in Malaya, July–September 1928," October 23, 1928, pp. 1–7, p. 6, CO 273/542.

demonstration to demand unemployment relief from the British authorities and then to incorporate those unemployed into the trade union:

> If police [are] coming to make arrests, the masses should gather together to shout slogans, and if someone is arrested, the masses should follow at once and demonstrate before the police station before the masses disperse into separate groups. If wholesale arrests are made, the more, the better. But their confession should be the same. They should say: "I am an unemployed and I went with the others to ask for relief. You authorities pay no attention to our life and death question and yet you have arrested me. How to deal with me is at your disposal but [for] you [to] fine me is unacceptable.[126]

Indeed, as a result of the MCP's strike on the Singaporean naval base on August 1, 1930, forty people were arrested. However, the MCP embraced both the legal and illegal methods that the Comintern suggested, although voices also spoke out "against the legalist movement."[127] The MCP planned to campaign for the legality of red trade unions, as was the case in Britain and as the Comintern also encouraged in China.[128]

The MCP's *huiguan*-style activities dovetailed with the Comintern's interests. At the founding conference, along with the establishment of a soviet republic in Malaya, the MCP promoted, as did locally born Chinese community leader Tan Cheng Lock, elections to the Legislative Councils of the Federated States and of the Straits Settlements. The MCP reforms advocated for a larger number of representatives and the appointment of "a Malay man" as the chairman in the "Political Discussing [sic] Bureau," that is, the Legislative Councils.[129] The MCP's plan to promote the representation of workers and peasants was strategic: if not successful, the MCP could say that this commission was only a tool of the imperialists.[130] In fact, the MCP didn't think much of the "men from the oppressed peoples" participating in the Legislative Councils, calling them "running dogs of the imperialists," and "the Chinese Political Affairs Department," that is, the Chinese Protectorate, was considered "the tool of the imperialists to overrule the

---

[126] "Central Circular no. 2," pp. 21–22. This is the text of the original document in English.
[127] "Central Circular no. 1. The Conclusion of the Third Delegate Conference of the C. P. of Malay," May 1, 1930, p. 9.
[128] Ibid. p. 14; "To the C. C. of the Chinese Party and the Comintern"; MCP, "To the English Komparty"; Titarenko and Leutner, *Komintern i Kitai* [*Comintern and China*], vol. 4, "Introduction."
[129] "Minutes of the Third Representative Conference of Nanyang," p. 29; Tregonning, "Tan Cheng Lock."
[130] "Central Circular no. 1. The Conclusion of the Third Delegate Conference of the C. P. of Malay," May 1, 1930, esp. p. 11; "To the C. C. of the Chinese Party and the Comintern."

Chinese."[131] When an unofficial Asian seat was again established in the Straits Settlements Legislative Council, it was occupied by a Malay, not a Chinese.[132]

Like other Chinese organizations, such as the Johor Overseas Chinese Office (Huaqiao gongsuo), the MCP campaigned against the Alien Registration Ordinance (1933).[133] In an attempt to solve the unemployment caused by the Great Depression, the British government introduced the ordinance on January 1, 1933, which complicated the immigration of Chinese to Malaya and put unemployed Chinese under the threat of deportation. The MCP distributed pamphlets to mobilize Chinese and other communities in all-Malaya protests, arguing that the ordinance was detrimental to the Malayan Revolution because it made the revolutionaries vulnerable to deportation and exacerbated contradictions among various people (*ge minzu*).[134] The MCP saw the Chinese laborers' fatalistic attitudes (*mingyun bu ji*) toward deportations, even welcoming being sent back home to China, as a "lack of confidence."[135] Meanwhile, police reported two protests against the ordinance organized by the MCP in Singapore, one in the Chinese high school and one in Johor in December 1932. In Singapore, fifty-nine participants were arrested, and in Johor, 300 Chinese assembled outside a coffee shop and distributed pamphlets, launched firecrackers, and clashed with police, during which two demonstrators were killed.[136]

The CYL too was criticized for not properly using anti-imperialist opposition to the Registration Ordinance,[137] as only the Chinese opposed it and

---

[131] "Minutes of the Third Representative Conference of Nanyang," p. 128; "Central Circular no. 1. The Conclusion of the Third Delegate Conference of the C. P. of Malay," May 1, 1930, p. 11.

[132] This expressed the anti-Chinese bias of the governor of the Straits Settlement, Cecil Clementi, who had taken office in 1930 and banned the GMD as his first order. His policy goal was to be loyal to earlier British–Malay treaties. Yong and McKenna, *The Kuomintang Movement in British Malaya*, pp. 134–146.

[133] Victor Purcell, *The Chinese in Malaya* (Oxford: Oxford University Press, 1967), p. 203, cited in Patricia Pui Huen Lim, "Between Tradition and Modernity: The Chinese Association of Johor Bahru Malaysia," in Kuah-Pearce and Hu-Dehart, eds., *Voluntary Organizations in the Chinese Diaspora*, pp. 29–52, esp. p. 33.

[134] "Magong lianzi tonggao di jiu hao. Dangtuan zhongyang youguan fandui xianzhi juzhu lü de jueyi [Central Circular no. 9. The Resolution of the CC of the MCP and CYL Regarding the Protests against the Restrictions on Residence]," September 10, 1933, RGASPI 495/62/20/31–33.

[135] Ibid.; "Magong lianzi tonggao di yi hao. Dangtuan zhongyang guanyu waiqiao dengji lüli yu women de gongzuo de jueyi [MCP Central Circular no. 1. Resolution of the CC of the MCP and CYL Regarding the Alien Registration Ordinance]"; Zhang Xia, "Xianyou xian lü Ma huaqiao yu geming huodong [Immigrants from Xianyou County in Malaya and Revolutionary Activities]," p. 36.

[136] Extract from *Straits Settlements Police Political Intelligence Journal* for December 1932, January 30, 1933, SMP D4443.

[137] "Magong zhongyang guanyu fan zhanzheng gongzuo de jueyi [CC MCP Resolution on the Antiwar Movement]," February 10, 1934, RGASPI 495/62/23/11–15.

organized protest rallies in Singapore and Johor.[138] The MCP's calls for Malayanization served the *huaqiao* community in practice and propagated the idea that Chinese interests were crucial for Malaya's Revolution and independence. This was not a case of disingenuous rhetoric but rather the result of the social experience of the MCP's leadership and its behavior as the de facto hybrid of an overseas Chinese organization and a communist party. Malaya represented a brave new world and a multilingual environment, so it should come as no surprise that there were gaps between intentions and results. The MCP's organization, activities, and self-explanations give us access to the divergent meanings and mechanisms that produced such unintentional results. Through this campaign, the MCP was able to indigenize as a Chinese organization while maintaining its Chinese identity by promoting the interests of Chinese immigrants for the sake of the Malayan Revolution, thus adopting a Malayan identity.

Nonetheless, the meaning of the Alien Registration Ordinance was clear: MCP members themselves were excluded from the official Malayan nation because they had been born outside Malaya. As the MCP reflected on the principles of immigration, the signifier *ji* (籍), which means "place of origin," "citizen," or "registration," started to appear after *Ma* (Malay) and *Yin* (Indian) in MCP texts.[139] The ordinance further juxtaposed Malaya-born residents against those born outside British Malaya and affirmed the MCP's connection to China. As a consequence, the MCP stopped using the phrase "Malayan nation," but continued to promote a Malayan Revolution that would emerge on the basis of a united front of Malaya's oppressed *minzu*. In about 1933, the term *Malaiya* started to exclusively denote Malaya as a nation, while the term *Malai* remained the signifier for Malays.[140] In 1933, the CYL referred to Malaya as *guo*, "country," and described Chineseness as a "nationality."[141] As a result of

[138] "Magong lianzi tonggao di yi hao. Dangtuan zhongyang guanyu waiqiao dengji lüli yu women de gongzuo de jueyi [MCP Central Circular no. 1. Resolution of the CC of the MCP and CYL Regarding the Alien Registration Ordinance]"; "United Chambers of Commerce. Malayan Chinese Topics. Alien Registration. Proposed New Bill Opposed," *Straits Times*, September 20, 1932, p. 18. "Extract from *Straits Settlement Political Intelligence Journal* for December 1932." In newspapers of the time, no protests by other communities are mentioned.
[139] "Tuan muqian de zhuyao renwu [Current Major Tasks of the CYL]," in "Malaiya qingshi fenxi yu dang de renwu. Jieshou Zhonggong zhongyang wu yue ershisan laixin de jueyi [The Analysis of the Situation in Malaya and the Tasks of the Party. Accepting the CC CCP Resolution from the CC CCP Letter Dated May 23]," September 20, 1933, RGASPI 495/62/21/31–48, esp. 42–44.
[140] "CC MCP Open Letter to Malay and Indian Comrades."
[141] "Report from Malaysia on the Organization of the Young Communist League," March 28, 1934, RGASPI 495/62/24/19; "Magong zhongyang tonggao di sijiu hao. Guoji qingnianjie de gongzuo jueyi [CC MCP Circular no. 49. Resolution Regarding the International Youth Day]."

the ordinance, the concept of the Chinese as aliens was reaffirmed and juxtaposed with the yet nonexistent country of Malaya.

Although fighting for the rights of the working class was undoubtedly a central item in its propaganda, the MCP in fact spoke for the rights of the Chinese community in general. The MCP's propaganda materials talked about the worsening situation of the Chinese exclusively during the Great Depression. Indeed, Malaya, a world producer of rubber and tin, was dominated by Chinese laborers who, although they were paid more than workers of any other nationality except Europeans,[142] were vulnerable to the conditions of the world economy. Chinese laborers were losing their jobs, and Chinese capitalists were going bankrupt. In contrast to Chinese remittances from the Dutch East Indies and the Philippines, remittances back home from Malaya decreased.[143] The MCP blamed the British policies of rationalization of production and monopolization to boost the competitiveness of British products on the world market for the bankruptcies of Chinese companies, especially in the tin and rubber industries. Taxes increased, and private lands were expropriated to build military facilities. Chinese immigration was curbed. The Chinese press was censored.[144] By 1933, the MCP noted that the revolutionized thinking of the masses (*qunzhong de geming sixiang*) had touched even the Chinese bourgeoisie in protests by seamen in Singapore and by rubber plantation workers in Johor Bahru.[145]

The MCP promoted the Malayanization (*Malaiyahua*) of the party as a way of mobilizing the support of the Malay and Indian communities in protest against the Alien Registration Ordinance, which targeted Chinese immigrants and led to the deportation of many suspected communists. This, it was argued, was for the sake of the revolutionary movement of the suffering working masses of Malaya (*Malaiya gongnong laoku qunzhong*) and the Malay nation (*Malai minzu*). Overall, this MCP call for Malayanization reflected the MCP's impulse as a Chinese overseas association to be embedded in the local environment. The MCP planned to establish a Malayan national united front organization of all oppressed *minzu* opposing limitations on the residence period for immigrants (*Fandui xianzhi juzhu datongmeng*).[146] Malayanization included

---

[142] Their salary was $12–25, as opposed to $10–20 paid to Indians and $11–22 paid to Malay rubber tree cutters. "Report from Malay."

[143] Ta Chen, *Emigrant Communities in South China*, p. 77.

[144] "Report from Malay."

[145] Dangtuan zhongyang [CC of the MCP and CYL], "Magong lianzi tonggao di ba hao: Guanyu yanmi dangtuan de zuzhi wenti [Circular no. 8 of the MCP Regarding the Organization of the Secret Work of the Party and CYL]," August 15, 1933.

[146] "Magong lianzi tonggao di yi hao. Dangtuan zhongyang guanyu waiqiao dengji lüli yu women de gongzuo de jueyi [MCP Central Circular no. 1. Resolution of the CC of the MCP and CYL Regarding the Alien Registration Ordinance]."

considering local conditions when designing party work, learning about the living conditions of the masses, and using slogans that originated with the masses. The party blamed its own immigrant mentality (*yimin yishi*), "incorrect tendencies," such as political stagnation (*zhengzhi kongshuai*), defeatism, pessimism, leftism, rightism, and fearful opportunism, for the unsuccessful Malayanization of the organization (*ge minzuhua*).[147]

Parallel to the indigenization directives of the Comintern and the CCP, but in fact as a reaction to anti-Chinese and pro-Malay legislation in 1932–1933, Tan Cheng Lock also promoted Malayanization (but not becoming Malay) and the unification of all "races." Tan's goal was to "Malayanise the children of the permanent population, i.e., to make them true citizens of Malaya," and "to unite all races in Malaya."[148] Moreover, both the MCP and Tan Cheng Lock echoed the official British discourse that in 1933 promoted the "Malayanisation of services as well as the Malayanisation of ideals."[149] A Malayanization of education took place, that is, Malay-language instruction was increasingly introduced for Straits-born Chinese.[150]

An inclusive Malayan identity had to be forged so that immigrants could be granted equal rights with Malays. In 1933, the Malay Reservation Enactment was amended to ensure that non-Malays were excluded from land traditionally held by Malays.[151] Apparently referring to the delegation of rice production to the Chinese and to the distribution of land plots without land titles to unemployed Chinese, the MCP viewed British intentions to oust the Malay peasants and to give land to Chinese as a common policy of divide and conquer.[152] Could the alert posture and eyes of the Chinese gardener give us a glimpse of those tensions? (See Figure 4.1.)

---

[147] "Dangwu wenti jueyian [Resolution on Party Work]."
[148] Tan Cheng Lock's Address at the Legislative Council, Malacca, February 12, 1934, in *Malayan Problems*, pp. 95–109, esp. pp. 95–97.
[149] "Inter-Racial Amity," *Malaya Tribune*, December 19, 1933, p. 3.
[150] Ta Chen, *Emigrant Communities in South China*, pp. 274–275.
[151] Francis Kok-Wah Loh, *Beyond the Tin Mines: Coolies, Squatters, and New Villagers in the Kinta Valley, Malaysia, c. 1880–1980* (Singapore: Oxford University Press, 1988), pp. 7–38, esp. p. 33.
[152] Another example of such a policy, in the MCP's opinion, was British enlistment of Malays in the army and police in order to utilize them against the Chinese workers' movement, presented as a Chinese attempt to conquer Malaya. A common Chinese view on British policies was as follows: "British policy was to lure Chinese with words like 'You go develop commerce in Malaya. We English take care only of administration.'" The author of the report lamented that even after Chinese producers of rubber and tin suffered from the economic crisis, they still hoped that the British would help them out: "In reality, Chinese merchants are like the cook-boy; the English master eats the fowl, giving the fowl's leg and head to the Chinese cook. The English further say, 'As long as the Chinese have rice to eat, cards to play, and opium to smoke, they are satisfied.'" "Report from Malay." Also, according to the MCP, as the British government centralized landownership, peasants went bankrupt. Every MCP report and the

Figure 4.1 A Chinese gardener, 1930.
Courtesy of National Archives of Singapore.

Comintern's letters to the MCP contained a section on work among peasants, talking about plans to organize peasants' unions (*nongmin xiehui*) to overthrow British imperialism and Malay feudalism. However, in reality, no practical work was done. The MCP planned to use farmers' cooperatives (*nongmin hezuoshe*) and peoples' schools (*pingmin xuexiao*) to promote the slogans of freedom of tilling, trade, belief, schooling, and husbandry. "Nongmin yundong jueyian [Resolution on the Peasant Movement]," in "Malai gongchandang di yi ci kuodahui jueyian" [The Resolutions of the First Enlarged Congress of the MCP], August 1934, RGASPI 495/62/21/1–21, esp. 18–19; "Central Circular no. 1. The Conclusion of the Third Delegate Conference of the C. P. of Malay," May 1, 1930, p. 8.

The emerging MCP discourse regarding an inclusive Malayan nation, and policies based on local conditions, occurred in conjunction with the changing social experience of immigrants, who felt a growing need to identify with Malaya, as many Chinese and Indians started to identify as Malays.[153] In 1933, propaganda on the "struggle for emancipation from British imperialism and the united front of Malaya's many weak nationalities (*duo ruoxiao minzu*) and toiling worker and peasant masses (*gongnong laoku dazhong*)" became more intensive.[154] Indigenizing tactics also became more pronounced in both the MCP and the CYL: the Central Committee was now to provide guidelines based on reports about each locality's specific situation. The MCP was to organize various revolutionary groups according to the various classes of the oppressed masses under the banner of the revolution and at the same time attract progressive elements into the party and the CYL. Those organizations included the Anti-Imperialist Union (Fandi datongmeng), the Malaya Independence Alliance (Malaiya minzu duli lianmeng), the red trade unions (*chise gonghui*), the peasants' committees (*nongmin weiyuanhui*), soldiers' committees (*shibing weiyuanhui*), the United Society of Revolutionary Students (Geming xuesheng lianhehui), the Women's Emancipation Association (Funü jiefang xiehui), the Toiling Children Corps (Laodong tongzituan), and the Proletarian Arts Union (Puluo yishu lianmeng).[155] The "Open letter to Malay and Indian comrades (*Ma Yin ji*)" is the only document available in which the MCP addresses Malay and Indian comrades.[156] This letter tells us that the MCP had an organizational basis among Chinese, Malays, and Indians (*Ma Yin zu*) that had to be strengthened and that the protests in support of the Chinese and Indian Revolutions had the goal of a Malayan Revolution. Yet the MCP said the anti-imperialist movement was stagnating (*daigong*). In 1934, the MCP connected the soviet movement in China to freedom of the "oppressed nations" (*xiaoruo minzu*) of the colonies and semi-colonies. All Malayan workers, peasants, soldiers, students, and small merchants (*xiao shangren*) of many ethnic groups (*duo minzu*) were supposed to oppose imperialism and support the establishment of CCP base areas in China, which was "its avant-garde" (*xianfeng*), and "the emancipation army for the world

[153] Yin Hua Wu, *Class and Communalism in Malaysia* (London: Zed Books, 1983), p. 51; Roff, *Origins of Malay Nationalism*, p. 208.
[154] CC MCP, "An Address to the Oppressed Peoples of Malaya."
[155] Ibid.; "Magong zhongyang guanyu jinnian guoji shiyejie yu jinhou dui shiye yundong de jueyi [Resolution of the CC MCP on the International Day of Unemployed and on the Future Work among the Unemployed]," January 1, 1930, RGASPI 495/62/23/1–5.
[156] "CC MCP, Open Letter to Malay and Indian Comrades." There is also a Malay version of this letter: "Surat Yang Terbuka Kepada Saudara-Saudara Kita Melayu dan Indian," undated, RGASPI 495/62/14–17.

proletariat and exploited masses."[157] The Comintern's rhetoric of colonial emancipation resonated with the MCP's discourse on the emancipation of oppressed peoples by the Chinese, which echoed Sun Yatsen's ideas. Ultimately, the MCP formula of Malayan independence was the indigenization of party organizations through internationalism:

> The Malayan Revolution [*Malaiya geming*] is a glimpse into the world of revolutionary movements. There are two choices – to continue living like horses and cows and protect capitalism or to unite peasants, workers, students, intellectuals, the proletariat, and oppressed weak and small nations [*bei yapo ruoxiao minzu*] of the world and together defeat world capitalism. Malay independence requires the unity of many ethnic groups. To achieve that, we must organize the oppressed masses of Malayan weak peoples, such as Malays, Chinese, and Indians, to struggle for Malayan independence and to organize an anti-imperialist front of multiple ethnic groups [*duo minzu qunzhong*].[158]

At the same time, China-born MCP members successfully used the MCP as a fundraising channel for the Chinese cause – that is, the Chinese Revolution, as seen in Chapter 7. The MCP used methods reminiscent of a Chinese association and had the goal of influencing China. In campaigning for a Soviet version of the revolution in Chinese associations (*shetuan*), the MCP sought mobilization for the Malayan Revolution. Not seeing that promoting empathy (*tongqing*) and participation (*can*) instead of promoting material aid ("preferably gold") was the goal of the campaign, the CC labeled this illustrative of an "immigrant mentality" (*Zhongguo minzu qunzhong de yimin guannian*).[159] The MCP was helping the Chinese Revolution for the sake of Malaya and it embraced two mechanisms for bringing change, that of a communist party, the revolution, and that of a Chinese association.

The Dutch East Indies had a comparable history of Chinese migration and a shared set of concepts of national belonging and language but

---

[157] "CC MCP, Open Letter to Malay and Indian Comrades."
[158] Magong zhongyang xuanchuanbu [CC MCP Propaganda Department], "Magong zhongyang fanzhanzheng gongzuo taolun dagang [CC MCP Plan for Antiwar Work]," February 10, 1934, RGASPI 495/62/24/5–9.
[159] "Magong zhongyang tongzhi. Zenyang qu jinxing yu fazhan yuanzhu Zhongguo suweiai geming yundong de gongzuo jueyi [CC MCP Circular. The Resolution on How to Carry Out and Develop Aid to the Soviet Revolutionary Movement in China]"; "Magong zhongyang gongzuo jueding [CC MCP Work Resolution Regarding the Fifteenth Anniversary of Liebknecht and Luxembourg's Death and the Tenth Anniversary of Lenin's Death]"; "Magong zhongyang baogao. Malaya de qingshi yu dang huodong cong 1933 nian yi yue dao ba yue. Dagang yu ximu. Magong zhongyang yonghu zhongguo suweiai geming xuanyan [Report of the CC MCP. Situation in Malaya and Party Activities from January to August 1933. General Outline and Details. CC MCP Statement on the Defense of the Chinese Soviet Revolution]," January 5, 1934, RGASPI 495/62/24/1–2.

different colonial masters and a communist party that had crashed and burned. There, the struggle for political rights among Chinese organizations paralleled that of Chinese organizations in Malaya. From the pro-Dutch Chung Hwa Hui (Chinese Association), which participated in various Dutch government bodies; to the radical Chinese Partai Tionghoa Indonesia (PTI) (the Chinese Party of Indonesia), which advocated for Indonesian nationalism; to the *Sin Po* newspaper, which embraced first-generation immigrant (*totok*) politics and allied with the "radical Indonesia nationalists," all Chinese political parties in Indonesia participated in elections and had different views on what legal status the Chinese should be accorded.[160] Yet among these organizations, the leftist party of the localized Chinese (the *Peranakans*), the PTI was the one that embraced indigenous nationalism.

Chinese Organizations and Indonesian Nationalism

The discourse of Indonesian and *Peranakan* political thinkers concerning the ambiguity of the terms "nation" (*natie*), *orang Indonesia*, and *bangsa Indonesia* was comparable to that in the MCP. The majority of these thinkers did not accept a nonracial concept of the Indonesian nation. Peranakans were excluded from Indonesian nationalist parties, and they identified with the Chinese nation (*bangsa Tionghoa*). After World War I, they even participated in the campaign against the Dutch nationality law because they did not want to serve in the militia.[161]

However, not having indigenous status, the Chinese could not own land. In 1927, in reaction to China's inability to protect the Chinese overseas, the idea of an Indonesian nation spread among *Peranakan* Chinese, advocated by the Indische Partij (Indies Party) based on a sense of belonging, but the majority of *Peranakans* objected to this, as it would lead to conflicts with the Europeans. In the early 1930s, this idea developed into the idea of Indonesian citizenship from Indies citizenship, but, similar to postwar Malaya,[162] locals were suspicious of it.[163] In the same years, few *Peranakans* from the leftist PTI party, as in Malaya, close to how Indonesian nationalists embraced both Chinese and Indonesian identities, and they used the term *Indonesier* to signify those having citizenship, including *Peranakan* Chinese, Dutch, and *Peranakan* Arabs in the future independent Indonesia. At the same time, attitudes toward Japan continued to be defined by Japan's bonds with China, as seen in

[160] Suryadinata, *Peranakan Chinese Politics in Java*, pp. 74–75, 145–151, 153, 169–170.
[161] Ibid., pp. 153, 158–160, 163, 168.
[162] Omar, *Bangsa Melayu*, pp. 45–50.
[163] Suryadinata, *Peranakan Chinese Politics in Java*, pp. 71–73.

Liem Koen Hian's debates with other thinkers over Japanese imperialism.[164]

As in Malaya, Chinese groups advocated for a multiethnic alliance. *Sin Po* and the PTI in 1932–1935 together promoted an anticolonial stance and cooperation between Chinese and indigenous Indonesians. The membership of the leftist PTI grew from 30 to 600 from 1932 to 1933 and thus was comparable to the MCP's membership. Their stance on the issue of Chinese was also comparable to that of the MCP members *Sin Po* wanted to re-Sinicize the *Peranakans*, to unite the *Peranakans* with the *totoks*, and to associate with China politically. The PTI believed that a true Chinese nationalist in Indonesia would be an Indonesian nationalist, because one could not fight for faraway China while in Indonesia. They embraced Sun Yatsen's ideas of pan-Asianism, as did "radical Indonesian nationalists" who also supported the rise of China. *Sin Po* organized joint pro-independence meetings together with the *Peranakan* Arab party and the Indonesia National Union. The Committee of Asian Unity and the Committee of Colored Races (*bangsa*) were established.[165]

However, as in Malaya, Chinese and indigenous radical movements went separate ways in the DEI. The PKI sought to organize themselves across different ethnic groups but appealed only to a small number of *Peranakans* (they comprised 1 percent of the exiled PKI in Boven Digoel) because of their Chinese identification and their business orientation, whereas *totoks* could not be attracted because of language barriers. The PKI advocated for the integration of *Peranakans* into Indonesia, but not for them to become indigenous, which was comparable to the MCP's stance. A few *Peranakans* from affluent families who studied in the Netherlands or at Dutch secondary schools in the Indies after joining the outlawed PKI gained influence in the 1930s in the PTI, became involved with the Comintern and cooperated with the Partai Arab Indonesia and with Gerindo, the only party that had opened its membership to *Peranakans* by 1939. The PTI, despite its Indonesian ambitions, remained a *Peranakan* party, while the PKI did not have much success attracting *Peranakans*.[166]

Conclusion

While the Comintern's policy of "one party, one country" stimulated the idea of a unified Malaya and a unified Indonesia through a national

[164] Ibid., pp. 78–79, 161, 169–170.
[165] Ibid., pp. 54–55, 70–71, 82, 87, 90, 96, 157–158.
[166] Ibid., pp. 130–131, 153–154, 166–168.

communist party, the Chinese movement for equal rights and the re-Sinicization of Chinese stimulated comparable debates about the place of Chinese in an indigenous nation, regardless of whether the ruling party was to be communist. Communist activity in the DEI was more difficult than in Malaya, and the PTI, the most arduous promoter of Indonesia nationalism, did not call itself communist despite using leftist language. Sun Yatsen's Asianist ideas about a Chinese alliance with the oppressed nations[167] were echoed in the MCP via its proletarian internationalism, and in the DEI, unlike in Malaya, those ideas had sympathizers among both radical Chinese and Indonesian "nationalists."

Although the MCP was uniquely positioned among Chinese organizations in British Malaya because of its "national" claim as the Chinese Malayan organization with a dual identity since the ban of the Malayan GMD, the MCP shared the problems and discourses of Chinese associations. The criticism of divisions in the party based on Chinese places of origin echoed the criticism of divisions between the Chinese overseas, criticisms that were voiced by contemporaneous GMD politicians. Among early 1930s' Singapore *huiguan*, who were reorienting from local concerns toward native place reconstruction projects under the leadership of China-born leaders who took the place of locally born and focused leadership, the MCP was not unique in its effort to indigenize in addition to propagate support for China.[168] Bryna Goodman's analysis of the role of native place associations in the 1930s as "the center of the reordering of the nation," as nationalism is necessarily built on preexisting loyalties and ideas of community,[169] thus equally applies to Malaya. The need among immigrants for a Malayan identity was the result of further British government suppression of the rights of the Chinese. These two goals of the MCP, revolution and political representation of the Chinese, were contradictory and would affect the MCP's constituency, which is discussed in Chapter 7.

The MCP's connections to Malaya and China were boosted by building into MCP propaganda the Comintern's vision of internationalism as expressed in the discourse of Malayan nationalism, that is, internationalist support for the Chinese Revolution for the sake of the world and Malayan Revolutions. Although the MCP's Malayan nationalism paralleled the popular British official discourse of an emerging Malayan nation, British legislation during these years further divided Malayan

---

[167] See Anna Belogurova, "Networks, Parties, and the 'Oppressed Nations': The Comintern and Chinese Communists Overseas, 1926–1933," *Cross-Currents: East Asian History and Culture Review* 6 (2)(November 2017), pp. 530–557.

[168] Wing Chung Ng, "Urban Chinese Social Organization," p. 485.

[169] Goodman, "The Locality as Microcosm of the Nation," p. 413.

society into locals and immigrants and thus strengthened the MCP's Chinese identity.

In all, this synthesis and the hybrid nature of the MCP show us one way in which globalizing forces could work in Asia and reflect the astonishing resilience of overseas Chinese organizations. The Comintern altered the indigenization pattern of the Chinese communists in Malaya through the involvement of non-Chinese in an internationally valid Malayan nationalism, which was needed locally. As a CCP branch, the MCP, the hybrid of a Chinese organization and a communist party, formally became a part of the Comintern's network. MCP propaganda thus was a case of an interwar ideological global moment with two lines of argument: connecting the world situation with the local situation, and adapting Comintern and CCP policies to Malayan local conditions. The Comintern–MCP connection worked for a time. In this process, Chinese networks were central and shaped how communists interacted with the local population, as seen in the MCP's attempts to bring non-Chinese into the party. Implementation of the Comintern's goals of building an indigenous and multiethnic communist movement in Southeast Asia and reviving the communist movement in Indonesia depended on Chinese communist networks and the MCP as a connecting hub. The Philippine communist party was in the transpacific orbit of the American communist party, the CPUSA. One channel of communication between the Philippines and the CPUSA ran through the Chinese immigrant networks.

5 The Comintern, Malaya, and Chinese Networks, 1930–1936

Chinese Communist Networks in the Nanyang

The CCP's Nanyang branch was a node in the expanding Chinese network in Southeast Asia. High school and middle school teachers who had graduated from teachers' colleges in Fujian and Guangdong, many of them already CCP members, were seeking employment in the Nanyang as teachers, newspaper editors, and writers.[1] During their cooperation in 1923–1927, the GMD and the CCP had dispatched cadres to foment revolution. After the end of their cooperation, however, especially after the failed Guangzhou uprising in 1927, many communists took refuge in the Nanyang. As a result, starting in the late 1920s Chinese communist organizations emerged throughout Southeast Asia, including Burma, the Philippines (discussed in Chapter 3), Vietnam, Phnom Penh, and Taiwan, where, unlike anywhere else, the communists were all Chinese born in Taiwan.[2]

Intersecting networks of multiple organizations and personal connections sustained CCP branches. These were the GMD, the CCP, as well as other societies uniting educated Chinese. One example was the society Engine (Yinqingshe, 引擎社), the name of which reflected the members' intentions to set things in motion across China. One of the founders of the MCP, Xu Tianbing, was a member of Tongmenghui and Engine in Hainan in the early 1900s,[3] and Wu Jingxin (吴景新), the founder of the CCP cell in Burma,[4] had been an Engine member in Shanghai. In a

---

[1] Zhang Xia, "Xianyou xiandai zhongxue de geming huoguang [The Revolutionary Fire of the Modern Middle Schools in Xianyou County]."

[2] Bertil Lintner, *The Rise and Fall of the Communist Party of Burma* (Ithaca, NY: Cornell University Press, 1990), p. 5; Gao Zinong, "Zhongguo gongchan qingnian tuan Feiliebin tebie difang gongzuo baogao [Work Report of the Philippine Special Local Committee of the Chinese Communist Youth League]"; Quinn-Judge, *Ho Chi Minh*, p. 164; Ben Kiernan, *How Pol Pot Came to Power: Colonialism, Nationalism, and Communism in Cambodia, 1930–1975*. 2nd edn. (New Haven, CT: Yale University Press, 2004), p. 15; Wang Naixin et al., eds., *Taiwan shehui yundong shi, 1913–1936 [History of Taiwan's Movement]*, 5 vols. Vol. 3, *Gongchanzhuyi yundong [The Communist Movement]* (Taibei: Chuangzao chubanshe, 1989), p. 105.

[3] Zhu Yihui, "Xu Tianbing," p. 143.

[4] Lintner, *The Rise and Fall of the Communist Party of Burma*, p. 5.

Shanxi high school, Engine was the breeding ground for the CCP. In 1933, in Putian (莆田) (Fujian), AIL and MCP member Zhang Yuanbao (张元豹) organized an Engine branch as a cover for party activity among teachers, journalists, and high school students. Several members of Engine who escaped the suppressed Fujian Rebellion (1933–1934) against the Nanjing GMD were also members of the CCP, the MCP, and the party front organization Hujishe (Mutual Aid Society).[5] They printed their literary periodical at a school run by a "revolutionary" GMD member Huang Liangjun (黄良骏), and many, similar to Xu Jie and Zhang Xia, continued to maintain connections with both parties even after the breakdown of cooperation and the start of bloody competition between the top leadership of both the CCP and the GMD.[6] The personal commitments of revolutionaries overruled their political ones.

The MCP, like members of Chinese associations, gained social capital by sending money back home and helping kinsmen to migrate. As a Chinese organization, it needed "to keep open a cultural, social and economic corridor to the old hometown" in order "to maintain a compatriot niche."[7] The CCP's migrant network expanded as party members helped their native place revolutionary compatriots from Xianyou County (仙游) and other places in southern Fujian escape the suppression of the Fujian Rebellion by issuing job invitations for those matching the list of professions required in colonial Malaya so as to facilitate colonial government approval upon arrival. Money for the journey, 50 yuan – or 120 to 150 yuan for a first-time traveler, a "new guest" (*xinke*) – was usually borrowed from a pawn house or from the director of the school where the migrant was to be employed.[8] Networks also expanded as party members lost their jobs and moved on to the Philippines, Burma, and Hong Kong. One such member was Chen Jiafei (陈贾飞), who planned to find a teaching job in one of these places after his arrest and

---

[5] Interview with a historian of the local CCP in Zhangzhou, Chen Fang (陈方, aka Fu Panfeng [傅泙锋]), December 21, 2010.
[6] Chen Junju, "Fandi datongmeng yu Xianyou Yinqing wenhuashe [The Anti-Imperialist League and Cultural Society Engine in Xianyou]," in Zhongguo renmin zhengzhi xieshang huiyi Fujian sheng Putian shi weiyuanhui wenshi ziliao yanjiu weiyuanhui, ed., *Putian shi wenshi ziliao di yi ji* [*Literary and Historical Materials of Putian City*, vol. 1] (1985), pp. 37–42; Jiang Hezhen, "Huiyi Xu Jie zai Jilongpo wenxue huodong [Remembering the Literary Activity of Xu Jie in Kuala Lumpur]," in Tiantai xian zhengxie wenshi ziliao yanjiu weiyuanhui, ed., *Tiantai wenshi ziliao di san ji: Xu Jie zhuanji* [*Literary and Historical Materials of Tiantai*, vol. 3: *Biography of Xu Jie*] (1987), pp. 81-88; Ke Pingping as related by Xue Jie, *Kanke daolu shang de zuji* [*Road Full of Misfortunes*].
[7] Kuhn, "Why China Historians Should Study the Chinese Diaspora," p. 168.
[8] Zhang Xia, "Xianyou xian lü Ma huaqiao yu geming huodong [Immigrants from Xianyou County in Malaya and Revolutionary Activities]."

deportation from Malaya in 1939.[9] Others went to the Dutch East Indies.[10]

By 1928, the Comintern, in pursuit of the world revolution and the building of its own networks, had also begun to push the reluctant CCP to establish connections with Java in order to reestablish the PKI.[11] The resolutions of the Sixth Congress of the CCP in 1928 regarding "the question of the connection between the CCP and the communist parties of other countries" (*Zhongguo gongchandang yu geguo gongchandang lianluo de wenti*) read as follows:

As for the relations between the workers' movement in Annam and the communist party of French Annam, between the Chinese workers' movement of the Nanyang archipelago and the party of the Malay archipelago [the communist party of Java], between the Mongolian question and the Mongolian Revolution and so on, the realistic ways of mutual connection with those parties should be discussed with the parties of the respective countries.[12]

Similarly, Li Lisan's letter encouraging the Nanyang communists to spur a Nanyang Revolution also redirected the Nanyang communists to the Comintern and Profintern to obtain resources to remedy their lack of cadres and money and for all matters involving "other nations," including the establishment of links with the Javanese party.[13]

The MCP was practical, as it sought to expand its jurisdiction at minimal cost in the nodes of Chinese networks. Much like the Chinese faction was to aid the parties in the Americas by organizing the *huaqiao* but was not to build local parties in Mexico or Canada, the MCP did not want to take responsibility for the party organization in Borneo, as doing so would be "very inconvenient"; the MCP proposed instead that it should fall under the jurisdiction of the Javanese party.[14] In the end, apparently following existing network connections, which in turn followed the boundaries of Western colonial possessions, the Chinese comrades in Borneo were considered

---

[9] Chen Jiafei, "Cong Malaiya Bile zhou dao Guangdong Huizhou [From Perak State in Malaya to Huizhou in Guangdong]," in Zhongguo renmin zhengzhi xieshang huiyi Fujian sheng Putian shi weiyuanhui wenshi ziliao yanjiu weiyuanhui, ed., *Putian shi wenshi ziliao di si ji* [*Literary and Historical Materials of Putian City*, vol. 4] (1989), pp. 28–36.

[10] Zhang Xia, "Xianyou xian lü Ma huaqiao yu geming huodong [Immigrants from Xianyou County in Malaya and Revolutionary Activities]."

[11] ECCI Letter to the FEB, October 23, 1930.

[12] "Zhongguo gongchandang di liu ci daibiao dahui de jueyian. Zhengzhi jueyian [The Resolutions of the 6th Congress of the CCP. Political Resolutions]," July 9, 1928, in *Zhonggong dangshi jiaoxue cankao ziliao (1)* [*CCP Teaching Materials, Vol. 1*] (Beijing: Renmin chubanshe, 1978), p. 171.

[13] CC CCP, "A Letter from the Central Committee of the CCP to the Nanyang Provisional Committee."

[14] "To the C. C. of the Chinese Party and the Comintern," p. 2; Letter to the Chinese Faction of the CPUSA, April 4, 1933.

under the jurisdiction of the Malayan party.[15] The MCP planned to help establish independent parties in Siam, Borneo, and Sumatra, which lacked their own cadres, to organize a study circle to educate cadres for work in the colonies[16] and to send an investigator to Annam to establish a party organization.[17] The MCP once sent a comrade to the East Indies to help solve a conflict there between Chinese and "Asian" workers over "national differences" and to "educate" them, arguing, "[t]he working classes in all countries are one family not divided by nationality."[18] In Burma, Chinese comrades spread propaganda among Chinese workers and planned to establish their own section in the Burmese party. As in the MCP, they proclaimed that the goal of the Burmese communist party was to unite and organize the Chinese workers into the Burmese party so as to lead the liberation of all Burmese people from British domination.[19]

Even if their intentions were to liberate locals from colonialism, Chinese communists remained in their China-oriented frame of thinking. For example, with regard to Siam, which was at the intersection of the Chinese and Vietnamese revolutionary networks,[20] Chinese communists reported to the Comintern: "The culture of Siam is backward because of feudal rule in the country. The residents are interested in Chinese novels. Although there is a European bourgeois culture, it is developing only in the cities."[21] In the imagination of CYL members, Siam was like China, a semi-colony, and so the object (*duixiang*) and essence of its revolution were similar to those of China and different from those of the rest of the Nanyang. In China, where every class had been affected by imperialist and feudal oppression in politics and the economy, especially oppression of peasants by landlords, every class needed a revolution to obtain its democratic rights. Similarly, Siam, an independent country in theory, was in reality controlled by British and French imperialists.[22] Unlike in China, the strongest oppressors in Siam were not landlords but monks.[23] Hainanese Chinese also dominated the Siamese party, in which there was not one "native."[24]

[15] Ho Chi Minh, "Economic Conditions in Malay."
[16] "Otchet o polozhenii v Nan'iane [Report about the Situation in Nanyang]," p. 27.
[17] In Sumatra, party members published two legal newspapers but did not have influence 'over the masses.' Ibid., pp. 16–17.
[18] Ibid., p. 21.
[19] "Report from Malay," p. 29.
[20] Goscha, *Thailand and the Southeast Asian Networks of the Vietnamese Revolution*, pp. 76–113.
[21] Untitled report about Siam, undated, RGASPI 495/16/51/19–21.
[22] Nanyang gongzuo baogao [Nanyang Work Report], 1929, p. 16.
[23] Ho Chi Minh, "Malay."
[24] Goscha, *Thailand and the Southeast Asian Networks of the Vietnamese Revolution*, p. 78; Ho Chi Minh used Comintern directives to guide the movement in Siam as a justification for Vietnamese leadership in the liberation of the Siamese masses. Ho reported that the

In 1930 the MCP asked the Comintern and the CCP for assistance with work among other ethnic groups. The MCP sought connections, instructions, and exchanges with "brotherhood parties" of China, Great Britain, Holland, and France.[25] Only the CCP acted upon this plea. The Comintern forwarded an MCP letter written in English to the British party on August 29, 1930, but since the British party had no Chinese section until the beginning of the Japanese aggression in China – the so-called Mukden Incident of 1931 – nobody cared.[26] Despite the Comintern's directives that the parties of the metropoles should help the parties of the colonies, the CCP took charge of two colonial parties consisting of Chinese members, the MCP and the Taiwanese party,[27] in place of the parties of the imperial center. Among other parties of the metropoles, the CPUSA took seriously the task of supervising the party of an American colony, the Philippines.

Yet MCP members who were also members of other overlapping networks of intellectuals and compatriots did not wish to follow Comintern directives in expanding their networks beyond what suited their survival needs. Thus, the Comintern simply reinforced the status quo, wherein the Chinese party imagined its jurisdiction as encompassing the entire Nanyang.

The Comintern's World: Establishing Connections, 1930–1934

Anti-Imperialist Leagues

In the interwar years, Chinese anti-imperialist networks expanded worldwide. Following the establishment of the LAI organization in Europe, AILs had been established in Shanghai, Canton, and Malaya as CCP front organizations and as a breeding ground for party members. The Taiwanese Communist Party's Comintern liaison, Weng Zesheng, and other members from Taiwan, Korea, Annam, the Philippines, and India established the Anti-Imperialist League of the East in Shanghai (1929–1930) under CCP leadership.[28] The CCP was supposed to supply arms and money, while the local office of the GMD also promised support

---

Siamese CC had also begun to "nativize" its organization, which apparently meant that two Annamites had joined the seven members of the CC. Ho Chi Minh, "Malay," p. 26.
[25] "Resolutions Adopted at the Third Congress of the Malaya Party," p. 10.
[26] MCP, "To the English Komparty"; Liao Huanxing, "Zhongguo gongchandang lü Ou zongzhibu, 1953 [European Branch of the Chinese Communist Party, 1953]."
[27] See Tertitskii and Belogurova, *Taiwanskoe kommunisticheskoe dvizhenie i Komintern*.
[28] Wang Naixin et al., eds., *Taiwan shehui yundong shi, 1913–1936* [*A History of Taiwan's Social Movements*], vol. 3: *Gongchanzhuyi yundong* [*The Communist Movement*], pp. 300–320.

to the revolutionary movements in India, Indonesia, and Korea independently of the central government.[29]

In November 1930, the Eastern Secretariat of the ECCI introduced the
idea of establishing a Far Eastern subsection of the LAI, the Far Eastern
Secretariat of the League Against Imperialism (FESLAI). The primary
reason for setting up the FESLAI was the initiative of the CCP and the
Chinese CYL to form the Eastern Anti-Imperialist League. The FESLAI
was to be set up as an international workers' relief aid organization and to
function as a front organization without explicit connections to either the
Profintern or the FEB of the Comintern in Shanghai. The FESLAI was to
coordinate the operations of the LAI in the Far East and to assist the
international secretariat of the LAI in maintaining and establishing contact with the anti-imperialist movements in China, Korea, Indochina,
Formosa, Malacca, Siam, Java, Indonesia, and Japan.[30]

Malaya's and Singapore's multiethnic populations were a fertile
ground for a multiethnic AIL organization. In Malaya, the Hainanese
had founded an anti-imperialist league in 1928. The league had published
the periodical *Bright Dawn*, addressing the oppressed nations of the East.
However, the British police stated that the Malayan AIL had no connection with the anti-imperialist league in Brussels, the LAI.[31] This was the
only Chinese-led organization in Malaya that had non-Chinese members
prior to 1930: 200 in all.[32] However, in 1931 the Singaporean AIL had no
non-Chinese among its 110 members, who were 50 percent Hainanese,
40 percent Hakka, and 10 percent Hokkien. Among these, 70 percent
were laborers and 30 percent were intellectuals, i.e., schoolteachers and
newspaper editors and writers.[33] In the Comintern's translation of the
MCP's report, the AIL in the Nanyang was said to be conducting "an
investigation of the work of the national commission" (*obsledovaniia
raboty natsionalnoi komissii*).[34] Here, *minzu* was translated as "national,"
while the authors intended for it to mean "nationality," thus conflating

[29] Quinn-Judge, *Ho Chi Minh*, pp. 166–167; Wang Naixin et al., eds., *Taiwan shehui
yundong shi, 1913–1936 [A History of Taiwan's Social Movements]*, vol. 3: *Gongchanzhuyi
yundong [The Communist Movement]*, pp. 354–372.

[30] "Plan of Work of the Far Eastern Secretariat of the Anti-Imperialist League, the Eastern
Secretariat," November 1930, RGASPI 542/1/37/248–250, quoted in Petersson, "'We
Are Neither Visionaries Nor Utopian Dreamers,'" pp. 414–415, n. 1047.

[31] Khoo, "The Beginnings of Political Extremism in Malaya," p. 312; "Kuo Min Tan and
Other Societies in Malaya (Continued), July–September 1928," October 23, 1928, pp.
9–10, CO 273/542.

[32] Hack and Chin, eds., *Dialogues with Chin Peng*, p. 72.

[33] MRCA, December 1931, pp. 48, CO 273/572.

[34] "Resoliutsia priniataia posle obsledovania raboty vremennogo komiteta v 1929
[Resolution Adopted after Investigation of the Work of the (Nanyang) Provisional
Committee in 1929]," pp. 25–26.

the Anti-imperialist League with the multiethnic nation.[35] The Nanyang AIL planned to develop a regional network as well, but it could not sustain even its existing influence in Singapore because of a lack of cadres and ever-decreasing ranks. Similar to the party organization, the lack of members in the AIL was attributed to the tendency to create a leading organization before the establishment of lower cells. Indeed, the AIL was run by party members.[36]

The MCP acted on the same aspirations of uniting the oppressed in the Nanyang under the leadership of Chinese immigrants. In the early 1930s, an MCP member, writer, and teacher from China, Ma Ning, the head of propaganda in the league, participated in a conference of Chinese immigrants from India, Vietnam, Burma, Malaya, and China held in the jungle near Johor Bahru. This was referred to as the All-Nanyang Colonial Peoples Delegate Congress (Quan Nanyang ge zhimindi ge minzu daibiao dahui).[37] In 1932, the Malayan AIL's leading committee of nine included two Malays and two Indians, and the 6,547 members from the communist-led labor, peasants', cultural, women's, and children's organizations included 135 Indians, 322 Malays, and 10 Javanese.[38]

In 1932, the Comintern planned to continue with the Far Eastern section of the LAI[39] as a network for communist connections in Southeast Asia. In the Philippines, it was the front organization uniting the members of trade unions, the party, and the movements of various ethnic and religious backgrounds.[40] In 1932, arrested members of the students' association in Singapore had with them Comintern publications printed in Germany and local AIL pamphlets.[41] The idea of Chinese leadership in the emancipation of the colonial peoples of Southeast Asia was put into practice in the organizational structure borrowed from the LAI based on Chinese networks.

---

[35] "Minutes of the Third Representative Conference of Nanyang," pp. 101–103.

[36] "Otchet o polozhenii v Nan'iane [Report about the Situation in Nanyang], [Report about the Situation in Nanyang]," pp. 24–25; MRCA, December 1931, pp. 48, 53, CO 273/572.

[37] Yu Yueting, "Ma Ning yige bei yiwang de liaobuqi de 'zuoyi' zuojia [A Forgotten Extraordinary Left-Wing Writer Ma Ning]," in Zhao Ting, ed., *Shifan qunying guanghui Zhonghua (di ershi juan)* [*Heroic Teachers, Shining China*, vol. 20] (Xi'an: Shaanxi renmin jiaoyu chubanshe, 1994), pp. 176–185.

[38] MRCA, March 1933, pp. 21, 24, CO 273/585.

[39] Petersson, "'We Are Neither Visionaries Nor Utopian Dreamers,'" p. 466.

[40] "Resolutsii s pervogo s"ezda ispolkoma TsK [Resolutions of the First Congress of the Executive Committee of the Central Committee]," in Letter from the Eastern Secretariat of the ECCI to the Communist Party of the Philippines, "Situation in the Philippines and Tasks of the CPPI," January 10, 1932, RGASPI 495/62/ 28/47–62, esp. 61–62.

[41] *Singapore Free Press*, February 6, 1932 and January 18, 1932, cited in Profintern press clippings from Singapore newspapers. RGASPI 534/3/811.

The Comintern and Chinese Immigrants, the Comintern and Malaya

The Comintern had relied on Chinese networks from early on. Since April 1927, the CCP had acted as the source of orthodoxy and as a liaison between the Comintern and the communists in Indochina.[42] Ho Chi Minh had thus relied on Chinese networks to implement Comintern directives.[43] However, the global scope of the Chinese networks on which the Comintern relied for communication among different parties did not come without costs. Immigrant party members were not useful for local mobilization, as they did not speak local languages and were vulnerable to deportation back to China, as was the case in the United States and in Malaya.[44] The Comintern criticized the MCP for its exclusively Chinese immigrant membership, and the MCP shared this criticism of itself, viewing party members' focus on China instead of on Malaya as indicative of an immigrant mentality (*yimin guannian*).

As previously discussed, Malayan communists inherited this criticism from the GMD. In a letter to the MCP, the Comintern said that the party in Malaya had decided correctly to transform itself from a party of Chinese immigrants into the communist party of Malaya, uniting all nationalities.[45] Since the Comintern built its policies on the reports and suggestions of local communists, immigrants were not useful in providing relevant and updated information with regard to the conditions in either their homeland or their host countries and parties. At the Comintern's Eastern Secretariat meeting in February 1929, the KUTV's director, Raiter, said, "[t]he Chinese group of the International Lenin School prepares materials, and we use them. We can accept or reject them, but we use the work done by these students. By doing so, we are preparing them for leadership work in China." Following an onrush (*naplyv*) of immigrant students in 1928–1929 in the KUTV, the Comintern decided to accept only recent immigrants.[46]

---

[42] Quinn-Judge, *Ho Chi Minh*, pp. 114, 117.
[43] Goscha, *Thailand and the Southeast Asian Networks of the Vietnamese Revolution*, p. 78.
[44] "How to Organize Chinese Communists in the US," undated, RGASPI 515/1/1111/12–14, esp. 12.
[45] Eastern Secretariat of the Comintern, Draft Letter to the MCP, February 20, 1931, RGASPI 495/62/18/6–10, esp. 8.
[46] "Vystuplenie Raitera o polozhenii Spetssectora KUTV na 7 fevr.1929 goda na zasedanii kollegii vostochnogo seckretariata [Raiter's Address about the Situation in the Special Sector of the KUTV on 7 February 1929 at the Meeting of the Collegiate of the Eastern Secretariat]," RGASPI 495/154/372/26–40, esp. 36. Iosif L'vovich Raiter (1893–1940), born in Mogilev, Belarus, had no formal education, became the director of the KUTV in October 1928, and was a member of the Central Asian Research Society in the KUTV. He was purged in 1938 and executed by a firing squad in 1940 for "espionage." He was posthumously exonerated in 1956. Vasil'kov, Iaroslav Vladimirovich and Marina Iur'evna Sorokina, *Liudi i sud'by, Biobibliograficheskii slovar' vostokovedov-zhertv politicheskogo terrora v sovetskii period [People and Lives. Bio-Bibliographical Dictionary of*

By 1930, with the construction of the British naval base there, Singapore had acquired greater importance for the Comintern. In March, Fu Daqing went to Singapore with instructions "to lay the foundation" for connections with Indonesia and India and to fix irregular connections with the Malayan states and with Singapore. For the role of liaison with Java, the Profintern considered another Chinese communist who had spent some time in Java as a representative of the Philippine party.[47] In January 1931, for the Profintern the most important countries were India, Indonesia, Indochina, and Japan. A Profintern boss wrote from London to the Pan-Pacific Trade Union Secretariat (PPTUS) representative in Shanghai that even though the overwhelming majority of red union members in Malaya were Chinese, the Profintern's goal was not only to organize the Singaporean Chinese "but also through them to reach out to the workers of Indonesia and India."[48] These Chinese immigrants from India and Indonesia would be educated while in Singapore and would then return to their countries to support the revolutionary trade union movements there.

Serious work was planned for Singapore because of the importance of its port for the pan-Pacific coast. Singapore and Hong Kong were important as bases of "British imperialism" in the Far East, and Hong Kong would be the main base of the British navy in the coming war.[49] Antiwar propaganda was thus important in these ports despite their small proletariat populations, in contrast to India and China.[50] In 1930, FEB cadre Ignatii Ryl'skii suggested that the CCP discuss "the attitude of the CCP to Chinese immigration in the Philippines and Indochina."[51] With regard to the MCP, the ECCI wrote to the FEB in Shanghai, "[t]he Chinese communists in a number of Eastern countries play and will play the largest role in the cause of the establishment of the organized communist movement."[52] The FEB was to train and recruit "reliable" (*proverennykh*) Chinese communist cadres for work in the Far East and the Middle East, where the number of Chinese migrant workers was growing.[53] In 1931, the Comintern used Chinese networks to communicate between the CPUSA and the Communist Party of the Philippine Islands (CPPI)

Orientalists: Victims of Political Purges during the Soviet Period (1917–1991)] (St. Petersburg: Peterburgskoe vostokovedenie, 2003). Online version accessed March 16, 2018: http://memory.pvost.org/pages/raiter.html.

[47] Stoliar's Letter to "Alex," March 27, 1931, RGASPI 534/4/370/34–35.

[48] Ibid.

[49] "Instructions to Com[rades] Leon [Stoliar] and Kennedy," January 20, 1931, RGASPI 534/4/106/18.

[50] Letter from London to the Shanghai Representative of the PPTUS, "Dear Niece," January 1, 1931, RGASPI 534/4/360/5–13, esp. 10.

[51] Titarenko and Leutner, *Komintern i Kitai* [*Comintern and China*], vol. 3, p. 828.

[52] ECCI Letter to the FEB, October 23, 1930.

[53] Ibid.

and promoted the CPPI's contacts with the revolutionary movements of China, Indonesia, and Malaya.[54]

The Comintern imagined a multinational network of communists in Southeast Asia and sought to revive the communist organization in the Dutch East Indies. However, the Comintern's attempts to establish connections with Indonesia through Indonesian communist Alimin, dispatched to China in 1931, were futile.[55] In 1932, the "CPUSA Suggestions for Work among Colonial Workers" stated that only the Chinese had connections with the local communist parties and other organizations under communist leadership in the colonies – the Philippines, India, and Indonesia.[56]

To achieve these goals, the Comintern promoted connections among the Chinese communists in the region beyond existing connections among organizations in Malaya, Siam, and Vietnam. The Comintern offered the opportunity for Chinese immigrant communists to carve out a niche and to expand this extended network of familial and community survival by providing a source of ideological legitimization and organizational resources through the fostering of migrant connections in the historical area of Chinese migration. However, this opportunity came with new expectations and requirements. In this way, the life of a Chinese organization, the network of Chinese immigrants, and the ideals and practices of the Comintern came together in the MCP and other revolutionary organizations in Malaya. The fit, of course, was far from

[54] "Draft Resolution on the Revolutionary Trade Union Movement in Philippines," August 16, 1931, RGASPI 495/66/23/ 59–67, esp. 67. There is a note on the back of the draft of the letter from the Eastern Secretariat of the ECCI to the Communist Party of the Philippines, "Situation in the Philippines and the Tasks of the CPPI," September 21, 1931, RGASPI 495/66/28/47–62: "*Kuusinen*. When [this letter is] approved, one copy [should be sent] to [the] CPPI, [and] one copy to [the] CPUSA through [the] American Chinese bureau to Philippines."

[55] Alimin found a helper, PKI member Alfonso, who had fled to Singapore following the suppression of the PKI rebellion. From there, Tan Malaka dispatched him to Shanghai as a representative of the Indonesian Youth League and as a past member of antigovernment student organizations and sport and friendship associations. In China, Alimin, fearing arrest, refused to go to Singapore and Hong Kong and was thus made responsible for publication in Malay of the PPTUS *Malayan Worker*. Alimin's approach, which he planned without any MCP reference materials in Germany in September 1930, was based on his assumption that there was no peasantry in Malaya. Alimin was in China until 1933. In 1934, he returned to Moscow. Alimin's letter, April 23, 1930, RGASPI 495/214/752/40–41; Alimin, "Avtobiografia [Autobiography]," April 29, 1932, RGASPI 495/214/67/1–7, esp. 3, 4; Stoliar's letter, sometime in late 1930–early 1931, RGASPI 534/4/370/1–12, esp. 10–11; "Santos Huan's Personal File," RGASPI 495/214/3/part 1/73, RGASPI 495/214/3/dossier/ 69, RGASPI 495/214/752/86.

[56] "Predlozheniia po rabote kompartii SASSh sredi kolonial'nykh rabochikh v Amerike [CPUSA Suggestions for Work among Colonial Workers]," January 16, 1932, RGASPI 532/4/2015/4, 5.

perfect or seamless. In practice, the MCP received funding without being accepted formally as a Comintern section, so the representatives of the MCP went to Shanghai to demand money, directives, and training from the Comintern. In fact, the way in which the MCP coped with Comintern demands was quite remarkable, as it produced large numbers of documents, the language of which was increasingly theoretical, Bolshevik, and self-critical in an effort to meet the Comintern's request for self-criticism. This engagement was reflected in MCP members' contacts with the Comintern.

The Comintern and the MCP in the Chinese Network

Maritime connections, steamships, and seamen played an important role in the CCP network in the Nanyang, connecting the party organizations in China and in the Nanyang as well as connecting the central committee of the MCP in Singapore with its branches in Malaya.[57] It was impossible to deliver propaganda materials and expensive to send envoys to areas where there were no seamen.[58] As in other places in the world, the Comintern relied on a network of seamen for communication within the Chinese communist network[59] and sought individual Chinese communists embedded in both the CCP and other local parties to foster links in its own Comintern network. This relationship required significant work from both sides.

Twenty-six-year-old sailor Wang Yung Hai was one of the representatives the MCP sent to the Comintern in Shanghai in 1930 "to report on the work done and present demands."[60] Wang, who was illiterate, dictated "My Brief Story" to a CCP cadre, and the document was then translated into English for the Comintern.[61] Wang was from a poor farming family. At twelve, he had gone to the Nanyang to work as a servant. At seventeen, he had joined a steamer as a fireman and then as a machinery worker. He joined the party in the Nanyang in 1926 and went from the leader of a party cell, to the leader of the nucleus in the trade union, to the secretary of the party organization on a steamer. He then became a member of the standing committee of the General Federation of Seamen, headquartered in Singapore. In November 1930, the federation

---

[57] Khoo, "The Beginnings of Political Extremism in Malaya," p. 295.
[58] "Otchet o polozhenii v Nan'iane [Report about the Situation in Nanyang]," p. 27; MRCA, December 1930, p. 53, CO 273/571.
[59] Benton, *Chinese Migrants and Internationalism*, pp. 53–56.
[60] Ho Chi Minh, "Letter to the MCP", November 25, 1930, RGASPI 495/62/6/5–7.
[61] Wang Yung Hai, "My Brief Story," December 8, 1930, RGASPI 495/62/4/1–2.

had a membership of 100 individuals, including the members in Penang.[62]

As in other cases of labor protests, the MCP tried to gain control of the sailors' activities already under way and ascribed success and failure respectively to "decisiveness" and the low political and cultural level of seamen. One of those activities was the unsuccessful 1932–1934 campaign to gain a legal status for Chinese sailors' own lodging houses (*haiyuan sushe*) for unemployed seamen and the campaign for abolition of the contract system.[63] A seasoned revolutionary, Wang Yung Hai had participated in the seamen's strike and even claimed to have killed two "reorganizationists."[64] In 1929, together with trade union cadre Huang Muhan, he was arrested for one month, released, and banished from the Nanyang. In April 1930, he was elected as a representative of the World Conference of the Red International Labor Union but said he was too busy to go. In his place, two other Nanyang communists, Huang Muhan and Fu Hung Chu (likely, 符鸿纪), went to Moscow.

Being a member of the Chinese Communist Party and trying to get in touch with international superiors was a nerve-racking matter requiring emotional commitment, and Wang did not last long in this role. After three months of waiting for promised money and instructions and for a plenary session of the executive committee of the General Federation of Seamen, Wang was frustrated that he had not even been introduced to a local CCP cell in Shanghai. Wang had a meeting with somebody from the FEB and the CCP, so the CCP convened a meeting of the comrades working in Malaya, Wang Yung Hai and Huang Muhan, and decided that MCP envoy Shieng Kien Chu, who had been dispatched to Shanghai for training, would return to the Nanyang at the expense of the FEB, paid through the CCP.[65] Shieng also waited in vain for three months, then

---

[62] Ibid.; Ho Chi Minh, "Malay," p. 26. The aim of this organization was to abolish the contract labor system as well as to back the right of recommendation and allow workers to work in turns. The organization covered fifty-two steamers in the Dutch colonies, Australia, and Africa, as well as several irregular petroleum steamers to Europe, South China, and Malaya, having twenty-two nuclei. Most were loyal to the red labor unions, and 80 percent paid membership fees. "Report of Labour Federation of Malaya no. 1 to the Profintern," March 25, 1934.

[63] In seamen's dormitories, out of 2,000 members, 50 percent were Cantonese (firemen), 25 percent Hainanese, and 25 percent Fukienese. Seamen demanded the right to land in Africa, to oppose the goods that were carried, to deny the company the right to change the work of a sailor at any time, to lift the ban on communication among various departments, to stop beatings by foremen, and to stop the splitting up of sailors along clan lines. "Report of Labour Federation of Malaya no. 1 to the Profintern," March 25, 1934; Tai Yuen, *Labour Unrest in Malaya*, pp. 45–52.

[64] Possibly, these were the members of the GMD Reorganization Comrades Association, established in 1928. Quinn-Judge, *Ho Chi Minh*, p. 135.

[65] Wang Yung Hai, "My Brief Story"; Wang Yung Hai, "To the Far Eastern Bureau."

asked the FEB directly for "travel expenses and instructions."[66] Wang also demanded that the FEB cover $45 as his living expenses for two months.[67] Although Wang requested to meet with the FEB twice a week and transferred reports coming from Malaya to the Comintern, in the end the FEB promised Wang that it would send the long-awaited instructions by mail.[68]

The CCP acted as an intermediary between the MCP and the Comintern as Chinese communists in the Nanyang continued to draw the Comintern's attention to the region. Wang sent to the Comintern reports prepared collectively by the members of the standing provisional committee of the MCP: Huang Muhan, Fu Hung Chu (who had just returned from Moscow), and Shieng Kien Chu. These reports were translated into Russian by the CC CCP in Shanghai and the Hong Kong Southern Bureau.[69] Wang wrote, "[i]t is my hope that our reports will be translated into different languages and sent to Moscow in order to attract the special attention of the Comintern to the work of the Nanyang."[70] Meanwhile, the Far Eastern Bureau of the Comintern in Shanghai had too much on its plate with the revolution in East Asia, so it gladly used the help of the Chinese communists. Frustrated that the Comintern paid little attention to the Nanyang, Wang Yung Hai sent letters criticizing the Comintern to the All-China Federation of Labor Unions and to the CC CCP.[71] Echoing earlier criticisms of the CCP, Wang wrote that the Comintern gave instructions that were "good on paper but hardly [effective] in action." "[The most urgent need is to have] a strong and regular connection with the FEB, which should understand the conditions in Malaya in order to guide more closely the work in the Nanyang. If there is no whole, concrete, practical instruction, as well as material assistance, the party of Malaya can never get from the present condition of half-living, half-dying."[72]

---

[66] Letter by Shieng Kien Chu to the Comintern FEB, December 26, 1930, RGASPI 495/62/4/3; Wang Yung Hai, "My Brief Story."

[67] These included $5 for bedclothes, $15 for clothes, and $25 for daily expenses, which Wang borrowed. Wang Yung Hai, "My Brief Story."

[68] Ibid.; Wang Yung Hai, "To the Far Eastern Bureau."

[69] "To the C. C. of the Chinese Party and the Comintern"; Wang Yung Hai, "To the Far Eastern Bureau"; Letter by Shieng Kien Chu to the Comintern FEB. According to British analysis, the MCP was first guided by this Southern Bureau of the CCP – "transmission and translation sub-agency of the FEB" – of which Ho Chi Minh was a member until his arrest in 1931. National Archives and Records Administration (NARA), Washington, D.C. RG263:D2527/4534–35.

[70] Wang Yung Hai, "To the Far Eastern Bureau."

[71] No such letters can be found in the RGASPI.

[72] Wang Yung Hai, "To the Far Eastern Bureau." Ho Chi Minh complained to the FEB during the same time period of the same lack of due attention from the Comintern to the

The Comintern's grand design for Southeast Asia became a resource for local communists organizing their own interests. As was the case with the Taiwanese Communist Party,[73] the Comintern based its suggestions and criticisms entirely on local reports, processing them and using the theoretical language of Marxism–Leninism to talk about them, and including the Comintern rhetoric or party line, which always revolved around Bolshevization. Wang, who was also in touch with the secretariat of the Pacific Labor Conference, suggested that the Malaya Executive Committee be set up under FEB guidance to handle regular connections between the Comintern and MCP comrades who understood conditions in Malaya and could provide accurate instructions.[74] Wang urged that a person from the MCP who understood local conditions should be appointed to work in the FEB rather than someone appointed by the FEB itself. Huang Muhan, an experienced Nanyang communist and a cadre in the All-China Federation of Seamen, was therefore appointed at Wang's suggestion.[75]

The Comintern line was produced both in Moscow and in the field in China and Southeast Asia by Comintern cadres and agents, both Chinese and foreigners. The general nature of Comintern and CCP directives was noted even by the British in their analysis of captured documents,[76] yet adhesion to the Comintern line did become the MCP's goal. The Comintern noted that, except for setting the general goals of building party leadership in localities, it was difficult to propose a "concrete work plan" for the MCP in chapters of the Malayan anti-imperialist league in cities, in factories and villages, and in the CYL. The FEB viewed the MCP program as "generally correct," unlike the ineffective "methods of work with the toiling masses," as the party did not have influence.[77] Iakov Rudnik, the administrative head of the FEB, wondered about the opinion of the MCP regarding the the FEB directives. He noted that the MCP

matters of the Indochinese party. According to a British analysis of captured FEB documents regarding Indochina, the most frequent themes in these letters to the Comintern were requests for recognition, directives, and financial assistance. A British report from February 21, 1931, quoted Ho: "Because there is no voice coming from Comintern [or any of its affiliated organisations], the masses of Indochina feel that their suffering and sacrifice [are ignored by] our organisations [and] that they are forgotten and lone, that they have no backing from international solidarity." "Communist Activities in China, Federated Malay States etc. (The 'Noulens Case')," March 7, 1932, NARA RG 263: D2527/45, p. 30.

[73] Tertitskii and Belogurova, *Taiwanskoe kommunisticheskoe dvizhenie i Komintern.*
[74] Wang Yung Hai, "To the Far Eastern Bureau."
[75] Ibid.
[76] "Communist Activities in China, Federated Malay States etc.," p. 26; MRCA, December 1930, p. 52, CO 273/571.
[77] FEB, "To the Malayan Comrades," December 17, 1930.

evaluated the FEB analysis to be "generally characterizing the situation correctly" and that the MCP would use the FEB directives as "a basis for future work."[78] The MCP indeed agreed with Comintern recommendations regarding its "method of work"[79] but refuted criticism of the MCP's calls for potentially dangerous open activity. The MCP explained that it used slogans of uprisings, general strikes, terrorism, and world revolution only for the purpose of propaganda and blamed a lack of cadres and finances as the obstacle that prevented it from achieving success.[80]

Similar to the CCP in the early 1920s, local party organizations continued to approach the Comintern on their own. Aside from Wang Yung Hai, three individuals claiming to represent the CC MCP went to Shanghai in the first half of 1931.[81] All of them in the past two to three years had left China for Malaya, to the Comintern's satisfaction. The Comintern gave all of them instructions and took their reports. In these reports, however, Nanyang communists wrote that they did not know the situation in the MCP. As a member of the executive committee of the central committee, Wang Yung Hai explained that this was because he did not regularly participate in the work of the standing committee. Again, these reports reflect a disconnect between upper and lower party organizations. In addition, Wang claimed he knew nothing about China or revolutionary work there. The MCP representatives also discredited one another's knowledge. Wang called Huang Muhan's report "incomplete and simple" because Huang did not know the current situation very well – unlike the history of the Nanyang party.[82] These disclaimers contributed to the Comintern's distrust of the information provided by immigrant communists as well as to its confusion over the Malayan party.

The MCP continued to promote the establishment of separate local communist organizations in Malaya based on ethnicity and temporarily subordinate to the central committee. To this effect, a three-person committee was established in Johor to lead a Malay committee consisting of ten people, and a five-person committee was established for the Indian committee, which originally had eighteen members. The communists in Perak

---

[78] FEB's Letter to Ducroux, May 20, 1931. For more on Rudnik, see Frederick S. Litten, "The Noulens Affair," *China Quarterly* 138 (June 1994), pp. 492–512.
[79] This was criticized in the FEB's letter "To the Malayan Comrades," December 17, 1930, p. 1.
[80] CC MCP, "From Malaya. To the FEB," February 7, 1931; Huang Muhan, "Worker Movement in Federated Malay States."
[81] FEB's Letter to Ducroux. There were other leftist Chinese organizations. In the summer of 1931, the Hainanese and Hokkien in Penang organized a socialist democratic party (*shehui minzhudang*), which was also called the Penang Labor Union of the CCP that was subordinate to the Amoy organization. MRCA, December 1931, pp. 31–32, CO 273/572.
[82] Wang Yung Hai, "To the Far Eastern Bureau."

thought that separate "racial" committees would affect the strength of the party, and in Selangor, Seremban, and Kuala Lumpur, the party did not have cadres to work among Malays and Tamils, nor did it have members of those ethnicities among its ranks.[83] In 1933, the MCP still advocated for trade unions based on ethnicity (*ge minzu de gonghui*) by gathering cadres working among those of other nationalities (*minzu huodong de rencai*) in order to build the Malayan Federation of Labor Unions.[84]

The FEB required party unification and acceptance of Comintern decisions, abolishing independent ethnic organizations and calling a joint party conference of Malayan, Chinese, Indian, and Javanese comrades to elect a central committee for all of the "Malay states" in April 1931, though this conference never took place.[85] Despite this gap between the required national multiethnic party and the de facto alliance of ethnic organizations that the MCP was building, as well as the predominance of Chinese in the party, the Comintern endorsed the existing CCP–MCP relationship. The ECCI wrote to the CC CCP in Moscow, "[t]he political commission of the CI decided on January 20, 1931, to pose the question of recognition of the CP of Malay states [and Singapore] as a CI section at the Seventh Congress. Until then, the leadership of this organization must be connected with the CC CCP."[86] The MCP continued to have close relations with the Guangdong provincial committee and the Amoy town committee of the CCP.[87] Moreover, while the Comintern was searching for a liaison with "the Malaya States," who would be "a good steady friend" comparable to "Quark" (Ho Chi Minh), the Chinese communists decided that "a Singapore Chinese" should be dispatched to implement the Comintern's grand plans regarding Southeast Asia and to spread the Comintern's message among Chinese and locals in India.[88]

Moreover, following the recommendations of Chinese comrades that Huang Muhan was unqualified for serious work, the Comintern decided not to send him, even though he had been recommended by Wang Yung Hai. A clearly false piece of information – that MCP secretary Fu Daqing had been arrested in Calcutta[89] – hints that it was Fu Daqing who was likely to be sent to India. The CC MCP indeed was in touch with the

[83] MRCA, December 1931, p. 36, CO 273/572.
[84] "Zhigong yundong jueyian [Resolution on the Labour Movement]," April 1933.
[85] FEB's Letter to Ducroux.
[86] ECCI Letter to the FEB, January 20, 1931, RGASPI 495 /62/10/1.
[87] MRCA, December 1930, p. 53, CO 273/571; MRCA, December 1931, pp. 31–32, CO 273/572.
[88] FEB's Letter to Ducroux, May 20, 1931.
[89] Fu allegedly communicated this to Zheng Chaoling when he ran into him in a Guangzhou prison in 1931. Zheng Chaoling, "Ji Fu Daqing [Remembering Fu Daqing]," *Bainian chao* [One Hundred Year Tide] 2 (1998), pp. 61–63, esp. 63.

Calcutta branch of the All-India Communist Party, which planned to send a representative to meet with French Comintern envoy Ducroux in Singapore.[90] Ducroux had to collect information from outside the MCP regarding the location and activities of party organizations. Two others were sent independently of Ducroux: these were "our friend" (Huang Muhan) and "clerk Sam for the PPTUS work" (Teo Yuanfu, a Hokkien speaker from Java, aliases Zhang Ranhe and Bassa).[91] The arrests in Singapore on June 1 of Ducroux, Huang, and Fu Daqing eventually led to the arrests of Ho Chi Minh and Rudnik and to the dismantling of the FEB.[92]

Although no trace of such a subsidy in 1931 was found, according to FEB accounts for the June quarter of 1931, 50,000 gold dollars were allocated for work in the Federated Malay States and 45,000 gold dollars for the work in Burma until the end of the year. Although the budget was not sufficient for the grand plans in East Asia, the FEB had freedom from the Comintern's head office to distribute financial aid to the "majority of the firms [i.e., communist parties] in the Far East" within a general directive to use money for travel expenses and meetings and to give money in small amounts.[93]

In March 1934, both the party and the labor movement were declining. From December 1933 to March 1934, membership in the MFLU dropped by 695 members to 6,035 in eight localities, excluding seamen: 4,513 were Chinese, 518 were Malay, and 52 were Indian. Among these, forty were female.[94] The party sounded desperate. All ranks of the party (*duoji dangbu*) had given up on reporting on the masses' protests; for the upper ranks of the party (*shangji dangbu fangmian*), the struggles of the masses were "even beyond our understanding" (*zai women de liaojie zhi wai*).[95] The MCP documents show that the party failed to handle a wave of spontaneous labor protests in 1934, and too-high standards for new trade unions, which had been in place since 1930, resulted in little

---

[90] Letter from the FEB to the "Center" Regarding Malaya, Indonesia and India, June 10, 1931. NARA RG263: D 2510/41–50.

[91] Ibid.; "Doklad tovarishcha Diukru [Report by Comrade Ducroux]," January 4, 1934, Ducroux's Personal File, RGASPI 495/270/809/30–34, esp. 31; Yong, *Origins of Malayan Communism*, p. 163.

[92] "Doklad tovarishcha Diukru [Comrade Ducroux's Report]," January 4, 1934, RGASPI 495/270/809/30–34.

[93] "Communist Activities in China, Federated Malay States etc.," pp. 35, 26; Letter from the FEB to the "Center" Regarding Malaya, Indonesia and India.

[94] "Report of Labour Federation of Malaya no. 1 to the Profintern," March 25, 1934.

[95] "Magong zhongyang tongzhi: Guanyu qunzhong douzheng de tongji he baogao de gongzuo de jueding [CC MCP Circular Regarding the Decision to Conduct a Survey of Mass Struggles]," March 21, 1934, RGASPI 495/62/23/31–35.

increase in membership.[96] Party membership had fallen by August 1934 to a total of 588. There were 136 members in Singapore, 135 in Johor, 160 in Malacca, 100 in Sembilan, 36 in *Kichow*, 8 in Kita, and 13 in Penang and Ipoh.[97] The MCP did not have clear regulations on acceptance into the party, but the procedure included a probation period of two to six months depending on class origin (*chengfen*), ranging from workers to those who were in reactionary organizations. The candidates had to have loyalty, "considerable" class consciousness (*xiangdang de jieji yishi*), and absolute acceptance of party leadership, and they had to be diligent and active in conducting revolutionary work.[98]

Overall, moods were pessimistic. MCP members were called "parlor revolutionists, if you please."[99] Local cells existed only on paper. The CC MCP reported, "[t]he party is unable to penetrate into the masses and lead their economic struggle. They looked at the struggles of the people with blank indifference and, furthermore, waited until the struggle developed its own course."[100] The party tried to take leadership of the protest actions already under way in order to build a party organization from those who participated in those struggles, as they should have, rather than attempting to build membership through everyday propaganda work. The MCP expressed this in the following way: despite radicalization of the masses, the party and red trade unions had failed to lead mass struggles. One example was the protest of Singaporean seamen who wanted to join the party, but the party could not expand the organization to include them; the same happened in Johor and Penang.[101]

Another problem was the party's inability to make use of "gray" auxiliary organizations and its lack of work in yellow unions, such as the mechanics' union.[102] In 1934, "some local committees considered it beyond their dignity to mingle with 'a bunch of gangsters [*liumang*

---

[96] Yong, *Origins of Malayan Communism*, pp. 210–216; Tai Yuen, *Labour Unrest in Malaya*; "Central Circular no. 9," 1930; Huang Muhan, "Worker Movement in Federated Malay States."

[97] "Magong laijian. Malaiya de qingshi yu dang de renwu [A Document Received from the MCP. The Situation in Malaya and the Tasks of the Party]," August 25, 1934; "Report of Labour Federation of Malaya no. 1 to the Profintern," March 25, 1934; "Resolution on the Labour Movement."

[98] "Magong zhongyang guanyu ru dang wenti de jueyi (dagang) [CC MCP on the Question of Acceptance into the Party (Draft)]," March 18, 1934, RGASPI 495/62/23/29–31.

[99] "Resolution of the C. C. of the C. P. of Malaya on the Activity of the Party in Key Industries. Abridged Translation," July 4, 1934, RGASPI 495/62/23/55–56.

[100] Ibid.; "Malaiya qingshi fenxi yu dang de renwu [The Analysis of the Situation in Malaya and the Tasks of the Party]," September 5, 1933.

[101] "Resolution of the C. C. of the C. P. of Malaya on the Activity of the Party in Key Industries."

[102] Ibid.

tuanti],'" such as members of the secret society Three Stars Party (Sanxingdang), and they denied the influence of yellow trade unions. To fix this, the party planned to send comrades to "study the actual living conditions of the workers and immediate needs which would be included in a program of struggle."[103] For propaganda in factories, the MCP planned to set up gray auxiliary organizations, such as factory and ship committees, music groups, and reading and sports clubs, as well as to publish a factory newspaper in simple language and to organize everyday economic struggles. In the next chapter, we will see what fruit these kinds of activities bore. The CC MCP advised local party committees to assist the cells but not impede their independent activity.[104]

The MCP continued to treat Comintern and CC CCP directives as guidance for its work.[105] All party leaders (*lingdao*) were "comrades from China" (*Zhongguo ji tongzhi*),[106] and the MCP referred to the CC CCP as the "CC" (*zhongyang*) beginning in 1933.[107] In 1935, when CCP members moved to Malaya, they were "transferred" (*zhuan*) between the MCP and the CCP.[108]

Indigenization and Regional Connections: The Comintern, the CCP, and the MCP in 1932–1936

The MCP was undoubtedly in dire straits, but it was also justifying its request for Comintern funding. In 1933–1934, both the MCP and the MFLU tried to reconnect with the Comintern and Profintern. The MFLU asked to send a Malayan, or at least a Chinese, comrade to help with work and, as always, promised the international authorities that it would call an

---

[103] Ibid.
[104] "Magong zhongyang guanyu zhongyao bumen gongren yundong de jueyi [CC MCP Resolution Regarding the Worker Movement in Important Industries]," July 4, 1933, RGASPI 495/62/20/7–14; "Decisions of the C. C. of the Malayan Party on the Intensification of the Labour Movement Passed on 20 March 1934."
[105] An example is the document "The Adoption by the Nanyang Provisional Committee of the Resolution of the Tenth Plenum of the [Executive Committee of the] Comintern and the Resolution of the CC about the Adoption of the Resolutions of the ECCI Tenth Plenum's Resolutions," March 15, 1930, RGASPI 495/62/1/28–44; "Malaiya gong-chandang di er ci kuodahui de zongjie [Summary of the Second Enlarged Congress of the MCP]," September 5, 1933, RGASPI 495/62/21/22–30; "Malaiya qingshi fenxi yu dang de renwu [The Analysis of the Situation in Malaya and the Tasks of the Party]."
[106] Guo Guang, "Magong laixin san hao [A Letter from the MCP no. 3]"; Guo Guang, "A Letter from Malaya No. 3" (English), RGASPI 495/62/22/8–12ob.
[107] "Malaiya qingshi fenxi yu dang de renwu [The Analysis of the Situation in Malaya and the Tasks of the Party]."
[108] Chen Yifei, "Jinian Minzhong tewei shuji Wang Yujie lieshi [Remembering the Secretary of the Special Committee of Fujian, Martyr Wang Yuji]," in Zhongguo renmin zhengzhi xieshang huiyi Fujian sheng Putian xian weiyuanhui, ed., *Putian wenshi ziliao di wu ji* [*Literary and Historical Materials of Putian*, vol. 5] (1983), pp. 45–52, esp. p. 48.

enlarged meeting and reorganize itself to rectify its errors.[109] The Comintern continued to work with the CCP in Southeast Asia and continued the course interrupted by the arrest of Rudnik and the dismantling of the FEB in 1931.[110] It is not clear whether the MCP received the letter from the Eastern Secretariat ECCI drafted between February and July 1931 by a number of Comintern cadres, including "Lilisian," as they scribbled Li Lisan's name in Russian on the list of Comintern cadres who were to receive a copy of the letter.[111]

In the fall of 1933, Wen Decai (阅德才) went to Shanghai, followed eight months later by Soong Tso Ming (Song Zhuoming, 宋卓明). There, the MCP had been promised a six-month Comintern subsidy after showing the Comintern that it desperately needed money, as there had not been enough people in the CC to prepare reports, do departmental work (*bu*), and publish party materials for several months. MCP cadre Guo Guang (国光) reported setting up training classes for Malay comrades at Malacca and Sembilan. However, local branches were uncooperative, and the main party activity remained the celebration of revolutionary anniversaries. A membership increase was reported in Johor and Johor Bahru, and in Singapore and Selangor in the factories, but arrests had decreased the numbers in Singapore and Sembilan. Guo Guang asked the Comintern to send propaganda materials in Malay, the Comintern's resolutions, and two experienced comrades, one with knowledge of both English and Chinese, as well as a Malay (*Malai ji tongzhi*) to do otherwise impossible work among non-Chinese (*Ma Yin ji tongzhi*) and youth.[112]

In 1934, the FEB's letter to the MCP was again based on MCP suggestions and criticisms as follows. The MCP was continuing to promote the involvement of non-Chinese and Chinese workers and peasants in the party, building the party in key industries and building the CYL, AIL, and unions into mass organizations. The FEB said that the MCP, the MFLU, and the CYL "stood aloof from the mass struggles," were lagging "behind revolutionary events," and were neglecting work among non-Chinese. The struggle had to be carried out under the slogans and

---

[109] "Report of Labour Federation of Malaya no. 1 to the Profintern," March 25, 1934.
[110] "Milton's" (Francis Waldron) Letter to the Eastern Secretariat of the ECCI, June 4, 1934, RGASPI 495/66/35/37–37ob.
[111] Eastern Secretariat of the Comintern's Letter to the MCP, April 14, 1931, RGASPI 495/62/18/42–53, esp. 42. Also see drafts from February 20, 1931, RGASPI 495/62/18/6–10, and "The Present Situation in Malaya and the Tasks of CPM," July 10, 1931, RGASPI 495/62/17/27–53.
[112] Guo Guang, "Magong laixin san hao [A Letter from the MCP no. 3]." Perhaps Song Zhuoming was "the fat Cantonese." Yong, *Origins of Malayan Communism*, p. 171.

demands of the masses.[113] Other points the Comintern repeated from the MCP reports, written in response to the Comintern's request for self-criticism, were as follows: insufficient struggles against reformists; a sectarian application of the united front from below; a lack of work in trade unions and in daily economic struggles; an inability to formulate and combine slogans to match the economic and political demands of the masses; inflexible and commanding methods of leadership; a lack of inner party democracy and life; a lack of daily activities in lower party committees; poor secret work; and a lack of illegal mass activities in combination with open legal methods of organization and struggle. The party had to eliminate opportunism, such as right opportunism and "tailism," passivity, and defeatism; to not underestimate the fighting spirit and capacity of Malayan, Chinese, and Indian workers; also to eliminate left opportunist sectarianism, putschism, "revolutionary phrase-mongering," and the disconnect between higher and lower party grades; and to simplify the sophisticated vocabulary of the party press in Malay and Indian languages, which was not "intelligible to the masses."[114]

The FEB expected the MCP to carry out its past directives and the CC MCP's decisions, and critically stated, "[t]he imperialist terror and lack of cadres cannot justify the weaknesses and shortcomings." Comintern recommendations not based on MCP letters included an organization of mass action under internationalist slogans, such as to oppose the shipment of troops and war supplies to China, India, and Burma as well as sabotage and strikes on Singaporean naval bases. The MCP should have taken into account the peculiar ethnic and social composition of the Malayan population in each region, urban center, and enterprise. Slogans based on Leninist policy regarding the national question and on specific local circumstances should have been put forward to encourage Malayan, Chinese, and Indian workers and peasants to rise up under the banner of proletarian internationalism and to fight against a common imperialist feudal oppressor. The national and class struggle in Malaya should also have been linked with solidarity protests in support of the Chinese and Indian Revolutions and in defense of the USSR. The FEB stated that "the party, by its practical mass work, [should] wed together the united revolutionary anti-imperialist front of the Malayan, Chinese, and Indian masses, at the same time exposing bourgeois nationalism, unmasking chauvinist propaganda like 'local autonomy for the Chinese in the Straits Settlement' and 'Malaya for the Malayans,' and struggling against the chauvinist propaganda of the British."[115]

---

[113] Comintern's Letter to the CC MCP, June 1, 1934, RGASPI 495/62/24/37–45.
[114] Ibid.
[115] Ibid.

The Comintern thus promoted the idea of an independent multiethnic Malayan nation-state. The party had to show that national oppression was inseparable from imperialist rule and that only communist party rule could fix that, as was the case in the USSR. The Comintern required the MCP to stop neglecting the peasant movement, stating, "[f]or the struggle for national liberation of the toiling masses of Malaya – Chinese, Indian, and Malay – to be successful, it must be linked up with the struggle for land and liquidation of all feudal remnants and then linked with the struggle of the proletariat. The agrarian revolution, to be successful, must be headed by the proletariat and linked with the struggle for national freedom." Other recommendations were to organize mass propaganda in certain important settings: railway centers (Sentul and Singapore); the most important tin mines and smelters; rubber factories and plantations, such as in the regions of Kuala Lumpur, Ipoh, and Seremban; and shipping lines and wharves in Singapore, Penang, Malacca, and Singapore's naval base. The MCP's success would depend on correct and skillful application of the united front from below. The MCP was thus "to radically reorganize the entire mass work of the party to rapidly transform into life the line and decisions of the Comintern and the CC of the CPM," to prepare the workers and peasants of Malaya "for the decisive struggle for Soviet power," and to become a strong mass Leninist party.[116]

Establishing Connections with Java and Indochina

In 1934, American Francis Waldron, aliases Eugene Dennis and Milton, the general secretary of the CPUSA in 1946–1957, was responsible for work "in South Seas countries" in the FEB – the Philippines, Malaya, Java, Siam, Burma, and Indochina.[117] The Comintern suggested that "one of the MCP's most vital international tasks" had to be "giving political guidance and organizational support to the communist groups and organizations in the Dutch East Indies, Siam, and Burma."[118] This was to include such activities as "creating contacts through the party and trade union, preparing cadres for these countries, mobilizing Malayan peasants and workers to support the revolutionary mass movement in these countries," and sending a detailed report with the next representative. The MCP was required to send a representative to the seventh world congress of the Comintern (July 25 to August 20,

---

[116] Ibid.
[117] Waldron's Letter, June 4, 1934.
[118] FEB, "Letter to the CC MCP about the 7th Congress of the Comintern etc."

1935), as well as a representative from the Dutch East Indies and three to five comrades for training, of which three would be Malay or Indian workers or poor peasants and two could be Chinese, provided they were "industrial workers and born in Malaya." This training would last for up to two years. In line with the amplified importance of Singapore, the Comintern promoted it as a place for the Politburo to sit and gave the MCP 1,500 American dollars as "material assistance" for six months but demanded a financial report. Seven hundred dollars were for the MCP, $300 for the MFLU, $200 for the CYL, and $300 for further development and strengthening of the work in the DEI, Siam, and Burma.[119] However, as police interrupted the rendezvous of Singaporean students Tan Sin Hoa (陈新华) and Li Kok Cheng (李国桢) in Shanghai in the summer of 1934 before they managed to meet with the Comintern, and as the MCP's receipt of the Comintern subsidy was intercepted in Singapore, the connection was lost.[120]

In an attempt to establish the regional relations pushed by the Comintern, the MCP connected with the CPUSA, thus closing the circuit of global connections of the Chinese communist network. The MCP had established connections with Siam but could not get in touch with those in Burma and Java, as it did not have cadres speaking Dutch, Malay, or English.[121] Later, the MCP reported that it had found a comrade who had been responsible for the work of a local committee in Java in 1926 and had just come back from Digoel Island, where captured PKI activists had been imprisoned after the suppression of the uprising in 1927. The MCP was not able to find a delegate from Indonesia to attend the Seventh Congress as the Comintern had requested, but it found an "Indonesian comrade" who had spent 1928–1933 in New York working in the American party. According to him, in Batavia there had been more than 100 comrades, some of whom had been briefly arrested, and about 500 revolutionary masses, but there was no party organization or program. The MCP planned to connect this comrade, whose name was erased, with a more able and energetic comrade to rebuild the party organization in Java. Again, as in the past, the MCP was reluctant to take responsibility for activities in Java: "In order to make those comrades agree with [zantong] what we say, complement our suggestions, and restore the organization, we will connect them directly to you, and you

[119] Ibid.
[120] Waldron's Letter to Moscow, August 19, 1934, RGASPI 495/66/35/88ob.; Guo Guang, Letter to the FEB, August 8, 1934, SMP D6152; Guo Wen, Letter to Guo Guang, August 27, 1934, SMP D7380.
[121] Guo Guang, Letter to the FEB, August 8, 1934.

will lead [*lingdao*] them directly."[122] The MCP reported, "[a]ccording to that Indonesian comrade, last year the party was not restored, but this year, according to what we've heard from sailors, in February, around the Chinese New Year [*huaren de xinnian*], there was a party that distributed leaflets. We are not sure which party it was, but as the sailor-comrade said, it was most likely our party [*wodang*]"[123] – that is, the CCP. Thus, the MCP finally established connections with Chinese-speaking communists in Java.

Indeed, Comintern cadre Musso reported to the Eastern Secretariat of the ECCI that in 1930, Chinese comrades were the only active communists in Indonesia, and their deportations back to China were covered by the media. As unlikely as it sounds, given MCP reports that it had no connections with Java, before they could start their mission, forty-six communists arriving from Singapore on instructions from the "South Seas communist party" had been arrested in Indonesia because of language problems and surveillance.[124] An anonymous report from October 1932 stated, "[n]ow, in Indonesia, we receive the impulse to work from our Chinese comrades. Here, pamphlets were confiscated from Chinese comrades, a certain number of them were arrested, and after trial several were deported to China."[125] The Chinese in Indonesia were sympathetic to the uprising in 1927, so it is quite likely that the Chinese were among the few active communists in Indonesia in 1933–1934.[126] However, fearing Chinese nationalism, the Dutch government labeled all Chinese who engaged in pro-China activities as communists. Thus, Reuters's report about 180 Chinese deported from the Dutch East Indies "as a result of police investigations into communist propaganda in the Riau Archipelago" did not mean that all of them were communists, *China Critic* argued.[127]

Compared to poor Malays and Indian immigrants, who rarely left their homes, the more affluent and mobile Chinese were suitable envoys. In accordance with Comintern demands, the MCP delegate for the Seventh Congress and the two students who were to go to Moscow to study were all locally born Chinese workers. The MCP could find neither an Indian

[122] Guo Guang, "Magong laixin san hao [A Letter from the MCP no. 3]."
[123] Ibid.
[124] Musso, "Situatsiia v Indonesii posle vosstaniia [The Situation in Indonesia after the Uprising]," September 22, 1930, RGASPI 495/214/752/53–76.
[125] "Polozhenie v Indonesii [Conditions in Indonesia]," September 8, 1932, RGASPI 495/214/756/43–49, esp. 49.
[126] "Programma deistviia kompartii Indonesii [The Program of the Communist Party of Indonesia]," late 1930s (after 1936), NIANKP materials, RGASPI 532/1/460/1–23, esp. 18–19.
[127] An article translated from *China Critic*, August 27, 1931, MRCA, September 1931, pp. 40–42, CO 273/572.

nor a Malay, as the two Malayan "poor peasants" who were recruited would not leave their families, and when they were sent for, they turned up but then ran away.[128] The MCP instead suggested that the Comintern use Malay and Indian networks, which would work in the manner of the Chinese chain migration. The MCP suggested that the Comintern find Malay and Indian comrades in Shanghai, who could send telegrams as a cover stating that they had found employment as sailors, if nothing else, for Malay and Indian MCP comrades.[129]

The FEB also pushed for connections with Indochina, but the MCP connected Vietnamese and Chinese networks because it was searching for a Comintern link. Notorious Sino-Vietnamese triple police informer and fake Comintern agent Lai Teck (Chinese name 莱特, Vietnamese name Nguyen Van Long) escaped to Singapore after the Siamese government's suppression of communists and got in touch with the MCP through the association of vegetable traders in 1934. Speaking good "Bolshevik," he rapidly achieved a top leadership position in the party. However, the Comintern report about prewar MCP leaders has no information about his studies in Moscow.[130] Coincidentally or not, the MCP dispatched a man to Bangkok in 1935 to search for contact with the Comintern,[131] and a letter from the communist party in Bangkok, which was mailed in March 1936, was intercepted by the Singapore police. Partly in legible English and partly in sympathetic "Annamite" (Vietnamese), it was written by a King (or Kong) in Bangkok and addressed to a Fong in Singapore. If Lai Teck were the only Vietnamese person in the MCP, the letter must have been addressed to him. The letter discussed money that the letter addressee, Mr. Choo in Hong Kong, was supposed to give to Fong in Singapore for travel – 100 "for his sister," 100 for the immigration tax, and 100 for a second-class ticket to Annam. In invisible ink on the back of the letter, Kong asked for "International Correspondence" published in 1936 and publications on political economy to send to a Xinhua bookstore

---

[128] Guo Guang, "Magong laixin san hao [A Letter from the MCP no. 3]."
[129] Guo Guang, Letter to the FEB, August 8, 1934.
[130] Yōji Akashi, "Lai Teck, Secretary General of the Malayan Communist Party, 1939–1947," *Journal of the South Seas Society* 49 (1994), pp. 37–103; Leon Comber, "'Traitor of all Traitors': Secret Agent *Extraordinaire*: Lai Teck, Secretary-General, Communist Party of Malaya (1939–1947)," *Journal of the Malaysian Branch of the Royal Asiatic Society* 83(2) (September 2010), pp. 1–25; "Biograficheskie svedeniia i kharakteristiki na rukovodiashchie kadry kompartii Malai, dannye v dokladakh Pen Haitan, byvshyi zav.otdelom propagandy singapurskogo gorodskogo komiteta partii Malai [Biographical Data and Personal References for the Leading Cadres of the MCP Provided by the Former Head of Propaganda of the Singapore City Committee of the MCP Peng Haitang]," RGASPI 495/62/30/1–10.
[131] Cheah, *From PKI to the Comintern*, p. 75.

address in Bangkok. The letter was addressed to Tran How Thanh (陈和诚) (who was also referred to as Tch'an Wo Sing by Cantonese speakers) in Shanghai, who forwarded letters to different addresses in Hong Kong and Singapore. Siamese communists had received 585 Hong Kong dollars from the MCP, but, apparently for establishment of the "Laos party" (via Brother Ly Tu Anh [李秀英], who was also referred to as Li Sao Ying in Cantonese), requested more money.[132]

In 1936, the need to connect with the Comintern and to sustain the Chinese communist "frontier enclave" (i.e., to bring in more cadres) in Laos encouraged connections between the Siamese party, the MCP, and China. In the same year, the MCP again asked the Siamese party to help it to reestablish a long-lost connection with the Comintern. The CC of the Siamese Communist Party (SCP) asked the MCP to help it to make connections with mainland China in order to recruit the Chinese into the party and reported in Vietnamese on conditions in the Indochinese peninsula and about major centers and mines and the "party" in Laos.[133] The Laos regional executive committee, comprised of Chinese, was reestablished in October 1935 (apparently after the suppression of the SCP in 1934),[134] but it was short of cadres. The Annam organization sent comrades to Laos, but those comrades were arrested and the connection with Annam was interrupted again. The SCP requested that the Comintern send back the two students who had been sent to Moscow to study as well as a Chinese comrade for translation work, and it additionally asked to be put in contact with the CCP or the Guangdong provincial organization so that it could recruit among Chinese, who comprised a quarter of the population of Siam and a large number of workers.[135] Thus, the need to connect with the Comintern fostered connections between Chinese communist cells in Indochina as well.

Likely inspired by the successful acquisition of a Comintern subsidy, the MCP started to report that the revolutionary movement (*geming yundong*) in Malaya was growing and would soon become a part of the world revolution.[136] Yet the MCP was also developing along the same trajectory as Chinese associations, and in 1934, regional lodges,

---

[132] "My mother is seriously ill, and I must return in order to look after her, but I do not know whether I have enough money for my journey. That is why I am pressing you for the money question." Letter of the CC SCP to the MCP, March 5, 1936, SMP D7376.

[133] Ibid.

[134] Goscha, *Thailand and the Southeast Asian Networks of the Vietnamese Revolution*, pp. 88–91.

[135] Letter of the CC SCP to the MCP, March 5, 1936.

[136] Guo Guang, Letter to the FEB, August 8, 1934.

huiguan, also started to recover following the depression.[137] The MCP revived leadership "investigation trips," supervisory tours to learn about the conditions in party cells, and thus finally got in touch with the lower grades of the party and the youth league. The CC ordered all party branches to survey party leadership in the protest actions in accordance with the survey plan (*tongjibiao*). Auxiliary "mass" organizations such as brotherhoods (*xiongdihui*) and sports societies (*tiyuhui*) also grew.[138]

Thus, in 1934–1936, the quest for Comintern resources and legitimacy pushed Chinese communists in Indochina to stay in touch with one another. During this time, the MCP finally established connections with Chinese-speaking communists in Java, but the Comintern did not receive that letter and the Comintern did not recognize the MCP as a Comintern section at the Seventh Congress in 1935.[139] For the Comintern, the struggle against fascism had become a priority after the Nazis rose to power in 1933, so the Seventh Congress announced yet another united front with social democrats and reformist labor unions and promoted the defense of political freedoms and parliamentary democracy.[140] On July 27, 1935, the Eastern Secretariat of the Comintern wrote the following note:

However, since in the last year and a half this organization [has] lost connections with the CI [Communist International] and CCP, under the direction of which it worked, and we don't know anything about its activity and organizational condition, until [the receipt of] further information about the condition in this party, the Eastern Secretariat will abstain from supporting its request to accept it into the CI as its section.[141]

By 1936, the PKI had still not been restored, and on January 6, 1936, Alimin asked the Comintern to send him to India to continue his efforts.[142] The Comintern and the CCP's interests in building parties in Southeast Asia came together during the time of the anti-Japanese united front. Zhou Enlai personally recommended that the Comintern "send comrade

[137] Wing Chung Ng, "Urban Chinese Social Organization."
[138] "C. C. MCP Circular Regarding the Decision to Conduct Survey of Mass Struggles," March 21, 1934; "Resolution on the Labour Movement."
[139] Letter of the C.C. SCP to the MCP, March 5, 1936; Guo Guang, "Magong laixin san hao [A Letter from the MCP no. 3]."
[140] Vatlin and Smith, "The Comintern."
[141] "Dokladnaia zapiska politicheskoi komissii IKKI [The Report of the Political Commission of the Eastern Secretariat of the ECCI]," July 27, 1935, RGASPI 495/14/385/12.
[142] Alimin ("Santos"), Letter, January 6, 1936, RGASPI 495/16/8/22–27; "Letter from Santos" (Alimin), 1937, RGASPI 495/16/8/63.

Santos [Alimin] to be at the disposal of the CCP."[143] At the same time, the Comintern was picking up on the growing importance of the *huaqiao* in wartime Southeast Asia because of their anti-Japanese efforts, and in the late 1930s the Comintern prepared a number of reports on conditions in Chinese communities in Burma, Malaya, and the Philippines.[144] Alimin worked in Moscow until mid-1939 in a foreign-language publishing house and as an editor of the translation of Lenin's writings into Malay. After that, he was dispatched to Indonesia but stayed in China, working in the CCP, and "struggled in the Chinese army against the Japanese."[145] Chin Peng met Alimin in 1945 while he continued to work on establishing a connection among Siam, Malaya, and the Dutch East Indies.[146]

The Comintern continued to promote the unity of the Chinese and other parties in Southeast Asia, and indigenization of the anti-Japanese China Salvation Movement was promoted in the Philippines. In a memorandum on the Philippine Islands discussed at a meeting of the Politburo of the Communist Party of the Soviet Union on June 9, 1938, the struggle of the Chinese people was mentioned in relation to the anti-Japanese struggle. The Philippine party was to support the struggle of the Chinese people, and the Friends of China organization was to be transformed into a mass organization of Filipinos and Chinese.[147] Furthermore, in the late 1930s, the Comintern continued to promote a pan-Asian and pan-Pacific vision based on communist networks. The basis of this network was networks of the Chinese and Indonesian Revolutions linked together:

We must establish connections between the national movement of Indonesians and the Chinese revolutionary movement in order to neutralize the attempts of

---

[143] "Zapiska ot zaveduiushchego otdela kadrov Guliaeva k sekretariu IKKI Dimitrovu [A Note from the Head of the Department of Cadres Guliaev to the Secretary of ECCI Dimitrov]," February 13, 1940, RGASPI 495/214/3bdossier/82.

[144] Vilkov et al., "Spravka o rabote"; "Spravka o Birme i o rabote sredi kitaiskikh emigrantov v Birme [Report about the Situation in Burma and about Work among Chinese Immigrants in Burma]," January 27, 1942, RGASPI 514/1/959/3–22; "Polozhenie kitaiskikh emigrantov na Filippinakh [The Conditions of the Chinese Immigrants in the Philippines]," January 28, 1942, RGASPI 514/1/929/3–25.

[145] "Santos Huan's Personal File."

[146] Chin Peng, *My Side of History as Told to Ian Ward and Norma Miraflor: [Recollections of the Guerilla Leader Who Waged a Twelve-Year Anti-Colonial War against British and Commonwealth Forces in the Jungles of Malaya]* (Singapore: Media Masters, 2003), p. 157.

[147] "Memorandum o filipinskikh obshchestvakh [Memorandum about Philippine Societies]," undated, RGASPI 495/20/564/8. The goal of "aid and unity with the USA and connection of the struggle of the Philippine people with the struggle of the people of China and Spain" was also promoted. "Resolution of CPPI," September 8, 1939, RGASPI 495/20/561/2–11, esp. 10.

Dutch and British imperialists to isolate the Indonesian liberation movement and suppress the Chinese revolutionary movement. Contact needs to be established with other national movements – in other colonies, such as in French Indochina and India. Then, friendly relations with leftist proletarian movements in Australia, New Zealand, and Japan must be established to round up the revolutionary bloc in the East, which will lead the struggle against military preparations that aim to prepare the new great war in this part of the world, which is led by Britain with the active support of Holland. All measures must be taken to strengthen the Pan-Pacific Workers' Secretariat.[148]

Thus, the Comintern and the CCP had similar rhetoric and activities in relation to the Chinese members of the CPPI and the Chinese workers, as well as the same promotion of internationalist support for the Chinese Revolution – in Malaya, in the Philippines, and in Indonesia.

The Eastern Secretariat of the executive committee of the Comintern was abolished in October 1936 as part of the centralization of Comintern apparatuses, making it more easily controlled by the general secretary of the ECCI, Stalin. Of the new secretariats established in its place, none was responsible for the work in Malaya.[149] Only the Academic Research Association for the Study of National and Colonial Problems (NIANKP) continued to collect materials on Malaya and Indonesia. Thus, no structure in the Comintern took a serious interest in the MCP until 1939, when the war pushed for drastic measures.

Thus, the Comintern and Chinese networks came together in the late 1930s. After the war, in 1949, the parties in Malaya, Indonesia, and Burma proposed to the CCP the organization of a Cominform of the East, but Mao rejected the proposal because of the civil war in China.[150] Leadership over the revolution in the East by the CCP was "granted" by Stalin and Liu Shaoqi's 1949 agreement on a Moscow–Beijing "division of labor" in fomenting the world revolution. Comintern–CCP relations in Southeast Asia were actually of mutual benefit and were not contradictory not only after[151] but even before the Second World War. Founded in

---

[148] "Programma deistviia kompartii Indonesii [The Program of the Communist Party of Indonesia]," late 1930s (most likely after 1936), NIANKP materials, RGASPI 532/1/460/1–23, esp. 18–19.

[149] Adibekov, Grant Mikhailovich, E. N. Shahnazarova, and Kiril K. Shirinya, *Organizatsionnaia struktura Kominterna, 1919–1943* [*Organizational Structure of the Comintern, 1919–1943*] (Moscow: ROSSPEN, 1997), pp. 186–190

[150] Shen Zhihua and Xia Yafeng, "Hidden Currents during the Honeymoon. Mao, Khrushchev, and the 1957 Moscow Conference," *Journal of Cold War Studies* 11(4) (Fall 2009), pp. 74–117.

[151] Chen Jian, "Bridging Revolution and Decolonisation: The 'Bandung Discourse' in China's Early Cold War Experience," in Christopher E. Goscha and Christian F. Ostermann, eds., *Connecting Histories: Decolonisation and the Cold War in Southeast Asia, 1945–1962* (Stanford, CA: Stanford University Press, 2009), pp. 137–171.

prewar times, communist networks continued to work: the parties of China, Vietnam, Laos, and Thailand helped the MCP in the 1950s.[152] The Comintern's network in Southeast Asia, into which the Chinese communist network was incorporated, laid the foundation for the MCP's postwar connections. Another circuit of the Chinese network ran through the transpacific network of the CPUSA and the Philippines.

The Philippines in the Orbit of the CPUSA

As we discussed in Chapter 2, the Philippine independence movement had had transnational connections since the late nineteenth century, having been a part of the vision of global liberation in anarchist and Asianist networks, which included none other but the "father of the Chinese nation," Sun Yatsen.[153] Established to protest the annexation of the Philippines, the first league against imperialism (1898) was revived by the Comintern in 1925; it became a CPUSA front organization. In the 1930s, the Chinese communists in the United States enthusiastically embraced this organization as a tool for fostering party organizations in the American empire, which included the Philippines. The newspaper of the Chinese section of the CPUSA, *The Chinese Vanguard* (*Xianfengbao*), reported about the struggles of the Chinese communities there and about the contributions of the Philippine Chinese to *The Chinese Vanguard*.[154]

Although the Comintern had already delegated the US party to supervise the party of the Philippines in 1924, "in close contact with the Eastern Department of the Comintern," and the Philippine labor movement leaders were already in contact with American communists in the Philippines,[155] before American communist Harrison George visited the Philippines in 1927, there had been no regular connection.[156] The Comintern planned to pay the US party $400 monthly to print a weekly

---

[152] Ang Cheng Guan, "Southeast Asian Perceptions of the Domino Theory," in Goscha and Ostermann, eds., *Connecting Histories*, pp. 301–331, esp. p. 318; Hara Fujio, *Mikan ni owatta kokusai kyōryoku: Maraya kyōsantō to kyōdaitō* [Unaccomplished International Co-operation: The Malayan Communist Party and the Fraternal Parties] (Tōkyō: Fūkyōsha, 2009).

[153] Anderson, *Under Three Flags*; Karl, *Staging the World*.

[154] "Wancheng sanbai fenxing dingyue da yundong [Fundraising Is Completed and Exceeded 300 Percent the Planned Amount]," "Feilübin kongqian weiyoude huaqiao dabagong [Unprecedented Strike of Chinese Workers in the Philippines]," *The Chinese Vanguard*, July 1, 1933; July 13, 1935.

[155] "The Philippines Independence Movement (by Hassan)," received on August 5, 1924, RGASPI 534/4/106; Cheah, *From PKI to the Comintern*, p. 9; "Immediate Tasks on the Work in the Philippine Islands," 1924, RGASPI 495/66/1/23.

[156] Undated, "The Philippine Islands," at least 1926, RGASPI 495/66/3/44.

party paper as well as to provide an allowance to fulltime organizers. A full-time American representative was to reside in the Philippines, and rallies against the sedition charges then placed against the leading members of the CPPI were to be organized among agricultural workers in California and Washington.[157]

For the Comintern, the importance of the Philippines in particular lay, as in the case of Malaya, in the anticipated imperialist war. The Comintern planned to work through labor unions, which operated legally in the Philippines and were organized separately by local Filipinos and Chinese migrants.[158] The independence of the Philippines was the main concern of the CPPI, and this fit the agenda of various pro-independence movements in the Philippines. The Comintern's suggestions for the Philippines were based on the 1927 suggestions of George and Evangelista, who had participated in the fourth congress of the Comintern.[159] A commission consisting of Mif, Vasiliev, Demard, Evangelista, Harrison George, and Humbert-Droz[160] developed "in Russian" a program for the establishment of a Philippine communist party, which was then to be discussed with "Philippine comrades,"[161] and a Comintern letter addressed to the workers' party of the Philippines was approved by American communists Lovestone and Foster.[162] Despite Harrison George's 1927 recommendation to evaluate the "possibility of the pan-Malaysian movement as an anti-imperialist base" in the Philippines, echoing Tan Malaka's pan-Malay aspirations, the Comintern relied on the Chinese network for its regional communications.[163]

The network of communication between the United States and Southeast Asia had run through China from early on. An American dubbed Conrad, likely Harrison George, suggested that the connection should run between the United States and Canton because the United States was planning to develop the production of rubber in the

---

[157] "Concrete Proposals regarding Philippines for Immediate Action," RGASPI 495/66/42/43.
[158] Letter from London, January 1, 1931, RGASPI 534/4/360/11.
[159] "Vopros o sozdanii sektsii kommunisticheskogo internatsionala na Filippinskikh ostrovakh [Question Regarding the Establishment of the Section of the Comintern in the Philippine Islands]."
[160] "Guiding Lines Concerning the Formation of a Communist Party in the Philippines Adopted at the Meeting of the Small Political Commission of the Secretariat of the ECCI on April 18th 1928," RGASPI 495/66/5/5–6.
[161] Theses Regarding the Formation of the Communist Party, April 21, 1928, RGASPI 495/66/5/14–16.
[162] "Letter to the Workers' Party," 1925, RGASPI 495/66/3/50–51.
[163] "Report by Comrade Harrison George on the Philippine Islands," October 17, 1927, RGASPI 495/66/4/1–14, esp. 11.

Philippines.[164] Starting from 1928, in order to establish connections with Filipino workers, Chinese communists asked the Comintern to send Gao Chenglie (高承烈) and Lin Qifeng (林啟锋) back to the Philippines from their studies in Moscow.[165] The Vladivostok bureau of the PPTUS, established in 1930, connected the Philippines and the United States, sending publications and asking for information from the Philippines.[166] In 1931, the Comintern communicated with the Philippine party through the Chinese section of the CPUSA, sending publications and directives to the CPPI, and in 1928, it planned to send Spanish-language propaganda from South America to the Philippines.[167] Likewise, Chinese comrades from the Philippines were sending suggestions to the Chinese faction of the CPUSA for its work among the Chinese migrants.[168] The Philippine–American network ran parallel to the Comintern–MCP network. Regional Chinese communist networks connected via individual communists moving along the immigration routes, banished by the authorities and looking for employment like Chen Jiafei, mentioned at the beginning of this chapter, who planned to find a teaching job in the Philippines after his arrest and deportation from Malaya in 1939.[169]

In the Corridors of *Minzu Guoji*: Money and Culture

The Comintern fostered connections amid the Chinese communist networks across Southeast Asia and the Pacific. These were the long-distance "extensions of the hometown that embraced men far away, realms of interests and affections" that were "both connective links and living cultural spaces."[170] Revolutionary networks formed a social and economic world more or less seamlessly for their Chinese inhabitants across some of these spaces. The migration of CCP members took place within the extended Chinese "nation" – the sojourning networks of overseas Chinese. In the internal operations of this new network, the Comintern

---

[164] Untitled document, undated, RGASPI 495/66/3/44.
[165] Gao Zinong, "Zhongguo gongchan qingnian tuan Feiliebin tebie difang gongzuo baogao [Work Report of the Philippine Special Local Committee of the Chinese Communist Youth League]."
[166] Carlis Johnson, Letter to Evangelista and Manahan, January 27, 1930, RGASPI 534/6/148/45.
[167] Draft Letter, "Situation in the Philippines and Tasks of the CPPI," October 21, 1931, RGASPI 495/66/28; Humbert-Droz, "Guiding Lines Concerning the Formation of a Communist Party in the Philippines," April 20, 1928, RGASPI 495/66/5/5–6.
[168] "A Letter from the Philippine Communists to the Chinese Bureau of the CPUSA," December 10, 1932, RGASPI 515/1/3181/5.
[169] Chen Jiafei, "Cong Malaiya Bile zhou dao Guangdong Huizhou [From Perak State in Malaya to Huizhou in Guangdong]."
[170] Kuhn, "Why China Historians Should Study the Chinese Diaspora," p. 168.

provided an additional sojourning channel, in Kuhn's terms, through which money, ideas, and people circulated between China, Malaya, and the international communist network and its center, the Comintern. We have already discussed the circulation of people in this chapter, so let us look at money and culture.

Money

The Chinese communist organization in Malaya, like other Chinese overseas organizations, which had included revolutionaries since the time of Sun Yatsen, existed on subscription money, school tuition, and "borrowing from the masses," that is, from affluent members of the Chinese community. Local branches passed money on to their superior organizations in a pyramidal manner, leaving an amount for their own expenses. However, that was never enough. For years, Comintern subsidies were desperately sought but were received only once in 1934 and possibly in 1928 from Fu Daqing, as discussed in Chapter 2. Remarkably, these subsidies were granted even though the MCP was not recognized as a Comintern section.

Until July 1929, the party had relied on outside sources. Apparently because the party could not repay its debt, voluntary contributions were introduced, while "the membership fees were exorbitant taxes and duties."[171] The Central Committee's monthly income was half of what was needed (60 out of 120 yuan), and it had to borrow the deficit "from the comrades."[172] At the founding conference, "income contributions" were introduced instead of voluntary contributions, half of which were to be passed on to the new CC.[173] The CC was disconnected from local economies and needed external support. The Singapore town committee complained that its monthly income from rent and comrades' school fees passed on to the central organization was only $40, which did not allow for printing, a secretariat, and branch offices. The monthly cost of 2,000 weekly copies of *Hong qi (Red Flag)* in Malay, "Hindustan," and Chinese was 135 Malayan dollars. In 1931, about $20 per month was the cost of having one or two comrades produce printed materials. None of the local committees had a regular press, and financial difficulties were consistently raised by representatives from all regions at the founding meeting.[174] In fact, the newly established MCP was a committee on top of the existing Chinese party

---

[171] Nanyang gongzuo baogao [Nanyang Work Report], 1929; "Minutes of the Third Representative Conference of Nanyang," p. 132.
[172] "Minutes of the Third Representative Conference of Nanyang," p. 123.
[173] Ibid., p. 142.
[174] At the time, 1 US dollar was equal to 1.65 Malayan dollars. "Informatsiia o Malaiskikh Shtatakh [Information about the Malay States]," p. 28ob.

organization that required additional funding. The MCP founding conference decided that the new Malayan party should pay $100 to the preliminary
committee of the Nanyang joint committee (or secretariat), organized
through the merging of separately organized ethnic parties, until it was
approved by the Comintern and could receive a Comintern subsidy.[175]

In August 1930, the MCP listed monthly party expenses through Ho
Chi Minh: the printing house required $110, propaganda $5, organizational expenses $50, the secretariat $50, communications $30, and work
among youth $10. The total was $300, with a monthly income of $200
and a deficit of $100, which the party asked to be covered. In October
1930, party CC required the following budget from the Comintern:
house rent and publishing expenses required 450 Malayan dollars,
expenses to hire five workers 40, communication expenses 10, paper
13, ink 3, and wax patterns (*voskovki*) 20, for a total of 135 Malayan
dollars.[176] The main source of revenue for the MFLU was membership
fees: a two-cent fee came to $2 per month plus donations. Clearly, that
was not enough. The trade union leaders, however, thought that it was
not appropriate to have a job other than organizing trade unions. In a
report on Malaya's labor movement, MCP–Comintern liaison Wang
Mei Hong (Huang Muhan) stated, "[t]he federation cadres have to have
jobs. How can we require that, under such circumstances, they invest
their souls into their work?"[177] Previously, in 1929, party leaders had to
find jobs in factories, when the financial situation was very difficult.[178]
In 1934, the MFLU asked for 100 Singapore dollars monthly as the
budget of the MFLU of $40 was not enough. The local union received
$10 per month.[179] MCP membership fees in Singapore were no
more than $90, which was not enough to pay the rent for party
headquarters.[180]

Any subsidy, especially that which came with international recognition,
like a Comintern subsidy, was important for the MCP. The Comintern
promoted the party's self-sufficiency based on fee collections that would
also "strengthen the organization and political connection between the
workers and the party" and finance publications in the Chinese, Indian,
and Malay languages, as well as fees from "sympathizers and broad toiling
masses."[181] The CYL decided to establish economic committees in

[175] "Minutes of the Third Representative Conference of Nanyang," pp. 119–120.
[176] "Informatsiia o Malaiskikh Shtatakh [Information about the Malay States]," p. 2.
[177] Huang Muhan, "Worker Movement in Federated Malay States."
[178] "Minutes of the Third Representative Conference of Nanyang," p. 132.
[179] "Report of Labour Federation of Malaya no. 1 to the Profintern," March 25, 1934.
[180] This was according to Ho Chi Minh, whose information came from the MCP. Ho Chi
    Minh, "Malay."
[181] FEB, "To the Malayan Comrades."

September 1931 for the collection of subscriptions,[182] as the amount of money the Comintern sent to the MCP was not large. In 1934, a Chinese "bourgeois," the son of silver and gold merchant Un, who is discussed in more detail in Chapter 6, "lent" $500, which was one-third of the Comintern subsidy, to the CC of the MCP.[183] By then, the party had accumulated a debt of $1,000 and thus did not have enough money for its activities, let alone for assistance to the parties in Indonesia, Siam, and Burma and to the CYL and labor unions. The MCP felt entitled to demand that the subsidy be calculated for a longer time period and that an additional sum be paid. The MCP had also borrowed money from funds in support of the Chinese "soviet" revolution, collected from "the masses."[184]

Thus, money was flowing through the corridors connecting enclaves in China and Malaya and through the center of the world revolutionary network, the Comintern. The MCP was sending money to the CCP as a contribution, while the CCP was also to give the MCP a "subsidy." The MCP wrote to the Comintern cadre in Shanghai, Guo Wen (国文), that the MCP had collected $1,000 for the support of the Chinese "soviet" revolution, which it intended to pass on to the CCP. The MCP requested that the FEB deduct $400 from the Comintern subsidy, and the MCP would send the remaining $600 later. As before, the MCP wanted the CCP to publish in its papers the amount it had collected or to provide a receipt.[185] Until the late 1930s, MCP members also sent money to party organizations to support the families of arrested communists back home in Fujian.[186]

Similar to how Chinese trade in the frontier enclaves of the European colonies had linked the Chinese economy to world markets of ideas and technology,[187] the Comintern incorporated the Chinese revolutionary enterprise into the global market of anticolonial liberation. By promising money to the MCP, the Comintern offered a hope of employment to higher-level party cadres. The promise of money and international legitimacy was the leverage extending the Comintern's influence over the MCP, while donations from the "masses" were crucial for the MCP's survival, as is discussed in the next chapter.

[182] MRCA, December 1931, p. 53, CO273/572.
[183] D. S. Jones, "Letter from H. B. M. Consulate-General Concerning Malayan Communists," August 30, 1935, SMP D6954.
[184] Guo Guang, "Magong laixin san hao [A Letter from the MCP no. 3]," March 24, 1934.
[185] Guo Guang, Letter to the FEB, August 15, 1934, SMP D6152. Memorandum, undated, RGASPI 515/1/4117/42–59.
[186] Chen Jiafei, "Cong Malaiya Bile zhou dao Guangdong Huizhou [From Perak State in Malaya to Huizhou in Guangdong]."
[187] Kuhn, "Why China Historians Should Study the Chinese Diaspora," p. 170.

Culture

Aside from money, language – in Kuhn's terms, culture – flowing in the corridors of *huaqiao* networks linked hometowns in China and cultural niches created by the Comintern in different places in Southeast Asia to one another and back to China. Self-criticism was the language of the relationship between the MCP and the Comintern and a part of Bolshevization as the only method of constant self-improvement of the communist parties: "Constant criticism by the communists of the mistakes committed, permanent control of their own actions, evaluation of the experiences gained in protests, examination of shortcomings and achievements in their work – this is extremely important for the development of the communist party."[188] Criticism and self-criticism had central roles in the organizational culture of the CCP[189] and among the Vietnamese communists. "By mutual criticism we can rectify our mistakes," said Ho Chi Minh at the founding conference meant to develop the MCP into a true communist party.[190] This criticism also involved criticism of superiors, including the Comintern itself. However, a 1960s' refugee from the PRC with experience under both the GMD and the CCP contrasted the catharsis achieved through criticism with the GMD's tendency to stifle the expression of grievances, leading to deepened conflict.[191] Whether criticizing their party for its lack of a mass following and its dearth of non-Chinese members or complaining about the need for funds and cadres to implement the Comintern's directives and therefore receive Comintern money and manpower, Malayan communists were active participants in the Comintern's policy making. In their correspondence with the Comintern, they expressed their agreement or disagreement with the Comintern's suggestions as well as criticizing it for not paying enough attention to the Nanyang, as did sailor Wang Yung Hai, or for not issuing special directives for the Nanyang through the CCP. At the time, the Comintern and the CCP represented a democratic institutional culture that appealed to the Chinese communists in Malaya. The Comintern's encouragement of criticism thus fed into what Hung-yok Ip calls the revolutionary intellectuals' self-construction as the deserving

---

[188] "The Philippines, Resolutions on the Trade Union Question," October 16, 1929, RGASPI 495/66/18/70–73, esp. 73.

[189] Frederick Teiwes, *Politics and Purges in China: Rectification and the Decline of Party Norms, 1950–1965* (Armonk, NY: M. E. Sharpe, 1979–1992). See also Liu Shaoqi's "Letter to the Party Centre Concerning Past Work in the White Areas, 4 March 1937," in Tony Saich and Benjamin Yang, *The Rise to Power of the Chinese Communist Party: Documents and Analysis* (Armonk, NY: M. E. Sharpe, 1996), pp. 773–786.

[190] "Minutes of the Third Representative Conference of Nanyang," p. 145.

[191] Lowell Dittmer, "The Structural Evolution of 'Criticism and Self-Criticism,'" *China Quarterly* 56 (October–December 1973), p. 709.

elite of the revolution, which elevated the party to a revolutionary vanguard most capable of self-reform.[192] Finally, the Comintern was "international," and international legitimacy was worth a lot.

Self-criticism fed into the employment and adaptation needs of Chinese
intellectuals who became party cadres. Wang Gung Wu has argued, "[t]he
Chinese had a keen sense of social leadership and they had traditionally seen
political leadership as deriving from deep-rooted ideas of status and the
potential for public office."[193] The Comintern provided one of few channels
for upward mobility for first-generation immigrants, who did not have
political rights, unlike their more affluent co-ethnics in centuries-old
Chinese communities in which Chinese were predominately owners of
family businesses of different sizes. The MCP's self-critical reports to the
Comintern had ritualistic meanings and functions. The MCP wrote,
"[r]eport-making is helpful in strengthening and developing party work."[194]
To report (baogao) was the orthopraxis and expression of loyalty. It was a
culture of exchange between the Comintern and local communists.

The Soviet Union was, for the MCP, an inspiration and a "bright
future," and the Comintern was the world revolution headquarters (shijie
geming de zongcan moubu), an administrative center established by
Lenin.[195] Baogao and self-criticism were performative in Austin's sense of
the word.[196] Reporting had a result on a functional level: the use of
communist ideology was a demonstration of loyalty to the Comintern,
and, as pointed out earlier, the content of the reports was often symbolic.
The number of participants in demonstrations, instead of being concrete
and verifiable, was usually a symbolic number representing many wan (tens
of thousands). For example, the number of people among the masses
awoken by the protests of the fall of 1939 was "one billion,"[197] and in the
Ipoh region after tin mines were closed and rubber production was sus-
pended, there were "one hundred thousand" unemployed miners.[198]

---

[192] Ip, Intellectuals in Revolutionary China, pp. 7, 79.
[193] Wang Gungwu, "Chinese Politics in Malaya," China Quarterly 43 (1970), pp. 1–30, esp.
p. 3.
[194] Guo Guang, "Magong laixin san hao [A Letter from the MCP no. 3]," March 24, 1934.
[195] "Magong zhongyang gongzuo jueding [CC MCP Work Resolution Regarding the
Fifteenth Anniversary of Liebknecht and Luxembourg's Death and Tenth
Anniversary of Lenin's Death."
[196] John L. Austin, How to Do Things with Words. 2nd edn. Edited by J. O. Urmson and
Marina Sbisá (Cambridge, MA: Harvard University Press, 1976).
[197] "Maijin [Forward]," December 1939–early 1941, RGASPI 495/62/28/53–84, esp. 59;
"Magong di er ci zhongzhihuiyi jueyian [The Resolutions of the Second Plenum of the
Executive Committee of the CC MCP]," February 20, 1940, RGASPI 495/62/28/18–
36, esp. 24.
[198] "An Open Letter from the C. C. of the C. P. of Malay to the Working Class of Malay,"
November 7, 1930, RGASPI 495/62/6/1a–4.

Self-criticism was a discourse, a mode of communication, and a form of praxis – a way to get things done. This practice, however, projected the impression that the party was always on the brink of collapse, let alone far from becoming the mass proletarian party the Comintern required.

Conclusion

Like other translation slippages,[199] the case of *minzu* reflected the balance of power. Yet in the end, the Comintern, which itself disbanded in 1943, developed CCP networks through the MCP as the connecting hub responsible for developing a regionwide communist network in Southeast Asia as well as transpacific networks of American communism. Despite adopting the Comintern's idea of a multiethnic national party, in practice the MCP continued to organize according to ethnicity. Comintern interactions with the MCP represented a case of synthesis. The Comintern's contribution to this process included promises of eagerly sought financial aid, propaganda materials, qualified cadres (especially those speaking English or Malay) to work among the different ethnic groups of Malaya,[200] ideological resources, and the "organizational culture" of the Bolsheviks. This was a democratic participation model outside of and alternative to that of the British state. It was based on a culture of self-criticism and on the suggestions of local party leaders, with the Comintern functioning as an international public sphere both requiring self-criticism and allowing room for criticism of itself by local communists. The Comintern's mutually reliant and beneficial regional relationship with the CCP and its local chapter, the MCP, was one of "obedient autonomy."[201] The Comintern pursued its interest in a revolution in Southeast Asia through CCP networks, of which the MCP was the connecting hub, with most of the leaders coming from China, often to be shortly thereafter banished and replaced by new arrivals.

To be sure, such a relationship between Chinese networks and the Comintern in Southeast Asia was unique in the atmosphere of Stalin's rising control in the Comintern. This relationship was also possible because the Comintern showed a lack of close attention and interest in the region. Illustrating this are the examples of Li Lisan, representing China, and Liao Huanxing, representing Germany and the League Against Imperialism, both areas of Soviet geostrategic interest, who

<hr/>

[199] See Lydia He Liu, *The Clash of Empires: The Invention of China in Modern World Making* (Cambridge, MA: Harvard University Press, 2006).
[200] CC MCP, "From Malaya. To the FEB," February 7, 1931.
[201] Erika Evasdottir, *Obedient Autonomy: Chinese Intellectuals and the Achievement of Ordinary Life* (Vancouver, BC: University of British Columbia/University of Hawaii Press, 2004).

were summoned to Moscow and held there without the right to leave and who were subjected to disciplinary punishments with Soviet and other foreign communists in Stalin's labor camps.

Meanwhile, far from these world centers of power, in Southeast Asia, like Chinese merchants, who, in Kuhn's words, "borrowed" European empires, the MCP borrowed the Comintern's empire to carve out its niche.[202] The MCP continued to respond to Comintern requests for propaganda for the defense of the Soviet Union and pitched policies that negatively impacted the Chinese community as British war preparations began against the Soviet Union.[203]

Similar to globalization reinvigorating old networks in other contexts, the Comintern fostered existing Chinese network connections and helped the CCP expand.[204] The Comintern used the Chinese Southeast Asian network to connect parties in the region because it was the only network available to the Comintern at the time. In the meantime, the CCP merged with the institutions of anti-imperialist leagues and thus became a kind of International of Nationalities in the Nanyang, as imagined by Hu Hanmin. Furthermore, in Southeast Asia, unlike the situation in other parts of the world, the internationalism of the Comintern matched that of the Chinese Nationalists, the GMD, in China. In contrast, European immigrant communist leader Victorio Codovilla, the founder of the South American Bureau of the Comintern in Buenos Aires in 1926, rejected the Comintern's suggestion to create an Indian republic in the South American Andes based on the pre-Columbian Inca empire and refused to embark upon an indigenous national project.[205] Unlike Japanese pan-Asianism and Enver Paşa's pan-Islamism – which, after a short-lived concord, clashed with Bolshevik internationalism in Central Asia, Manchuria, and Siberia[206] – the Chinese and Comintern internationalisms remained in harmony until after the Second World War.

The MCP, due to a lack of language skills, not only established connections between Chinese communists in Southeast Asia and in the United States but also recruited second-generation Chinese students in Malaya for study in Moscow. The MCP "indigenized," but only within the Chinese community, extending *huaqiao* networks as part of the

[202] Kuhn, "Why China Historians Should Study the Chinese Diaspora," p. 163.
[203] Guo Guang, "Magong laixin san hao [A Letter from the MCP no. 3]," March 24, 1934.
[204] Timothy N. Harper, "Empire, Diaspora and the Languages of Globalism, 1850–1914," in Anthony Gerald Hopkins, ed., *Globalization in World History* (London: Pimlico, 2002), pp. 141–166. Hong Liu, "Old Linkages, New Networks: The Globalization of Overseas Chinese Voluntary Associations and Its Implications," *China Quarterly* 155 (1998), pp. 582–609.
[205] Becker, "Mariátegui, the Comintern, and the Indigenous Question in Latin America."
[206] Aydin, *The Politics of Anti-Westernism*, pp. 145–149.

Comintern's plan to connect Southeast Asia through a communist network. The Comintern's demand for locally born Chinese was in tune with the Nanjing policy of "nationalizing" the overseas Chinese, especially in strengthening locally born Chinese identification with China. We will see in the next chapter that this was part and parcel of the Nanjing GMD's policy of promoting the expansion of Chinese influence in Southeast Asia, the localization of Chinese migrants, and the idea of establishing a *minzu guoji*.

Part III

The GMD, the MCP, and the Nation: *Minzu* Cultivated, *Minzu* Lost

6   *Minzu* Cultivated, 1928–1940

Countering Japan's Southward Expansion: The GMD and the Education of the Chinese Overseas

As we have seen, internationalism created nationalism during the interwar period and became the vehicle for the anticolonial and colonial goals of aspiring nations. China was not unique at the time in its aspirations to win the Darwinian race to be first among nations. As Protestant missionary civilizational discourse, colonial aspirations dressed up in civilizational goals were also a part of the internationalist project of the interwar period.[1] Colonialism, like socialism, was an accepted aim among leading actors. Famously, in October 1922, lecturer Juin Li at Ji'nan University called on the *huaqiao* to unite and stand up against colonial governments instead of asking for help from the Chinese government. This attitude, he said, was the reason why China had fallen behind Europe in colonial possessions. He prophesied the revolt and independence of the Malay Peninsula and implored students: "Shoulder this big burden … Now is the time for you students to build up your political ability, because the future masters of the Malay Peninsula are you students of this college."[2]

For the Nanjing GMD government, the allegiance of Chinese communities in the Nanyang became vitally important with the onset of Japanese aggression in 1928, and it intensified its policy of indoctrinating the overseas Chinese and promoting the colonization of Southeast Asia, which had long been seen in China as a Chinese sphere of influence.[3] The GMD cultivated identification with China and anti-Japanese activities, such as boycotts, as well as pan-Asian ideas. The idea of a pan-Asian *minzu guoji*, an International of the East, or a Three Principles International headed by China, advocated first by the left wing of the GMD, including Chen

---

[1] Robert, "First Globalization?"
[2] Guillemard to Duke of Devonshire, November 18, 1922, MBPI No. 8, October 1922, item 41, CO273/518, cited in Khoo, "The Beginnings of Political Extremism in Malaya," p. 174.
[3] Liu Jixuan and Shu Shicheng, *Zhonghua minzu tuozhi Nanyang shi* [*The History of the Chinese Colonization of Nanyang*] (Shanghai: Guoli bianyi guan, 1935).

Gongbo, was a key element in the GMD's policy of countering Japan's southward expansion and was promoted in overseas Chinese schools.[4] In November 1929, at a public meeting called by the GMD regarding the education of overseas Chinese (*huaqiao jiaoyu huiyi*), it was resolved to promote national consciousness (*minzuxing*) and citizen education (*guomin jiaoyu*), including Mandarin education (*guoyu jiaoyu*), resisting "slave education," and making China the avant-garde of world development.[5]

In reaction to the ban of the Malayan GMD in 1930, Hu Hanmin called for a strengthening of Chinese nationalism in overseas communities and an end to Western domination in China.[6] In 1930, under the supervision of Dai Jitao, a new periodical called *Xin Yaxiya* (*New Asia*) espoused pan-Asianism in order to justify China's sovereignty over the peoples of the hinterland. In addition to Hu Hanmin's piece, this journal whose goal was to keep Sun Yatsen's ideas alive, published many articles on *minzu guoji*.[7] By propagating Chinese nationalism among overseas Chinese communities in the Nanyang, the GMD aimed to ward off Japanese expansion in the region in a manner reminiscent of the United States' Monroe Doctrine, which Kawashima Shin refers to as the policy of "restoring the tribute states."[8]

[4] So Wai-Chor, *The Kuomintang Left in the National Revolution, 1924–1931: The Leftist Alternative in Republican China* (Oxford: Oxford University Press, 1991), pp. 84–85, 92, 234; Li Yinghui, *Huaqiao zhengce yu haiwai minzuzhuyi (1912–1949)* [*The Origin of Overseas Chinese Nationalism (1912–1949)*], pp. 506–507. Essays about *minzu guoji* appeared in various periodicals. See Hu Hanmin (recorded by Zhang Zhenzhi), "Minzu guoji yu disan guoji [International of Nationalities and the Third (Communist) International]," *Xin Yaxiya* [*New Asia*] 1(1) (1930), pp. 23–27; Han Hui, "Minzu yundong yu minzu guoji [The Nationalist Movement and the International of Nationalities]," *Xin Dongfang* [*New East*] 3(8) (1932), pp. 108–129; Hong Weifa, "Guanyu minzu guoji [About the International of Nationalities]," *Xin Yaxiya* [*New Asia*] 3(4) (1932), pp. 48–54; Tian Ren, "Tongxun: Gouzhu Dongfang minzu guoji de jichu shi women weida de shiming [News Report: To Build the Foundation of the International of Nationalities of the East Is Our Great Mission]," *Xin Dongfang* [*New East*] 3(8) (1932), pp. 156–165; Tong Xuenan, "Minzu guoji de xuyao [The Need for an International of Nationalities]," *Jingguang* [*Unwinking Light*] 1(1) (1932), pp. 69–72; Cheng Shengchang, "Tongxun: Zuzhi Dongfang minzu guoji wenti zhi taolun [News Report: Discussing the Question of the Organization of the International of Nationalities of the East]," *Xin Dongfang* [*New East*], Anniversary Issue (1931), pp. 404–413; Guo Sizheng, "Bei yapo minzu guoji zuzhi wenti [The Question of Organization of the International of Nationalities of the Oppressed Peoples]," *Xin Ping* [*New Peace*] (1931), pp. 10–11, 92–116. For *minzu guoji* as constructed in opposition to the Comintern, see Craig A. Smith, "China As the Leader of the Small and Weak: The *Ruoxiao* Nations and Guomindang Nationalism," *Cross-Currents* 6(2) (November 2017), pp. 36–60.
[5] Li Yinghui, *Huaqiao zhengce yu haiwai minzuzhuyi (1912–1949)* [*The Origin of Overseas Chinese Nationalism (1912–1949)*], pp. 505–507.
[6] Yong and McKenna, *The Kuomintang Movement in British Malaya*, pp. 160–161.
[7] Prasenjit Duara, *Sovereignty and Authenticity: Manchukuo and the East Asian Modern* (Lanham, MD: Rowman & Littlefield Publishers, 2003), pp. 102–103.
[8] Kawashima Shin, "China's Reinterpretation of the Chinese 'World Order,' 1900–1940s," in Anthony Reid and Zheng Yangwen, eds., *Negotiating Asymmetry: China's Place in Asia* (Singapore: National University of Singapore Press, 2009), pp. 139–158.

A British translation of a 1931 address by the president of the Institute of Culture in Shanghai and the president of the Control Yuan of the GMD government, Yu Yujin, reads as follows: "The only fault of the weak races of the East is that they are not united. They must form an organisation for the overthrow of Imperialist [*sic*], and China must be its centre." To achieve this, the GMD would establish "the organisation of an Eastern International by the Chinese Kuomintang with the Three People's Principles of Dr. Sun Yat Sen as the revolutionary doctrine for all weak Eastern races who are struggling for international, political and economic equality." This was to be a league against imperialism in the East and would have connections with the Eastern proletariat. The document goes on: "In his will, Dr. Sun urged us to help the weak races and to lead the world's revolution in order to set up a 'utopia' for the world ... Only then can we be in a position to offer resistance to the imperialistic encroachments and be vanguards of the world revolution."[9]

On September 3, 1931, the central standing committee of the GMD resolved to promote education on the Three People's Principles among overseas Chinese and the idea of a relationship between overseas Chinese and the Chinese Revolution, as well as between Japan's southward expansion and the livelihood of overseas Chinese. To achieve the goal of raising the status of overseas Chinese to parity with other races, "racial consciousness" (i.e., Chinese nationalism) was to be cultivated, and the "standard of living and self-managing and productive ability" among overseas Chinese was to be improved. Regarding the relationship between the "weak races" of the world and the Three People's Principles, students were "to understand their local environment and their own position with the object of extending the influence of the overseas Chinese." Otherwise, ethics were to be modeled on "old-time Chinese culture" and "physical culture education," with "lectures on current events in Chinese [to] be frequently delivered so as to arouse the patriotism of overseas Chinese." Knowledge essential to local existence was also to be promoted.[10]

This GMD policy prepared the ground for acceptance of the Comintern's indigenization ideas, which fused the global and the local to create the national. The emancipation of the oppressed peoples of the Nanyang through a *minzu guoji* and Chinese overseas unity and strength were tied together in the discourse of the Nanjing GMD's policy toward the *huaqiao*, which aimed to cultivate the Chinese identity of locally born

---

[9] "A Review of the Misery of the Weak Races of the East," *Wenhua banniankan* [*Culture Biannual*] (February 1931), MRCA, June 1931, pp. 49–51, CO 273/572.
[10] MRCA, December 1931, pp. 21–24, CO 273/572.

Chinese. Thus, the GMD promoted indigenization with the goal of empowering the Chinese community, just as the MCP was doing in its campaign against the Alien Registration Ordinance in 1932–1933. Around the same time, the Comintern relied on the Chinese to foster a world revolution in Southeast Asia and promoted cooperation between Chinese immigrants and locals. Regarding anti-imperialism, Chinese nationalism, and the localization of Chinese in the Nanyang, the goals of the GMD and the MCP were identical.

As in Malaya, Chinese communists in the United States were also embedded in the GMD policy of "Chinese colonization" and expansion. *The Chinese Vanguard*, produced by Chinese communists in the United States, like other Nanjing-era publications targeting the Chinese overseas, devoted much space to introducing the life of the *huaqiao* in the Americas and around the world and promoted campaigns for the rights of Chinese laborers and the idea of Chinese leadership in the revolution, such as in Cuba, where laws against foreign laborers adopted in the early 1930s, similar to Malaya's discriminatory laws, ignited the concerns of the Chinese.[11]

In China, students were writing essays on the topic of *minzu guoji*.[12] "General principles of propaganda for the overseas Chinese to study," a document by the GMD central propaganda department, stressed the importance of complying with Nanjing's educational policies to develop identification with China.[13] Understandably, the British government resisted the introduction of Chinese nationalist education in schools and banned the importation of textbooks.[14]

The agents of Nanjing nationalism were schoolteachers who had graduated from China's new teachers' colleges, first established by the GMD in the 1920s as part of its policy of establishing control of the countryside.[15] Teachers' colleges and schools were set up when the GMD and the CCP shared a commitment not only to patriotism and revolution but also to political institutions. The Central China Teachers' College in Wuhan in the mid-1920s maintained that every new teacher was a member of the GMD. In Guangdong, Chen Jiongming appointed one of the founders of the CCP,

[11] Benton, *Chinese Migrants and Internationalism*, pp. 42–45.
[12] "Gaozhong weiwen zhi bu: Minzu guoji [High School Essay: International of Nationalities]," *Xuesheng wenyi congkan* [*Anthology of Student Writings*] 6(9) (1931), pp. 79–90.
[13] MRCA, March 1931, CO 273/571, pp. 4–6.
[14] Ta Chen, *Emigrant Communities in South China*, p. 279.
[15] Ibid., p. 277. A Nanjing GMD regulation prescribed that Chinese school prefects had to be recruited in China. Li Yinghui, *Huaqiao zhengce yu haiwai minzuzhuyi (1912–1949)* [*The Origin of Overseas Chinese Nationalism (1912–1949)*], p. 508; Cong Xiaoping, *Teachers' Schools and the Making of the Modern Chinese Nation-State, 1897–1937* (Vancouver, BC: University of British Columbia Press, 2007), p. 128.

Chen Duxiu, to oversee education prior to 1923. School reform was one of the first initiatives of the GMD government after it came to power in Guangdong, and in 1925 the GMD published textbooks on the history and principles of the party.[16] In the 1930s, teachers' schools in Shandong and Hebei were centers for communist organizing.[17] Many communist teachers from Fujian, even those who had formally been members of the GMD, found employment in the Nanyang. Teachers born and trained in China promoted patriotic ideas in Chinese schools in the language of revolution, anti-imperialism, and protection of overseas Chinese. It is not surprising that teachers in Chinese schools in 1927 were referred to as "emissaries from Moscow."[18] Although financed by dialect communities (*bang*) and run by regional lodges (*huiguan*), Chinese schools were hotbeds of communism.[19] Schools were often raided by the police, who, upon discovering copious communist propaganda, revoked their registration.[20] Intellectuals had been the most active communists in Malaya since 1927, but they engaged in little protest activity, at least before 1930.[21]

As in mainland China, students were central to the nationalist and communist movements in Malaya. Often, teachers were just four years older than their pupils, so college students were also teachers.[22] Propagated by these teachers, cosmopolitan yet patriotic communist ideas attracted Chinese students. Member of the MCP Zhang Xia was teaching Esperanto and Western music in Malaya, while in his native Fujian he would sing revolutionary songs such as "La Marseillaise" with his students. This was a common – in fact, as the MCP lamented, the most common – activity of MCP members among workers in Singapore.[23] Communist propaganda

---

[16] Fitzgerald, *Awakening China*, p. 268.
[17] Cong, *Teachers' Schools and the Making of the Modern Chinese Nation-State*, p. 17; Zhang Xia, "Xianyou xian lü Ma huaqiao yu geming huodong [Immigrants from Xianyou County in Malaya and Revolutionary Activities]."
[18] *Straits Times*, March 16, 1927, p. 9, cited in Kenley, *New Culture in a New World*, p. 55.
[19] Yen, *A Social History*, pp. 301–304. In Indonesia, regional associations, *huiguan*, also promoted education and financed schools. Ta Chen, *Emigrant Communities in South China*, p. 159; Mary Somers Heidhues, "Chinese Voluntary and Involuntary Associations in Indonesia," in Kuah-Pearce and Hu-Dehart, eds., *Voluntary Associations in the Chinese Diaspora*, pp. 77–97; Yong, *Origins of Malayan Communism*, p. 133.
[20] MRCA, May 1931, pp. 20–22, CO 273/572.
[21] Ching Fatt Yong, "Closing Questions," in Hack and Chin, eds., *Dialogues with Chin Peng*, p. 237; "Minutes of the Third Representative Conference of Nanyang," pp. 96–97.
[22] Yu Dafu, "Private Classes and a Modern School," in *Nights of Spring Fever and Other Writings* (Beijing: Panda Books, 1984), pp. 174–180.
[23] "Report from Malay," p. 29; Zheng Tingzhi and Li Ruiliang, "Yige jianding de wenhua Zhanshi: Chen Junju tongzhi de yisheng [The Life of an Exemplary Cultural Warrior: Chen Junju]," in Zhongguo renmin zhengzhi xieshang huiyi Fujian sheng Putian shi weiyuanhui wenshi ziliao yanjiu weiyuanhui, ed., *Putian shi wenshi ziliao di qi ji* [*Literary and Historical Materials of Putian City*, vol. 7] (1991), pp. 122–128, esp. p. 123; Zhang

such as *World Weekly* (*Shijie zhoukan*), *How to Study the New Socialism* (*Ruhe yanjiu xin shehuizhuyi*), *Pioneer* (*Tahuangzhe*), and *Lenin Youth* called students to study the social sciences and current events and instructed them on how to fix world social problems and organize science societies for the study of Marxism and materialism instead of reading "the histories of heroes," that is, Chinese novels. Students were encouraged to leave their books behind and join the movement of the masses.[24]

Overall, however, it was the nationalist message that stayed with the students attending Chinese schools. A salesman from a Chinese rubber factory in Singapore said the following:

Since I graduated from the Chinese school, I have become more and more sympathetic toward China. I hope that our countrymen at home will whole-heartedly co-operate with one with another to save the country in this national crisis. I have been living in the Nanyang for many years, and I admire the colonial administration for its ability to maintain peace and safety and to conduct clean politics, but I hope that political stability will soon prevail in China, too, so that China may steadily advance on the road toward becoming a strong nation.[25]

Concerns about Second-Generation Chinese and Their Connections to China

Concerns with the Chinese identification of locally born Chinese became paramount when colonial governments restricted Chinese immigration.[26] Besides, as a *Peranakan* Chinese teacher from Java explained, the Chinese did not want to assimilate into local culture as that culture was "so very much simpler than that of the Chinese."[27] No wonder the Chinese communists in Malaya saw the second-generation Chinese as crucial for the Malayan Revolution.

Chinese communist teachers promoted Nanjing official nationalism among their students. The CYL looked down on students who had no "democratic liberties" and were "bound with all kinds of inherited morality and doctrine." Their minds were corrupted (*mazui*) with superstitions and British Christian education that made them slaves, using the Bible as a textbook.[28] The CYL criticized those young Chinese who wanted to learn only English and math and to go overseas or back to China to study. These

Xia, "Xianyou xiandai zhongxue de geming huoguang [The Revolutionary Fire of the Modern Middle Schools in Xianyou County]," p. 44.
[24] *Lenin Youth*, no. 18, May 6, 1931, MRCA, May 1931, p. 24, CO 273/572.
[25] Ta Chen, *Emigrant Communities in South China*, p. 160.
[26] Wang, "The Limits of Nanyang Chinese Nationalism."
[27] Ta Chen, *Emigrant Communities in South China*, p. 159.
[28] "Report of the CC of the CYL of Malaya to the League International," March 28, 1934, RGASPI 495/62/23/20–22ob, 60–66; CC MCP, "An Address to the Oppressed Peoples

students did not want to read Chinese, as their textbooks praised New York, Washington, and London.[29] Xu Jie, an immigrant writer who, as discussed earlier, ridiculed the Nanyang capitalist world, was skeptical about young Chinese, who spoke Malay and English, had a "full mouth of coffee and betel nut," and could cry out "Long live the king" but were embarrassed that their fathers were *Taishan ashu* (uncles from Taishan, China).[30]

In his novels, Xu Jie made clear that to remedy that lack of awareness, to be anti-imperialist and progressive, was to become more Chinese and communist. In one of his stories, Xu Jie contrasts the majority of locally born Chinese with his two protagonists. He was surprised to find that there were communists among second-generation Chinese who had received English-language education. For Xu, the lack of enthusiasm among the young Chinese for learning Chinese was an indicator of a slave mentality, while being able to speak Chinese meant being revolutionary and progressive. The novel is based on the real story of two locally born Chinese youth in Kuala Lumpur, Li De and Ai Lian, who were contributors to *Yiqunbao* and students at a Methodist English-language school and who later joined the Youth Revolutionary Party (Qingnian geming dang), which was apparently meant to represent the CYL. In the story, possibly an homage to Comintern criticism of Li Lisan's line, the two youths failed because of their "childish attitude"; they were arrested while distributing communist pamphlets in the streets.[31] However, despite its critical attitude, the MCP felt responsible for the youth. It was concerned about the students' future employment and livelihood, as impoverished families could not send their children to school to acquire a profession to secure their future. Another concern was British military training and expanding boy scout organizations in the schools as part of war preparations.[32] The CYL also complained in 1929 that Chinese students had capitalist outlooks, believed in new warlords and Chiang Kai-shek, and were concerned only about making money, not about politics in China.[33]

Yet despite the fact that for Straits-born Chinese, English-language education provided access to positions of power in the colonial system, the number of students in Chinese schools also grew over the 1930s.

---

of Malaya"; "Magong zhongyang tonggao di sijiu hao. Guoji qingnianjie de gongzuo jueyi [CC MCP Circular no. 49. Resolution Regarding the International Youth Day]."

[29] Nanyang gongzuo baogao [Nanyang Work Report], 1929, pp. 56–57.

[30] Xu Jie, "Liang ge qingnian [Two Youths]," pp. 18–33.

[31] Ibid.; Ke Pingping as related by Xue Jie, *Kanke daolu shang de zuji* [*Road Full of Misfortunes*], pp. 173–175.

[32] CC MCP, "Notice Issued by the C. C. of the Communist Party of the Malay States Relating to the Conclusion of the III Delegate Congress of the Nanyang Communist Party," p. 24; CC MCP, "An Address to the Oppressed Peoples of Malaya"; "Central Circular no. 1. The Conclusion of the Third Delegate Conference of the C. P. of Malay," May 1, 1930.

[33] Nanyang gongzuo baogao [Nanyang Work Report], 1929, pp. 65, 66.

Moreover, enrollment in English-language schools dropped in 1938, likely because of the start of the war in China and growing Chinese nationalism. In the Straits Settlements in 1932, the number of students in Chinese schools was double that in English schools, with an enrollment of 16,533 male and 5,495 female students. In the Malayan Federation at the time, Chinese schools had an enrollment of 14,384 males and 5,446 females. In 1938, the number in Chinese schools in the Straits Settlements reached 34,373 male and 12,794 female students, and in Malaya 32,272 and 12,095. English numbers grew steadily from 13,066 male and 4,812 female students in 1932 to 17,792 males and 6,844 females in 1937, then dropped to 12,444 males and 5,404 females in 1938. In 1933, in all of British Malaya, there were 373 Chinese schools, with a total student body of 18,000 boys and 6,000 girls. In Singapore in 1935, there were 183 staff members and 1,373 students in schools established by Tan Kah Kee (Chen Jiageng), and 588, or 42 percent, came from "emigrant families."[34]

The GMD's concern with the patriotic education of the Chinese overseas coincided with the Comintern and MCP's goal of seeing locally born Chinese in the MCP[35] and reflected their shared goals of indigenization. By 1934, when the MCP sent several locally born Chinese to Moscow[36] at the request of the Comintern,[37] the second generation of Malayan Chinese had become involved in the Nanyang Revolution – which the MCP now referred to as the Malayan Revolution – even if they were not MCP members. They launched struggles against school authorities and contributed money and language skills to the revolution. There are many examples, but one typical case is that of Un Hong Siu (Yin Hongzhao in Mandarin, 尹鸿兆, also known as Lau Ma, 老马, or Ma Tsu, 马祖), the son of a silver and gold merchant, who financially supported the MCP and for several years translated communist propaganda from the United States and from Comintern documents.[38] This is another example of how the MCP became localized through the involvement of locally born Chinese.

Un was educated in a Confucian school in Kuala Lumpur, was a member of the Kuala Lumpur Young Men's Progressive Society, and attempted to establish a branch at Ji'nan University, where he also participated in the

---

[34] Ta Chen, *Emigrant Communities in South China*, p. 161; Fan Ruolan, *Yimin, xingbie yu huaren shehui: Malaixiya huaren funü yanjiu (1929–1941)* [*Immigration, Gender, and Overseas Chinese Society: A Study of Chinese Women in Malaya, 1929–1941*] (Beijing: Zhongguo huaqiao chubanshe, 2005), pp. 128–129, 121.

[35] FEB, "To the Malayan Comrades," December 17, 1930; Comintern's Letter to the CC MCP; FEB, "Letter to the CC MCP about the 7th Congress of the Comintern etc."

[36] Guo Guang, "Magong laixin san hao [A Letter from the MCP no. 3]"; Guo Guang, Letter to the FEB, August 15, 1934, SMP D6152.

[37] FEB, "Letter to the CC MCP about the 7th Congress of the Comintern etc.," p. 13.

[38] Jones, "Letter from H. B. M. Consulate-General Concerning Malayan Communists."

movement to overthrow Ten Hong Lian, the university chancellor. In 1932, in Malaya, he organized several short-lived "subversive" societies independent of the MCP, but the following year he corresponded with Bun Teck Chai (Wen Decai), the ex-secretary of the MCP, who was imprisoned at the time in Hainan. Un was considering funding the reorganization of the MFLU Railway Branch in the Federated Malay States Railways workshop in Sentul, Kuala Lumpur.[39] Un was among the 20 percent of children of emigrant families who had been sent to study in China as a result of the Great Depression, as the Chinese overseas had started to look for economic opportunities in China. A middle-class wholesaler with few children set forth his views as follows: "Formerly we used to send our children to the government schools so that after graduation they could become government clerks or commercial salesmen in some European business. But these opportunities have decreased in recent years. Therefore, some of us have come to send our children to the Chinese schools to later find employment in China."[40] This was an important reason why the Chinese made efforts to improve education in their home communities. This was also their response to Nanjing's calls for the "re-nationalization" of the Chinese overseas. There was little surprise that the 1934 MCP campaign to aid the Chinese "soviet" revolution was supported by some in the Chinese community, which will be discussed in the next chapter.

To a considerable extent, the growth of nationalist feeling among overseas Chinese was heavily dependent on expatriate intellectuals, agents of GMD policy.[41] One of them was Xu, who promoted the Nanjing government's Chinese nationalist message in local Chinese schools. Like the Chinese politicians of the late Qing who toured the Nanyang, as described by Prasenjit Duara, the GMD thus "succeeded in cultivating a vague, contextual and ambivalent yearning for a Chineseness that reminds us of the 'national' in transnational."[42]

The Communists and the Youth

The Students: Communism as a Youth Subculture and Channel for Protest

Among overseas Chinese, communist ideas were part of the world outlook of diasporic nationalism and they had an appealing aura of

---

[39] Ibid.
[40] Ta Chen, *Emigrant Communities in South China*, p. 279.
[41] Wang, "The Limits of Nanyang Chinese Nationalism," pp. 417–419.
[42] Prasenjit Duara, "Transnationalism and the Predicament of Sovereignty: China, 1900–1945," *American Historical Review* 102(4) (October 1997), pp. 1030–1051, esp. p. 1043.

cosmopolitanism and modernity.[43] Students were the ones with the ability to understand the Aesopian references used to avoid censorship in literary supplements and Chinese newspapers (*fuzhang*), which the MCP criticized for not speaking the language of the "masses." At the same time, the MCP promoted propaganda that would appeal to the target audience with its content and easy language – that is, would be popular (*tongsu*).[44] Even the British government pointed out that "most [communist] propaganda must be above the intelligence of the masses."[45] Communist ideas were easily accessible to those who could read and decipher hidden meanings, but those were themselves the writers of these articles and those already familiar with communist discourse, like the protagonist in Xu Jie's story, Liang Yulian, a real Malayan-born young Chinese. In the story, published in the literary supplement *Desert Island* (*Kudao*) (枯岛), edited by Xu Jie, Liang Yulian is contacted by and drawn into the CYL because of an article he has written.[46]

For students, who were rarely MCP members, communist ideas served to channel youth iconoclasm and to protest for the overthrow of disliked schoolteachers both in China and in Malaya.[47] In 1930, more than forty students were expelled from Nanyang Overseas Chinese School in Singapore (Xinjiapo Nanyang huaqiao zhongxuexiao) for disturbances. In 1931, the students at that school demanded "revolutionary" holidays on May 4 (Student Movement Day) and May 5 (Sun Yatsen's assumption of office, President's Day) for school union meetings, at which they demanded reinstatement of the expelled students. In the same year, students at the overseas Chinese high school in Singapore launched a self-government movement.[48] Communism and protests against GMD indoctrination, and simply against teachers, were the subculture of the Nanyang second-generation Chinese. In 1934–1935, a father writing to his son, who was living in the Chinese settlement of Cholon, near Saigon,

[43] C. M. Turnbull, "Overseas Chinese Attitudes to Nationalism in Malaya between the Two World Wars," in Ng Lun Ngai-ha and Chang Chak Yan, eds., *Liangci shijie dazhan qijian zai Yazhou zhi haiwai huaren* [*Overseas Chinese in Asia between the Two World Wars*], pp. 367–374.

[44] "Tuan muqian de zhuyao renwu [Current Important Tasks of the CYL]," in "Malaiya qingshi fenxi yu dang de renwu. Jieshou Zhonggong zhongyang wu yue ershisan laixin de jueyi [The Analysis of the Situation in Malaya and the Tasks of the Party. Accepting the CC CCP Resolution from the CC CCP Letter of May 23]," 20 September 1933, RGASPI 495/62/21/31–48, pp. 42–44.

[45] MRCA, December 1930, p. 59, CO 273/571.

[46] Xu Jie, "Liang ge qingnian [Two Youths]," pp. 18–33; Ke Pingping as related by Xue Jie, *Kanke daolu shang de zuji* [*Road Full of Misfortunes*], pp. 173–175.

[47] See, for instance, John Israel, *Student Nationalism in China, 1927–1937* (Stanford, CA: Stanford University Press, 1966), p. 92.

[48] Zheng Liren, "Overseas Chinese Nationalism," pp. 306–307; MRCA, May 1931, pp. 20–25, CO 273/572.

warned, "[d]on't permit yourself to be disturbed in your work by talk about communism and other unworthy subjects."[49]

Despite such warnings, some sons of *huaqiao* ended up in Comintern schools in Moscow. One of them was an Indonesian Chinese, Van Sen (b. 1907), who started to work with a Chinese merchant at the age of six to help his family make ends meet. He learned how to be a tailor from his mother, but because of her cruel punishments, he left home at the age of seventeen and worked different jobs. In 1927, he became a sailor in Singapore, but in 1933, because of the cruelties toward sailors on his ship, he escaped and, with the help of local communists, went to Moscow. He was exposed to communist activities in Java and helped to organize party meetings, then on his own initiative propagandized what he heard, but he was not accepted into either the party or the CYL because he was too young.[50]

Another student, from Amoy, whose father was a returned immigrant from Indonesia, in Moscow had the Russian alias Liderov, meaning "Leaderson." Comrade "Leaderson" (b. 1904), at the age of seventeen, was the head of a primary school in Amoy, from which he was expelled for participation in a movement to overthrow the director of the school. At twenty-two, he was the head of a department at a secondary school in Shanghai. His employment did not last longer than a year, and the rest of the time he lived "as a dependent of his family" – his father was a merchant in Indonesia but went bankrupt and returned home to become a farmer. Then Liderov worked at the Amoy Academy of Literature (Amoiskaia Akademia Slovesnosti) and, after a year, was fired for demanding the celebration of May 1. He studied at Shanghai University, was a GMD member (1919–1922), joined the CCP in 1927, worked as a party organizer in a school, was arrested, fled to Wuhan, and from there was sent to Moscow by the CC CCP.[51]

Tan Kah Kee did not approve of the Chinese youths' interest in communism, specifically student protests against teachers in the Overseas Chinese School in Singapore, which he had established.[52] However, the combination of Tan Kah Kee's educational efforts in line with Nanjing's policy, the Comintern's requests in 1933 for second-generation Chinese to be sent to Moscow in 1934 to study, and Chinese organizations' needs to involve those in their ranks who were born locally contributed to the social significance of the MCP's mobilization campaign among youth. Like other MCP endeavors, it was not successful. Instead, the predominantly Chinese

[49] Ta Chen, *Emigrant Communities in South China*, p. 154.
[50] "Avtobiografiia tov. Van-Sena [Autobiography of Comrade Van Sen]," undated, RGASPI 495/214/43/14.
[51] "Biografiia studenta Liderova [A Biography of Student Liderov]," undated, RGASPI personal file 1930, not numbered.
[52] Zheng, *Overseas Chinese Nationalism*, pp. 306–307.

CYL and the party were rival communist organizations contrary to organizational hierarchy.[53] At the MCP's establishment conference, the league had almost as large a membership as the party, 1,000 people, 60 percent of whom were "foreign affairs workers" (i.e., servants in foreigners' houses), 20 percent shop employees, and 20 percent industrial workers.[54] The CYL and the MCP, in Kuhn's terms, attempted to carve out the same niche – that of the political party leading Malaya to emancipation and legitimized by international authority. This led them to conflict with each other.

"Youth" Organization: The CYL, the Party, and the Youth, 1928–1930

In March 1926, the founder of the CYL in Singapore, Pan Yunbo, claimed that when the Guangdong CCP committee sent him and two other natives of Wenchang County, Hainan, Xu Xiafu (许侠夫) and Huang Changwei (黄昌伟), to build an organizational network in the Nanyang in order to acquire aid for the revolution in China, they found neither a communist party nor the GMD, only the CYL organization directly subordinate to Ren Bishi, the head of the CYL in China. A graduate of a teachers' school, Pan Yunbo was active in the student movement in Guangdong and became the secretary of the CYL at Sun Yatsen University. In 1925, he transferred to the party and became the principal of Huanan School in Malacca.[55] Many CYL members had white beards and were more than thirty and even forty years old, similar to the CYL in China, where Youth League members simply did not join the party as their next step for fear of government persecution.[56] There was no age limit for those entering the CYL before

---

[53] Ho Chi Minh, "Malay."

[54] "Minutes of the Third Representative Conference of Nanyang," p. 107.

[55] In 1927, Pan Yunbo represented the Nanyang provisional committee at the fifth conference of the CYL in Hankou and at the third conference of labor unions. In 1929, he went to Annam and Siam to find members of the military who had fled to the Nanyang after defeat in the Guangzhou Uprising. In 1930, he handled the finances of the CCP's Southern Bureau (*Nanfangju*) in Hong Kong. Huang Xunyan, Lin Zhi, and Qi Wen, "Pan Yunbo tongzhi geming de yisheng [The Revolutionary Life of Comrade Pan Yunbo]," in Du Hanwen, Hainan zhengxie wenshi ziliao weiyuanhui, eds., *Hainan wenshi, di shijiu ji* [*The History of Hainan*, vol. 19] (Haikou: Hainan chuban gongsi, 2005), pp. 57–64, esp. pp. 58–60; Pan Yunbo, "Canjia geming de pianduan huiyi [Fragments of a Memoir about Participation in the Revolution]," in Zhongguo renmin zhengzhi xieshang huiyi Guangdong sheng Guangzhou shi weiyuanhui wenshi ziliao yanjiu weiyuanhui, ed., *Guangzhou wenshi ziliao di shiba ji* [*Guangzhou Literary and Historical Materials*, vol. 18] (1980), pp. 1–13.

[56] Henricus Sneevliet, Letter to Zinoviev, Bucharin, Radek, and Safarov, June 20, 1923, in Saich, ed., *The Origins of the First United Front in China*, pp. 611–619, esp. p. 613; Huang Xunyan, Lin Zhi, and Qi Wen, "Pan Yunbo tongzhi geming de yisheng [The Revolutionary Life of Comrade Pan Yunbo]," p. 57; Pan Yunbo, "Canjia geming de pianduan huiyi [Fragments of a Memoir about Participation in the Revolution]."

it was set at the MCP's founding conference: those under twenty were to join the CYL, and those older than twenty-three were to join the party. Those in between could join either.[57] In the summer of 1928, the CYL had a quite developed organization: the secretariat of the CYL in Singapore had four regional committees (two in Penang, one each in Malacca and Kuala Lumpur); special divisions in Seremban (Negeri Sembilan), Muar, and Batu Pahat (Johor); special branches in Johor, Soa Boey Kang (DEI), the naval base in Singapore, Pa Seng (DEI), and Chung Lam Kong; and the Siam special committee.[58]

The CYL did not recognize the authority of the party in the Nanyang and the CC CCP, argued about ideological questions such as the nature of the revolution in the Nanyang, and refused to hand over money to the provisional committee. Yet the CYL expected money from the party and complained about a lack of party directives and cooperation in the labor movement. In 1929, it refused to submit to the party's directive to transfer members with concurrent membership in both organizations and labor unions. The head of the CYL, Lung, escaped to Guangdong (allegedly absconding with party funds), and many left the league. CYL members held the view that, according to Marx, conflict between the communist party and the communist youth league was inevitable. In 1929, with the exception of the secretary of the Kuala Lumpur organization – "an intellectual with a petty bourgeois outlook" who engaged in a conflict with the party (perhaps Lung) – the rest of the city committee's leaders were reported as workers. In January 1929, 80 percent of the CC CYL's members were workers, and 20 percent were intellectuals. Workers were all "free laborers" or professionals (*ziyou zhiyezhe*) or were unemployed. Relatively few (*jiaoshao*) were industrial workers; note that the Chinese expression *jiaoshao* often means "none."[59] Table 6.1 gives an idea of the CYL membership based on available sources. Disciplinary measures, such as banning CYL members from voting, threatening party excommunication for disobeying the revolutionary hierarchy, and Ho Chi Minh turning down the CYL's request to be recognized by and directly subordinate to the Youth International at the founding conference eventually bore fruit, and the relationship between the party and the CYL improved.[60]

---

[57] "Minutes of the Third Representative Conference of Nanyang," p. 143.
[58] "Kuomintang and Other Societies in Malaya," July–September 1928, pp. 5, 6, CO 273/542.
[59] "Minutes of the Third Representative Conference of Nanyang," pp. 107–109, 123–127, 141; Nanyang gongzuo baogao [Nanyang Work Report], 1929; Nanyang gongzuo baogao [Nanyang Work Report], 1928.
[60] In May and September 1930, the CYL received letters from the Communist Youth International. MRCA, May 1931, p. 28, CO 273/572; "Central Circular no. 1. The Conclusion of the Third Delegate Conference of the C. P. of Malay," May 1, 1930, pp. 16–17; "Minutes of the Third Representative Conference of Nanyang," pp. 107, 143, 146.

Table 6.1 *CYL membership*[61]

	Place, vocation, origins, and gender	Total
1928	Singapore, 428 Penang, 55 Malacca, 102 Kuala Lumpur, 30 Johor, 84 Dutch East Indies, 14 Siam, 45	758
January 1929	Industry, 310 Unemployed, 190 Professionals (*ziyou zhiyezhe*), 390 871 males and 19 females	890
October 1930	The largest organizations were in Singapore, Sembilan, and Johor	441
1934	20 Malay 431 Chinese: 356 Hainanese and 75 from Fuzhou, Xiamen, and Chaozhou, as well as Hakka 140 "shop employees" and "waiters for foreigners" (洋务), 228 workers on rubber plantations, some workers in tea factories 16 yellow-pear planters, 2 blacksmiths (铁厂), 65 students 419 males and 12 females	451

The CYL and the Youth, 1931–1934

Large portions of MCP documents seized in 1932 by the police dealt with the youth rather than with the labor movement.[62] The party observed that students' thinking (*sixiang*) had undergone an "active leftist revolutionarization" (*jiji zuoxiang geminghua*) and that hatred toward the British among intellectuals (*zhishi jieji*) had increased.[63] However, despite making efforts to adapt its propaganda to the target audience, the party did not

---

[61] Nanyang gongzuo baogao [Nanyang Work Report], 1928; "Minutes of the Third Representative Conference of Nanyang," pp. 100, 106; "Report from Malaysia on the Organization of the Young Communist League"; "Magong zhongyang laijian. Zhengge tuan dezuzhi gaikuang [A Document Received from the CC MCP. The Organizational Situation in the CYL]," August 25, 1934; "Kuomintang and Other Societies in Malaya," pp. 5, 6; "Informatsiia o Malaiskikh Shtatakh [Information about the Malay States]"; "Report of the CC of the CYL of Malaya to the League International."
[62] Khoo, "The Beginnings of Political Extremism in Malaya," p. 305.
[63] Guo Guang, "A Letter from Malaya no. 3" (English).

succeed in attracting them to communist youth organizations.[64] The CYL blamed its "research institution" work style, as it focused on internal CYL work instead of spreading propaganda among youth.[65] The party criticized the CYL as it had criticized its own comrades in the 1930s for its lack of activity; its mechanistic, formalistic, and "bureaucratic" tendencies; its factionalism, pessimism, and leftism; its lack of Bolshevik self-criticism; and its insufficient propaganda against the British government and the war, about the advantages for youth in the Soviet Union,[66] and about the alliance with youth of the "various oppressed nations in Malaya." Like the MCP, the CYL blamed its failures on the backwardness of the masses and on the complex ethnic layout of the region: "Malaya is a very backward colony. The cultural level of the youth is very low; therefore, it is difficult to carry out propaganda and agitation . . . Peoples in Malaya are too complicated and have different languages, habits and customs, so we cannot smoothly do our work."[67]

The CYL spread communist messages on wall newspapers (*bibao*), the propaganda journals *Political Economy* (*Zhengzhi jingji xue*), *Proletariat* (*Puluo*), and *War Drum* (*Zhangu*), and in the Singapore Nanyang Overseas Chinese School. They also held meetings and drama performances.[68] Drama was the most popular form of public entertainment, and its message could reach the illiterate.[69] Dramatic performances were thus sites for a demonstration of "theoretical struggle" against reactionaries and of the "correct theory of the party and [the] CYL," and they included scenes meant to overcome incorrect thinking, imperialist education, and backwardness,[70] which the CC had routinely called an "-ism," using a transliteration of the Russian word for tailism, *khvostism*, in the linguistic polyglot manner of the youthful protagonists in Kubrick's *A Clockwork Orange*.

---

[64] "Magong zhongyang laijian. Zhengge tuan de zuzhi gaikuang [A Document Received from the CC MCP. The Organizational Situation in the CYL]," August 25, 1934.

[65] "Tuan muqian de zhuyao renwu [Current Important Tasks of the CYL]."

[66] "Malaiya qingshi fenxi yu dang de renwu [The Analysis of the Situation in Malaya and the Tasks of the Party]"; "Address by Singapore Committee of Malaya Comparty and League of Communist Youth of Malay in the Leaflet to the Youth," undated, RGASPI 495/62/5/2.

[67] "Report of the CC of the CYL of Malaya to the League International."

[68] MRCA, April 1931, p. 22, CO 273/572.

[69] Ta Chen, *Emigrant Communities in South China*, p. 169.

[70] He Siren, "Bingcheng de Nanyang xingxin xiju yundong (1930–1931): Xin Ma xiju yundong zuoqing yishi de kaiduan [The New Drama Movement in Penang (1930–1931): The Beginnings of Leftist Thinking in the Drama Movement of Chinese in Singapore and Malaya]," in Yang Songnian and Wang Kangding, eds., *Dongnanya huaren wenxue yu wenhua* [*The Culture and Literature of the Chinese in Southeast Asia*] (Xinjiapo: Yazhou yanjiu xuehui, 1995), pp. 109–133; "Report of the CC of the CYL of Malaya to the League International"; "Report from Malaysia on the Organization of the Young Communist League."

The New Drama Society published sixteen issues of *Drama Leading Press* until police surveillance and financial difficulties put an end to its distribution. It targeted young people interested in proletarian culture and reading societies in Singapore, Mopore (DEI), Fuyong, and Penang. The New Drama Society started from the Moluo (Moloch, 摩洛) society in Penang and included Little Bomb (Xiaodan, 小弹), Thousand Masses (Qianzhong, 千众), Spitting Horse (Sima, 嘶马), Standing on Heaven (Tianli, 天立), Snow White (Xuewa, 雪娃), Fragrant Chaste (Fenzhen, 芬贞, maybe not a pseudonym), Cold Current (Lengliu, 冷流), and Residual Cold (Canleng, 残冷). They aspired to establish a just and better world.[71]

The CYL was trying to convert youth through individual conversations and at meetings of workers, reading and football clubs, as well as through "red recreation centers." It established Young Pioneer organizations and youth detachments in red trade unions.[72] There, to compete with the rival military-style sports associations established by the British government, athletic CYL comrades were to conduct antiwar propaganda.[73] The Malayan CYL had children's corps (up to twelve years of age), a student federation (twelve to fifteen years of age), a women's division (fifteen to twenty-three years of age), and a young workers' department (eighteen to twenty-three years of age). The CYL's tactic was to turn economic struggles (the demand for clothing and houses) into political struggles (opposition to arrest, beatings, imprisonment, and deportation as punishment for protests).[74] Propaganda materials distributed and sold (*tuixiao*) were mostly in Chinese, and among Comintern-collected materials there were only one or two leaflets in Malay, with a few more in English, for instance, *Lenin's Youth and Training*. Some Malay handbills were distributed in Penang, Malacca, Selangor, and Negeri Sembilan. The goal was to talk about various problems of the youth in simple language and to have pictorial material to keep readers interested. The party also published *Minors' Avant-Garde* (*Shaonian xianfeng*) and a children's pictorial.[75]

Apparently as a consequence of the arrests and of the economic downturn that affected all Chinese organizations, the party was not able to support the

[71] He Siren, "Bingcheng de Nanyang xingxin xiju yundong (1930–1931). Xin Ma xiju yundong zuoqing yishi de kaiduan [The New Drama Movement in Penang (1930–1931): The Beginnings of Leftist Thinking in the Drama Movement of Chinese in Singapore and Malaya]"; "Report of the CC of the CYL of Malaya to the League International."

[72] "Minutes of the Third Representative Conference of Nanyang," pp. 140–141; "Report of the CC of the CYL of Malaya to the League International"; MRCA, May 1931, pp. 26–28, CO 273/572.

[73] CC MCP, "An Address to the Oppressed Peoples of Malaya."

[74] "Report of the CC of the CYL of Malaya to the League International."

[75] "Magong zhongyang tonggao di sijiu hao. Guoji qingnianjie de gongzuo jueyi [CC MCP Circular no. 49. Resolution Regarding the International Youth Day]"; MRCA, December 1931, p. 52; MRCA, May 1931, p. 27, CO 273/572.

CYL, and sometime in 1933–1934, the MCP and the CYL reorganized their central committees into a nine-member joint central committee (*dangtuan zhongyang*).[76] Section committees of the CYL in Singapore were canceled, and nuclei were directly subordinated to municipal committees. The Singaporean town committee of the MFLU closed down some departments, as well.[77] During that same period, the CYL twice wrote to the Youth International to request recognition as a section, English-speaking cadres to help with CC work (or sending five comrades to receive training), and a monthly subsidy of 100 American dollars. The CYL's monthly expenses were more than $150, with a monthly income of $80. In response to this request, a Comintern cadre wrote "$35" between the lines.[78]

The CC had ten organizations under its control: Selangor, Singapore, Penang, Malacca, Perak, Sembilan, Johor Bahru, Mopore (DEI), Pahang, and Siam. Like other communist organizations, the CYL was in dire straits. Eight of nine CC members had been arrested, and the CYL did not accept new members. It also did not have a newspaper in suitable simple language and did not proselytize in local branches. The members were still overage, and propaganda corps (*xuanchuandui*) did not go beyond talking (*quming wu qushi*). The CYL, like the MCP, explained that its lack of political propaganda regarding the Malayan Revolution and its inability to lead the youth masses were a result of an immigrant mentality and political suppression. The majority of its members were Chinese domestic servants in foreigners' households, shop employees, and workers on rubber plantations. There was a large turnover (*liudong*) of cadres, as many left the organization, did not attend meetings or pay membership fees, did not read the printed materials of the league, did not have work responsibilities, argued (*nao yijian*) and settled personal accounts at the expense of party interests (had a non-proletarian consciousness), lacked discipline and secret work, had "vacillations" in Malacca and Selangor, and engaged in "romantic actions" (*liangman xingwei*).[79]

---

[76] Yong, *Origins of Malayan Communism*, p. 154; "Malaiya qingshi fenxi yu dang de renwu [The Analysis of the Situation in Malaya and the Tasks of the Party]."

[77] MRCA, December 1931, p. 45, CO 273/472; "Magong lianzi tonggao di yi hao. Dangtuan zhongyang guanyu waiqiao dengji lüli yu women de gongzuo de jueyi [MCP Central Circular no. 1. Resolution of the CC of the MCP and CYL Regarding the Alien Registration Ordinance]"; "Dangtuan zhongyang [CC of the MCP and CYL], "Magong lianzi tonggao di ba hao: Guanyu yanmi dangtuan de zuzhi wenti [Circular no. 8 of the MCP Regarding the Organization of the Secret Work of the Party and CYL]," August 15, 1933.

[78] "Report of the CC of the CYL of Malaya to the League International."

[79] "Report from Malaysia on the Organization of the Young Communist League"; "Magong zhongyang tonggao di sijiu hao. Guoji qingnianjie de gongzuo jueyi [CC MCP Circular no. 49. Resolution Regarding the International Youth Day]"; "Report of the CC of the CYL of Malaya to the League International"; Guo Guang, "A Letter from Malaya no. 3" (English); "Magong zhongyang laijian. Zhengge tuan de zuzhi

The MCP made efforts to mobilize different groups of the population as promoted in every Comintern letter from 1930 to 1937, and its strength lay in its front organizations.[80] Although women figured prominently in the workforce in British Malaya in the 1930s,[81] the MCP's women's associations appealed to "girls who [were] dissatisfied with the feudal system of the ruling class," who comprised 60 percent of the members.[82] In Johol, the Negeri Sembilan General Labor Union promoted freedom of divorce and marriage.[83] In the Singapore women's association in 1932–1933, of a total of eighty-one members, 50 percent were "girls from families" (housewives), 33 percent were students, and 17 percent were factory workers. Of these female members, 70 percent were Hainanese and the rest were Cantonese and Khes (i.e., Hakka).[84] The CYL propagated its ideas among sisterhoods of girls at public schools and in reading classes and encouraged all relations of the revolutionaries (wives, sisters, relatives, and friends) to become involved in women's associations. The MCP listed the same deficiencies in women's work that it found in students' work: inactivity, bureaucratism, a low level of the masses, a lack of understanding of the needs of the lower ranks of the CYL and women, and Chinese membership.[85]

Despite relatively developed communist organizations and the popularity of communist ideas among students, the student protest movement in Chinese schools remained outside the grasp of the MCP or the CYL. Occasionally, communists were involved in student skirmishes, as in 1930 when the MCP was involved in cyclostyling materials of the Singaporean student association based at the Nanyang Chinese High School in Singapore during protests, as discussed earlier in this chapter.[86] The CYL proposed to protest against the system of schools (*xuexiao zhidu*), to advocate for free education for young workers, to prepare young cadres, and to improve everyday education (*richang jiaoyu*) in order to raise the political and cultural consciousness of the youth (*tigao*

gaikuang [A Document Received from the CC MCP. The Organizational Situation in the CYL]," August 25, 1934.
[80] Yong, *Origins of Malayan Communism*, p. 152.
[81] See Fan Ruolan, *Yimin, xingbie yu huaren shehui: Malaixiya huaren funü yanjiu (1929–1941)* [*Immigration, Gender and Overseas Chinese Society: A Study of the Chinese Women in Malaya, 1929–1941*].
[82] "Report of the CC of the CYL of Malaya to the League International."
[83] MRCA, September 1931, p. 37, CO 273/572.
[84] MRCA, December 1931, p. 49, CO 273/572.
[85] "Magong zhongyang tonggao di sijiu hao. Guoji qingnianjie de gongzuo jueyi [CC MCP Circular no. 49. Resolution Regarding the International Youth Day]"; "Report of the CC of the CYL of Malaya to the League International."
[86] MRCA, March 1931, CO 273/571, cited in Khoo, "The Beginnings of Political Extremism in Malaya," p. 275.

qinggong de zhengzhi yu wenhua shuiping). The CYL had five local units of student organizations under its leadership. The Student Association consisted of 154 Chinese members, among whom 38 were Chinese girls. The CYL also established the highest organ of the student union in Malaya, the Federation of the Revolutionary Students in Malaya, on November 9, 1933, to work in Johor Bahru and Singapore.[87]

The CYL criticized student unions for their superficial daily lives, their low political level, and the empty content of their publications, yet the CYL could not lead the student movement because of its "infantile tactics."[88] Overall, student union membership also declined in Singapore,[89] with forty-five members compared to more than eighty the year before, and in Penang, with thirteen members in 1933 compared to forty members the year before. Pioneer (Shaonian xianfengdui) organizations, all Chinese, existed in Singapore, Penang, and Selangor, totaling 133 members, 90 percent of whom were male and 83 percent were students (the rest were workers). The life of such organizations was "superficial and dry," meaning that for children, membership was boring and some children even left the organizations. The CYL admitted that it had undermined the student protests, so the MCP proposed that no one interfere with the independent student movement and the student self-governing societies.[90] During a rally on September 7, 1931, on Youth Day in Singapore, fifty Hainanese members of the Malaya Youth Party (perhaps a cover name for the CYL) distributed handbills published by the Singapore Student Federation and the periodical *Zhenglibao* (*Truth*), an apparent allusion to the Soviet newspaper *Pravda* ("truth" in Russian). The September issue of *Truth* criticized Chinese high schools for disciplinary measures applied to students for reading socialist literature.[91]

To improve work and increase membership, the CYL planned to introduce a revolutionary competition, the Stakhanovite movement, as well as to lower the requirements for new members to just two conditions:

---

[87] "Tuan muqian de zhuyao renwu [The Important Tasks of the CYL at Present]," September 20, 1933. RGASPI 495/62/21/42–48; "Report of the CC of the CYL of Malaya to the League International."
[88] "Report of the CC of the CYL of Malaya to the League International."
[89] In 1931, the Singapore Student Union had ninety members; 30 percent were Hakka, 20 percent Hainanese, 20 percent Cantonese, 10 percent Hokkiens, 10 percent Teochews, and 10 percent other groups. Of these, 70 percent were boys. The union was not well organized and did not carry out many activities. The aid society existed in name only. AIL membership was 110, with 50 percent Hainanese, 40 percent Hakka, and 10 percent Hokkiens. MRCA, December 1931, p. 49, CO 273/572.
[90] "Report of the CC of the CYL of Malaya to the League International."
[91] MRCA, September 1931, p. 36, CO 273/572.

some knowledge of the revolution and loyalty to the league.[92] In order to co-opt the student movement, the MCP and the CYL, as other groups, planned to use indigenizing tactics. These involved promoting "everyday life" slogans, such as stopping tuition increases, permitting males and females to study together, creating student organizations in government English-language schools, and, among Indian and Malayan students, opening up student unions (*xueshenghui*) and uniting the organizations and activities of students, young peasants, and workers so that students could help in the revolutionary movement. The CYL planned to send comrades to schools to organize student unions, to "understand the students and make [their] work fit for them." To strengthen class consciousness in children, the CYL was to cultivate collective life habits and bravery. The key point, it emphasized, was to make this fun rather than "inflexible propaganda."[93] Indeed, sports and art clubs were the places where the MCP was able to bring together youth of different ethnic groups and thus cultivate its multinational united front.[94]

Schoolteachers were the conduits of communist ideas to students. Their activities as MCP cadres show that communism for them was as much an intellectual and patriotic endeavor as an aspiration for violent revolution. Their imagined global, utopian, just world consisted of the intersecting images of modernity of the time. These were science, a world language (Esperanto), utopian images originating in Christianity, traditional Chinese public communication techniques in the form of drama, and novel artistic forms and tropes.

Teachers: The Crossing Worlds of the Chinese Revolution

> The honorable historical task of the revolutionary intellectual is to help to develop industrial workers who are the backbone of the communist movement and who can help to bring the working class to the actual place of hegemony in the revolution of the Malayan people against British imperialism.
>
> "What Workers Should Stand For," 1930, p. 12

It was the "progressive" intellectuals who connected the center and the periphery, their native places in China and the migrant associations overseas, to borrow the imagery from Kuhn, of the revolutionary Chinese world.[95]

---

[92] Ibid.; "Magong zhongyang laijian. Zhengge tuan de zuzhi gaikuang [A Document Received from the CC MCP. The Organizational Situation in the CYL]," August 25, 1934.
[93] "Tuan muqian de zhuyao renwu [Current Important Tasks of the CYL]."
[94] Onraet, *Singapore: A Police Background*, p. 115.
[95] Kuhn, "Why China Historians Should Study the Chinese Diaspora."

The agents of GMD nationalism were a new professionalized intelligentsia comprising mostly teachers and writers from China who were looking for employment in Malaya. The MCP too placed responsibility for cultivating the working class on intellectuals, that is, teachers and newspaper writers and editors. The number of Chinese schools in the Straits Settlements and the Federated Malay States increased from 252 in 1921, to 716 in 1930, to 933 in 1937. The number of teachers also increased from 589, to 1,980, to 3,415, respectively.[96] Many of them were dispatched by the GMD as agents of party propaganda, and the GMD presented them as courageously fighting under "the iron heel of a foreign government" and against the oppression of South Seas Chinese by the imperialists. Mobile Chinese teachers were ideal agents for propaganda work in the South Seas and comprised the network that not only the GMD but also the Comintern, as we have seen, was eager to tap into.

Public propaganda, verbal or written, immediately engages the attention of the local authorities, but teachers are in a better position and can easily carry out propaganda. They are intellectual and widely distributed over the countries in the South Seas. It is possible for them to carry out verbal propaganda among the young and by this means to influence the families of students, which is of great assistance to our party organisations. The teachers in the lower schools in West Borneo are nearly all party leaders. Since most of them have their families in China, they can, if deported, go elsewhere without much hardship, but the seed of the revolution is then already sown in the place they leave. Propaganda conducted by teachers has met with great success and [has aroused] the enthusiasm of the overseas Chinese and it is precisely due to this reason that overseas Chinese schools are oppressed by colonial governments.[97]

Many were deported, and their protection was declared to be of "paramount importance" to the Chinese government.[98] The Dutch government also prohibited the importation of communist literature to the East Indies and restricted the immigration of "undesirable" Chinese intelligentsia. However, *China Critic*, a journal published in English by Chinese students abroad, argued that most of those deported were nationalists who promoted the independence of the Dutch East Indies from the Dutch government rather than communists:

In the Dutch East Indies, communism may mean two entirely different things, when a Chinese is strong pro-GMD, or even merely an ardent nationalist, he or she is likely to be labelled a "communist," and the native who is opposed to the Dutch rule is just as much a "communist," though the lawyer of one of the

---

[96] Leong, "Sources, Agencies and Manifestations of Overseas Chinese Nationalism in Malaya," p. 121.
[97] *Huaqiao xianfeng* [*Avant-garde of the Chinese Overseas*], July 15, 1931, Canton, cited in "Extracts from Chinese Newspapers," in MRCA, September 1931, p. 39, CO 273/572.
[98] Ibid.

arrested leaders of the "communist" movement pointed out that what that defendant did was no more than what William of Orange did for the Spanish there hundreds years ago [sic].[99]

The relations of many MCP intelligentsia with both the GMD and the CCP demonstrate ideological flexibility through which party affiliations were subsumed under the strong emotional appeal of patriotic sentiments and survival strategies. Xu Jie was a CCP member but claimed to have no strong sense of party identity. The MCP seconded the complaint of a weak party identity (dang guannian) and a non-rigid organization.[100] Despite Li Lisan's warning for the Nanyang party to distance itself from the GMD after the breakdown of the united front in 1927,[101] maintaining contacts with both communists and the GMD was not uncommon. Because Xu Jie was sent to the Nanyang by the CC GMD, he could not openly be a communist, but the CCP knew "deep in the bones" that he was a revolutionary.[102] Indeed, Xu Jie's story "Mansion in the Coconut Grove" is essentially a record of his attempt to persuade a Chinese rubber producer that the Nanyang's prosperity, peacefulness, public safety (until a few years earlier, it had not been necessary to lock one's doors at night), and supposedly superior labor conditions were illusions. Xu argued that world capitalism was globally connected and would inevitably fall, of which the rising unemployment was evidence.[103]

Overall, because both Chinese parties had been banned, the GMD and the CCP in Malaya had common ground based on their anti-imperialist ideology. For example, in Malacca, communists propagated violent protests against the GMD in 1928, while 900 GMD members (many belonging to the left wing of the party) in fact "did not hinder party work" because they "did not pay attention to [it]."[104] Zhang Xia's life is another good example. He was a member of the intelligentsia migrant network from Xianyou County, Fujian, which did not send as many migrants to Malaya as the Fuzhou region or southern Fujian, but many of such migrants worked as teachers and participated in revolutionary work (geming gongzuo) and patriotic movements (aiguo yundong), including Xu Yuqing

---

[99] China Critic, August 27, 1931, quoted in MRCA, September 1931, pp. 40–42, CO 273/572.
[100] "Zhigong yundong jueyian [Resolution on the Labour Movement]," April 1933.
[101] CC CCP, "A Letter from the Central Committee of the CCP to the Nanyang Provisional Committee."
[102] Ke Pingping as related by Xue Jie, Kanke daolu shang de zuji [Road Full of Misfortunes], pp. 212, 217.
[103] Xu Jie, "Yelin de bieshu [Mansion in the Coconut Grove]," pp. 18–33.
[104] "Protokol der.3. Delegierten Konferenz von Nanyang (Malayische) [Protocol of the Third Representative Conference of the Nanyang Party (Malayan)]," p. 91.

(许彧青), Zhang Zhaohan (张兆汉), Cai Mingshan (蔡明善), Chen Hongbin (陈鸿宾), and Huang Ming (黄明).[105]

Zhang was from a "farming" family and was descended from three generations of paper lantern painters. In 1927, Xianyou County's middle school founded a teachers' class (*gaozhong shifanban*) for the purpose of training schoolteachers for overseas communities, sometimes funded by Chen Jiageng. Zhang studied there for one year and joined the GMD. In 1929, he started to teach art classes at the middle school. From 1932, Zhang participated in the Mutual Aid Society (Hujihui), which was a front organization of the CCP, and in the Anti-Imperialist League he spread communist ideas among students. In 1935, Zhang narrowly escaped arrest by the GMD. His compatriot and MCP member Zhang Yuanbao found him a job in Sitiawan, near Zhang Yuanbao's school in Perak Province.[106]

Zhang Xia then became an art teacher and a secretary at the Nanhua middle school. He taught there what he had taught himself – Western music theory, acoustics, violin, and guitar. He organized student orchestras and composed pieces in which Western and Chinese musical instruments performed together. For art classes, he took students outside for sessions *en plein air* and hired an Indian worker as a model for drawing, for there was a shortage of plaster replicas suitable for the early stages of learning. He also taught embroidery and basket-weaving during craft lessons, as well as Esperanto to two students, one of whom was future MCP leader Wu Tianwang (伍添旺). Zhang maintained an impressive international penpal network. He was in contact with Ukrainian children, airport workers, Austrian and Swedish teachers, the Spanish Esperanto association, telegraph and telephone communication workers in Japan and America, and a British merchant in Tibet. They exchanged illustrated journals from different countries, stamps, and their own works of art.[107] How much more cosmopolitan could one get?

In 1936, because he did not receive the pay he expected, he quarreled with the principal of the school, Wang Shujin (王叔金), the head of the local branch of the GMD, and moved to a different primary school. Together with the editor of the literary supplement for *China Publishing* (*Zhonghua baoshe*), Wang Xuanhua (王宣化), in Ipoh Zhang established the Association of Overseas Chinese Culture Workers of Northern Malaya

---

[105] Zhang Xia, "Xianyou xian lü Ma huaqiao yu geming huodong [Immigrants from Xianyou County in Malaya and Revolutionary Activities]," pp. 34–39.

[106] Zhang Jinda, "Mianhuai Zhang Xia xiansheng [Remembering Mr. Zhang Xia]," in Zhongguo renmin zhengzhi xieshang huiyi Fujian sheng Xianyou xian weiyuanhui wenshi weiyuanhui, ed., *Xianyou wenshi ziliao di shiyi ji* [*Literary and Historical Materials of Xianyou County*, vol. 11] (1994), pp. 47–61.

[107] Ibid.

(Bei Ma huaqiao wenhua gongzuozhe xiehui). Their revolutionary fervor attracted the attention of the authorities, and Zhang had to leave Perak. In 1937, through a recommendation by a colleague from the 1932 communist underground in Xianyou County, Fu Naizhao (傅乃超), Zhang found a position as an art teacher in Johor's Kota Tinggi. After the start of the anti-Japanese war, Zhang was the head of the propaganda department organized by the MCP's "Anti-Enemy Backing-Up Society of the Overseas Chinese Workers" (AEBUS) (Huaqiao gongren kang di houyuanhui). In 1937, Zhang joined the MCP, and one year later he organized an anti-Japanese propaganda traveling drama troupe as well as a local chapter of the AEBUS. In 1938, after Zhang was arrested, his wife, also a teacher, was transferred by the MCP to a workers' evening school.[108]

The stories of MCP members' prison experiences reveal the scope of the "revolutionary activities" they engaged in. After his arrest, Zhang was put in jail in Johor Bahru together with three other MCP members and started spreading among the prisoners communist propaganda about the international situation and the Chinese war of resistance. He established an AEBUS branch in which, in addition to Chinese, there were also Malays and Indians. By the time of the Chinese New Year, Zhang had instigated prisoners to demand a more bountiful meal in celebration: coffee with milk, two eggs, an increase in the ration of oil to three *qian*, and three *liang* of pork. Malays and Indians who did not eat pork demanded lamb or beef. When the authorities refused, the prisoners went on a successful hunger strike.[109] After spending six months in jail, Zhang was deported to China. On the ship to Hong Kong, there were about 100 other banished travelers with him. Among them he began a "propaganda organization." During their six days on board, Zhang, Zhu Zonghai (朱宗海), and Zhang Guisheng (张贵生) translated Zhang's speeches into Hainanese and Cantonese, propagating unity and anti-Japanese resistance. They also organized a commemoration of the death of Sun Yatsen. As a result, the group raised and donated more than 200 Malayan dollars for the needs of Chinese war refugees. The endeavor was overseen by the captain of the ship and the policemen on board, who apparently did not attempt to stop this activity.[110]

Back home, the overseas ventures of people like Zhang were suspected by the CCP and persecuted by the GMD. After returning to China, Zhang could not stay in his native Xianyou County because of GMD government surveillance, so he worked in neighboring Dehua County (德化) in a middle school as a music teacher. He taught his students how to make wind and

---

[108] Ibid.
[109] Zhang Jinda, "Mianhuai Zhang Xia xiansheng [Remembering Mr. Zhang Xia]."
[110] Ibid.

string instruments during war scarcities. In 1940, his wife brought him a recommendation letter from the AEBUS in Singapore, but since it was not an MCP recommendation, Zhang had trouble with the underground CCP at home too. Yet overseas Chinese networks helped at home as well: Zhang's wife found a job in a school established by a Burmese *huaqiao*. In 1942, the GMD accused Zhang of being a "party traitor" (*dangjian*), and only his sister's connections helped to refute the accusations. In 1943, he returned to his native Xianyou County and established a connection with the CCP after eight years of being out of touch.[111]

Zhang Xia was known in southern Fujian as the only person who could play Western musical instruments, and a violin, along with a wind instrument, was specially ordered for him from Hong Kong. In 1945, when Zhang was arrested by the GMD in Putian city, a prison guard saw his works and suggested that he take part in the provincial exhibition in Fujian and later took his paintings there. Specifically for this exhibition, Zhang made a painting in the dry-brush style (*ganbi*), adding color; the painting was entitled *Garden of Eden* and it was based on the creation story from the Bible. The painting depicted Adam and Eve, and on the apples in the trees, the Esperanto word *KOMUNISMO* was written.[112]

Cosmopolitanism was a part of the overall intellectual and cultural eclecticism that was a characteristic feature of the world of Chinese communism in Malaya. To be sure, Zhang Xia, who also played the organ, obviously having learned it in church, was critical of Christianity. However, this did not prevent him from imagining and depicting the world of communism in the language of Christianity. Christianity was one of the intersecting worlds, among others, to be discussed in the next section, which shaped South Seas communism, as the recruitment of the labor needed in the British colony from Zhang's native Xianyou County to the Nanyang was carried out by missionaries.[113]

The Places of Revolution and How to Get There: Roads, Crossroads, and Temples

Christian temples were a part of the world of Chinese communists in the greater realm of the South Seas, which included the Nanyang and South China. In southern China, Christian temples were the places to go for free meals and to exchange information with fellow comrades.[114] In these

---

[111] Ibid.
[112] Ibid.
[113] Zhang Xia, "Xianyou xian lü Ma huaqiao yu geming huodong [Immigrants from Xianyou County in Malaya and Revolutionary Activities]."
[114] Interview with Chen Fang.

temples, GMD and CCP members mingled and left their political dis-
agreements behind. The future head of Perak County's MCP branch and
the head of the fifth guerrilla unit of the Malayan Peoples Anti-Japanese
Army (MPAJA), Zeng Shaowu (曾绍舞), escaped arrest by the GMD
during the Fujian Rebellion because he was a Christian, as was the head of
the 36th division of the 102nd regiment of the GMD army, Li Liangrong
(李良荣), who was sent to Yongchun to suppress the rebels. Li, to avoid
carrying out an arrest in the temple and giving a fellow Christian a
warning, invited Zeng to join him in the military club during a Sunday
service, which, to Zeng, was the indication that his CCP activities had
been exposed. He then made arrangements with Wang Nanzi (王南子) to
leave for Malaya.[115]

Wang, the librarian in the same school where Zeng was a teacher, was a
worthy reference. He had an impeccable revolutionary pedigree since he
had studied at the Communist University of the Toilers of the East
(KUTV). Zeng's father was another illustration of the intersecting networks of Christians and revolutionaries in southern China. He was a local
priest at Datong Church, an engineer, and a teacher, and he became the
representative of Yongchun County in the National People's Congress, a
standing member of the Political Consultative Committee, and a member
of the committee of overseas Chinese after 1949. Zeng was decorated by
the British government after the war, but he participated in the
Emergency and perished in combat in 1951.[116]

In a Sikh temple in Singapore, the MCP disseminated *Red Flag*, propaganda about the Three People's Principles and the USSR, and materials published by the Eastern Oppressed Peoples' Association in
Nanjing.[117] Aside from temples, Chinese schools, newspaper houses,
and associations, the three pillars of the Chinese community were places
where one could be exposed to communist ideas in the Nanyang. They
were meeting points, places for the exchange of ideas and information.
Roads and crossroads in dramas and fiction by MCP activists illustrated
how these intellectuals, who propagated communist ideas in prisons,
while sailing ships, and while attending church, imagined a revolutionary
road for the masses. Engine, an intellectuals' society with chapters in
China and overseas, as discussed earlier, was the engine to get to those

[115] Sun Jianbin, "Jue bu dang Wangguonu: Mianhuai kang Ri xianbei Jiang Qitai, Zeng
Shaowu, Lin Boxiang [Don't Become Slaves: Remembering the Elders in the Anti-
Japanese Resistance, Jiang Qitai, Zeng Shaowu, Lin Boxiang]," in Zhongguo renmin
xieshang huiyi Fujian sheng Quanzhou shi weiyuanhui wenshi ziliao weiyuanhui, ed.,
Quanzhou wenshi ziliao di ershisi ji [*Literary and Historical Materials of Quanzhou*, vol. 24]
(2005), pp. 123–131.
[116] Ibid.
[117] MRCA, September 1931, p. 64, CO 273/572.

imagined places. Engine member Chen Junju (陈骏驹) was among the students with whom Zhang Xia organized musical and theatrical performances of European music, including the music of Soviet composers and "La Marseillaise."[118] As seen, Zhang Xia himself imagined the revolutionary destination as the Garden of Eden.

Roads to emancipation were a common motif in plays by Chinese Malayan writers. *Ma hua wenxue*, the literature of the Chinese in Malaya, had two trends: Nanyang local color (*Nanyang caise*) and proletarian works (*puluo wenxue*).[119] The MCP's communist ideas and their indigenization fit both currents. In early 1931, schools and *huaqiao* associations across Malaya declared that the stage was to become a weapon in the anticolonial struggle. The New Drama Movement (Xinxing xiju de yundong) opposed the artsy style (*wenming fengge*) and instead promoted bringing real life onto the stage. A proponent of the movement, in which CYL members were active, was the MCP's head of propaganda in 1933, writer Ma Ning (马宁), who held a meeting of the AIL in the forest of Johor Bahru. Two years previously, in 1931, Ma Ning, a founder of the Chinese Leftist Writers Union (Zhongguo zuoyi zuojia lianmeng), had fled Shanghai and found a job as a school prefect in Singapore, where he published *Mapu* (*Malaya Proletariat*) and the monthly *Nanyang Wenyi* (*Nanyang Literary*) and established the Proletarian Art Union of Malaya (Malaiya puluo yishu lianmeng).[120] In Singapore, he participated in the biggest youth literary organization there, the Inspiration Society (Lizhishe, 励志社) (est. 1920), which, after the Mukden Incident of September 18, 1931, organized an anti-imperialist propaganda campaign in a school and was closed down. He staged a few one-act plays about Malayan Chinese society in which he attacked the backward feudal society (*luohou huaqiao fengjian shehui*) and thinking (*yishi*) of the Chinese.[121]

One of Ma Ning's plays featured an Indian worker who shared his piece of bread with an unemployed Chinese rubber worker. Also on the road, Xu Jie met a Malay whose gaze frightened him with its expression of colonial oppression. Another story set on a road was by Lin Xianqiao (林仙峤), who, in November 1930, was banished for his play *Crossroad*

---

[118] Zheng Tingzhi and Li Ruiliang, "Yige jianding de wenhua zhanshi: Chen Junju tongzhi de yisheng [The Life of an Exemplary Cultural Warrior: Chen Junju], p. 123.

[119] Yu Yueting, "Ma Ning yige bei yiwang de liaobuqi de 'zuoyi' zuojia [A Forgotten Extraordinary Left-Wing Writer Ma Ning]."

[120] Chen Yutang, ed., *Zhongguo jinxiandai renwu minghao da cidian: quanbian zengdingben* [*Dictionary of Names in Modern China: A Revised Edition*](Hangzhou: Zhejiang guji chubanshe, 2005), p. 22; Yu Yueting, "Ma Ning yige bei yiwang de liaobuqi de 'zuoyi' zuojia [A Forgotten Extraordinary Left-Wing Writer Ma Ning]."

[121] Ibid.

(十字街头). It was the story of a rubber worker and a miner (two categories of workers the MCP most wanted to recruit) who decided to commit suicide to solve their problem of making a living. They lay down on the road to be run over by a car. A road worker tried to rob them, thinking that they were dead. When he realized that he was trying to steal from miserable people like himself, his thinking turned progressive (*sixiang jinbu*), and together they decided to struggle against the imperialists, who monopolized their road in life. After the arrest of Lin Xianqiao, between 100 and 150 newspapers across Malaya did not dare to publish literary supplements.[122] Lin's arrest caused an outcry in the Chinese community and provided the MCP with an illustration of the damage that the Alien Registration Law had caused the Malayan Revolution.[123]

In the early 1930s, Malayan Chinese communists imagined new roads to Malayan national emancipation: those of proletarian unity and internationalism. Tragically, it was the war and, ironically, GMD propaganda that brought the MCP's aspirations to mobilize the youth to fruition.

War and Flowers for China: The GMD, Communists, and Youth in China and Malaya

Young Chinese learned Esperanto and French revolutionary music, along with Marxism, from their teachers and revolted against school authorities and teachers affiliated with the GMD who promoted Chinese nationalism. Yet, ironically, similar to the GMD in China, the MCP unsuccessfully attempted to channel patriotic student movements, which remained an independent force and had similar structural problems, such as overage members and rivalry between the party and its youth corps.[124] Chinese immigrant schools and newspapers were the GMD's center of activity.[125] While cultivating Chinese nationalism, GMD propaganda also caused protests. In Kuala Lumpur, student MCP members boycotted classes and petitioned Chinese community leaders as well as British authorities to eliminate GMD party education and "reactionary teachers" in local schools.[126] While the GMD had to

---

[122] Ibid.
[123] "Ma Ning. Zai Nanyang fazhan Zhongguo de xinxing juyun [Ma Ning. Chinese New Drama Movement in Nanyang]," in Zeng Qingrui, ed., *Zhongguo xiandai huaju wenxue wushijia zhaji [Chinese Modern Drama. Notes on Fifty Writers]* (Beijing: Zhongguo chuanmei daxue chubanshe, 2008), pp. 259–268. Also see Chapter 4.
[124] Huang Jianli, *The Politics of Depoliticization in Republican China: Guomindang Policy towards Student Political Activism, 1927–1949* (Bern: Peter Lang AG, 1996), pp. 92–147.
[125] Vilkov et al., "Spravka o rabote," pp. 10, 17.
[126] "Xuelan'e Jiaying de xuesheng yundong [The Student Movement in Kajang, Selangor]," in Ershiyi shiji chubanshe bianjibu, ed., *Zhanqian dixia douzheng shiqi.*

curtail the student movement, for the communists the movement was a chance to mobilize, and they to encourage student activism. From 1927 to 1937, students in China were bored by GMD indoctrination and mostly felt alienated from the GMD.[127] Similar to China, where the CCP appropriated the December 9, 1935, student movement,[128] the MCP appropriated the student movement in Malaya, where the Malay student union and other public organizations advocated for a united front of the GMD and the CCP.[129]

After the beginning of full-fledged war in 1937 in China, various groups of Chinese in Malaya, including students, became actively involved in the worldwide China Salvation Movement. The Straits Chinese Relief Fund Committee of Singapore (Xinjiapo Haixia huaren chouzhenhui), established in 1938 and chaired by a prominent leader of the Chinese community, Lim Boon Keng, organized activities such as selling flags, flowers, and souvenirs and hosting fairs, variety shows, and magic shows featuring local and foreign artists. The flowers were made by students, members of civic associations, and individuals. More than 180 schools and clan associations participated. According to the explanatory text of one photo from an exhibition about the occupation of Singapore by the Japanese, the unexpected outcome of the activities of this fund was the solidarity of the Chinese-born and Straits-born communities.[130]

Children and teenagers who sold flowers for the China Salvation, Movement, organized by teachers like Zhang Xia,[131] joined the MCP

Jiandang chuqi jieduan, Magong wenji, congshu xilie, di yi ji [*The Prewar Period of the Underground Struggle: The Founding of the Party. Documents of the MCP*, vol. 1] (Kuala Lumpur: (Ershiyi shiji chubanshe, 2010), pp. 138–146.

[127] Israel, *Student Nationalism in China*, pp. 184–187, cited in Huang, *The Politics of Depoliticization in Republican China*, p. 193; Yeh Wen-hsin, *Alienated Academy: Culture and Politics in Republican China, 1919–1937* (Cambridge, MA: Harvard University Press, 1990), pp. 124, 87.

[128] Israel, *Student Nationalism in China*, pp. 101, 154, 178.

[129] Vilkov et al., "Spravka o rabote," p. 25.

[130] The photo of the fundraising campaign for China's anti-Japanese resistance depicting students holding paper flowers from the late 1930s was shown at the exhibition organized by the Singapore National Archives, "Syonan Years: Singapore Under Japanese Rule, 1942–1945," at the Old Ford Factory exhibition gallery, Singapore, in December 2010.

[131] "Half a Million Blood Flowers in Commemoration of the Double Tenth. Tenth Day of the Tenth Month Anniversary of the Chinese Republic, Are Being Sold in 65 Town and Rural Districts in Singapore Today. Anti-Japanese Campaign: Double-Tenth Being Celebrated Quietly 200,000 Chinese Selling 'Blood Flowers,'" *Straits Times*, October 10, 1939, p. 10; Zhang Jinda, "Mianhuai Zhang Xia xiansheng [Remembering Mr. Zhang Xia]." For more about the same fundraising campaign, see Huang Yifei, "Huiyi Xin Ma huaqiao lieshi Zhang Yuanbao [Remembering the Martyred Overseas Chinese of Singapore and Malaya Zhang Yuanbao]," in Zhongguo renmin zhengzhi xieshang huiyi Fujian sheng Xianyou xian weiyuanhui wenshi weiyuanhui, ed., *Xianyou wenshi ziliao di si ji* [*Literary and Historical Materials of Xianyou County*, vol. 4] (1986), pp. 38–43.

after Singapore was occupied in February 1942. This generation of young students who became teenagers during the war and had been infused with GMD nationalist propaganda joined the MCP-led guerrillas after the start of the war. After the Japanese atrocities against the Chinese communities in Singapore and Malaya, many people from the student movement influenced by the MCP became party guerrillas leaders as the MCP organized the anti-Japanese resistance.[132] The Japanese occupation therefore shifted the loyalties of patriotic youth toward the MCP. Chin Peng first considered joining the GMD military college, but he read Mao's *On Protracted War* and found it more convincing.[133] The Malayan-born daughter of a GMD official, Ling Hanmei (凌寒梅), who joined the MCP propaganda troops after the start of the Japanese invasion as a teenager, would have gone to study in China on a GMD scholarship if it had not been canceled.[134] Many women joined the MCP due to its patriotic appeal during and before the war.[135] In 1939, among the middle-level leaders of the MCP in Singapore nine out of twenty-one were women.[136] Huang Wenhua (黄文华), whose father migrated to Malaya's Perak Sitiawan and became a rubber tree cutter, joined the MCP after the Japanese occupation began, became a leader in the guerrilla resistance, and, after the war, became the CC secretary.[137] Chen Chengzhi (陈诚志), born in China, went to Malaya with his father. When the war started, he worked at a restaurant, but he joined the "dog-eliminating squads" organized by the MCP that targeted the Japanese.[138]

A large portion of MCP members in the late 1930s were young people and students.[139] Teachers and student cadres took short-term courses during school vacations and studied *The Communist Manifesto*, Lenin's

[132] Yong, *Origins of Malayan Communism*, p. 257.
[133] Chin Peng, *My Side of History*, pp. 47–48.
[134] Interview with Ms. Ling Hanmei in Fuzhou on December 22, 2010.
[135] Agnes Khoo, *Life as the River Flows: Women in the Malayan Anti-Colonial Struggle* (Petaling Jaya: Strategic Information Research Development [SIRD], 2004); Mahani Musa, "Women in the Malayan Communist Party, 1942–89," *Journal of Southeast Asian Studies* 44 (2013), pp. 226–249.
[136] "Biograficheskie svedeniia i kharakteristiki na rukovodiashchie kadry kompartii Malai, dannye v dokladakh Pen Haitan, byvshyi zav.otdelom propagandy singapurskogo gorodskogo komiteta partii Malai [Biographical Data and Personal References for the Leading Cadres of the MCP Provided by the Former Head of Propaganda of the Singapore City Committee of the MCP, Peng Haitang]," RGASPI 495/62/30/1–10.
[137] Zhang Xia, "Xianyou xian lü Ma huaqiao yu geming huodong [Immigrants from Xianyou County in Malaya and Revolutionary Activities]," pp. 34–39.
[138] Chen Chengzhi, "Wangshi huiyi [Reminiscences about Past Things]," in Zhongguo renmin zhengzhi xieshang huiyi Fujian sheng Tong'an xian weiyuanhui wenshi ziliao gongzuozu, ed., *Tong'an xian wenshi ziliao di si ji* [Literary and Historical Materials of Tong'an County, vol. 4] (1984), pp. 57–76.
[139] Khoo, "The Beginnings of Political Extremism in Malaya," p. 354.

State and Revolution, Stalin's *Short Course of the History of the Communist Party of the Soviet Union*, Mao's *On Protracted War* and *On New Democracy*, Liu Shaoqi's *How to Be a Good Communist*, Edgar Snow's *Red Star over China*, and Ai Siqi's *Mass Philosophy*.[140] Large numbers of students worked for the AEBUS.[141] In 1939–1940, eight out of eighteen leaders of the Singaporean party organization worked for the AEBUS,[142] yet the majority of the MCP-led guerrilla army of the MPAJA were not party members.[143] The MCP's too-strict criteria for CYL membership had prevented the CYL from growing in 1934,[144] but now the MPAJA received many new recruits because it was the MCP that led the anti-Japanese resistance, and it was the only choice for young Chinese who witnessed the Japanese massacre of the Chinese, Sook Ching, in Singapore and Malaya.[145] The majority of the MCP's wartime cadres came from Chinese-language schools.[146] Thus, the GMD's project in Malaya succeeded: it boosted the number of MCP members during the war.

Conclusion

The meaning of communism in Malaya for students lay in getting rid of resented teachers and curricula. For teachers, it meant patriotism and an idealistic belief in communist ideas – for which they were not hesitant to commit violence. The MCP's attempt to co-opt the student movement

---

[140] "Xuelan'e Jiaying de xuesheng yundong [The Student Movement in Kajang, Selangor]," p. 140.

[141] Yong, *Origins of Malayan Communism*, pp. 246–248.

[142] "Biograficheskie svedeniia i kharakteristiki na rukovodiashchie kadry kompartii Malaii, dannye v dokladakh Pen Haitan, byvshyi zav.otdelom propagandy singapurskogo gorodskogo komiteta partii Malai [Biographical Data and Personal References for the Leading Cadres of the MCP Provided by Former Head of Propaganda of Singapore City Committee of the MCP Peng Haitang]." For more information on prewar MCP leaders, see Fujio Hara, "Riben zhanling xiade Malaiya gongchandang [The MCP during the Japanese Occupation]," *Nanyang ziliao yicong* [*Compendia of Nanyang Materials*] 161(1) (2006), pp. 26–47, "Di'erci shijie dazhan qiande Malaiya gongchandang [The MCP before the Second World War]," and "Malaiya gongchandang yu Zhongguo [The MCP and China]," *Nanyang ziliao yicong* [*Compendia of Nanyang Materials*] 144 (4)(2001), pp. 26–39.

[143] Karl Hack, "The Malayan Emergency," in Hack and Chin, eds., *Dialogues with Chin Peng*, pp. 3–37, esp. p. 8.

[144] "Report of the CC of the CYL of Malaya to the League International."

[145] Hirofumi Hayashi, "Massacre of Chinese in Singapore and Its Coverage in Postwar Japan," in Yoji Akashi and Mako Yoshimura, eds., *New Perspectives on the Japanese Occupation in Malaya and Singapore, 1941–1945* (Singapore: National University of Singapore Press, 2008), pp. 234–249; Heng, *Chinese Politics in Malaysia*, p. 37; Hack, "The Malayan Emergency," pp. 3–4.

[146] "Xuelan'e Jiaying de xuesheng yundong [The Student Movement in Kajang, Selangor]."

was ineffective until the China Salvation Movement, despite the popularity of communist ideas among students and teachers. At the local level, attracting youth and locally born Chinese into the organization was a matter of organizational survival for the MCP in its role as a Chinese organization and it was essential in order for it to fulfill its goal as a communist party to mobilize all social groups. The CCP's indigenization therefore succeeded among the second-generation Chinese thanks to the educational efforts of the GMD.

The success of the communists in Malaya was comparable in one aspect to that of those in China. John Israel has stated, "[i]dealistic youth [had] been psychologically driven to seek a totalistic ideological orientation that the party of Sun [Yatsen] was unable to provide. Communists were fortunate to be out of power during these years. The CCP won the allegiance of an impatient generation."[147] This chapter has shown that the rise of communism in Malaya was not a result of the MCP's efforts but rather was an unintended consequence of GMD education policies promoting identification of the overseas Chinese with China and of Japanese atrocities against Chinese communities. Immediately before that occurred, however, the MCP's revolution had failed on a national, that is, Malayan, level.[148] Once the MCP became rigid in its anti-bourgeois and anti-British language and narrowly defined its "nation," it lost its base of support. We turn in the next chapter to the role of language and discourse in understanding why the MCP would do this. At the same time, the Japanese aggression and wartime propaganda helped to cultivate Chinese identification with Malaya.

---

[147] Israel, *Student Nationalism in China*, p. 194.
[148] Wang, "Closing Comments: Chin Peng and the Malayan Nationalist Cause," Session XI, in Hack and Chin, eds., *Dialogues with Chin Peng*, pp. 226–232.

The Power of Language

The MCP's Minzu: Sojourning Nation

By the start of the Second World War, English-educated Chinese elites were talking about the emerging Malayan nation, as the younger generation of Chinese, Malays, and Indians had been brought up in similar lifestyles of combined education in English schools. The *Straits Times* reported that harmony already existed in Malaya, yet the concern was whether Malaya would remain a peaceful society. Despite the rise of "narrow nationalism" and "racial prejudices," the hope was that citizens were "building up a Malayan unity, an affinity of morals, of thoughts, of aspirations" – in other words, a Malayan nation.[1]

Members of the Chinese community imagined themselves as part of the Malayan nation but retained their Chinese identity. After the start of the Japanese invasion of China, Chinese writers in Singapore and Malaya abandoned their search for "Nanyang color" and devoted their writing to China.[2]

Yet, according to Chin Peng, MCP members identified with Malaya and felt responsible for fighting for its independence.[3] Maintaining an allegiance to both Malaya and China was the way Chinese overseas communities functioned, namely by establishing links at both ends of their sojourning corridors: China and their host environments. The MCP's embeddedness in the local environment and its connection to China were expressed in its documents, where *minzu* referred to either or both Malaya and China in different sentences. The overlapping meanings of *minzu* continued to mean different things in different contexts. *Minzu* was also

---

[1] "A Malayan Nation: Always a Land of Harmony?" *Straits Times*, August 3, 1939, p. 10.
[2] Yeo Song Nian and Ng Siew Ai, "The Japanese Occupation as Reflected in Singapore–Malayan Chinese Literary Works after the Japanese Occupation (1945–49)," in Patricia Pui HuenLim and Diana Wong, eds., *War and Memory in Malaysia and Singapore* (Singapore: Institute of Southeast Asian Studies, 2000), pp. 106–122, esp. pp. 107–108.
[3] Chin Peng, *My Side of History*, p. 9.

used to mean "nationalities" for the various ethnic groups living in Malaya, who were to comprise the "national united front." In addition, *minzu* was used in the context of class divisions and referred to the proletariat.

The word *minzu* resembles what literary theory has called a floating signifier. We can see its meaning as moving, or sojourning, between Malaya and China. This ability to use one word to represent what would seem to be significantly different concepts reflected the MCP's comfort with these multiple or overlapping ideas of national identity and to which nation, *minzu*, it belonged. What appears to us as a logical contradiction or confusion was not so for MCP authors. One of my goals has been to recover the world in which the activists of the MCP lived and to sufficiently translate their experience to readers today to show how such a multivalent use of the word *minzu* could serve the MCP leadership quite satisfactorily, and more so that such use of *minzu* could come quite naturally to people in that environment. The MCP's use of *minzu* in this way also provided flexibility, gave the MCP the opportunity to participate in both Malayan and Chinese national projects, and reconciled these two identities within the MCP.

Minzu *as China and Malaya*

One example is the discourse of "national interests" (*minzu liyi*). In the context of the MCP's decision to change its policy from pro-British to anti-British, *minzu* meant both China and Malaya or it was ambiguous. The MCP described the point of view among members of the Chinese bourgeoisie in the "MCP Resolutions of the Second Enlarged CC Plenum," published in February 1940: the bourgeoisie saw Britain as China's "international friend" (*guoji youren*) in the same manner as Malays and Indians saw Britain as a protector and Hitler as an enemy. The document stated: "Hence, for national interests [*minzu liyi*], we must not fight against the British or carry out protests, and during the hardship of war we must all bear the burden." In the same document, the MCP described Malaya's special characteristics as follows: "Feudal forces in each of Malaya's nationalities [*Malaiya ge minzu*] sell off national interests [*minzu liyi*] and join the front of national traitors."[4] The national traitors were those who had established legal labor organizations and yielded to British demands, diminishing the revolutionary influence among the masses and suppressing the revolution.[5] Here,

---

[4] "Magong di er ci zhongzhihuiyi jueyian [The Resolutions of the Second Plenum of the Executive Committee of the CC MCP]," p. 30.
[5] Ibid., p. 23.

minzu refers to Malaya, yet in establishing a democratic republic, the MCP wanted to "rely not on British running dogs, but on [its] own 'national forces' [*minzu ziji de liliang*]."[6] Whether *minzu* refers to Malaya or China here is ambiguous.

In the MCP brochure "Forward!" the term "Malayan people" (*Malaiya renmin*), clearly echoing CCP and Soviet discourse, was juxtaposed with the idea of national traitors (*minzu pantu*): "Day by day the anti-imperialist struggle of the whole Malayan people deepens [*quan Ma renmin de minzu fandi douzheng*]." However, in the preceding sentence, the idea of national traitors was used together with the term *hanjian*. The Malayan people were the Malayan nation, whereas the term "national traitor" (*minzu pantu*) referred to those collaborating with the Japanese.[7] Here, *minzu* refers to the Chinese.

Minzu *as a National Front of "Various Peoples"*

The MCP promoted its united front through the Racial Emancipation League (Minzu jiefang lianmeng), established in 1936.[8] In 1937, prior to the outbreak of war in China, the MCP changed its own name and the names of the CYL and the MFLU by adding the words *ge minzu* (all nationalities) to them. Its new name was *Malaiya ge minzu gongchandang* (All-Nationalities Communist Party of Malaya). At the same time, the outbreak of war in 1937 intensified MCP concerns over Japanese aggression in China and China salvation work among the Chinese community.[9] In 1938, the MCP abolished the Multiracial Liberation Youth League (Ge minzu jiefang qingniantuan).[10] However, the rhetoric of Chinese liberation through the liberation of colonial peoples, Malays in this case, continued, and ultimately helped to shape the identification of the Chinese community with the territory of Malaya shared with other ethnic communities, Malays and Indians.

Minzu also referred to Malaya and to all three ethnic groups (Malayan, Indian, and Chinese) in the expression *minzu tongyi zhanxian*, "national united front" or "united front of nationalities." The Malayan *minzu* was to be liberated through the liberation of the Chinese (*Zhongguo minzu*), both *huaqiao* and in China, and other oppressed nations. The MCP's nation, as in the national movement, was the national united front (*minzu*

---

[6] Ibid., p. 28.
[7] "Maijin [Forward]," p. 60.
[8] Yong, *Origins of Malayan Communism*, p. 204.
[9] Ibid., pp. 196–197.
[10] "Zhanqian dixia douzheng shiqi xuesheng yundong de ruogan qingkuang [The Situation in the Student Movement during the Underground Prewar Period]," p. 138.

tongyi zhanxian) that the MCP claimed to have established before the war. It included all ethnic groups (*ge minzu*) and all classes (*ge jiceng renmin*) – workers and peasants, shop workers, clerks (literally the "urban petty bourgeoisie," *chengshi xiao zichan jieji*), and soldiers – but excluded the "capitulationist" bourgeoisie.[11]

The MCP was skeptical about the alleged harmony in Malayan society, as it was British dominance that provided a check to hostilities among the different ethnic groups. Malays were poor, and they could not compete with the Chinese, who outnumbered them in Singapore by a factor of two even in agriculture, where they had been predominant, because "their tools [were] dated." Indians mostly worked on rubber plantations, and Japanese owned the richest iron mines in Malaya, in Johor, and in Trengganu, while Arabs and Jews were real estate owners in the cities.[12] In 1935–1940, even in legal workers' organizations, there was no united front of different ethnic groups, and the Chinese comprised most of the labor movement. For example, of 33,000 members of the Malayan Federation of Labour, 5,002 were Indian immigrants and 150 were Malays.[13]

Despite the various international engagements of the Nanyang communists, the discourse of internationalism (*guoji zhuyi*) appeared in MCP documents for the first time in the late 1930s and it had several meanings. One was allying with the Soviet Union because it supported China and with the workers and peasants of capitalist countries for the anticolonial emancipation movement in the Far East, the Nanyang, and China, as well as the effort to form a joint labor movement among Malaya's ethnic groups.[14] It was manifested in the following strikes with the participation of non-Chinese: at a rubber plantation near Malacca in 1931, at a coal mine in 1937 with 5,000 to 6,000 participants, at a strike involving 2,000 tram workers in 1938, and at two strikes in 1939, one at a government heavy machinery factory and one involving the refusal to unload cargo from Japanese vessels at a Singapore port.[15]

The MCP, as before, imagined political organization along ethnic lines and presented itself to the Comintern as the only "real political party" in Malaya, as Malays and Indians did not have one.[16] Although its influence

---

[11] "Maijin [Forward]," p. 58.
[12] Li, Tun-go, *Sokrashchennyi perevod broshury Malaia segonia, sostavlennoi na kitaiskom iazyke v 1939 g.* [*Abridged Translation of Brochure "Malaya Today" Compiled in Chinese*], December 23, 1941; the original text was compiled on December 7, 1939, RGASPI 495/62/29/65–86, esp. 67–68 (henceforth "Malaya Today").
[13] Vilkov et al., "Spravka o rabote," pp. 30–31.
[14] "Magong di er ci zhongzhihuiyi jueyian [The Resolutions of the Second Plenum of the Executive Committee of the CC MCP]," pp. 21, 23.
[15] Li, "Malaya Today," p. 68.
[16] Vilkov et al., "Spravka o rabote," pp. 16–17.

among Malays and Indians was not "as strong as among the Chinese,"[17] the MCP argued that it could become a central factor in multiethnic Malayan politics. The MCP proclaimed that in the "strategy of the anti-imperialist united front, in order to solve the nationalities question [*minzu wenti*], the party [had] to pay attention to the common interests of different *minzu* and the particular interests of particular *minzu* to redefine the strategy in accordance with the revolutionary situation."[18] The MCP set the following program for Malays (*Malai minzu*): to focus on their independence movement and the establishment of an independent democratic republic, and to get rid of British puppet sultans and landlords. The party had to lead workers, peasants, and urban residents (*shimin*) in small, everyday struggles from their economic awakening (*jingji juewu*) into an awakening of the independence movement (*duli yundong de juewu*) and into fraternal feelings toward and a united movement with the Chinese and Indians.[19]

The MCP regarded Chinese "patriotic" anti-Japanese actions as acts of internationalism.[20] If in the early 1930s Comintern internationalism meant support for the communist Chinese Revolution, in 1939 it justified support for the liberation of China from the Japanese. The MCP's multi-ethnic united front, promoted by the Comintern, was also a continuation of its earlier impulse as a Chinese organization to embed itself in the local environment (as was the discourse of Malayan nationalism):

Today, in order to help the anti-Japanese war of our motherland, we need national liberation [*minzu jiefang*]. That means we must support the Chinese anti-Japanese war and the democratization and constitutional movement; isolate capitalists so they don't dare capitulate; achieve liberty of residence and business for *huaqiao* in Malaya and protest deportations; participate in the Malaya all-peoples liberation movement and antiwar struggle [*ge minzu de jiefang yundong* and *fanzhan dou-zheng*]; aid the independence movement of Malays [*Malai minzu de duli yundong*]; and fight together for the establishment of the Malayan democratic republic.[21]

In MCP discourse, to liberate Southeast Asia was to help the liberation of China. One MCP document said, "[t]he pressing need of today's China is to aid the revolutionary struggle of the peoples of the colonial countries of the Nanyang. The liberation movement of the Chinese people [*Zhongguo renmin de jiefang yundong*] supports the anti-imperialist struggle of the colonial countries of the Far East and the Nanyang [*peihe*

---

[17] In the Russian original *natsional'nost'*. Li, "Malaya Today," p. 83.
[18] "Magong di er ci zhongzhihuiyi jueyian [The Resolutions of the Second Plenum of the Executive Committee of the CC MCP]," p. 29.
[19] Ibid., p. 28.
[20] Li, "Malaya Today," p. 68.
[21] "Magong di er ci zhongzhihuiyi jueyian [The Resolutions of the Second Plenum of the Executive Committee of the CC MCP]," p. 26.

*yuandong Nanyang ge zhimindi guojia minzu de fandi douzhen*g]." The struggles of the oppressed peoples (*minzu geming douzheng de bei yapo minzu*) and their national liberation (*minzu jiefang*) were possible only if those peoples opposed imperialist wars and allied with the Soviet Union. The MCP stated, "[t]he slogan of the rising together of the national revolutions of China and of the colonies in the Nanyang [*Nanyang ge zhimindi de minzu geming tong Zhongguo de minzu geming*] has a pressing meaning today." This was why it argued that:

> Not only for the interests of the independence of the motherland [*zuguo duli*] but also for their own security, *huaqiao* in the colonial countries of the Nanyang must stand together with brothers of all other oppressed nations [*ge bei yapo minzu xiongdi*] and carry out an antiwar and anti-imperialist movement to overthrow their local rulers [*dangdi de tongzhi*] and establish an independent and free country ... This is the most realistic, the most powerful way to help the anti-Japanese war of the motherland [*zuguo kangzhan*]; nobody can do this honorable duty for us.[22]

The MCP's continuing discourse on the cooperation of various peoples was also reinforced by a CCP–GMD united front rhetoric of cooperation between the *huaqiao* and the Nanyang peoples (*Nanyang ge minzu*) in working toward their common goal of establishing a multiethnic (*ge minzu de*), antifascist, national united front (*minzu tongyi zhanxian*).[23] Thus, the communist party, the avant-garde of the proletariat of all of the colonial countries of the Nanyang, for the success of the national liberation movement (*minzu jiefang yundong*) had to organize the China Salvation Movement and the revolutionary unity of the *huaqiao*, promote the friendship and joint struggle of the *huaqiao* with local brothers from oppressed nations or peoples (*dangdi bei yapo minzu xiongdi*), and aid the Chinese resistance.[24] For the success of the resistance and the national revolution in China, as well as to boost China's international prestige, the colonies in the Nanyang had to be liberated through a joint struggle by the *huaqiao* and the local oppressed nations. One example of such cooperation was the fact that the Indian branch of the MCP in Singapore adopted a new name, the Friends of China Society.[25]

However, in practice, despite the MCP's goal of creating "a joint organization of workers of various *minzu* in the spirit of internationalist solidarity,"[26] the MCP was not able to attract Malays into its ranks; it only

---

[22] "Maijin [Forward]," pp. 58–59.
[23] Ren Guixiang and Zhao Hongying, *Huaqiao huaren yu guogong guanxi* [*Chinese Overseas and CCP–GMD Relations*], p. 156.
[24] "Maijin [Forward]," p. 59.
[25] Ibid.; Yong, *Origins of Malayan Communism*, p. 204.
[26] "Magong di er ci zhongzhihuiyi jueyian [The Resolutions of the Second Plenum of the Executive Committee of the CC MCP]," p. 23.

attracted some Indians who were connected with the Indian Communist Party, the Indian National Congress, and other Indian independence organizations. The MCP blamed this on British "divide and rule" policies that had resulted in Malays and Indians joining reformist unions during the protest wave of 1939.[27] However, MCP propaganda, even when written in English, in fact talked only to the Chinese. For example, although the address beginning "To fellow commercial countrymen of all nationalities," which urged readers to protest the introduction of a commercial enactment act, addressed "commercial circles of all nationalities" (*ge minzu shangjie tongbao*), it called on them to go to the Chinese protectorate and make a petition against the act.[28]

In practice, internationalism at times contradicted the MCP's Chinese patriotism, but the orthodoxy prescribed that CCP members overseas had to be both Chinese and internationalist. In 1939, MCP members lamented, "[s]ome comrades adopt a neutral attitude toward the imperialist war; some comrades call themselves *huaqiao* and forget they are internationalists [*guojizhuyizhe*]!"[29] This new *guojizhuyi* of the MCP was likely borrowed from CCP discourse. For example, the influence of Mao's speech at the sixth plenum is obvious: "Can an internationalist [*guojizhuyizhe*] communist party member also be a patriot [*aiguozhuyizhe*]? I think he not only can, but he must."[30] Similarly, Bo Gu argued that there was no contradiction between revolutionary nationalism and internationalism.[31] Another source stated that the nationalism of the GMD (*Guomindang de minzuzhuyi*) and communist internationalism (*gongchandang de guojizhuyi*) had to merge (*heqilai*).[32] Starting with the internationalist brigades in Spain, internationalism had been prescribed by the Comintern, and now the CCP was carrying it out on the international scene.

---

[27] Li, "Malaya Today," p. 82.
[28] Malaiya gongchandang Xingzhou shiwei [Singapore City Committee of the MCP], "Wei fandui shangye zhuce tiaolie gao ge minzu shanglei tongbao shu," November 18, 1939, RGASPI 495/62/28/6; Malayan Communist Party Singapore Executive Committee, "To Fellow Commercial Countrymen of All Nationalities. Strong Protest Against the Commercial Enactment Act," November 18, 1939, RGASPI 495/62/28/103–4.
[29] "Magong di er ci zhongzhihuiyi jueyian [The Resolutions of the Second Plenum of the Executive Committee of the CC MCP]," p. 26.
[30] Mao Zedong, "Zhongguo gongchandang zai minzu zhanzheng zhong de diwei [The Role of the CCP in the National War]," Speech at the 6th Plenum of the CC, October 14, 1938, in *Mao Zedong xuanji, di er juan* [*Collected Works of Mao Zedong*, vol. 2] (Beijing: Renmin chubanshe, 1991), pp. 519–536, esp. p. 520.
[31] Bo Gu, "Guojizhuyi he geming de minzuzhuyi [Internationalism and Revolutionary Nationalism]," *Jiefang* [*Liberation*] 36 (1938), pp. 16–20.
[32] Heng De, "Guoji xingshi lun minzu zhanzheng zhong de Zhongguo gongchandang [Discussing the CCP in the National War and the International Situation]," *Xinli* [*New Force*] 12 (1938), pp. 6–8.

In the same manner as in the 1920s and 1930s, the MCP's focus on the *huaqiao* and its new discourse on internationalism, *guojizhuyi*, were connected to the discourse on the combined emancipation of the *huaqiao* and the oppressed nations. This "internationalism," built on the Comintern's proletarian internationalism, represented modernity and progressiveness juxtaposed against the backwardness (*luohou*) and "narrow nationalism" of the masses. Internationalism was also the new translation of the idea of Sun Yatsen that the rise of the colonies and the rise of China were connected. Emancipating the *huaqiao* from the oppression of the colonial governments of the Nanyang and emancipating the oppressed peoples of the Nanyang and of China proper from imperialism fit the impulse to be embedded in the local environment while also staying connected to China, and it reconciled nationalism and internationalism in MCP ideology. The MCP was self-critical for focusing too much on the *huaqiao*, an orientation that was not sufficient to represent the needs of the whole nation,[33] and on China Salvation work, just as in 1929 when Li Lisan had accused the Nanyang party of "making a Chinese Revolution in the Nanyang."

Yet the propaganda concerning a multiethnic anti-Japanese united front in fact cultivated the association of Chinese with Malaya. For example, as traveling communist theatrical troupes performed anti-Japanese propaganda to racially mixed *kampung* audiences, they shaped local Chinese notions of Chinese as one of three races within a shared national territorial space. This was a crucial shift in the development of the anti-Japanese resistance, first for the purpose of Chinese salvation, then to protect Malaya as a sovereign territory. As the troupes performed Malay songs and plays about Malay and Indian experiences, Chinese realized that the anti-Japanese united front was not only about the defense of China but also about the common struggle with all Malayan *minzu* against Japanese aggression.[34]

Another meaning of *minzu* in MCP texts, "proletariat," showed how the MCP limited its "nation" by excluding the Chinese "comprador bourgeoisie" in Malaya, who were the MCP's most important constituency in reality but not in discourse.

---

[33] "Dui liu zhong kuodahui jueyi celüe bufen de jiancha [Partial Examination of the Resolutions of the 6th Enlarged Plenum of the Central Committee]," undated, early 1940, RGASPI 495/62/28/86–89, esp. 87.

[34] Li Xiaodian, Chen Liang, and Wen Gang, "Xin, Ma renmin wuzhuang kang Ri shiqi de kang Ri juyun [Drama Troupes of the Malayan and Singaporean Chinese during the Anti-Japanese Resistance]," in *Du Bian yu Ma hua (Xin Ma) juyun* [*Du Bian and the Drama Movement of the Malayan and Singaporean Chinese*] (Jiulong: Jinwei yinshua youxian gongsi, 1994), pp. 67–82, esp. p. 69.

The MCP's Proletarian Nation, the Bourgeoisie, and the British

The Bourgeoisie and the MCP before the War

> Only under the leadership of the proletariat and the party is national emancipation [*minzu jiefang*] possible.
>
> CC MCP, 1940[35]

In 1921, Comintern envoy Sneevliet, while visiting Shanghai, noted that Chinese immigrants comprised "the capitalist elements of the Kuomintang."

[They] have always financed the workers' party and expect it to reunify China, to establish law and order, to eradicate the divisive influence of the constantly fighting Tuchuns [warlords] and the defence of China's independence from foreign domination. This Chinese bourgeoisie is situated in the colonies and has only begun very recently to set up firms in China. It has no clear political goal. The leadership of the Kuomintang can never really express the needs of this group.[36]

During the 1930s, this disappointment of the Chinese overseas with the GMD increased as Japanese aggression escalated and as Chiang Kai-shek's policy with regard to Japan was more widely seen as appeasement.

In contrast, the MCP offered a new Bolshevik language with which to speak about the needs of the Chinese community. Many of the MCP's members were "shop employees" (*dianyuan*), and the MCP made efforts to conduct communist propaganda among small traders. In 1929, the MCP wrote to the Comintern that the ban by the British government on the sale of food in the streets of Malaya could be used as a propaganda opportunity.[37] However, it was no exaggeration to say that every Chinese immigrant had come to the Nanyang to become a "bourgeois," so communist propaganda did not make much sense to them. In 1928–1929, Xu Jie, in an attempt to convince a *huaqiao* merchant to embrace communist ideas, tried in vain to explain to him that the world economy had an impact on the Malayan situation, but the attitude of Chinese migrants was that everybody came to the Nanyang to get rich.[38] Similarly, Philippine Chinese communist Gao Zinong complained that Chinese immigrants in the Philippines cared only about becoming rich (*renao qiucai*),[39] and Chinese

---

[35] "Magong di er ci zhongzhihuiyi jueyian [The Resolutions of the Second Plenum of the Executive Committee of the CC MCP]," p. 25.

[36] "Report of Comrade H. Maring to the Executive," esp. p. 318.

[37] "Report from Malay."

[38] Xu Jie, "Yelin de bieshu [Mansion in the Coconut Grove]," pp. 18–33; Ke Pingping as related by Xue Jie, *Kanke daolu shang de zuji* [*Road Full of Misfortunes*], p. 190.

[39] Gao Zinong, "Zhongguo gongchan qingnian tuan Feiliebin tebie difang gongzuo baogao [Work Report of the Philippine Special Local Committee of the Chinese Communist Youth League]," pp. 141, 157–159.

communists in San Francisco had difficulty explaining to the workers who were members of Chinese associations, *tong* and *gongsi*, that they were being exploited,[40] for they "usually [became] bourgeoisie or petty-bourgeoisie when they [went] back to China." Additionally, Chinese students were "usually the sons of wealthy and official families, so they [were] opportunistic and reactionary."[41] However, the Cuban Communist Party, which had a strong base among immigrant communities, including the Chinese, was popular among not only workers but also among petty peddlers (*gongren yu xiao shangren*).[42]

Ho Chi Minh's report about the situation in the MCP in November 1930 stated that: "[Among 1,500 members], the great majority are workers: seamen, builders, rubber workers, miners, etc. There is a small number of intellectuals (schoolteachers and students) and independents (such as restaurant keepers). To a certain extent, they follow the communal economic process of the emigrating Chinese: either trying to save some money to develop what little they possess in their home land or to possess something if they have nothing."[43] For example, it was common for those with a "low cultural level" (*wenhua shuiping dide*) to open bicycle repair shops or to become drivers because the chances to become capitalists were relatively few (*nengcheng zibenjia de jiaoshao*). These migrants, as a rule, did not take part in revolutionary activities, in contrast to intellectuals such as Zhang Xia who became party members.[44]

Among this constituency, national salvation was the cause. In 1928, the NPC considered commemorating the three-month anniversary of the clash between Japanese and GMD troops in Ji'nan, which had resulted in a Japanese expansion after the GMD retreated, to be its most important activity. This event had been commemorated by both the GMD and the CCP, and while the NPC could not do it openly and therefore rather planned a rally and boycott of Japanese products under the name of the Anti-Japanese Chinese Residents' Association, it also planned to distribute propaganda advocating the return of the foreign concessions to China, the anti-imperialist unity of "all oppressed nationalities and classes," and the freedoms of speech, print, assembly, and strike. It also

---

[40] "May First Manifesto of the Chinese Faction of the Workers (Communist) Party of America"; Letter to Comrade Gomez.

[41] "Report of the Bureau of the Chinese Faction. Translation from Chinese," August 5, 1928.

[42] "Guba geming chaojia shen tongzhi jieji liehen [Class Rift Deepens in Cuba]," *The Chinese Vanguard*, April 1, 1934, p. 2; Benton, *Chinese Migrants and Internationalism*, pp. 42–45.

[43] Ho Chi Minh, "Malay."

[44] Zhang Xia, "Xianyou xian lü Ma huaqiao yu geming huodong [Immigrants from Xianyou County in Malaya and Revolutionary Activities]," pp. 34–39.

promoted a wage increase, an eight-hour workday, and the abolition of unjust taxes and the registration of Chinese schools.[45] On August 3, some Singapore Chinese workers stopped working, students skipped classes, and Chinese businesses, schools, and organizations lowered their flags. A rally of 300 participants, mostly Hainanese, resolved to pressure the "national [Chinese] government" to conduct an open foreign policy, to carry out a boycott of Japanese goods, to punish speculators, and to protest the adoption of five points of the Japanese Demands. The police dispersed the rally and arrested several, including an "important communist." After a second five-month anniversary rally, a number of Hainanese night schools were closed. Reflecting on these activities, members of the Fujianese masses, who were most patriotic and were often looked down on as reactionary, believed that national salvation was the right cause, whether led by communists or others.[46]

At least since 1928–1929, the Nanyang party had borrowed money from the "masses" and had not always been able to repay it.[47] Li Lisan warned that the communists might join forces with the revolutionary bourgeoisie in anti-imperialism, but this cooperation should be political, not economic.[48] In 1930, 20 percent of the 1,400 party members were "liberal businessmen." In Singapore, among the Chinese community, 20 percent were merchants and 60 percent were "toiling masses and liberal businessmen."-[49] Both were the main targets of the MCP's propaganda, as many small business owners had gone bankrupt during the depression, while laborers had lost their jobs. In the early 1930s, among party leaders, there were petty bourgeoisie, intellectuals, and members of the working class.[50]

Despite all these illustrations of the importance of a business-minded community to communist activities, from the beginning the bourgeoisie were to be excluded from the revolutionary Malayan nation led by the Malayan national communist party. Fu Daqing, representing the Comintern's opinion, stated that the national bourgeoisie were not a revolutionary force in Malaya,[51] despite the definition of the Nanyang Revolution as a bourgeois democratic revolution.[52] The MCP was left

[45] Vremennyi komitet malaiskogo arkhipelaga [Nanyang Provisional Committee], "V tsentral'nyi komitet. Otchet Malaiskogo Komiteta profsoiuzov [To the Central Committee. The Report of the Soviet of Trade Unions of the Malay Archipelago]."
[46] Ibid.; "Kuomintang and Other Societies in Malaya, July–September 1928," pp. 7, 8.
[47] Nanyang gongzuo baogao [Nanyang Work Report], 1928.
[48] CC CCP, "A Letter from the Central Committee of the CCP to the Nanyang Provisional Committee."
[49] "To the C. C. of the Chinese Party and the Comintern."
[50] Yong, *Origins of Malayan Communism*, p. 167.
[51] "Minutes of the Third Representative Conference of Nanyang," pp. 136–137.
[52] "Resolutions Adopted at the Third Congress of the Malaya Party," p. 2; "Report from Malay."

with the unresolved contradiction that the bourgeoisie were helping to finance the party but had to be excluded from the Malayan Revolution. However, at the founding conference, before Fu Daqing announced his resolution, attendees attempted to solve this contradiction between the two models – one of a Bolshevik party and the other of a Chinese association – and decided not to exclude the bourgeoisie from their revolution. It was clear to them that the national bourgeoisie were oppressed and weak, except for in the Philippines and Ceylon (they likely meant the Chinese), and "demanded independence to develop their class interest," which the MCP interpreted as "a sort of anti-imperialist revolutionary action."[53]

In Burma, Siam, Java, Annam, and Malaya, the MCP stated, "[t]he exploitation is so severe that there is no national bourgeoisie beyond agents of imperialist wholesale dealers. They are counterrevolutionary, but they are so weak, although we cannot say they are not bourgeoisie and do not have thoughts of a patriarchal society ... Yet we have to oppose the imperialists and work hard to secure freedoms of assembly, speech, press, commerce, organization, education, and strike."[54] Furthermore, this movement for democratic freedoms would be carried out by the proletariat, who would seize power. The minutes of the MCP's founding meeting state that: "We should not forsake the democratic movement because of the counterrevolution of the bourgeoisie. We must lead the majority of the oppressed masses to secure their true democratic rights. Therefore, we have to attempt to establish democratic republics in the Malayan states. This is an essential condition to make a united front of the oppressed peoples."[55] Thus, the bourgeoisie, specifically small business owners – or independents, as Ho Chi Minh called them – had a role to play because they were interested in a political force that would represent them in their movement for democratic rights in the countries where they were living. Comintern representative Fu Daqing translated the "democratic movement" advocated by the MCP into the Bolshevik "demands of the masses,"[56] which became the most important slogan of MCP indigenization promoted by the Comintern.

Despite its antibourgeois rhetoric, Nanyang communists had ties with "merchants and intellectuals" who admittedly had a strong national ideology.[57] British analysts pointed out that communist propaganda was effective because "of the anti-imperialist cry, which [had] its appeal to all Chinese whether Communist or not."[58] The AIL's strategy focused

[53] "Minutes of the Third Representative Conference of Nanyang," p. 118.
[54] "Resolutions Adopted at the Third Congress of the Malaya Party," p. 3.
[55] "Minutes of the Third Representative Conference of Nanyang," p. 119.
[56] Ibid., p. 137.
[57] "To the C. C. of the Chinese Party and the Comintern," p. 2.
[58] MRCA, December 1930, p. 59, CO 273/571.

mainly on the "national and petty bourgeoisie as on the main mass of [its] organization."[59] According to an article in *La Dépêche Indochinoise* of March 7, 1933, Comintern agent Joseph Ducroux had been arrested together with Fu Daqing, the secretary of the MCP, and the Comintern–MCP liaison, Huang Muhan, on June 1, 1931, in the company of "rich Chinese who had a book about communism with them."[60]

In 1932, during the campaign against the Alien Registration Ordinance, the MCP argued that although the national bourgeoisie of all *minzu* (*ge minzu zichan jieji*) were not usually a revolutionary force, and although they feared a worker–peasant revolution, during times of economic crisis, they, like others, were dissatisfied with the British imperialists. They therefore became useful to the anti-imperialist movement. Hence, the MCP was to use this attitude among the bourgeoisie. However, the party had to make sure not to compromise the goals of the Malayan Revolution but rather to lead the bourgeoisie to abandon their capitalist mentality in order to develop an anti-imperialist organization and engage with the small bourgeoisie (*xiao zichan jieji*). Throughout, the MCP insisted that the driving force of the Malayan Revolution (*Malaiya geming*) remained the proletariat the and peasants, not the petty urbanites and the national bourgeoisie.[61]

It did not take long for the MCP to realize that the bourgeoisie were also its rival for the allegiance of the masses. In 1932, to prevent the Chinese community from siding with the Chinese bourgeoisie, the MCP planned to explain that Chinese capitalists had exploited the discourse on national interests to convince other classes to sell out their own interests and to support the capitalists to achieve the interests of the capitalist class. National interests (*minzu liyi*) were those of the Chinese, and their representative was the MCP. Thus, the MCP's proletarian nation was emerging. The MCP also began to argue that the bourgeoisie were using the backward masses (*luohou qunzhong*) "to walk the road of peace under their leadership." Yet again, after the Chinese community protested the ordinance, the MCP considered the national bourgeoisie to be oppressed by the fascist British imperialists.[62]

The MCP's campaign in support of the Chinese "soviet" revolution was successful among the most unlikely constituency of a communist party – not

---

[59] "Otchet o polozhenii v Nan'iane [Report about the Situation in Nanyang], [Report about the Situation in Nanyang]," pp. 24–25.

[60] Ducroux's Personal File, RGASPI 532/1/460/39.

[61] "Dangwu wenti jueyian [Resolution on Party Work]."

[62] "Magong lianzi tonggao di yi hao. Dangtuan zhongyang guanyu waiqiao dengji lüli yu women de gongzuo de jueyi [MCP Central Circular no. 1. Resolution of the CC of the MCP and CYL Regarding the Alien Registration Ordinance]."

the MCP's imagined destitute masses or members of the communist party, who, in contrast, did nothing beyond "issuing circulars and empty talk [kongtan zhuyi],"[63] but the most natural supporters of a Chinese association: the bourgeoisie. They could afford to invest in a political force that claimed to be more nationalist and modern than the GMD and that would form a better government in their country of heritage, that is, China, and they sought to improve their position in Malaya. In the Malayan economy of 1933, which had barely started to show signs of recovery, the alleged successes in the Soviet Union looked appealing, especially as the CCP in China was perceived as struggling for China's national independence and freedom (Zhongguo minzu zhi duli yu ziyou).

The MCP rhetoric offered a way to deal with China's present national crisis, while the imperialists, as the MCP explained, were eager to divide China into colonies, and the GMD government appeared inefficient and was selling off China's national interests in exchange for imperialist loans. Aside from establishing the Union to Aid China's Soviet Revolution, the MCP also planned, on behalf of a community school (shetuan xuexiao), to send a telegram to protest the GMD's attack on the CCP base areas and to congratulate the Red Army on its victories. The MCP also planned to organize tours in CCP base areas: "[There, workers and peasants] build a free and happy life, and all participate in political and cultural life, enjoy real [shijide] freedom and political rights, an eight-hour working day, and Sundays off." In contrast, the GMD-occupied areas (tongzhi zhixia) were ravaged by unemployment, exploitation, conflicts among warlords, cold, hunger, and natural disasters. The MCP therefore implied that the GMD had exhausted its Mandate of Heaven.[64]

The MCP was concerned about the general economic position of the Chinese community in Malaya, not only the economic position of the proletariat. In describing the effect of British policies on Malaya since 1930, the MCP talked only about the deterioration of Chinese economic interests. It was concerned about the big Chinese bourgeoisie in Malaya losing their economic position. Besides unemployment, salary cuts, and an increase in working hours, in 1939 the MCP reported a dramatic decline in Chinese ownership of rubber plantations (from a "majority" down to 16 percent) and tin mines (down from 80 percent to 34 percent since

---

[63] "Magong zhongyang tongzhi. Zenyang qu jinxing yu fazhan yuanzhu Zhongguo suweiai geming yundong de gongzuo jueyi [CC MCP Circular. The Resolution on How to Carry Out and Develop Aid to the Soviet Revolutionary Movement in China]."

[64] "CC MCP Statement on the Defence of the Chinese Soviet Revolution," January 5, 1934; "Magong zhongyang tongzhi. Zenyang qu jinxing yu fazhan yuanzhu Zhongguo suweiai geming yundong de gongzuo jueyi [CC MCP Circular. The Resolution on How to Carry Out and Develop Aid to the Soviet Revolutionary Movement in China]."

1912–1913). Big plantations were growing in size, while small plantations, owned by Chinese and Indians, had disappeared.[65] Although it is unclear from where the MCP obtained these figures, the MCP likely blamed the effects of the Great Depression as well as long-term British efforts. Since the late nineteenth century, the British government had outlawed Chinese secret societies and regulated the labor contract system, thereby eroding relations between Chinese employers and employees, monopolized a lucrative trade in opium, spirits, and tobacco, and banned gambling, which had previously made mining lucrative even on poorer-yielding tin land.[66]

The 1937 economic crisis likewise affected the export of tin and rubber. The Chinese, unlike the British, were not allowed to use the latest mining equipment. After the start of the war, the government banned the import of tin, iron, and rubber without government permission, instituted government control over overseas money remittances, imposed new taxes, and limited Chinese production of rice and tea. The British "deprived the *huaqiao* of the liberty to save China (*jiuguo ziyou*)." This manifested in the closure of Chinese organizations, deportations, press censorship, the abolition of unemployment aid, and the introduction of mandatory military training for men. The MCP explained that although the Chinese played an important role in the Malayan economy, they remained dependent on British imperialism because the British could take Chinese property at any time. The Malayan Chinese were interested in a strong China that would be able to protect their property,[67] and the MCP shared this interest.

The bourgeoisie's interest in a better government in China and the MCP's ambiguous attitude toward the bourgeoisie facilitated the latter's support of the party in 1934. However, the Bolshevik concept of a proletarian nation and its anticolonial attitude translated into antibourgeois language, which the MCP had adopted as a communist party from the time of its establishment. This radical language intensified with the beginning of the anticipated world war and mass protests, which apppeared to be the impending revolutionary era and which undermined the MCP's support base.

War, Mass Protests, the United Front, and Anti-British Policy   The MCP's goal was to overthrow the British government in Malaya as a part of the world proletarian revolution. Anti-imperialism made sense to the MCP as a form of protest against the British government's discrimination of Chinese migrants. In 1930, an officeholder of the British Malayan branch

[65] Li, "Malaya Today," pp. 71–72.
[66] Donald M. Nonini, *British Colonial Rule and the Resistance of the Malay Peasantry, 1900–1957* (New Haven, CT: Yale University Southeast Asia Studies, 1992), p. 67.
[67] Li, "Malaya Today," pp. 71–72; Vilkov et al., "Spravka o rabote," pp. 18–19; "Maijin [Forward]," p. 60.

of the GMD, Fang Chih-cheng, explained the reasoning behind anti-imperialism while discussing the banning of the GMD with the governor of Malaya, Cecil Clementi. In 1927, Hong Kong *GMD News* had called for the overthrow of the British, and in reference to this, Fang said, "[a]nti-imperialism [does] not mean we oppose the British, it means we oppose the people who encroach upon Chinese ... Imperialists do not mean any particular nation but those people who encroach upon Chinese."[68] This explanation sheds light on the layers of meaning in the MCP's anti-British attitudes too.

However, not everyone in the Chinese community shared anti-British sentiments. In order to earn the support of overseas Chinese in Hong Kong, in 1923 Sun Yatsen had to ally with those who were on good terms with the British government, since his anti-British stance had alienated many.[69] Since the early days of its establishment, the MCP had to explain to fellow Chinese why they had to oppose the British. A pamphlet distributed in 1930 on the anniversary of Lenin's death is an example of the adaptation of the communist message to local cultural codes, which was the MCP's goal and was reminiscent of Li Lisan's techniques while mobilizing workers in the Anyuan mines.[70] The pamphlet opened with a question: "Why shall we protest against imperialism?" It then explained that imperialism was like a tiger sitting in front of one's house, where one's wife and children were: "You call for a friend, and you must either force the tiger to leave or kill it. Our Malaya [*women de Malaiya*] is exactly in this situation ... British imperialism is the tiger that prevents us from improving our own lives."[71]

As a part of the CCP's united front policy, in 1938 the MCP adopted a pro-British stance because Great Britain was "China's friend,"[72] and in 1939, it pledged its cooperation on the condition that universal franchise and other democratic freedoms would be granted to all ethnic communities. However, it reserved the right to mobilize workers against the British.[73] At the same

---

[68] "Conference Held at Government House, Singapore, on the 20th February 1930 at 2.30 P.M.," Foreign Office Records 371/14728/2083, cited in Yong and McKenna, *The Kuomintang Movement in British Malaya*, pp. 247–252, esp. p. 252.

[69] Henricus Sneevliet, "Report on the Situation in China and on Work during the Period 15–31 May 1923," in Saich, ed., *The Origins of the First United Front in China*, pp. 535–542, esp. p. 535.

[70] Perry, *Anyuan*, pp. 46–75.

[71] Singapore City Committee of the MCP, "Shijie wuchan jieji geming lingxiu Liening tongzhi qushi di qi zhounian jinian [Commemorating the Seventh Anniversary of the Death of the Leader of the World Proletarian Revolution Comrade Lenin]."

[72] This was documented at an AEBUS meeting and was published in *Nanyang Siang Pau* on July 30, 1938, as "Our Attitudes." The AEBUS was the venue for the MCP's China Salvation Movement and had many local branches across Malaya. Yong, *Origins of Malayan Communism*, p. 246.

[73] Yong, *Origins of Malayan Communism*, pp. 261–262.

time, following the line of the CCP, the MCP celebrated the Soviet–Nazi nonaggression pact of August 23, 1939, and touted the USSR as a model liberator of oppressed nations that helped the national liberation movements of oppressed peoples (*bei yapo renmin he minzu jiefang yundong*) in the annexed territories in Poland, Finland, the Baltic region, and Bessarabia. "In accordance with the Comintern resolutions' spirit and Malaya's internal situation," the MCP promoted overthrowing the British government and establishing a democratic republic of Malaya (*minzhu gongheguo*).[74]

Also contradictory were the assorted goals of the MCP. These included a parliament consisting of an assembly of all parties and anti-imperialist organizations, selected by all people in each state; freedoms of assembly, speech, print, belief, and strike, as well as the opportunity for wage increases, unemployment aid, and disaster payments; development of the national economy (apparently the Malayan economy) and self-government of customs; an eight-hour workday; social security, male–female equality, maternity leave, and abolition of the Mui Tsai system;[75] democratization of the military; education in the national language (*minzu yuwen*) as well as free education for the impoverished; the unification of all oppressed nations of the world; opposition to war, defense of the Soviet Union by all peace-loving nations, and punishment of fascists, national traitors, and corrupt bureaucrats; national independence and the development of a national culture; support for the resistance in China and the national liberation movement of India; and a united anti-imperialist front of all nationalities. On the margins of this page, a Comintern Chinese reader asked: "What are the tactics [*celüe*] to carry this out?"[76]

The reaction to British wartime economic measures after Britain's entry into the war on September 3, 1939, which resulted in longer working hours, price increases, and disproportionally smaller pay increases in Singapore,[77] was widespread protests. The MCP reported "more than one hundred thousand workers" participating in strikes from September 1939 to January 1940.[78] In October, the MCP sounded victorious, as its June resolutions had correctly predicted the imperialist war that triggered

---

[74] "Magong di er ci zhongzhihuiyi jueyian [The Resolutions of the Second Plenum of the Executive Committee of the CC MCP]," p. 21; "Maijin [Forward]," pp. 54–56; Lyman P. van Slyke, *Enemies and Friends: The United Front in Chinese Communist History* (Stanford, CA: Stanford University Press, 1967), p. 121.

[75] For more on the Mui Tsai system, see Rachel Leow, "'Do You Own Non-Chinese Mui Tsai?' Re-examining Race and Female Servitude in Malaya and Hong Kong, 1919–1939," *Modern Asian Studies* 46 (2012), pp. 1736–1763.

[76] "Magong di er ci zhongzhihuiyi jueyian [The Resolutions of the Second Plenum of the Executive Committee of the CC MCP]," p. 28; Li, "Malaya Today," pp. 46–48.

[77] Vilkov et al., "Spravka o rabote," pp. 29–34.

[78] Ibid., pp. 34–35.

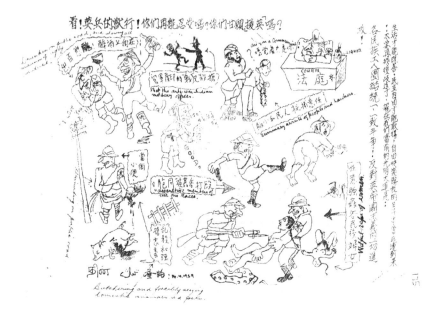

Figure 7.1 Anti-British drawing, 1940.[82]
Published with permission of the National Archives, UK.

the national liberation movement.[79] The MCP interpreted these wide-spread protests to be a result of the growing anti-imperialism of the toiling masses and small bourgeoisie and as an opportune time to start a revolution in the Nanyang. The MCP proclaimed, "[t]he only road for the people of Malaya is to overthrow the British to achieve national independence [*minzu duli*]."[80] The MCP now resented its infantile (*youxiang*) prewar policy of cooperation with the British (*yu Ying hezuo*). The MCP decided that as the political party of class interests and national and social liberation (*minzu and shehui jiefang*), it could not cooperate with the main enemy of all nationalities (*ge minzu*), which was suppressing Malaya's rights in politics, the economy, and culture. Yet the MCP did not rule out cooperation with the British in the future.[81]

[79] "Zhongyang changwei dui dangqian gongzuo xin de jueyi [New Resolutions on the Party Work of the Standing Committee of the CC]," April 6, 1940, RGASPI 495/62/28/45–52, esp. 47 (henceforth, "CC New Resolutions").

[80] Li, "Malaya Today," p. 66; "Magong di er ci zhongzhihuiyi jueyian [The Resolutions of the Second Plenum of the Executive Committee of the CC MCP]," p. 25.

[81] "Dui liu zhong kuodahui jueyi celüe bufen de jiancha [Partial Examination of the Resolutions of the 6th Enlarged Plenum of the Central Committee]"; Yong, *Origins of Malayan Communism*, p. 198.

[82] *Qianfengbao* [*Avant-garde*] (5), January 1, 1940, CO 273/662/50336.

An anti-British MCP drawing (see Figure 7.1) addresses the compatriots of "all peoples" (*ge minzu tongbao*) and promotes "national" unity (*minzu tuanjie*), demonstrating the continuing multiple meanings of *minzu*. Whether intentionally or unintentionally, the message is that Chinese national unity and Malayan national unity concern the same nation (*minzu*). This is another example of anti-British propaganda that targeted common Chinese with simple and understandable language. It was built around the British breaching of social norms, such as raping, butchering, and forcibly seizing domestic animals, relieving themselves in public, drinking, and summarily arresting and suppressing protesters.

Soon, however, the MCP recognized that its anti-British policy was inadequate: "In an unfavorable situation, the party must not call the masses under its slogans, such as 'Overthrow British imperialism' and 'Oppose the imperialist war' but work from the slogans initiated by the masses and in accordance with the 'degree of awakening' of the masses [*juewu chengdu*], for only in this case can the masses come to the party."[83] The MCP's anti-British policies were at odds with the mood of the Chinese community. Although those who upheld the anti-Japanese resistance movement had more influence "than the capitulationists," they did not resist British imperialism. The MCP had tried to recruit among the Corps for the Resistance to Japan and Salvation of the Motherland, comprising small bourgeoisie, traders, intellectuals, students, workers, and shop clerks, by explaining how in fact British policy "indirectly compromised with Japan and sold out anti-Japanese war interests."[84] However, the party's radicalism prevented the masses from joining. The MCP had been outlawed, and participants in protests were sometimes killed by police, as during the rally on May 1, 1940 or during the coal miners' strike in 1937 in Batu Arang, which was a major MCP success in organizing labor.[85]

The MCP decided to stop its anti-British policy prior to October 1940, when the CCP in Hong Kong, which coordinated the united front in Southeast Asia, instructed it to do so.[86] In fact, the MCP had started to doubt the effectiveness of the policy in February of that year, although it continued to put forward the slogan of independence.[87] The MCP changed its policy based on local conditions: "We do not say in our program to

[83] "Maijin [Forward]," p. 82.
[84] Li, "Malaya Today," p. 81; "Magong di er ci zhongzhihuiyi jueyian [The Resolutions of the Second Plenum of the Executive Committee of the CC MCP]," p. 29.
[85] Vilkov et al., "Spravka o rabote," p. 37; Li, "Malaya Today," p. 68; Yong, *Origins of Malayan Communism*, pp. 220–227.
[86] Yong, *Origins of Malayan Communism*, p. 232; Glen Peterson, *Overseas Chinese in the People's Republic of China* (London: Routledge, 2011), p. 20.
[87] "Magong di er ci zhongzhihuiyi jueyian [The Resolutions of the Second Plenum of the Executive Committee of the CC MCP]," p. 34; "Maijin [Forward]," p. 88.

kick the British out of Malaya, because at least they do not help the fascists. We say, 'Establish a democratic system' rather than 'Kick out the British.' However, in the long run, we must plan to kick out the British and establish a self-determined democratic republic, because British interests are incompatible with the interests of all Malaya's oppressed peoples [*ge bei yapo minzu*]."[88]

Although on the wave of unrest the MFLU's membership grew from 20,000 in April 1939 to 50,000 in 1940,[89] the picture of the MCP's triumphant leadership in the labor unrest of 1937–1939 and its strengthened power base[90] is undermined by its own reflections. When the struggles "had already become a part of everyday life for various nationalities ... the party did not work at the lower level of the united front,"[91] had a "disdainful" (*prezritel'noe*) attitude toward the labor movement organization, and was at the tail of the working masses. Overall, the MCP portrayed the workers' movement as having been under its leadership since its beginning, but because the communists "did not always correctly understand the conditions and tasks of the workers' movement, they often remained without the leadership of communists, and failed." Workers' protests were economic struggles and were not anti-imperialist. In 1935–1940, labor organizations in Malaya operated legally, and since workers' struggles were sometimes successful, workers were under the

---

[88] "Magong di er ci zhongzhihuiyi jueyian [The Resolutions of the Second Plenum of the Executive Committee of the CC MCP]," p. 28, Leong, "Sources, Agencies and Manifestations of Overseas Chinese Nationalism in Malaya," pp. 557–573; the earliest MCP party history, "Nandao zhichun [The Spring of Southern Islands]," is found in Cheah, *From PKI to the Comintern*, pp. 103–124.

[89] Yong, *Origins of Malayan Communism*, p. 234.

[90] Ibid., pp. 216–233, esp. pp. 231–232. In the celebratory reports compiled by the Comintern's Chinese cadres based on MCP reports, from September 1939 to January 1940, the "majority" of workers' strikes had been under the MCP's leadership. These included the following strikes: the strike at the Malacca plantation in 1931; the strike of construction workers in Singapore in 1937; the Singapore tram workers' strike for a salary increase and the Singapore port workers' refusal to accept Japanese cargo in 1938; a January 9, 1938, rally of Chinese immigrants in Singapore on the International Day of Aid to China; a Kuala Lumpur machinery factory workers' strike involving 2,500 government factory workers; and a gathering of 500 to 600 workers and clerks in a May 1 rally. In November and December 1939, 1,500 woodcutters and several thousand workers in a rubber factory protested for a wage increase and a decrease in working hours. The MCP reported its leadership in more than 300 workers' protests, with more than 80,000 participants, between April and September 1939. After the British entrance into the war in that same month, the MCP reported an increase in the number of people involved in activities organized by the party. In Pahang, it increased seven times, in Selangor four times, in Penang three times, and in other places more than two times, with the exception of Malacca, which saw only a 30–35 percent increase. Vilkov et al., "Spravka o rabote," pp. 34, 35, 45; Li, "Malaya Today," pp. 68, 75, 84–85.

[91] Vilkov et al., "Spravka o rabote," p. 46.

illusion that they could improve their lot without a political struggle against British imperialism.[92]

In 1940, as an effect of growing pro-British attitudes, the labor union registration law, and the Industrial Court Ordinance, meant to settle industrial disputes via industrial courts and to refuse registration if a union had participated in unlawful activity,[93] there was an overall downturn in labor protests.[94] The MCP campaigned against the ordinance (see Figure 7.2) but nonetheless had to adjust its tactics to this new situation. Since February, the party's following and membership had plummeted, especially in north Malaya, in Penang, and in Perak.[95] Some had joined yellow trade unions, and this was in addition to the fact that previously reported numbers of the "masses" had been exaggerated by 20–30 percent. The party was connected only with the upper strata of mass organizations. Most activities occurred in Singapore, which was the only place where the masses were not considered backward by the MCP. The party did not have a basis in urban centers, the most important rubber plantations, mines, or big industries. The party's discussion movement (*taolun yundong*) and "legalist" protests were "superficial lectures."

Figure 7.2 MCP propaganda against the trade union registration ordinance introduced by the government of the Straits Settlements in 1939, ca. 1940.[96] Published with permission of the National Archives, UK.

[92] Ibid., pp. 37–39.
[93] Yong, *Origins of Malayan Communism*, p. 277.
[94] Tai Yuen, *Labour Unrest*, p. 172.
[95] The number increased in Malacca, Johor Bahru, and Kedah. In south Malaya, Singapore, and Johor Bahru, the "masses" who participated in protests became more "reliable." "Maijin [Forward]," pp. 62–63; "CC New Resolutions."
[96] CO 273/662/50336.

In March 1940, the MCP started a political unity movement (*zhengzhi tongyi yundong*) to improve the party's connection with the masses. To improve comrades' insufficient understanding of CC resolutions and of lower-level comrades (*xiaceng tongzhi*) in party and labor unions, the party was to participate in yellow unions and other "organizations of the masses," to promote non-party activists to positions of leadership, to guide the masses to places where protests were to take place and encourage them to participate, and to "fit the education to the moods of the masses."[97] Each member had to establish connections with ten or several tens of members of the masses. To succeed, comrades needed only "not to fear difficulties" (*bu pa mafan*) and to creatively (*chuangzaode*) lead the masses, especially after the suppression of the struggles.[98] For the first time, the party organization was called backward (*dang zuzhi de luohou*): "If the party doesn't Bolshevize, it will be behind the masses."[99] The party was torn between the ideology of a Bolshevik party and the specific context of its situation and constituency. Even where the party organized small groups of five to twenty people not only could it not handle the masses but instead the masses handled the party (*bawo*). Where there used to be more than ten comrades and hundreds of masses, there now remained only tens of masses and just over ten comrades. Closed doors based on class outlook (*jieji guandian*), or on a narrow-minded rightist outlook, did not let party membership grow.[100]

While continuing to promote development of the organizations of other ethnic groups (*ge minzu zuzhi*)[101] and continuing to criticize its own "immigrant mentality,"[102] as a part of the CCP's united front the MCP focused mainly on *huaqiao* in its efforts to fundraise for China's anti-Japanese resistance in Chinese associations. Since the early 1930s, organizations based on native place and dialect connections had become "an indispensable operational framework for any large-scale social campaign," as patriotism had become a necessary quality for any status claimant in Singapore.[103] During the China Salvation fundraising campaign, CCP envoys launched

---

[97] "Maijin [Forward]," p. 65; "Magong di er ci zhongzhihuiyi jueyian [The Resolutions of the Second Plenum of the Executive Committee of the CC MCP]," p. 34; "CC New Resolutions," p. 47.

[98] "CC New Resolutions," p. 47.

[99] "Maijin [Forward]," p. 65.

[100] Ibid.

[101] "Magong di er ci zhongzhihuiyi jueyian [The Resolutions of the Second Plenum of the Executive Committee of the CC MCP]," p. 34; "CC New Resolutions," p. 47.

[102] "Maijin [Forward]," p. 61.

[103] Wing Chung Ng, "Urban Chinese Social Organization."

propaganda among Chinese overseas communities worldwide through Chinese associations.[104] The MCP was establishing a network of secret study societies (*yanjiuhui*) and small groups (*xiaozu*), such as newspaper reading groups (*dubaoban*) in Chinese associations.[105] In 1936, the MCP formed a united front with the Singapore Overseas Chinese Anti-Japanese Union (Xinjiapo huaqiao kang Ri lianhehui) and founded the All-Malaya Overseas Chinese Anti-Japanese National Salvation Union (Quan Malaiya huaqiao kang Ri lianhehui). The MCP's active participation in the China Salvation Movement thus boosted its support base.[106]

However, the traditional role of Chinese associations in Singapore as intermediaries with the Chinese community, resolving conflicts and mobilizing community support in close connection with the British government,[107] contradicted the anti-British and anti-bourgeoisie MCP discourse, and thus the party slogans did not attract the members of the Chinese associations. Blaming this again on the backwardness of the masses, the MCP abandoned its work in China Salvation organizations (*kang yuan zuzhi*) and ceased to carry out open propaganda in some Chinese associations (*gongkai shetuan gongzuo*), as in Perak, because it was afraid that its propaganda would push the masses the way of reactionaries despite their anti-imperialist moods.[108] Some had overestimated the progressiveness and revolutionary spirit (*gemingxing yu jinbuxing*) of the masses.[109] The CC thus insisted on reviving propaganda and fundraising in those organizations.[110]

Complications in the MCP's relations with the bourgeoisie were a result of tension between its two sides: one as a Chinese organization and the other as a Bolshevik party. As a Chinese organization, the MCP relied on community members for support, but as a Bolshevik party, it had to exclude them. This tension is clear in MCP texts. Before the war, the MCP, like other Chinese organizations, had promoted the slogan of labor–capital cooperation (*laozi hezuo*). Chinese guilds traditionally included both owners and employees.[111] While some argued that this slogan meant abandoning class interests, proponents argued that the slogan was a part of the party's national united front tactics (*minzu*

[104] Ren, Zhao, and Mao, *Chinese Overseas and CCP–GMD Relations*, pp. 157–164.
[105] "Magong di er ci zhongzhihuiyi jueyian [The Resolutions of the Second Plenum of the Executive Committee of the CC MCP]," p. 32.
[106] Yong, Origins of Malayan Communism, pp. 180, 184.
[107] Wing Chung Ng, "Urban Chinese Social Organization."
[108] "Maijin [Forward]," pp. 67–68.
[109] "Magong di er ci zhongzhihuiyi jueyian [The Resolutions of the Second Plenum of the Executive Committee of the CC MCP]," pp. 27, 28.
[110] "Maijin [Forward]," pp. 55–56.
[111] Yong, *Origins of Malayan Communism*, p. 246.

tongyi zhanxian celüe), used to bring the revolutionary part of the bourgeoisie to the national liberation movement (*minzu jiefang yundong*), and it did not mean promoting "unconditional cooperation with capitalists."[112]

The MCP's attitude toward the bourgeoisie was optimistic in the beginning, since the national economy (*minzu jingji*) and the position of the bourgeoisie had been greatly affected by British wartime policies, as had all other strata of the population (*ge jieji renmin*), including *huaqiao* workers and small bourgeoisie. The MCP argued, "Fascists under the mask of nationalism suppress the national liberation movement [*minzu jiefang yundong*] ... Sultans are [therefore] helping the British, but the national bourgeoisie [*minzu zichan jieji*] are not satisfied with the British policy and are progressive [*jinbu pai de*] like Tan Kah Kee."[113] Notably, though Tan Kah Kee had always been critical of the communists, he was never criticized by the communists in return and was likely sympathetic to their cause.[114]

By February 1940, the MCP declared that the call for concord between labor and capital by the Chinese chamber of commerce and Chinese consul Gao Lingbai was nothing else but a selling off of the national interest (*minzu liyi*), because the bourgeoisie presented their class interest as the national interest. The Nanyang merchants' theory of labor and capital cooperation meant "selling out *minzu liyi* and sacrificing the interests of the workers."[115] Clearly, *minzu* in this sentence referred to the workers. The MCP concluded that the united front of various nationalities represented the interests of all strata of the population (*ge jieceng renmin*) but that the concessionist bourgeoisie had to be opposed. Thus, the MCP's *renmin* did not include the bourgeoisie despite the fact that the MCP supposedly promoted a cross-class alliance. Even Comintern reader Wang Ming, judging from the handwriting, was not convinced by this logic and scribbled a comment against this paragraph: "Where is the united front [*tongyi zhanxian hezai*]?"[116]

---

[112] Maijin [Forward], p. 28.

[113] Li, "Malaya Today," p. 76. For examples of British nationalist propaganda, see "New G. O. C. on Growing Strength of Empire," *Straits Times*, July 29, 1939, p. 12; "Britain's Crusade for Liberty," *Singapore Free Press and Mercantile Advertiser*, September 25, 1939, p. 4.

[114] Zheng, *Overseas Chinese Nationalism*, pp. 306–307, 313; Ye Zhongling [Yeap Chong Leng], "Chen Jiageng [Tan Kah Kee] dui Magong taidu de zhuanyi: Cong 'ruoji ruoli' dao gongkai chongtu [Changing Attitudes Toward the Malayan Communist Party: From 'Ambiguity' to Open Conflict]," in *Yazhou wenhua* [*Asian Culture*] 28 (June 2004), pp. 94–108.

[115] "Magong di er ci zhongzhihuiyi jueyian [The Resolutions of the Second Plenum of the Executive Committee of the CC MCP]," pp. 30–31.

[116] Ibid., p. 26.

At the same time, the MCP argued that capitalists had become the "loyal stooges" of British policy because the aforementioned Chinese consulate in Singapore and Perak's Chinese chamber of commerce promoted Sino–British friendship. To the MCP, this meant that the interests of Malayan Chinese capitalists (*Ma hua da zichan jieji*) were the same as British interests: to put China into a position of colonial slavery.[117] To a Comintern reader, the MCP's discourse about the bourgeoisie was confusing, and Wang Ming scribbled on the margins of the same MCP document: "The attitude toward the bourgeoisie is unclear [*dui zichan jieji de taidu shi mohude*]."[118]

In 1939–1940, in addition to its negative effects, such as the soaring prices of daily necessities, the war also brought an economic boom beneficial for the bourgeoisie.[119] Perhaps this was the reason that by 1940, the MCP had begun to identify the national interest exclusively with the interests of the proletariat despite the rhetoric of the united front, which was supposed to conflate national and class interests (*jieji liyi*). The MCP's nation, like Li Dazhao's imagined China in 1920, was a "proletarian nation."[120] As such, the MCP's *minzu* was its anti-imperialist front. That included residents of central cities – the urban masses, such as shop workers, coolies, and handicraftsmen, as well as the proletariat and peasants and petty bourgeoisie (*xiao zichan jieji*). To the MCP, to mobilize these people meant to mobilize (*dongyuan*) the whole nation (*quan minzu*), "without which we can't speak about mobilization of most of the people [*daduoshu renmin de liang*]."[121] However, this nation was not under the MCP's influence.

The party bitterly admitted that it was not influential even among Chinese immigrants and reported that in Trengganu, Selangor, and Johor its organizations were weak and communist influence was almost unnoticeable. The number of Malays and Indians in the party was negligible, and the number of workers among its leaders, from the CC to lower-level cells, was very small. The leaders of the party organization were, "as a rule," Chinese communists.[122] The situation regarding the MCP's influence in the Chinese community was gloomy. The party's view on this deserves to be quoted in full:

---

[117] "Maijin [Forward]," p. 79.
[118] "Magong di er ci zhongzhihuiyi jueyian [The Resolutions of the Second Plenum of the Executive Committee of the CC MCP]," p. 28.
[119] Tai Yuen, *Labour Unrest*, p. 134.
[120] Fitzgerald, *Awakening China*, pp. 88, 175.
[121] "Maijin [Forward]," pp. 76–77; "Magong di er ci zhongzhihuiyi jueyian [The Resolutions of the Second Plenum of the Executive Committee of the CC MCP]," p. 23.
[122] Vilkov et al., "Spravka o rabote," pp. 50–51.

Figure 7.3 Street scene in Singapore, ca. 1940.
Singapore Federation of the Chinese Clan Associations Collection.
Courtesy of the National Archives of Singapore.

There are two forces among the broad masses of workers and peasants, only around
seventeen thousand people; all are Malay sprouts [*Malai douhua*], immigrants from
bankrupt villages back home [*guonei*]. [They are] middle class, poor peasants, and
agricultural laborers, bankrupt middle business owners from the cities, and lower-
level [*xiaceng*] laborers. Since the 1929 world economic depression, a lot of local
[*bendi*] petty capitalists have gone bankrupt and become proletariat [*wuchanzhe*].
For these historical factors, the revolutionary force of the masses of Chinese
immigrants in Malaya [*Ma huaqiao zhong*] for the most part cannot have a proletarian class consciousness [*meiyou nenggou juyou danchun de wuchan jieji yishi*].
There are about several tens of thousands of [*shu wan*] workers under the party's
influence who have gone through training via economic struggles, and their class
consciousness [*jieji juewu*] has risen. However, we must admit that the greater part
of the masses has strong nationalist ideas [*nonghou de minzu guannian*], which,
because of British oppression ... grow day by day. They support the anti-Japanese
war, unity, and progressiveness. However, party influence over this force is not
common [*bu pubiande*], and what is common [*pubiande*] is backwardness
[*luohouxing*].

   Another force is the urban petty bourgeoisie, urban residents, students, and
intellectuals [*chengshi xiao zichan jieji shimin xuesheng zhishi fenzi*]. This force has
been oppressed by the British for years. The national bourgeoisie are almost all
bankrupt and are more and more disappointed with Malaya as the war unfolds
and they see the resistance war [*kangzhan*] as an investment opportunity in China.
They support the anti-Japanese war and unity [*tuanjie*] and are progressive, but

they are pessimistic about its perspectives; they are dissatisfied with the British imperialists but lack self-confidence and have vacillation and fear.

The comprador capitalists and defeatists have influence over the masses with their ideology of nationalism and its backward [*minzu guannian ji qi luohouxing*] and opportunist policy [*touji zhengzhi*]. Because of all this, and the narrow class-mindedness of the comrades and mechanistic application of the party line … it makes the job of defeatists easier. For instance, because comrades everywhere raise anti-British slogans, masses support concessionist [*toujian tuoxie pai*] slogans … Also, the slogan of class struggle helped the activity of concessionist organizations. This is a grave warning that if the party doesn't abandon its class narrowmindedness, the danger of breaking from the masses is looming.[123]

Thus, anti-British, antiwar,[124] and anti-bourgeoisie slogans alienated the masses. Although the party claimed to have a symbolic large number of followers, "several tens of thousands," the workers' economic awakening superseded a class awakening (*jingji juewu chaoguo jieji juewu*)[125] and the masses feared (*haipa xinli*) the party because of the "enemy's propaganda."[126] Open displays of anti-British sentiment caused police reprisals, and by July 1940, 229 communist leaders, mostly students and trade union agitators, had been arrested.[127] The MCP was to lead Malaya's proletarian nation in the "national" movement, yet the MCP's united front remained an objective, not a reality. As a result, the MCP was leading a national movement without a nation.

National Party without a Nation

Now the situation in the party is like when one has just crossed a bridge and has set out to travel on a big road to a faraway destination.
CC MCP, early 1940[128]

The MCP's participation in the China Salvation Movement likely boosted its membership. In February 1937, among the twelve-member committee of the Singapore Overseas Chinese National Salvation Association (Xinjiapo qiao kang Ri lianhehui), six were MCP members and one was a CYL member. Until September 1940, the MCP continued to use the AEBUS, which had been organized in December 1937, as its front organization. In 1939, AEBUS membership was estimated at 38,848.[129] In spite of this, the narrative of the MCP's uninterrupted growth in popularity, which resulted

[123] "Maijin [Forward]," pp. 79–81.
[124] Ibid., p. 81.
[125] "Magong di er ci zhongzhihuiyi jueyian [The Resolutions of the Second Plenum of the Executive Committee of the CC MCP]," p. 24.
[126] "Maijin [Forward]," p. 67.
[127] Heng, *Chinese Politics in Malaysia*, p. 32.
[128] "Maijin [Forward]," p. 67.
[129] Yong, *Origins of Malayan Communism*, pp. 245, 247–248, 267.

in estimates of 5,000 members in 1941,[130] invites questions, because regardless of the very likely increase in the influence of communist ideas, the party was losing its membership, not only its constituency. The MCP's claim of 10,000 members in 1937 was obviously an exaggeration,[131] as MCP documents reveal a different order of membership figures, and its growth relied on "persuading opportunists" in Singapore.[132] Party membership was 379 in March 1937, 1,000 in April 1939, and 500 later in 1939, since we know that the membership doubled to 1,000 by January 1940. Membership again increased to 1,700 in May 1940.[133] Even though the development of party organizations was made a priority over the development of mass organizations, it was halted by arrests, inaction, expulsions, and abolition of the category of reserve member (*houbu*).[134]

The MCP's exclusion of small bourgeoisie was also the reason it was losing members. Because the MCP did not recruit petty bourgeoisie and did not let new members enter the party ("narrow closed-doorism"), it became "a secret organization with a narrow class outlook" (*mimi de xiaai de jieji guandian*)[135] instead of promoting the unity of classes and national interests (*jieji liyi he minzu liyi shi yizhide*).[136] "Narrow-minded patriotism" (*aiguozhuyi*) was linked to narrow-minded class ideas: "Many comrades think that the core of the national liberation struggle is workers and peasants (although there are a lot of factories, plantations, etc. where there is no party nucleus), and they overlook the petty bourgeoisie [*xiao zichan jieji*]. They think they are the core of the national liberation struggle, while in fact they exercise closed doorism." They focused on workers and peasants and labeled the "petty bourgeoisie and the backward masses [*luohou qunzhong*]" as having "vacillation" and "defeatism."[137] As a result, the MCP broke "national" unity [*fenhua minzu de tuanjie*]: "If

---

[130] Ibid., p. 202.

[131] "Malayan Reds also Plan 'United Front,'" *Straits Times*, October 25, 1937, p. 13.

[132] "Maijin [Forward]," p. 59; "Magong di er ci zhongzhihuiyi jueyian [The Resolutions of the Second Plenum of the Executive Committee of the CC MCP]," p. 24.

[133] Yong, *Origins of Malayan Communism*, p. 202; Vilkov et al., "Spravka o rabote," pp. 44, 45.

[134] The procedure for accepting new members (*dang duixiang*) into the party started with giving them party materials to read and discuss. At the same time, the party had to understand each person's family background, social connections (*shehui guanxi*), personal habits, and positive and negative sides and thereby decide whether each person was ready to become a party member. The purpose was to filter out the moles in the party. Once a person became a party member, the party had to help him or her complete a reserve (*houbu*) period and, with class warmness (*jieji reqing*), educate the candidate to determine whether he or she could be accepted into the party. The person who introduced the new party member held full responsibility toward the party. "CC New Resolutions," pp. 49–50.

[135] "Maijin [Forward]," pp. 67–68.

[136] Ibid., p. 68. This idea can be traced back to 1932 in China. Van Slyke, *Enemies and Friends*, pp. 11–12.

[137] "Maijin [Forward]," pp. 68, 74.

our party counts on workers' and peasants' movements and not on an all-national movement [*quan minzu yundong*], how can we struggle against the enemies?"[138] Thus, to neutralize the effect of the British hiring labor unions (*gonghui dang*) to break up workers' struggles, the MCP even decided to work among secret societies (*sihuidang*) and to apply a "warm national feeling" (*qingqie de minzu ganqing*) in order to unite the workers (*lianjie*), much as the CCP had sought nonideological methods of attracting new members with its united front tactics.[139] At the same time, summarily advocating (*luantichu*) the slogan that workers had no motherland (*gongren wu zuguo*) was also against the anti-imperialist united front (*fandi tongyi zhanxian*).[140]

"Reactionary capitalists" attacked the party for representing narrow class interests[141] and stated that the GMD was more successful in China Salvation work and attracted the same constituency the MCP was targeting. These were the immigrant bourgeoisie, the petty bourgeoisie, workers, and cultural workers. The MCP argued that the GMD had attracted a following because it offered career and investment opportunities in China, as it existed semi-legally and worked through legal mass social organizations, newspapers, and Chinese schools. The GMD started to hold drama performances and meetings and "lied to the masses" that the CCP no longer existed. On the other hand, the Corps for the Resistance to Japan and Salvation of the Motherland recruited Chinese to serve as officers in the army in China, with a support base among the petty bourgeoisie, traders, intellectuals, and students. In Kuala Lumpur, even "big capitalists" and writers only "reluctantly accepted" workers and shop clerks.[142] The MCP implied that there was an audience that could be receptive to its propaganda.

Instead, the MCP had never sounded so desperate, for it had been defeated by the bourgeoisie and the GMD, whom the MCP had excluded from its "nation" in the battle for the allegiance of the masses. The organizations of the masses "became the tools of capitalists," and the party lost its independence.[143] The capitalists, in contrast, had put forward slogans of capital–labor cooperation, cooperation with the British (*Zhong Ying qingxi*), and a people's diplomacy (*guomin waijiao*).[144] To deal with these, the party was to abandon its narrow-minded class

---

[138] Ibid., pp. 73–74.
[139] Ibid., p. 76; Van Slyke, *Enemies and Friends*, p. 120.
[140] "Maijin [Forward]," pp. 68, 74.
[141] Ibid., pp. 73–74.
[142] Vilkov et al., "Spravka o rabote," pp. 17, 20; Li, "Malaya Today," pp. 78–82.
[143] "Magong di er ci zhongzhihuiyi jueyian [The Resolutions of the Second Plenum of the Executive Committee of the CC MCP]," p. 32.
[144] "Maijin [Forward]," pp. 73–74.

outlook, implement open Chinese organizations (*gongkai shetuan*), and establish party organizations according to territorial divisions (streets), as it had been advocating since 1931,[145] not according to industry, as had been the Comintern's policy. In February 1940, the MCP reverted to the slogans of encouraging the development of national capitalist enterprises and again advocated the establishment of a parliamentary republic. However, the MCP argued: "[This will not be] a soviet republic, as Malays' national liberation [*minzu jiefang*] is not at the stage of the national struggle of workers and peasants [*gongnong minzu douzheng*], so it is still in the period of bourgeois revolution [*zichan jieji geming*]." The question of land reform, however, remained a point in the MCP's program.[146]

The MCP alluded to Mao to explain that the party was weak because it did not have a strong theoretical standpoint, neither did it carry out its activities based on practical conditions:

As our teachers taught us . . . a Bolshevik party does not fall from the sky [*yi ge Buershiweike dang bing bu shi cong tiankong diaoxialai de*] but appears through struggles and suffering. However, until now there have been comrades who treat revolutionary theory [*geming de lilun*] as something off topic [*mobuzhao bianji de dongxi*]. They are fatalistic [*tongtian youming*]. Struggles are not initiated by comrades from smaller struggles . . . Because of comrades' ideological [*yishi*] vacillations, the party doesn't have the power to change the environment [*gaizao huanjing*]. The party is weak. The results of political mobilization have shown that the party cannot become the political leader of the national liberation movement. The party is so backward [*luohou*] that it has become an obstacle to the forward development of the national liberation movement.[147]

The Language of Power

The Comintern's requirements that the MCP embrace the goals of Bolshevization both empowered and hindered the party. Reinhart Koselleck's *Begriffsgeschichte*, or history of concepts, tells us that a concept, a "word representing an idea that is both powerful enough in a certain discourse to direct thought and ambiguous enough to hold within it a range of meanings," "establishes a particular horizon for potential experience and conceivable theory and in this way sets a limit."[148] Concepts both empower and hinder social actors. Bolshevik language deprived the MCP of its nation, yet it also provided the MCP with a discourse that justified its

---

[145] "Report from Malay," p. 28ob; "Maijin [Forward]," pp. 76–77.
[146] "Magong di er ci zhongzhihuiyi jueyian [The Resolutions of the Second Plenum of the Executive Committee of the CC MCP]," p. 28.
[147] "Maijin [Forward]," pp. 65, 66.
[148] Koselleck, "*Begriffsgeschichte* and Social History," pp. 82–83.

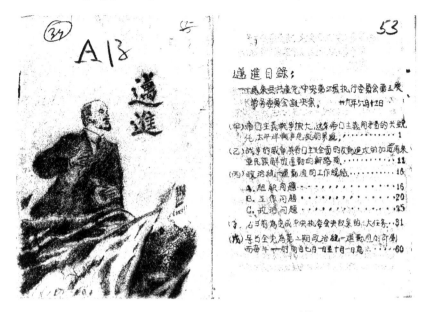

Figure 7.4 MCP publication "Forward!" 1939.[149]
Published with permission of the RGASPI.

ambitions to govern and to become a state. This change in the MCP's
language was first triggered by its wish to be accepted as a Comintern
section, something that required it to become a Bolshevik party. The MCP
learned how to speak Bolshevik from the CCP.

On the eve of the war, the MCP amplified the discourse of strengthening its theoretical level and discipline as well as the discourse of sacrifice
for the party. All three elements had been promoted by the Comintern
since 1934.[150] In the CCP, the Eighth Route Army's spirit of self-sacrifice
had been crucial for the success of the Red Army,[151] and thus sacrifice for
the party and sacrifice for the nation converged. The publication
"Forward!" stated that: "As Malaya's revolutionary situation is ripening,
the party must raise the comrades' theoretical level of Marxist–Leninism
and their decisiveness to sacrifice."[152] The MCP resolutions similarly
argued: "If party members today do not understand communism, how
can there be a guarantee that tomorrow they will be willing to sacrifice and

---

[149] "Maijin [Forward]," p. 53.
[150] FEB, "Letter to the CC MCP about the 7th Congress of the Comintern etc."
[151] Van Slyke, *Enemies and Friends*, p. 136.
[152] "Maijin [Forward]," p. 65.

shed their blood for it?"[153] Party membership was not uniform. The same "Forward!" publication said, "[s]ome comrades are ready to sacrifice for the party; some comrades do not read the party program carefully." Lack of discipline and irresponsible chatter (*luan tan*) destroyed many party organizations.[154]

The MCP worked to achieve its ideal of a Bolshevik party organization wishing for Comintern recognition and funding. The goals of Bolshevization included having a coherent, simple, and homogenous language, a centralized structure, armed forces, and the ability to penetrate all groups of society. This transformation had begun within the MCP by the beginning of the war in 1939–1940. Most significant, superior Bolshevik organizational capacity brought with it further aspirations, and realizing all these aspects of its goals drove the MCP to strive for the role of a state and a bureaucratized government, an effort that, simply put, backfired, as we have seen in this chapter. This echoes Kuhn's thesis about the Taiping vision: imported ideas and organizational models "fit" local needs but also introduce new aspirations that might not work in the long run.[155]

The MCP also increased propaganda in the army and contemplated armed action. In 1940, the MCP started to talk about building its own armed forces. Since 1933, the MCP had advocated for the expansion of the Correction and Investigation Troops (Jiucha dui) as "the only armed force of the workers," which it argued should have stopped being "a tool in the struggle against the Three Star Party." The party was also to learn the peasants' psychology (*xinli*) and their needs in order to organize peasant self-defense committees.[156] The party criticized those members who thought that because the party was antiwar, it should not participate in the army.[157] Citing Togliatti's speech at the seventh Comintern congress, the CC advocated propaganda in the army to "learn how to use arms and turn the rifle onto the enemies of the nation [*minzu diren*] and how to organize the unemployed and other masses into the army."[158] The enemies of the nation in this sentence were clearly the Japanese, and *minzu* referred to both Malaya and China. Like a millenarian Chinese organization, the MCP was awaiting an imperialist war, and when that war broke out, the MCP called for taking up arms against the British

[153] "Magong di er ci zhongzhihuiyi jueyian [The Resolutions of the Second Plenum of the Executive Committee of the CC MCP]," p. 25.
[154] "Maijin [Forward]," pp. 73–74.
[155] Kuhn, "Origins of the Taiping Vision."
[156] "Malaiya qingshi fenxi yu dang de renwu [The Analysis of the Situation in Malaya and the Tasks of the Party]."
[157] "Maijin [Forward]," pp. 77–78.
[158] "New CC Resolutions," p. 48.

government, which it had contemplated since 1930: "As the British imperialists are confused because of the rise of revolutions in China and India, we should call upon all the oppressed peoples of Malaya to fight against the imperialists' interference in China and India, and we should prepare for our own revolutionary armed force to oppose the imperialist war. This is our unforgettable task!"[159]

Conclusion

The tension between the MCP's goals as a Chinese organization (the mediator between the Chinese vis-à-vis the British colonial government) and its goals as a Bolshevik party (the overthrowing of the rule of the British government and of the capitalists) resulted in its lack of support. Radical Bolshevik language was at odds with the goals of Chinese associations, whose methods the MCP applied and to whose constituency it tried to appeal. The majority of the Chinese community was neither anti-British nor anticapitalist.

At first, MCP members enjoyed the communist language of the cult of the proletariat, which came with the global prestige of the Comintern and the prospect of cash support. By 1934, they had gotten a dose of reality and had abandoned their metaphorical language of excluding the bourgeoisie as a potential "revolutionary force." They therefore practiced united front tactics, as did the CCP during the same time period, the early 1930s, in Shanghai.[160] This was dictated by the MCP's logic of survival as an overseas Chinese organization. The united front strategy, as well as the changing policy toward the British government, was born locally, not imposed by the Comintern or by the CCP. Over the course of the 1930s, the MCP was supported by some affluent members of the Chinese community, as were other parties in Southeast Asia, such as in Taiwan,[161] because the overseas bourgeoisie were concerned about a better government in China.

The Bolshevik concept of a proletarian nation and anti-British rhetoric hindered the MCP in its ability to attract a following and excluded the Chinese bourgeoisie as potential members of its communist party. That happened, ironically, when the MCP redirected its attention back toward Chinese associations in the Nanyang as part of its united front tactics.

---

[159] "Central circular no. 4," August 8, 1930, RGASPI 495/62/13/27–30.
[160] Patricia Stranahan, *Underground: The Shanghai Communist Party and the Politics of Survival, 1927–1937* (Lanham, MD: Rowman & Littlefield Publishers, 1998); Titarenko and Leutner, *Komintern i Kitai [Comintern and China]*, vol. 4, "Introduction," pp. 25–61.
[161] The Taiwanese communist party was also supported by wealthy party members, such as landowner Lin Rigao and merchant Li Shanhuo. He Chi, *Weng Zesheng zhuan [A Biography of Weng Zesheng]*, pp. 204–205, 239.

Moreover, the bourgeoisie became the party's rival for the allegiance of the masses during the protest wave of 1939.

The MCP's work among non-Chinese was unsuccessful. A multi-ethnic united front was therefore a means to reach the MCP's main goal: Malaya's national independence and a Malayan multinational nation-state. The MCP's all-*minzu* united front, promoted by the CCP–GMD united front for the benefit of the China Salvation Movement, echoed the indigenization of a Chinese organization, or its double rootedness in the host and sending societies. At the same time, organizational indigenization was in fact an aspect of Bolshevization that the Comintern required.

Other aspects of Bolshevik discourse empowered the MCP to become a state that could be legitimately rooted in both Malaya and China. *Minzu* was a key word in MCP rhetoric, a signifier of MCP members' national allegiance, which was split between China and Malaya. After the creation of the MCP in 1930, *minzu* invariably referred to Malaya. Then, after the MCP's campaign against the Alien Registration Ordinance, which stressed the divide between those born and those not born in Malaya, *minzu* more often signified China than Malaya. By the start of the war, the MCP's *minzu* was China again. This occurred because the MCP, as the organization representing the interests of the Chinese, was responding to the negative impact of the British wartime policies toward the *huaqiao* bourgeoisie. Although the MCP propagated the united front of all *minzu* of Malaya and stimulated Chinese identification with Malaya, in the documents, the MCP continued to refer to China as motherland, *zuguo*, and to Malaya as "All-Malaya," *quan Ma*.[162]

In July 1941, the MCP proclaimed that the victory in the Malayan anti-Japanese war and the Malayan national liberation (*minzu jiefang*) movement enhanced the prospects of independence for the Malayan nation. This was conditioned by the progress of the national liberation movement and the victory of the resistance both in China and in the Soviet Union. Thus, the Malayan anti-Japanese war and the Chinese resistance were of one accord (*yizhi de*).[163] The MCP had two goals: to liberate Malaya and to liberate China. Bolshevik discourse also empowered the MCP in its ambitions to govern and to become the state. This was reflected in an

---

[162] "Magong di er ci zhongzhihuiyi jueyian [The Resolutions of the Second Plenum of the Executive Committee of the CC MCP]," pp. 23, 24.

[163] "Magong de zhuzhang he celüe (1939–1943) [The Standpoint of the MCP and Its Tactics]," in Ershiyi chubanshe bianjibu, ed., *Zhanqian dixia douzheng shiqi. Jiandang chuqi jieduan, Magong wenji, congshu xilie, di yi ji* [*The Prewar Period of the Underground Struggle: The Founding of the Party. Documents of the MCP*, vol. 1] (Kuala Lumpur: Ershiyi shiji chuban she, 2010), pp. 67–83. pp. 67–83, esp. p. 81.

amplified discourse of sacrifice for the party, significantly more theoretical Marxist–Leninist language, the importance of propaganda in the army, and finally the call to arms, which became crucial for the MCP during the war. The MCP drama propaganda and anti-Japanese activity helped shape Chinese community identification as one of the three *minzu* living in the territory of Malaya, which echoed and helped to facilitate the three races (*san da zhongzu*) notion of Malayan nationalism.[164]

---

[164] For an example of the discourse of *san da zhongzu*, see Liang Yingming, "Malaixiya zhongzu zhengzhi xia de huaren yu Yinduren shehui [Chinese and Indians under Malaysian Racial Policy]," in *Huaqiao huaren lishi yanjiu* [*Studies of Chinese Overseas*] 1 (1992), pp. 1–7.

8   Epilogue

The experience of the Japanese occupation first in China and then in Malaya further shaped the territorial notion of Malaya for the MCP. Structural, contextual, and contingent factors led to the improbable survival of the MCP in the interwar years. The British–MCP concord was endorsed on December 20, 1941, twelve days after the Japanese invasion of Malaya, when communist detainees were released from British detention.[1] This and the training of some by the British helped the MCP to form the Malayan Peoples' Anti-Japanese Army (MPAJA), which became the main anti-Japanese resistance. Through its prewar and wartime anti-Japanese organization, the MCP regained its following as Malayan-born Chinese, educated in GMD Chinese schools with nationalist ideas and identification with China, joined the MCP's guerrilla forces. Among those who joined were the sons and daughters of bourgeoisie who themselves did not support the MCP. These included Chin Peng, the future head of the MCP during the Emergency, whose family, like many other Chinese immigrants, owned a bicycle shop.[2] Similar to other communist parties around the world, the MCP gained its strength during the Second World War.[3]

When the Japanese invaded Malaya, the MCP's influence was strongest among the Chinese community.[4] A few Malays, including the MCP's postwar leader, Abdullah C. D., joined the MCP-led anti-Japanese resistance army but they were often distrusted because of Malay–Japanese collaboration.[5] Unlike in Indonesia, where the communist party had from its outset consisted of local nationalists,[6] in Malaya, Malay and Indian labor activists and members of the Kesatuan Melayu Muda (KMM) did not join the MCP until 1947–1948. This came as a

[1] Yong, *Origins of Malayan Communism*, pp. 198–201.
[2] See Chin Peng, *My Side of History*, p. 31.
[3] Smith, "Introduction."
[4] Vilkov et al., "Spravka o rabote," p. 50.
[5] Cheah, *Red Star over Malaya*, pp. 71, 322, n. 37.
[6] McVey, *The Rise of Indonesian Communism*.

reaction to the British government's arrests of KMM members in the Malay Nationalist Party, which had allied with the MCP in agitating for political reform. Nonetheless, the MCP's Malayan National Liberation Army was 95 percent Chinese in the 1950s.[7]

The MCP itself admitted a lack of clarity in its political position, which resulted from "the fact that the party was in essence coming from the position of the interests of Chinese immigrants, but in its organization (po forme) was taking care of the interests of all of the country's oppressed."[8] In the second half of the 1930s, the MCP viewed its own Chinese nationalism and exclusive Chinese membership as an embarrassing cause of its failure to attract non-Chinese members, such as Indians and Malays, to the ostensibly "national" party, which was supposed to include members of all communities.[9] Chinese nationalism was further compromised because the MCP was viewed as fighting for the cause of the CCP, not Malaya.[10] Identification with China has been viewed in the postwar period as siding with the communists,[11] and China's involvement in the Emergency continues to be ambiguous. Overall, the politics of China's efforts to embrace overseas Chinese, recruit their loyalties, and attract their resources back to China,[12] as well as the MCP's failure to attract non-Chinese in the 1930s, added to the image of the party as a pawn of the CCP. The MCP's internationalist, that is, Comintern, origins were blamed for its lack of consideration for the local Chinese community.[13] The Emergency aggravated the relationship between the Chinese community and the British government, and historians have portrayed the MCP as exploiting Chinese nationalism and "failing to appreciate" Malay nationalism.[14] After the 1989 peace agreement with the Malaysian government, MCP General Secretary Chin Peng ascribed the failure of the MCP insurgency to a

---

[7] Hack and Chin, eds., *Dialogues with Chin Peng*, p. 74, n. 13.

[8] Vilkov et al., "Spravka o rabote," p. 50.

[9] Cheah, *From PKI to the Comintern*, p. 32.

[10] See Wang, "Chinese Politics in Malaya."

[11] Wang Gungwu, *The Chinese Overseas: From Earthbound China to the Quest for Autonomy* (Cambridge, MA: Harvard University Press, 2000), p. 86.

[12] James Jiann Hua To, *Qiaowu: Extra-Territorial Policies for the Overseas Chinese* (Leiden: Brill, 2014).

[13] Ng Sin Yue, "The Malayan Communist Party and Overseas Chinese Nationalism in Malaya, 1937–1941" (MA dissertation, University of Hull, 1981); Leong, "Sources, Agencies and Manifestations of Overseas Chinese Nationalism in Malaya"; Zheng Liren, "Overseas Chinese Nationalism in British Malaya, 1894–1941"; Wang, "Chinese Politics in Malaya."

[14] Leong, "Sources, Agencies and Manifestations of Overseas Chinese Nationalism in Malaya," p. 819; Ng Sin Yue, "The Malayan Communist Party and Overseas Chinese Nationalism," p. 55; Wang, "Chinese Politics in Malaya," pp. 18, 29.

lack of Malay support as well as to unsuitable geography and premature conditions for Marxism in Malaya.[15]

Yet from their transitional organizational base – part communal organization of Chinese, part new-style political organization speaking through various front organizations – the MCP contributed to the discourse of an emerging Malayan nation and attempted to appropriate it. The Malaya conceived of by the MCP would be a multiethnic nation through the efforts of a national communist party comprising Chinese immigrants. As such, the MCP, whose leaders were CCP members, did not have a mass following because of its constraints as a Chinese organization: it did not speak the necessary languages and was condescending to its potential constituency, the "masses," both Chinese and non-Chinese. When the MCP followed the communist ideology, openly propagating the overthrow of the British government and excluding the bourgeoisie – which meant the majority of the Chinese "masses" because of the entrepreneurial culture of the Chinese communities – it failed. Wang Gungwu has argued that: "[The] democratic impulses of the communist movement went against the interests of the nationalist elites, whereas the capitalists' offerings to the nationalist elites appealed to them much more readily."[16]

The MCP did not pioneer local–external hybridization in the political culture of the Chinese community in Malaya. From the mid-nineteenth century on, Chinese political culture in Malaya was rooted both in Chinese characteristics and in a hybrid local culture.[17] Another Chinese organization, the pro-British Malayan Chinese Association, established in 1949 by Chinese community leaders from across Malaya as a response to the Malayan Emergency, was a "Janus-like organization which displayed the characteristics of both a modern political party and a traditional association in organization, function and ideology."[18]

Chinese organizations acting as mediators between the Chinese community and the local environment were natural ardent promoters of equal rights for immigrants in the Malayan nation. During the 1920s and 1930s, when the British government was cultivating the concept of a Malayan nation exclusive of immigrants, a Chinese organization, the MCP (indeed, a Nanyang branch of the CCP), influenced by the American and Soviet models and building on GMD internationalism and Malayan multiethnic conditions, pioneered the concept of a political organization consisting of ethnic parties as the government of Malaya's multiethnic population. After the experience of the Japanese invasion, the

[15] Hack and Chin, eds., *Dialogues with Chin Peng*, p. 226.
[16] Wang, "Closing Comments," p. 231.
[17] Heng, *Chinese Politics in Malaysia*, p. 3.
[18] Ibid., p. 54.

British government started to promote the creation of a united, independent, Malayan multiethnic state.[19] However, after the war, the British government weakened the MCP's control over the labor unions, which had already comprised an alternative structure to traditional association networks.[20] At the same time, after several unsuccessful attempts to institutionalize intercommunity political cooperation, the MCA formed an alliance with the United Malays National Organization (UMNO) and the Malayan Indian Congress on a nationwide scale, where it jointly contested and won the elections, leading Malaya to independence in 1957 in cooperation with the British government.[21]

The MCP and the MCA were opposed in their attitudes toward the British and drew their support from networks belonging to competing classes. The MCP networks comprised journalists, teachers, and students in Chinese schools and labor unions, and the MCP had the support of lower-income urban Chinese, who had been educated in Chinese schools. The MCA combined in its political culture the Chinese who had been in Malaya for generations and the descendants of nineteenth-century migrants, who accordingly represented the GMD, the Chamber of Commerce, and the *huiguan* circles, and thus were oriented toward China as well as the Straits Chinese British Association.[22] In 1949, the MCA claimed a membership of 103,000, the majority in rural areas. In 1962, when the Emergency had quieted down, the MCA's membership of 67,700 comprised 35 percent businessmen, 3 percent shopkeepers, and 48 percent members of the working class, including rubber tappers, mine and construction workers, hawkers, miscellaneous laborers, and handicraftsmen. Many MCA and MCP members were former GMD members.[23] The MCA was supported by businessmen from big to small shop owners. While lower grassroots members of the MCA were rural and Chinese-educated, and grassroots leaders were poorly paid Chinese

[19] Karl Hack, "Screwing Down the People: The Malayan Emergency, Decolonisation, and Ethnicity," in Hans Antlöv and Stein Tønesson, eds., *Imperial Policy and Southeast Asian Nationalism, 1930–1957* (London: Curzon Press, 1995), pp. 83–109, at p. 98; Heng, *Chinese Politics in Malaysia*, pp. 200–201.

[20] Heng, *Chinese Politics in Malaysia*, p. 163. In 1947, the MCP-led Pan-Malayan Federation of Trade Unions claimed to control 80 percent of all trade unions in Malaya, with a membership of more than 263,000, comprising more than 50 percent of the workforce. Yong, "An Overview of the Malayan Communist Movement to 1942," p. 250. In contrast, the number of MCP guerrillas was much smaller. In 1952, the Malayan National Liberation Army, led by the MCP, had 7,000 to 8,000 members – a number that would drop dramatically during the following few years. C. C. Chin, "In Search of the Revolution: A Brief Biography of Chin Peng," in Hack and Chin, eds., *Dialogues with Chin Peng*, p. 366.

[21] Heng, *Chinese Politics in Malaysia*, pp. 179–250.

[22] Ibid., p. 54.

[23] Ibid., pp. 78, 81–82.

schoolteachers and doctors, either trained in China or self-trained, the higher echelon of MCA leaders comprised Malayan-born, English-educated wealthy businessmen and professionals who held positions in government, Chinese associations, and multiethnic bodies. The MCA was thus referred to as a party of merchants who used it opportunistically to further their business interests.[24] A sinologist and British official in Malaya, Victor Purcell, called the MCA an elitist organization unable to express the interests of lower-class Chinese, similar to the GMD in China.[25]

The MCA members embraced the GMD, traditional *huiguan*, and a Westernized outlook,[26] and had no ideology comparable to that of the MCP. However, the MCP and the MCA both shared the vision of an inclusive Malayan nation and the goal of Chinese political participation. After the start of the Emergency, Tan Cheng Lock, the first president of the MCA, promoted the discourse of a Malayan nation consisting of all ethnic communities. In 1949, Tan said, "[t]he people of Malaya can only constitute a nationality if the different communities making up its mixed population are united among themselves" and live "under equal rights and laws." Furthermore, he stated, "[t]he Chinese in Malaya have come to stay and must wake up and unite not only among themselves but also with the Malays and other communities to make this land … one country and one nation."[27] In 1951, Tan emphasized that the MCA had been formed "to foster and to engender a truly Malayan outlook, consciousness, and patriotism among the domiciled Malayan Chinese in order to forge and fortify their ties with this country and unite as an integral part and parcel of the Malayan people."[28] In his earlier speech of 1949, also echoing the GMD discourse of the 1930s, Tan promoted the dual goal of unity among Chinese and cooperation with locals. He stated that the MCA was "an organisation on a pan-Malayan basis with the twin fundamental objectives of bringing about cohesion and unity among the Malayan Chinese of all classes and promoting interracial good will, harmony, and cooperation for the sole good of this country and its inhabitants as a whole."[29] In 1951, Tan envisioned the MCA as a Chinese association that would be the basis of a broader Malayan party unifying other ethnic parties:

---

[24] Ibid., pp. 59–60, 74–75.
[25] Cited in ibid., p. 75.
[26] Ibid., p. 84.
[27] Tan Cheng Lock, "Speech on the 27th February 1949 at the Inaugural Meeting of the Proposed Malayan Chinese Association at Kuala Lumpur," in Tan Cheng Lock, *Malayan Problems from the Chinese Point of View*, p. 1.
[28] Tan Cheng Lock's speech at the MCA annual Central General Committee meeting, April 21, 1951, cited in Heng, *Chinese Politics in Malaysia*, p. 86.
[29] Tan Cheng Lock, "Speech on the 27th February 1949," p. 1.

Perhaps what is needed, and the first and most practical step to be taken under existing conditions and in the present stage of the development of Malayan consciousness among the people of this land, would be to create a new united Malaya national organisation or party with a new constitution in which members of all the races are assembled and meet on a common ground and on an equal footing to discuss the affairs of the country purely as Malayans ... This would be the way to prepare the ground for the merging of the existing communal associations into the proposed non-communal and national organisation.[30]

Tan's discourse of a Malayan nation was connected to his goal of achieving citizenship rights on behalf of the Chinese majority, who had been deprived in the citizenship provisions of 1948.[31] He argued that the political transformation of Chinese into true Malayans could only come about if they were accorded constitutional rights equal to those of the Malay community.[32]

The MCP and the MCA both measured their success by activities that fostered a united Malaya, a Malayan consciousness, and cooperation between the Chinese and other ethnic communities.[33] Aside from the MCA's own efforts, the establishment of the PRC played a great role in the indigenizing of Chinese politics in Malaya, as overseas Chinese businesses abandoned their intentions to resettle in China.[34] However, many MCP members, in contrast, were drawn to return to the new communist China. The MCP's indigenization efforts of 1945–1948 continued to be futile, and the MCP stood aloof even from its own front organizations.[35] The MCA is credited with producing a Malaya-centered view among ethnic Chinese and with introducing coalition politics as a way to enhance Malayan unity.[36]

---

[30] Tan Cheng Lock, "We Need a New United Malaya National Party," pamphlet reprinted from the *Sunday Standard*, April 22, 1951, pp. 1, 6–7.

[31] Only in 1957 did the MCA fight off these citizenship provisions. Heng, *Chinese Politics in Malaysia*, pp. 46–50.

[32] Ibid., p. 86.

[33] However, both struggled in this process. Cheah, *Red Star over Malaya*, p. 68. One form of indigenization was the welcoming of non-Chinese into Chinese organizations. Tan advised that the MCA "must interest itself in the masses, whether Malays, Chinese, or Indians," and explained that the MCA's motto could not be "For Chinese only." Tan Cheng Lock, "Malayan Mirror," June 28, 1953, pp. 1, 2, cited in Bee Khim Lim, "Tan Cheng Lock, Tan Siew Sin and the MCA (1949–1974)" (BA honors dissertation, National University of Singapore, 1991), p. 19. Much like local GMD members and the MCP, who earlier had aspired to involve non-Chinese but had been unsuccessful, the MCA added non-Chinese associate members from 1951 to 1953. However, they could not hold office, and then their voting rights were canceled. After 1967, the MCA again became closed to non-Chinese. Heng, *Chinese Politics in Malaysia*, p. 159.

[34] Heng, *Chinese Politics in Malaysia*, pp. 251–252.

[35] Hack and Chin, eds., *Dialogues with Chin Peng*, pp. 257, 267.

[36] Heng, *Chinese Politics in Malaysia*, p. 54.

Conclusion

The MCP's and the MCA's efforts were on parallel tracks. These were the outcome of the Malayan multiethnic environment and British policies. The GMD's internationalism and localization efforts, the Comintern's internationalism, the Comintern's promotion of national parties and independence, based on the US communist ethnic parties model, also shaped the MCP's idea of Malaya. The CCP chapter in Malaya made efforts to localize Chinese communism by involving Malay and local Chinese participants and by making communism relevant to the Chinese immigrants' struggle for political rights in a specific historical context when immigrants needed a local identity. The Malayan nation, like the staple food of Southeast Asia, the durian, was key in the Chinese community's logic of survival. At the same time, it was nurtured by global utopian, regional, and nationalist imaginations. Tan Liok Ee has argued that the GMD's idea of *minzu* was transformed into a discourse of "minzu as communities within a [Malaysian] nation," which was promoted by various Chinese associations in Malaya/Malaysia in the 1950s and by the MCA.[37] Was the MCP's translation slippage the missing link in this transformation?

The history of the MCP is a chapter in the story of Southeast Asia's modern transition. A part of this transition was the search for an alternative to empire in China during the first half of the twentieth century via Chinese nationalism, experienced predominantly through revolution. Malaya's multiethnic population presented a potential miniature model of pan-Asian liberation under Chinese leadership. While attempting to localize its organization, the MCP simultaneously aspired to an ethnically inclusive pan-Asian liberation. This regional vision was common among Asian revolutionaries such as Tan Malaka and Ho Chi Minh, and it also resonated with the GMD's vision.

The MCP connects the Chinese Revolution to world history through world revolutionary activity, particularly as aided and abetted by the Comintern, not only in Southeast Asia but in the Americas as well. The role of the Comintern was ironic: it failed to provide the groundwork for a communist revolution but it helped to promote a nationalist revolution that took place in Malaya after the Second World War. The Malayan Revolution was the Chinese overseas revolutionary experience created by Soviet internationalism operating in a local area, in the world of the *huaqiao* struggling for political rights in Southeast Asia. At the same time, from Li Lisan's late 1920s ideas about adapting the Chinese Revolution to Southeast Asian conditions in the Nanyang revolution, to

[37] Tan Liok Ee, "The Rhetoric of Bangsa and Minzu," p. 34.

the Nanjing government's idea of the pan-Asian International of Nationalities as promoted in Chinese schools in the 1930s, to Sun Yatsen's call for an alliance with the oppressed nations of the world for the purpose of China's revival, the goals and means of these projects were shaped by the historical ideas of China's role in Southeast Asia and by the experience of Chinese communities and colonialism there.

One cannot fully understand revolution and nationalism either in China or in Malaya except in conjunction with one another. In Malaya, the Chinese Revolution was not simply divided into hostile GMD and CCP forces as the official historiographies of the CCP and the GMD present it. But they overlapped, as they did in South China. Moreover, an unintended consequence of the GMD's educational and propaganda efforts to cultivate Chinese nationalism was the participation of locally born Chinese in the anti-Japanese resistance led by the MCP, which was crucial for the party's survival, as were the MCP's dual nationalisms and the Japanese occupation for fomenting the identification of the Chinese with a territorial sovereign Malaya.

The MCP's history demonstrates Philip Kuhn's point that "the modern history of Chinese emigration and the modern history of China are really aspects of the same social-historical process."[38] This is not to say that Chinese migrant revolutionaries were nationalistic only for China and that the internationalist element was entirely alien to them. The MCP members' links to native places did not preclude cooperation with non-Chinese and non-compatriots, nor did they preclude the development of dual loyalties in their host environments.

Moreover, the transnational setting of the Nanyang and the ideology of an alliance of the oppressed for the benefit of China resulted in a lack of contradiction between nationalism and internationalism in Chinese revolutionary networks, where nationalism and internationalism became one. Shaped by the logic of migrant survival and by China's revival, the historical roles of Chinese communist networks defy the existing scholarly understanding of the interwar communist movement as based exclusively on the goals and means of a proletarian revolution in industrialized countries (or even a peasant revolution) and on tensions between proletarian internationalism and nationalism. Indeed, the Chinese Revolution and internationalism were linked in Chinese transnationalism when Chinese revolutionaries participated in non-Chinese local labor organizations as they fought for their rights overseas.[39]

---

[38] Kuhn, "Why China Historians Should Study the Chinese Diaspora," p. 163.
[39] Gregor Benton, "The Comintern and Chinese Overseas," in Tan Chee-Beng, ed., *Chinese Transnational Networks* (London: Routledge, 2007), pp. 122–150.

As in the case of Christianity, through which missionaries incorporated local churches into a global network,[40] the Comintern incorporated Chinese networks into global networks of international communism and strengthened them as the MCP borrowed the Comintern's ideological, organizational, and financial resources. Built on those networks, the world of international communism was a public sphere wherein policies were designed based on local conditions and implemented in a third country.[41] As we have seen, the very idea of the organization of ethnic communist parties in Malaya also was drawn on US communist organizing experience. The idea of organizing a chapter of the CCP traveled from Europe to the United States via the networks of the League Against Imperialism. At the same time, the LAI originated in the United States, was reestablished by the Comintern there and staffed by Chinese communists, while the LAI was also planted in Europe on the basis of a pro-China campaign. On the basis of the LAI in the Americas and Southeast Asia, Chinese communists imagined regional liberation polities for the sake of the Chinese Revolution, world liberation, and Chinese immigrant rights.

Between the enclaves of the Chinese revolutionary network in Singapore, Berlin, San Francisco, and Manila, in the context of contingent events and experiences in Chinese communities, the interactions between Chinese and Comintern networks created different outcomes in different contexts in Southeast Asia. Their workings were driven by survival strategies and conditioned on historical contingencies rooted in indigenous political cultures, organizations, different colonial policies, and the configurations of a continuous Chinese identity. These workings were pragmatic, as the laws of institutional isomorphism would have it.[42] The revolutionaries adopted organizational forms, such as those of communist parties and anti-imperialist leagues, which had already proven to work in other places. The story of Chinese communist organizations in

---

[40] Carol Lee Hamrin, *Salt and Light, Vol. 3: More Lives of Faith That Shaped Modern China* (Eugene, OR: Pickwick Publications, 2011), p. 15. Hamrin cites John Barwick, "Chinese Protestant Elites and the Quest for Modernity in Republican China" (PhD dissertation, University of Alberta, 2011), ch. 1, pp. 57–58; ch. 3, pp. 144–146.

[41] For the CCP as a public sphere, see Timothy Cheek, "From Market to Democracy in China: Gaps in the Civil Society Model," in Juan David Lindau and Timothy Cheek, eds., *Market Economics and Political Change: Comparing China and Mexico* (Lanham, MD: Rowman & Littlefield Publishers, 1998), pp. 219–252. For how this international public sphere worked in the case of the Taiwanese communists, see Anna Belogurova, "The Civic World of International Communism: The Taiwanese Communists and the Comintern (1921–1931)," *Modern Asian Studies* 46(6) (2012), pp. 1–31.

[42] Paul J. DiMaggio and Walter W. Powell, "The Iron Cage Revisited: Institutional Isomorphism and Collective Rationality in Organizational Fields," *American Sociological Review* 48(2) (1983), pp. 147–160.

Malaya is unique among other nodes of Chinese networks, but it also highlights patterns of Chinese indigenization through the discourses of indigenous national identities, as in the Philippines and the Dutch East Indies. This conclusion raises more questions about the local histories of Chinese communists in the Philippines and Indonesia and about the role of Chinese in indigenous nationalism in various Southeast Asian contexts.

Hybridization was a feature of these interwar communist networks. The MCP provides a window into the transformation of a hybrid organization in the interwar global moment in the context of the Southeast Asian response to imperialism. An understanding of the MCP in the 1930s as a hybrid with its constituent parts, and of its role as one of the revolutionary international organizations active in Southeast Asia connecting the various peoples living in the area to the rest of the world, makes the case that local developments – whether in Singapore or Shanghai or Manila – cannot be understood without a basic understanding of global interactions. Moreover, it demonstrates how Chinese practices were intertwined with global tendencies that produced the embeddedness of nations in global discourses, which are often mistaken for national discourses.[43] To understand how Sun Yatsen's pan-Asian internationalism, with China at its center, worked apart from Chinese experiences, we need to consider different contexts in colonial spaces in Southeast Asia as well as various visions of the region and identities based on a community of descent, including the transnational Malay Unity, the territorial idea of Indonesia, the transnational Islam community, Christianity, and the Freemason world as well as indigenous organizations there. Sun Yatsen's vision of a regional Asian organization provides a glimpse into the long-term vision shared by both GMD and CCP leaders regarding China's role in the Nanyang, in Asia, and in the larger international environment. It also sheds light on the conceptual origins of the CCP's ambition to lead the world – and regional anticolonial movements – in the second half of the twentieth century.[44]

The story of Chinese participation in anti-imperialist leagues, together with the "imperial" borrowings of Chinese overseas engagements with local politics, would have looked like imperial ambition to local governments, especially because the PRC's united front department from early

---

[43] Prasenjit Duara, "Globalization in China's 20th Century," *Modern China* 34(1) (2008), pp. 152–164.
[44] Alex Cook, "Third World Maoism," in Timothy Cheek, ed., *A Critical Introduction to Mao* (New York, NY: Cambridge University Press, 2010), pp. 288–312.

on dealt with the PRC's policy of engagement with overseas Chinese.[45] Former MCP cadres who returned to Fujian received not only top positions in united front organizations, such as the Overseas Chinese Association (Qiaolian), which was the successor of the overseas Chinese work of the GMD, but also posts in the Fujian provincial government.[46] Zhang Xia held high positions in Xiamen City's united front committee, was the secretary of the city's consultative committee and of the Overseas Chinese Association, and was the head of the city's Culture Department.[47] The founder of the communist organization in Malaya, Pan Yunbo, became the head of the Hong Kong native place association of Wenchang County in 1949.[48] Xu Jie became the first dean of the Department of Chinese Literature at Shanghai's East China Normal University in 1951.[49] The PRC retained the GMD's overseas Chinese policy and nationality laws and continued not to discern between PRC nationals and other overseas Chinese.[50] After the war, Chinese overseas support for the CCP grew among educated students who were oriented toward the internationalist movement, which transcended local concerns and aspired to be an alternative to bourgeois Western civilization.[51] Some were disillusioned with Chiang Kai-shek after the war and therefore turned to the CCP and supported Mao.[52] Again, the Chinese policy regarding overseas Chinese involved a familiar appeal to go indigenous. This was reflected in the PRC's call for overseas Chinese to adopt local citizenship after 1956, with simultaneous efforts by the PRC to co-opt such Chinese into the PRC's economy as economic resources as well as to pursue a policy of peaceful coexistence with the Southeast Asian countries in order to counter American and GMD efforts to isolate China in Southeast Asia.[53]

---

[45] Jiann Hua To, *Qiaowu*, pp. 19–20.

[46] Ibid., pp. 65–66.

[47] Zhang Xia, "Xianyou xian lü Ma huaqiao yu geming huodong [Immigrants from Xianyou County in Malaya and Revolutionary Activities]."

[48] Huang Xunyan, Lin Zhi, and Qi Wen, "Pan Yunbo tongzhi geming de yisheng [The Revolutionary Life of Comrade Pan Yunbo]"; "Revolutionary Memoir: An Oral History of Pan Yunbo."

[49] Jiang Hezhen, "Xu Jie zhuanlüe [A Brief Biography of Xu Jie]," in Tiantai xia wenshi ziliao weiyuanhui, ed., *Tiantai wenshi ziliao, di san ji, Xu Jie zhuanji* [*Literary and Historical Materials of Tiantai*, vol. 3: *Biography of Xu Jie*] (1987), pp. 4–12.

[50] Jiann Hua To, *Qiaowu*, pp. 58–59.

[51] Charles Patrick Fitzgerald, *The Third China: The Chinese Communities in South-East Asia* (Vancouver, BC: Publications Centre, University of British Columbia, 1965), pp. 62–64; Benedict Anderson, *The Spectre of Comparisons: Nationalism, Southeast Asia and the World* (London; New York, NY: Verso, 1998), p. 289; Esther Cheo Ying, *Black Country Girl in Red China* (London: Hutchinson, 1980) and Pamela Tan, *The Chinese Factor* (Dural Delivery Centre, NSW: Rosenberg Publishing, 2008), all cited in Jiann Hua To, *Qiaowu*, p. 62.

[52] Ningkun Wu and Li Yakai, *A Single Tear: A Family's Persecution, Love and Endurance in Communist China* (1993), cited in Jiann Hua To, *Qiaowu*, p. 62.

[53] Peterson, *Overseas Chinese in the People's Republic of China*, p. 124.

The CCP continued to elicit support from Chinese overseas business-men. Aside from the development of the economy and the culture, the CCP set goals for such businessmen to promote patriotic unity and a spirit of internationalism in their local environments and to serve as a diplomatic front for China through the associations set up by the united front department.[54] After the Cultural Revolution, PRC policy turned back to mobilization of support among overseas Chinese, and as late as 1973, the PRC government encouraged overseas Chinese to advance revolutionary pro-communist activity abroad and to continue building relations between China and the world. In the reform era, the PRC government did not see overseas Chinese as supporters of China's international revolutionary struggle but rather as supporters of China's modernization, national reuni-fication, and advancement of CCP interests and as economic, cultural, and political intermediaries with ASEAN member countries.[55] In 1989, over-seas businessmen were referred to as a part of the Chinese nation (*Zhonghua minzu*) on the pages of the national weekly *Beijing Review*.[56]

***

The visionaries and key actors in interwar Chinese overseas revolutionary networks remain on the fringes of China's revolutionary history. Liao Huanxing's post as Wang Ming's secretary, in which he dealt with ques-tions of *huaqiao* CCP organizations beginning in 1931, confined him to marginal references. Like Li Lisan, Liao was sent to one of Stalin's labor camps in 1938 and he returned to China after 1951.[57] Malaysia still has the largest proportion of a Chinese population outside China.[58] The MCP's aspirations for Malayan unity – indeed, the aspirations of the Chinese community in general – are expressed in contemporary por-trayals of the MCP as patriotic and loyal to the interests of the Chinese community but not to the CCP or the GMD, and they are portrayed as an integral part of the Malayan liberation movement.[59]

---

[54] Jiann Hua To, *Qiaowu*, pp. 65–66.
[55] Ibid., pp. 69, 40.
[56] Michael Godley, "Reflection of China's Changing Overseas Chinese Policy," *Solidarity* 123 (July 1989), cited in Jiann Hua To, *Qiaowu*, pp. 67–68.
[57] Liao Huanxing's Personal File RGASPI 495/225/1043.
[58] Kuhn, *Chinese among Others*, p. 148.
[59] He Qicai, "Zhanqian Malaiya zuoyi yundong de xingqi yu fazhan: Malaiya gongchan-dang he Malai qingnian xiehui de guanxi tanjiu [The Rise and Development of the Prewar Leftist Movement in Malaya: Relations between the MCP and the Malay Youth Association]," in Ershiyi shiji chubanshe bianjibu, eds., *Zhanqian dixia douzheng shiqi: Magong wenji, congshu xilie, di erji: Fan Faxisi, yuan Hua kang Ri jieduan* [*The Prewar Period of the Underground Struggle. Documents of the MCP*, vol. 2: *The Anti-Fascist and Aid China Anti-Japanese Struggle*] (Kuala Lumpur: Ershiyi shiji chubanshe, 2010), pp. 305–320.

In the meantime, the durian and the imagination of Zheng He's explorations have remained the tropes of Malayan communism. Huang Jinshu, a popular postmodernist Malaysian Chinese writer, was raised in one of the Malayan New Villages, the barbed wire Chinese communities resettled as a part of the British counterinsurgency measures that shaped the nostalgic memories of some Chinese in Malaysia. Huang Jinshu now writes from the safety of another China: Taiwan. His novel, *Memorandum of the People's Republic of Nanyang*, is a fictional account of the connections between the MCP and China during the Emergency. In Huang Jinshu's imagined path of the "Garden of Forking Paths" of the Chinese network, the People's Republic of Nanyang that had been conceived of in discussions between the Indonesian and Malayan communist parties in 1945 was finally put into practice by the MCP when it settled in southern Thailand. The coin of the People's Republic of Nanyang has someone looking like Zheng He imprinted on one side and a durian on the other.[60]

---

[60] Huang Jinshu, *Nanyang renmin gongheguo beiwanglu* [*Memorandum of the Nanyang People's Republic*] (Taibei: Lianjing, 2013), pp. 63, 64, 239.

Selected Bibliography

21 uslovie priema v Komintern [*Twenty-One Conditions of Acceptance into the Comintern*]. 2nd edn. Introduction by O. Piatnitskii (Izdatel'stvo TsK VKP (b), 1934).

Adibekov, Grant Mikhailovich, E. N. Shahnazarova, and Kiril K. Shirinia, *Organizatsionnaia struktura Kominterna, 1919–1943* [*Organizational Structure of the Comintern*] (Moscow: ROSSPEN, 1997).

Anderson, Benedict Richard O'Gorman, *Imagined Communities: Reflections on the Origin and Spread of Nationalism*. Revised Edition. (London; New York, NY: Verso, 1991).

The Spectre of Comparisons: Nationalism, Southeast Asia and the World (London; New York, NY: Verso, 1998).

Under Three Flags: Anarchism and the Anti-Colonial Imagination (London; New York, NY: Verso, 2005).

Ang Cheng Guan, "Southeast Asian Perceptions of the Domino Theory," in Christopher E. Goscha and Christian F. Ostermann, eds., *Connecting Histories: Decolonisation and the Cold War in Southeast Asia, 1945–1962* (Stanford, CA: Stanford University Press, 2009), pp. 301–331.

Austin, John L., *How To Do Things with Words*. 2nd edn. Edited by J. O. Urmson and Marina Sbisá (Cambridge, MA: Harvard University Press, 1976).

Aydin, Cemil, *The Politics of Anti-Westernism in Asia: Visions of World Order in Pan-Islamic and Pan-Asian Thought* (New York, NY: Columbia University Press, 2007).

Bai Dao, "Dong Chuping: Wode geming yinlu ren [Dong Chuping: My Revolutionary Fellow Traveler]," in *Bai Dao wenji di qi ji* [*Collected Works of Bai Dao*, vol. 7] (Beijing: Zhongguo xiju chubanshe, 2002), pp. 549–569.

Barrett, David P., "Marxism, the Communist Party, and the Soviet Union: Three Critiques by Hu Hanmin," *Chinese Studies in History* 14(2) (Winter 1980–1981), pp. 47–75.

Barwick, John, "Chinese Protestant Elites and the Quest for Modernity in Republican China" (PhD dissertation, University of Alberta, 2011).

Becker, Marc, "Mariátegui, the Comintern, and the Indigenous Question in Latin America," *Science & Society* 70(4) (October 2006), pp. 450–479.

Belogurova, Anna, "The Civic World of International Communism: The Taiwanese Communists and the Comintern (1921–1931)," *Modern Asian Studies* 46(6) (2012), pp. 1602–1632.

"Networks, Parties, and the 'Oppressed Nations': The Comintern and Chinese Communists Overseas, 1926–1933," *Cross-Currents: East Asian History and Culture Review* 6 (2)(November 2017), pp. 558–582.

Benton, Gregor, *Chinese Migrants and Internationalism* (London: Routledge, 2007).

"The Comintern and Chinese Overseas," in Tan Chee-Beng, ed., *Chinese Transnational Networks* (London: Routledge, 2007), pp. 122–150.

Breuilly, John, *Nationalism and the State* (Chicago, IL: University of Chicago Press, 1994).

Carstens, Sharon A., "Chinese Culture and Policy in Nineteenth-Century Malaya: The Case of Yap Ah-loy," in David Ownby and Mary Somers Heidhues, eds., *"Secret Societies" Reconsidered: Perspectives on the Social History of Modern South China and Southeast Asia* (Armonk, NY: M. E. Sharpe, 1993), pp. 120–153.

Chatterjee, Partha, *Nationalist Thought and the Colonial World: A Derivative Discourse* (London: Zed Books, 1986).

Cheah Boon Kheng, *From PKI to the Comintern, 1924–1941: The Apprenticeship of the Malayan Communist Party. Selected Documents and Discussion.* (Ithaca NY: Southeast Asia Program, Cornell, University, 1992).

Red Star over Malaya: Resistance and Social Conflict during and after the Japanese Occupation of Malaya, 1941–1946 (Singapore: Singapore University Press, 1983).

Cheek, Timothy, "From Market to Democracy in China: Gaps in the Civil Society Model," in Juan David Lindau and Timothy Cheek, eds., *Market Economics and Political Change: Comparing China and Mexico* (Lanham, MD: Rowman & Littlefield Publishers, 1998), pp. 219–252.

The Intellectual in Modern Chinese HIstory (Cambridge: Cambridge University Press, 2015).

"The Names of Rectification: Notes on the Conceptual Domains of CCP Ideology in the Yan'an Rectification Movement." *Indiana East Asian Working Paper Series on Language and Politics in Modern China*, no. 7, East Asian Studies Center, Indiana University, January 1996.

Chen Chengzhi, "Wangshi huiyi [Reminiscences about Past Things]." in Zhongguo renmin zhengzhi xieshang huiyi Fujian sheng Tong'an xian weiyuanhui wenshi ziliao gongzuozu, ed., *Tong'an xian wenshi ziliao di si ji* [Literary and Historical Materials of Tong'an County, vol. 4] (1984), pp. 57–76.

Chen Jiafei, "Cong Malaiya Bile zhou dao Guangdong Huizhou [From Perak State in Malaya to Huizhou in Guangdong]," in Zhongguo renmin zhengzhi xieshang huiyi Fujian sheng Putian shi weiyuanhui wenshi ziliao yanjiu weiyuanhui, ed., *Putian shi wenshi ziliao di si ji* [Literary and Historical Materials of Putian City, vol. 4] (1989), pp. 28–36.

Chen Jian, "Bridging Revolution and Decolonisation: The 'Bandung Discourse' in China's Early Cold War Experience," in Christopher E. Goscha and Christian F. Ostermann, eds., *Connecting Histories: Decolonisation and the Cold War in Southeast Asia, 1945–1962* (Stanford, CA: Stanford University Press, 2009), pp. 137–171.

Chen Junju, "Fandi datongmeng yu Xianyou Yinqing wenhuashe [The Anti-Imperialist League and Cultural Society Engine in Xianyou]," in Zhongguo renmin zhengzhi xieshang huiyi Fujian sheng Putian shi weiyuanhui wenshi ziliao yanjiu weyuanhui, ed., *Putian shi wenshi ziliao di yi ji* [*Literary and Historical Materials of Putian City*, vol. 1] (1985), pp. 37–42.

Chen Ta, *Emigrant Communities in South China: A Study of Overseas Migration and Its Influence on Standards of Living and Social Change* (New York, NY: Secretariat, Institute of Pacific Relations, 1940).

Chen Yifei, "Jinian Minzhong tewei shuji Wang Yuji lieshi [Remembering the Secretary of the Special Committee of Fujian, Martyr Wang Yuji]," in Zhongguo renmin zhengzhi xieshang huiyi Fujian sheng Putian xian weiyuanhui, ed., *Putian wenshi ziliao di wu ji* [*Literary and Historical Materials of Putian*, vol. 5] (1983), pp. 45–52.

Chen Yutang, ed., *Zhongguo jinxiandai renwu minghao da cidian: Quanbian zengdingben* [*Dictionary of Names in Modern China: A Revised Edition*] (Hangzhou: Zhejiang guji chubanshe, 2005).

Chen Zhenchun, "Xinjiapo binggan gongchang gongren de douzheng [Struggle of the Workers at a Cookie Factory in Singapore]," in Zhongguo renmin zhengzhi xieshang huiyi Guangdong sheng weiyuanhui wenshi ziliao yanjiu weiyuanhui, ed., *Guangdong wenshi ziliao di wushisi ji* [*Literary and Historical Materials of Guangdong*, vol. 54] (Guangzhou: Guangdong renmin chubanshe, 1988), pp. 155–161.

Chin Peng, *My Side of History as Told to Ian Ward and Norma Miraflor: [Recollections of the Guerilla Leader Who Waged a Twelve-Year Anti-Colonial War against British and Commonwealth Forces in the Jungles of Malaya]* (Singapore: Media Masters, 2003).

Choi, Susanne Yuk Ping, "Association Divided, Association United: The Social Organization of Chaozhou and Fujian Migrants in Hong Kong," in Khun Eng Kuah-Pearce and Evelyn Hu-Dehart, eds., *Voluntary Organizations in the Chinese Diaspora: Illusions of Open Space in Hong Kong, Tokyo, and Shanghai* (Hong Kong: Hong Kong University Press, 2006), pp. 121–140.

Chow, Kai-wing, *Ethics, Classics and Lineage Discourse* (Stanford, CA: Stanford University Press, 1994).

"Narrating Nation, Race, and National Culture: Imagining the Hanzu Identity in Modern China," in Kai-wing Chow, Kevin Michael Doak, and Poshek Fu, eds., *Constructing Nationhood in Modern East Asia* (Ann Arbor, MI: University of Michigan Press, 2001), pp. 47–84.

Chu, Richard T., *Chinese and Chinese Mestizos of Manila: Family, Identity and Culture, 1860s–1930s* (Leiden: Brill, 2010).

Comber, Leon, "'Traitor of all Traitors': Secret Agent *Extraordinaire*: Lai Teck, Secretary-General, Communist Party of Malaya (1939–1947)," *Journal of the Malaysian Branch of the Royal Asiatic Society* 83(2) (September 2010), pp. 1–25.

Cong, Xiaoping, *Teachers' Schools and the Making of the Modern Chinese Nation-State, 1897–1937* (Vancouver, BC: University of British Columbia Press, 2007).

Conrad, Sebastian and Klaus Mühlhahn, "Global Mobility and Nationalism: Chinese Migration and the Re-territorialization of Belonging, 1880–1910," in Sebastian Conrad and Dominic Sachsenmaier, eds., *Competing Visions of World Order: Global Moments and Movements, 1880s–1930s* (New York, NY: Palgrave Macmillan, 2007), pp. 181–212.

Conrad, Sebastian and Dominic Sachsenmaier, "Introduction: Competing Visions of World Order: Global Moments and Movements, 1880s–1930s," in Sebastian Conrad and Dominic Sachsenmaier, eds., *Competing Visions of World Order: Global Moments and Movements, 1880s–1930s* (New York, NY: Palgrave Macmillan, 2007), pp. 1–25.

Cook, Alex, "Third World Maoism," in Timothy Cheek, ed., *A Critical Introduction to Mao* (New York, NY: Cambridge University Press, 2010), pp. 288–312.

Dawahare, Anthony, *Nationalism, Marxism, and African American Literature between the Wars: A New Pandora's Box* (Jackson, MI: University Press of Mississippi, 2002).

DiMaggio, Paul J. and Walter W. Powell, "The Iron Cage Revisited: Institutional Isomorphism and Collective Rationality in Organizational Fields," *American Sociological Review* 48(2) (1983), pp. 147–160.

Dittmer, Lowell, "The Structural Evolution of 'Criticism and Self-Criticism,'" *China Quarterly* 56 (October–December 1973), pp. 708–729.

Doak, Kevin M., "Narrating China, Ordering East Asia: The Discourse on Nation and Ethnicity in Imperial Japan," in Kai-wing Chow, Kevin Michael Doak, and Poshek Fu, eds., *Constructing Nationhood in Modern East Asia* (Ann Arbor, MI: University of Michigan Press, 2001), pp. 85–116.

Duan Yunzhang, *Zhongshan xiansheng de shijieguan* [*The Worldview of Mr. Sun Yatsen*] (Taibei: Xiuwei zixun keji, 2009).

Duara, Prasenjit, "Globalization in China's 20th Century," *Modern China* 34(1) (2008), pp. 152–164.

Sovereignty and Authenticity: Manchukuo and the East Asian Modern (Lanham, MD: Rowman & Littlefield Publishers, 2003).

"Transnationalism and the Predicament of Sovereignty: China, 1900–1945," *American Historical Review* 102(4) (October 1997), pp. 1030–1051.

Edwards, Brent Hayes, *The Practice of Diaspora: Literature, Translation, and the Rise of Black Internationalism* (Cambridge, MA: Harvard University Press, 2003).

Elson, Robert Edward, *The Idea of Indonesia: A History* (Cambridge: Cambridge University Press, 2008).

Esherick, Joseph, *Ancestral Leaves: A Family Journey through Chinese History* (Berkeley, CA: University of California Press, 2011), p. 173.

"How the Qing Became China," in Joseph Esherick, Hasan Kayalı, and Eric van Young, eds., *Empire to Nation: Historical Perspectives on the Making of the Modern World* (Lanham, MD: Rowman & Littlefield Publishers, 2006), pp. 229–259.

Evasdottir, Erika, *Obedient Autonomy: Chinese Intellectuals and the Achievement of Ordinary Life* (Vancouver, BC: University of British Columbia/University of Hawaii Press, 2004).

Fan Quan, "Ji Ai Wu yige kule yibeizi, xiele yibeizi de zuojia [Remembering Ai Wu: A Bitter Life, a Writer of a Lifetime]," in Fan Quan, ed., *Wenhai xiaoyan [The Smoke of the Sea of Literature]* (Ha'erbin: Heilongjiang renmin chubanshe, 1998), pp. 68–91.

Fan Ruolan, *Yimin, xingbie yu huaren shehui: Malaixiya huaren funü yanjiu (1929–1941) [Immigration, Gender, and Overseas Chinese Society: A Study of Chinese Women in Malaya, 1929–1941]* (Beijing: Zhongguo huaqiao chubanshe, 2005).

Fang Chuan and Zhang Yi, eds., *Zhongguo xiandai mingren zhenwen yishi [Stories of Famous People in Modern China]* (Beijing: Zhongguo huaqiao chubanshe, 1989).

Fei Lu (Roland Felber), "Jiezhu xinde dang'an ziliao chongxin tantao Sun Zhongshan zai ershi niandai chu (1922–1923) yu Su E guanxi yiji dui De taidu de wenti [Regarding Sun Yatsen's Views on Relations with the Soviet Union (1922–1923) and His Attitudes toward Germany Based on New Archival Materials]," in *Sun Wen yu huaqiao: Jinian Sun Zhongshan danchen 130 zhounian guoji xueshu taolun-hui lunwenji [Sun Yatsen and Overseas Chinese: Proceedings of the International Academic Conference Commemorating the 130th Anniversary of the Birth of Sun Yatsen]* (Kobe: Caituan faren Sun Zhongshan jinianhui, 1997), pp. 57–69.

Fitzgerald, Charles Patrick, *The Third China: The Chinese Communities in South-East Asia* (Vancouver, BC: Publications Centre, University of British Columbia, 1965).

Fitzgerald, John, *Awakening China: Politics, Culture, and Class in the Nationalist Revolution* (Stanford, CA: Stanford University Press, 1998).

Big White Lie: Chinese Australians in White Australia (Sydney, NSW: University of New South Wales Press, 2007).

Fitzgerald, Stephen, *China and the Overseas Chinese: A Study of Peking's Changing Policy, 1949–1970* (Cambridge: Cambridge University Press, 1972).

Fowler, Josephine, *Japanese and Chinese Immigrant Activists Organizing in American and International Communist Movements, 1919–1933* (New Brunswick, NJ: Rutgers University Press, 2007).

Fuller, Ken, *Forcing the Pace: The Partido Komunista ng Pilipinas: From Foundation to Armed Struggle* (Diliman, Quezon City: University of the Philippines Press, 2007).

Gallicchio, Marc, *The African American Encounter with Japan and China: Black Internationalism in Asia, 1895–1945* (Chapel Hill, NC: University of North Carolina Press, 2000).

Gao Hua, *Hong taiyang shi zenyang shengqide: Yan'an zhengfeng yundong de lailong qumai [How the Red Sun Rose: The Yan'an Rectification Movement]* (Xianggang: Zhongwen daxue chubanshe, 2011).

Geertz, Clifford, *The Interpretation of Cultures* (London: Fontana, 1973).

Gellner, Ernst, *Nations and Nationalism* (Oxford: Blackwell Publishing, 2006).

Goodman, Bryna, "The Locality as Microcosm of the Nation? Native Place Networks and Early Urban Nationalism in China," *Modern China* 21(4) (1995), pp. 387–419.

Goscha, Christopher E., *Going Indochinese: Contesting Concepts of Space and Place in French Indochina* (Copenhagen: Nordic Institute of Asian Studies, 2012).

Thailand and the Southeast Asian Networks of the Vietnamese Revolution, 1885–1954 (Richmond: Curzon Press, 1999).

Guillermo, Ramon, "Andres Bonifacio: Proletarian Hero of the Philippines and Indonesia," *Inter-Asia Cultural Studies* 18(3) (2017), pp. 338–346.

Hack, Karl, "The Origins of the Asian Cold War: Malaya 1948," *Journal of Southeast Asian Studies* 40(3) (2009) pp. 471–496.

"Screwing Down the People: The Malayan Emergency, Decolonisation, and Ethnicity," in Hans Antlöv and Stein Tønesson, eds., *Imperial Policy and Southeast Asian Nationalism, 1930–1957* (Richmond: Curzon Press, 1995), pp. 83–109.

Hack, Karl and C. C. Chin, eds., *Dialogues with Chin Peng: New Light on the Malayan Communist Party* (Singapore: National University of Singapore Press, 2004).

Hamrin, Carol Lee, *Salt and Light, Vol. 3: More Lives of Faith That Shaped Modern China* (Eugene, OR: Pickwick Publications, 2011).

Hanrahan, Gene Z., *The Communist Struggle in Malaya*. With an introduction by Victor Purcell (New York, NY: Institute of Pacific Relations, 1954).

Hara, Fujio, "Di'erci shijie dazhan qiande Malaiya gongchandang [The MCP before the Second World War]," *Nanyang ziliao yicong* [*Compendia of Nanyang Materials*] 160(4) (2005), pp.56–70.

"Malaiya gongchandang yu Zhongguo [The MCP and China]," *Nanyang ziliao yicong* [*Compendia of Nanyang Materials*] 144(4) (2001), pp. 26–39.

Mikan ni owatta kokusai kyōryoku: Maraya kyōsantō to kyōdaitō [*Unaccomplished International Cooperation: The Malayan Communist Party and Its Fraternal Parties*] (Tōkyō: Fūkyōsha, 2009).

"Riben zhanling xiade Malaiya gongchandang [The MCP during the Japanese Occupation]," *Nanyang ziliao yicong* [*Compendia of Nanyang Materials*] 161(1) (2006), pp. 26–47.

Harper, Timothy N., ed., "Empire, Diaspora and the Languages of Globalism, 1850–1914," in Anthony Gerald Hopkins, ed., *Globalization in World History* (London: Pimlico, 2002), pp. 141–166.

Harrington, Fred H., "The Anti-Imperialist Movement in the United States, 1898–1900," *Mississippi Valley Historical Review* 22(2) (1935), pp. 211–230.

Hayashi, Hirofumi, "Massacre of Chinese in Singapore and Its Coverage in Postwar Japan," in Yōji Akashi and Mako Yoshimura, eds., *New Perspectives on the Japanese Occupation in Malaya and Singapore, 1941–1945* (Singapore: National University of Singapore Press, 2008), pp. 234–249.

He Chi, *Weng Zesheng zhuan* [A *Biography of Weng Zesheng*] (Taibei: Haixia xueshu, 2005).

He Qicai, "Zhanqian Malaiya zuoyi yundong de xingqi yu fazhan: Malaiya gongchandang he Malai qingnian xiehui de guanxi tanjiu [The Rise and Development of the Prewar Leftist Movement in Malaya: Relations between the MCP and the Young Malay Union]," in Ershiyi shiji chubanshe bianjibu, ed., *Zhanqian dixia douzheng shiqi: Magong wenji, congshu xilie, di er ji: Fan Faxisi, yuan Hua kang Ri jieduan* [*The Prewar Period of the Underground Struggle. Documents of the MCP, vol. 2: The Anti-Fascist and Aid China Anti-*

Japanese Struggle] (Kuala Lumpur: Ershiyi shiji chubanshe, 2010), pp. 305–320.

He Siren, "Bingcheng de Nanyang xingxin xiju yundong (1930–1931): Xin Ma xiju yundong zuoqing yishi de kaiduan [The New Drama Movement in Penang (1930–1931): The Beginnings of Leftist Thinking in the Drama Movement of Chinese in Singapore and Malaya]," in Yang Songnian and Wang Kangding, eds., *Dongnanya huaren wenxue yu wenhua* [*The Culture and Literature of the Chinese in Southeast Asia*] (Xinjiapo: Yazhou yanjiu xuehui, 1995), pp. 109–133.

Heidhues, Mary Somers, "Chinese Voluntary and Involuntary Associations in Indonesia," in Khun Eng Kuah-Pearce and Evelyn Hu-Dehart, eds., *Voluntary Organizations in the Chinese Diaspora: Illusions of Open Space in Hong Kong, Tokyo, and Shanghai* (Hong Kong: Hong Kong University Press, 2006), pp. 77–97.

Heng, Pek Koon, *Chinese Politics in Malaysia: A History of the Malaysian Chinese Association* (Singapore; New York, NY: Oxford University Press, 1988).

Henley, David, "Ethnogeographic Integration and Exclusion in Anticolonial Nationalism: Indonesia and Indochina," *Comparative Studies in Society and History* 37(2) (1995), pp. 286–324.

Hirsch, Francine, *Empire of Nations: Ethnographic Knowledge and the Making of the Soviet Union (Culture and Society after Socialism)* (Ithaca, NY: Cornell University Press, 2005).

Hobsbawm, Eric J., *Nations and Nationalism since 1780: Programme, Myth, Reality* (Cambridge: Cambridge University Press, 2012).

Hobsbawm, Eric J. and Terence Ranger, eds., *The Invention of Tradition* (Cambridge: Cambridge University Press, 1983).

Hong Liu, "Old Linkages, New Networks: The Globalization of Overseas Chinese Voluntary Associations and Its Implications," *China Quarterly* 155 (1998), pp. 582–609.

Hu Hanmin, "Minzu guoji yu disan guoji [International of Nationalities and the Third (Communist) International]," in Cuncui xueshe, ed., *Hu Hanmin shiji ziliao huiji, di si ce* [*Hu Hanmin's Works*, vol. 4] (Xianggang: Dadong tushu gongsi, 1980), pp. 1395–1401.

Hu Xianzhang, ed., *Ziqiang buxi houde zaiwu: Qinghua jingshen xunli* [*Self-Discipline and Social Commitment Are the Tsinghua Spirit*] (Beijing: Qinghua daxue chubanshe, 2010).

"Hu Zhiming de shehuizhuyi sixiang [The Socialist Thought of Ho Chi Minh]," in He Baoyi, ed., *Shijie shehuizhuyi sixiang tongjian* [*World Socialist Thought*] (Beijing: Renmin chubanshe, 1996).

Huang Jianli, *The Politics of Depoliticization in Republican China: Guomindang Policy towards Student Political Activism, 1927–1949* (Bern: Peter Lang AG, 1996).

Huang Jinshu, *Nanyang renmin gongheguo beiwanglu* [*Memorandum of the Nanyang People's Republic*] (Taibei: Lianjing, 2013).

Huang Xunyan, Lin Zhi, and Qi Wen, "Pan Yunbo tongzhi geming de yisheng [The Revolutionary Life of Comrade Pan Yunbo]," in Du Hanwen and

Hainan zhengxie wenshi ziliao weiyuanhui, eds., *Hainan wenshi, di shijiu ji* [*The History of Hainan*, vol. 19] (Haikou: Hainan chuban gongsi, 2005), pp. 57–63.

Huang Yifei, "Huiyi Xin Ma huaqiao lieshi Zhang Yuanbao [Remembering the Martyred Overseas Chinese of Singapore and Malaya Zhang Yuanbao]," in Zhongguo renmin zhengzhi xieshang huiyi Fujian sheng Xianyou xian weiyuanhui wenshi weiyuanhui, ed., *Xianyou wenshi ziliao di si ji* [*Literary and Historical Materials of Xianyou County*, vol. 4] (1986), pp. 38–43.

Ileto, Reynaldo Clemeña, *Pasyon and Revolution: Popular Movements in the Philippines, 1840–1910* (Quezon City: Ateneo de Manila University Press, 1979).

Ip Hung-yok, "Cosmopolitanism and the Ideal Image of Nation in Communist Revolutionary Culture," in Kai-wing Chow, Kevin Michael Doak, and Poshek Fu, eds., *Constructing Nationhood in Modern East Asia* (Ann Arbor, MI: University of Michigan Press, 2001), pp. 215–246.

Intellectuals in Revolutionary China, 1921–1949: Leaders, Heroes and Sophisticates (London: Routledge Curzon, 2005).

Ishikawa Yoshihiro *The Formation of the Chinese Communist Party*, trans. by Joshua Fogel (New York, NY: Columbia University Press, 2012).

Israel, John, *Student Nationalism in China, 1927–1937* (Stanford, CA: Stanford University Press, 1966).

James, Harold, *The End of Globalization: Lessons from the Great Depression* (Cambridge, MA: Harvard University Press, 2001).

Jiang Hezhen, "Huiyi Xu Jie zai Jilongpo wenxue huodong [Remembering the Literary Activity of Xu Jie in Kuala Lumpur]," in Tiantai xian zhengxie wenshi ziliao yanjiu weiyuanhui, ed., *Tiantai wenshi ziliao di san ji, Xu Jie zhuanji* [*Literary and Historical Materials of Tiantai*, vol. 3: *Biography of Xu Jie*] (1987), pp. 81–88.

"Xu Jie zhuanlüe [A Brief Biography of Xu Jie]," in Tiantai xian wenshi ziliao weiyuanhui, ed., *Tiantai wenshi ziliao, di san ji, Xu Jie zhuanji* [*Literary and Historical Materials of Tiantai*, vol. 3: *Biography of Xu Jie*] (1987), pp. 4–12.

Jiann Hua To, James, *Qiaowu: Extra-Territorial Policies for the Overseas Chinese* (Leiden: Brill, 2014).

Karl, Rebecca E., *Staging the World: Chinese Nationalism at the Turn of the Twentieth Century* (Durham, NC: Duke University Press, 2002).

Kawashima Shin, "China's Reinterpretation of the Chinese 'World Order,' 1900–1940s," in Anthony Reid and Zheng Yangwen, eds., *Negotiating Asymmetry: China's Place in Asia* (Singapore: National University of Singapore Press, 2009), pp. 139–158.

Ke Pingping as related by Xu Jie, *Kanke daolushang de zuji* [*Road Full of Misfortunes*] (Shanghai: Huadong shifan daxue chubanshe, 1997).

Kenley, David, *New Culture in a New World: The May Fourth Movement and the Chinese Diaspora in Singapore (1919–1932)* (London: Routledge, 2003).

Khoo, Agnes, *Life as the River Flows: Women in the Malayan Anti-Colonial Struggle* (Petaling Jaya: Strategic Information Research Development [SIRD], 2004).

Khoo, Kay Kim, "The Beginnings of Political Extremism in Malaya, 1915–1935" (PhD dissertation, University of Malaysia, 1973).

Kiernan, Ben, *How Pol Pot Came to Power: Colonialism, Nationalism, and Communism in Cambodia, 1930–1975*. 2nd edn. (New Haven, CT: Yale University Press, 2004).

Kishkina, Elizaveta (Li Sha), *Iz Rossii v Kitai – put' dlinoiu v sto let* [*From Russia to China – Hundred Years' Journey*] (Moscow: Izdatel'skii proekt, 2014).

Koselleck, Reinhart, "*Begriffsgeschichte* and Social History," in *Futures Past: On the Semantics of Historical Time* (Cambridge, MA: MIT Press, 1985), pp. 73–91.

Kotkin, Stephen, *Magnetic Mountain: Stalinism as a Civilization* (Berkeley, CA: University of California Press, 1997).

Krüger, Joachim, "Die KPD und China," in Mechthild Leutner, ed., *Rethinking China in the 1950s (1921–1927)* (Münster: LIT Verlag, 2000), pp. 107–116.

"A Regular China Voice from Berlin to Moscow: The China Information of Liao Huanxin, 1924–1927," in Mechthild Leutner, Roland Felber, Mikhail L. Titarenko, and Alexander M. Grigoriev, eds., *The Chinese Revolution in the 1920s: Between Triumph and Disaster* (London: Routledge, 2002), pp. 177–186.

Kuah-Pearce, Khun Eng and Evelyn Hu-Dehart, eds., *Voluntary Organizations in the Chinese Diaspora: Illusions of Open Space in Hong Kong, Tokyo, and Shanghai* (Hong Kong: Hong Kong University Press, 2006).

Kuhn, Philip, *Chinese among Others: Emigration in Modern Times* (Lanham, MD: Rowman & Littlefield Publishers, 2008).

Origins of the Modern Chinese State (Stanford, CA: Stanford University Press, 2001).

"Origins of the Taiping Vision: Cross-Cultural Dimensions of a Chinese Rebellion," *Comparative Studies in Society and History* 19(3) (July 1977), pp. 350–366.

"Why China Historians Should Study the Chinese Diaspora, and Vice-Versa." Liu Kuang-ching Lecture, 2004. *Journal of Chinese Overseas* 2(2) (2006), pp. 163–172.

Lai, H. Mark, *Chinese American Transnational Politics* (Urbana, IL: University of Illinois Press, 2010).

Laqua, Daniel, *Internationalism Reconfigured: Transnational Ideas and Movements between the World Wars* (London: I. B. Tauris, 2011).

Leibold, James, "Searching for Han: Early Twentieth-Century Narratives of Chinese Origins and Development," in Thomas Mullaney, ed., *Critical Han Studies: The History, Representation and Identity of China's Majority* (Berkeley, CA: University of California Press, 2012), pp. 210–233.

Leong, Stephen Mun Yoon, "Sources, Agencies and Manifestations of Overseas Chinese Nationalism in Malaya, 1937–1941" (PhD dissertation, UCLA, 1976).

Leow, Rachel, "'Do You Own Non-Chinese Mui Tsai?' Re-examining Race and Female Servitude in Malaya and Hong Kong, 1919–1939," *Modern Asian Studies* 46 (2012), pp. 1736–1763.

Levine, Marilyn, *The Found Generation: Chinese Communists in Europe during the Twenties* (Seattle, WA: University of Washington Press, 1993).

Li Minghuan, *Dangdai haiwai huaren shetuan yanjiu* [*Contemporary Associations of Overseas Chinese*] ([Xiamen]: Xiamen daxue chubanshe, 1995).

Li Weijia, "Otherness in Solidarity: Collaboration between Chinese and German Left-Wing Activists in the Weimar Republic," in Qinna Shen and Martin Rosenstock, eds., *Beyond Alterity: German Encounters with Modern East Asia* (New York, NY: Berghahn Books, 2014), pp. 73–93.

Li Xiaodian, Chen Liang, and Wen Gang, "Xin, Ma renmin wuzhuang kang Ri shiqi de kang Ri juyun [Drama Troupes of the Malayan and Singaporean Chinese during the Anti-Japanese Resistance]," in *Du Bian yu Ma Hua (Xin Ma) juyun* [*Du Bian and the Drama Movement of the Malayan and Singaporean Chinese*] (Jiulong: Jinwei yinshua youxian gongsi, 1994), pp. 67–82.

Li Yinghui, *Huaqiao zhengce yu haiwai minzuzhuyi (1912–1949)* [*Overseas Chinese Policy and Overseas Chinese Nationalism (1912–1949)*] (Taibei: Guoshiguan, 1997).

Li Yuzhen, "Fighting for the Leadership of the Chinese Revolution: KMT Delegates' Three Visits to Moscow," *Journal of Modern Chinese History* 7(2) (2013), pp. 218–239.

Liang Yingming, "Malaixiya zhongzu zhengzhi xia de huaren yu Yinduren shehui [Chinese and Indians under Malaysian Racial Policy]," *Huaqiao huaren lishi yanjiu* [*Studies of Chinese Overseas*] 1 (1992), pp. 1–7.

Liao Huanxing, "Zhongguo gongchandang lü Ou zongzhibu, 1953 [The European Branch of the Chinese Communist Party, 1953]," in Zhongguo shehui kexueyuan xiandaishi yanjiushi, Zhongguo geming bowuguan dangshi yanjiushi, eds., *Zhongguo xiandai geming shi ziliao congkan. "Yi Da" qianhou. Zhongguo gongchandang di yi ci daibiao dahui qianhou ziliao xuanbian* [*Series of Materials on Chinese Modern Revolutionary History Around the Time of the First Congress: A Selection of Materials*, vol. 2] (Beijing: Renmin chubanshe, 1980), pp. 502–510.

"Zhongguo renmin zhengqu ziyou de douzheng: Guomindang zhongyang changwu weiyuanhui daibiao de jiangyan [The Righteous Struggle of the Chinese People: Speech by the Representative of the Standing Committee of the GMD]," in Zhonggong Hengnan xianwei dangshi ziliao zhengji bangongshi, eds., *Zhonggong Hengnan difang shi: Xin minzhuzhuyi geming shiqi* [*The History of the CCP in Hengnan County: The Revolutionary Period of New Democracy*] (Beijing: Zhonggong dangshi chubanshe, 1995), pp. 142–145.

Liao, Shubert S. C., ed., *Chinese Participation in Philippine Culture and Economy* (Manila: Bookman, 1964).

Lim, Bee Khim, "Tan Cheng Lock, Tan Siew Sin and the MCA (1949–1974)" (BA honors dissertation, National University of Singapore, 1991).

Lim, Patricia Pui Huen, "Between Tradition and Modernity: The Chinese Association of Johor Bahru Malaysia," in Khun Eng Kuah-Pearce and Evelyn Hu-Dehart, eds., *Voluntary Organizations in the Chinese Diaspora: Illusions of Open Space in Hong Kong, Tokyo, and Shanghai* (Hong Kong: Hong Kong University Press, 2006), pp. 29–52.

Lintner, Bertil, *The Rise and Fall of the Communist Party of Burma* (Ithaca, NY: Cornell University Press, 1990).

Litten, Frederick S., "The Noulens Affair," *China Quarterly* 138 (June 1994), pp. 492–512.

Liu Changping and Li Ke, *Fengyu Wanqingyuan: Buying wangque de Xinhai geming xunchen Zhang Yongfu* [*Trials and Hardships of Wangqing Garden: Meritorious Official of the Xinhai Revolution Zhang Yongfu Should Not Be Forgotten*] (Beijing: Zhongguo wenshi chubanshe, 2011).

Liu Jixuan and Shu Shicheng, *Zhonghua minzu tuozhi Nanyang shi* [The History of Chinese Colonization of Nanyang] (Shanghai: Guoli bianyiguan, 1935).

Liu Lüsen, "Zhongcheng jianyi de gongchandang ren: Geming xianqu Liao Huanxing tongzhi zhuanlüe [Loyal and Persistent CCP Member: A Biography of the Revolutionary Avant-Garde Comrade Liao Huanxing]," in Zhonggong Hengnan xianwei dangshi lianluo zhidaozu, Zhonggong Hengnan xianwei dangshi bangongshi, ed., *Yidai yingjie xin minzhuzhuyi geming shiqi Zhonggong Hengnan dangshi renwu* [An Era of Heroes: Party Members during Hengnan Revolutionary Period of New Democracy] (1996), pp. 3–11.

"Zhongcheng jianyi de gongchandang ren Liao Huanxing [Loyal and Persistent CCP Member Liao Huanxing]," *Hunan dangshi yuekan* [*Hunan CCP History Monthly*] 11 (1988), pp. 20–22.

Liu, Lydia He, *The Clash of Empires: The Invention of China in Modern World Making* (Cambridge, MA: Harvard University Press, 2006).

Translingual Practice: Literature, National Culture, and Translated Modernity: China, 1900–1937 (Stanford, CA: Stanford University Press, 1995).

Liu Shaoqi, "Letter to the Party Centre Concerning Past Work in the White Areas, 4 March 1937," in Tony Saich and Benjamin Yang, eds., *The Rise to Power of the Chinese Communist Party: Documents and Analysis* (Armonk, NY: M. E. Sharpe, 1996), pp. 773–786.

Lockard, Craig A., "Chinese Migration and Settlement in Southeast Asia before 1850: Making Fields from the Sea," *History Compass* 11(9) (2013), pp. 765–781.

Loh, Francis Kok-Wah, *Beyond the Tin Mines: Coolies, Squatters, and New Villagers in the Kinta Valley, Malaysia, c. 1880–1980* (Singapore: Oxford University Press, 1988).

Louro, Michele, "India and the League Against Imperialism: A Special 'Blend' of Nationalism and Internationalism," in Ali Raza, Franziska Roy, and Benjamin Zachariah, eds., *The Internationalist Moment: South Asia, Worlds, and World Views 1917–39* (New Delhi: SAGE Publications India, 2014), pp. 22–55.

"Magong de zhuzhang he celüe (1939–1943) [The Standpoint of the MCP and Its Tactics]," in Ershiyi shiji chubanshe bianjibu, ed., *Zhanqian dixia douzheng shiqi. Jiandang chuqi jieduan, Magong wenji, congshu xilie, di yi ji* [The Prewar Period of the Underground Struggle: The Founding of the Party. Documents of the MCP, vol. 1] (Kuala Lumpur: Ershiyi shiji chubanshe, 2010), pp. 67–83.

"Ma Ning. Zai Nanyang fazhan Zhongguo de xinxing juyun [Ma Ning. The Chinese New Drama Movement in Nanyang]," in Zeng Qingrui, ed., *Zhongguo xiandai huaju wenxue wushijiu zhaji* [*China's Modern Drama. Notes of Fifty Writers*] (Beijing: Zhongguo chuanmei daxue chubanshe, 2008), pp. 259–268.

Manela, Erez, *The Wilsonian Moment: Self-Determination and the International Origins of Anticolonial Nationalism* (Oxford: Oxford University Press, 2007).

Mao Zedong, "Zhongguo gongchandang zai minzu zhanzheng zhong de diwei [The Role of the CCP in the National War]," Speech at the 6th Plenum of the CC, October 14, 1938, in *Mao Zedong xuanji, di er juan* [*Collected Works of Mao Zedong*, vol. 2] (Beijing: Renmin chubanshe, 1991), pp. 519–536.

Martin, Terry, *The Affirmative Action Empire: Nations and Nationalism in the Soviet Union, 1923–1939* (Ithaca, NY: Cornell University Press, 2017).

McDermott, Kevin and Jeremy Agnew, *The Comintern: A History of International Communism* (Houndmills: Macmillan, 1996).

McLane, Charles B., *Soviet Strategies in Southeast Asia: An Exploration of Eastern Policy under Lenin and Stalin* (Princeton, NJ: Princeton University Press, 1966).

McVey, Ruth Thomas, *The Rise of Indonesian Communism* (Ithaca, NY: Cornell University Press, 1965).

Menasse, Robert, *Das war Österreich: Gesammelte Essays zum Land ohne Eigenschaften* (Frankfurt am Main: Suhrkamp, 2005).

Miller, Nicola, "Latin America: State-Building and Nationalism," in John Breuilly, ed., *The Oxford Handbook of the History of Nationalism* (Oxford: Oxford University Press, 2013), pp. 388–391.

Milner, Anthony, *The Invention of Politics in Colonial Malaya: Contesting Nationalism and the Expansion of the Public Sphere* (Cambridge: Cambridge University Press, 1994).

Murray, Dian, "Migration, Protection, and Racketeering: The Spread of the Tiandihui within China," in David Ownby and Mary Somers Heidhues, eds., *"Secret Societies" Reconsidered: Perspectives on the Social History of Modern South China and Southeast Asia* (Armonk, NY: M. E. Sharpe, 1993), pp. 177–189.

Murray, Jeremy A., *China's Lonely Revolution: The Local Communist Movement of Hainan Island, 1926–1956* (Albany, NY: State University of New York Press, 2017).

Musa, Mahani, "Women in the Malayan Communist Party, 1942–89," *Journal of Southeast Asian Studies* 44 (2013), pp. 226–249.

Ng, Sin Yue, "The Malayan Communist Party and Overseas Chinese Nationalism in Malaya, 1937–1941" (MA dissertation, University of Hull, 1981).

Ng, Sze-Chieh, "Silenced Revolutionaries: Challenging the Received View of Malaya's Revolutionary Past" (MA thesis, Arizona State University, 2011).

Ng, Wing-chung Vincent, "Huiguan: Regional Institutions in the Development of Overseas Chinese Nationalism in Singapore, 1912–41" (MA dissertation, University of Hong Kong, 1987).

"Urban Chinese Social Organization: Some Unexplored Aspects in Huiguan Development in Singapore, 1900–1941," *Modern Asian Studies* 26(3) (July 1992), pp. 469–494.

Nicolaevsky, Boris, "Russia, Japan, and the Pan-Asiatic Movement to 1925," *Far Eastern Quarterly* 8(3) (1949), pp. 259–295.

Nonini, Donald M., *British Colonial Rule and the Resistance of the Malay Peasantry, 1900–1957* (New Haven, CT: Yale University Southeast Asia Studies, 1992).

Omar, Ariffin, *Bangsa Melayu: Malay Concepts of Democracy and Community, 1945–1950* (Kuala Lumpur; New York, NY: Oxford University Press, 1993).

Ong, Aihwa and Donald Nonini, *Ungrounded Empires: The Cultural Politics of Modern Chinese Transnationalism* (London: Routledge, 1997).

Onraet, Rene H., *Singapore: A Police Background* (London: Dorothy Crisp, 1947).

Owen, Norman G., ed., *The Emergence of Modern Southeast Asia: A New History* (Honolulu, HI: University of Hawaii Press, 2005).

Ownby, David, "Chinese Hui and the Early Modern Social Order: Evidence from Eighteenth-Century Southeast China," in David Ownby and Mary Somers Heidhues, eds., *"Secret Societies" Reconsidered: Perspectives on the Social History of Modern South China and Southeast Asia* (Armonk, NY: M. E. Sharpe, 1993), pp. 34–67.

Ownby, David and Mary Somers Heidhues, eds., *"Secret Societies" Reconsidered: Perspectives on the Social History of Modern South China and Southeast Asia* (Armonk, NY: M. E. Sharpe, 1993).

Pan Yunbo, "Canjia geming de pianduan huiyi [Fragments of a Memoir about Participation in the Revolution]," in Zhongguo renmin zhengzhi xieshang huiyi Guangdong sheng Guangzhou shi weiyuanhui wenshi ziliao yanjiu weiyuanhui, ed., *Guangzhou wenshi ziliao di shiba ji* [*Guangzhou Literary and Historical Materials*, vol. 18] (1980), pp. 1–13.

Peng Zhandong, "Cong aiguo qiaoling Peng Zemin zhandou yisheng kan huaqiao huaren zai Zhongguo geming lichengzhong de tuchu gongxian [The Life of Patriotic Overseas Chinese Peng Zemin as an Example of the Contributions of Overseas Chinese to the Chinese Revolution]," in *Qiaowu huigu* [*Overseas Chinese Reminiscences*, vol. 2] (Beijing: Guowuyuan qiaowu bangongshi, 2006).

Perry, Elizabeth J., *Anyuan: Mining China's Revolutionary Tradition* (Berkeley, CA: University of California, 2012).

Shanghai on Strike: The Politics of Chinese Labor (Stanford, CA: Stanford University Press, 1993).

Peterson, Glen, *Overseas Chinese in the People's Republic of China* (London: Routledge, 2011).

Petersson, Fredrik, "'We Are Neither Visionaries Nor Utopian Dreamers': Willi Münzenberg, the League Against Imperialism, and the Comintern, 1925–1933" (PhD dissertation, Åbo Akademi University, 2013).

Piazza, Hans, "Anti-Imperialist League and the Chinese Revolution," in Mechthild Leutner, Roland Felber, Mikhail L. Titarenko, and Alexander M. Grigoriev, eds., *The Chinese Revolution in the 1920s: Between Triumph and Disaster* (London: Routledge, 2002), pp. 166–176.

Pittman, Don A., *Toward a Modern Chinese Buddhism: Taixu's Reforms* (Honolulu, HI: University of Hawaii Press, 2001).

Price, Don, *Russia and the Roots of the Chinese Revolution* (Cambridge, MA: Harvard University Press, 1974).

Purcell, Victor, *The Chinese in Malaya* (Oxford: Oxford University Press, 1967).

Quinn-Judge, Sophie, *Ho Chi Minh: The Missing Years, 1919–1941* (Berkeley, CA: University of California Press, 2003).

Ratnam, Kanagaratnam Jeya, *Communalism and the Political Process in Malaya* (Kuala Lumpur: University of Malaya Press, 1965).

Records of the Colonial Office, Commonwealth and Foreign and Commonwealth Offices, Empire Marketing Board, and Related Bodies Relating to the Administration of Britain's Colonies (Kew, Surrey: National Archives, 2009).

Rees, Tim, "1936," in Stephen A. Smith, ed., *The Oxford Handbook of the History of Communism* (Oxford: Oxford University Press, 2014), pp. 125–139.

Rees, Tim and Andrew Thorpe, eds., *International Communism and the Communist International, 1919–1943* (Manchester: Manchester University Press, 1998).

Reid, Anthony, "Melayu as a Source of Diverse Modern Identities," in Timothy Barnard, ed., *Contesting Malayness: Malay Identity across Boundaries* (Singapore: Singapore University Press, 2004), pp. 1–24.

Ren Guixiang and Zhao Hongying, eds., *Huaqiao huaren yu guogong guanxi* [*Chinese Overseas and CCP–GMD Relations*] (Wuhan: Wuhan chubanshe, 1999).

Riddell, John, *To the Masses: Proceedings of the Third Congress of the Communist International, 1921* (Leiden: Brill, 2015).

Robert, Dana, "First Globalization? The Internationalization of the Protestant Missionary Movement between the World Wars," in Ogbu U. Kalu and Alaine Low, eds., *Interpreting Contemporary Christianity: Global Processes and Local Identities* (Grand Rapids, MI: William B. Eerdmans Publishing Company, 2008), pp. 93–130.

Roff, William R., *The Origins of Malay Nationalism* (New Haven, CT: Yale University Press, 1967).

Sahlins, Marshall, *Historical Metaphors and Mythical Realities: Structure in the Early History of the Sandwich Islands Kingdom* (Ann Arbor, MI: University of Michigan Press, 1981).

Saich, Tony, "The Chinese Communist Party during the Era of the Comintern (1919–1943)," unpublished manuscript.

The Origins of the First United Front in China: The Role of Sneevliet (Alias Maring). 2 vols. (Leiden: Brill Academic Publishers, 1991).

Saich, Tony and Hans J. van de Ven, eds., *New Perspectives on the Chinese Communist Revolution* (Armonk, NY: M. E. Sharpe, 1995).

Schoenhals, Michael, *Doing Things with Words in Chinese Politics: Five Studies* (Berkeley, CA: Institute of East Asian Studies, University of California, 1992).

See, Teresita Ang, "Integration, Indigenization, Hybridization and Localization of the Ethnic Chinese Minority in the Philippines," in Leo Suryadinata, ed., *Migration, Indigenization and Interaction: Chinese Overseas and Globalization* (Singapore: Chinese Heritage Centre, World Scientific Publishing, 2011), pp. 231–252.

Shanghai Municipal Police Files, 1929–1945 (Wilmington, DE: Scholarly Resources, 1989).

Share, Michael, *Where Empires Collided: Russian and Soviet Relations with Hong Kong, Taiwan, and Macao* (Hong Kong: Chinese University Press, 2007).

Shen Zhihua and Yafeng Xia, "Hidden Currents during the Honeymoon: Mao, Khrushchev, and the 1957 Moscow Conference," *Journal of Cold War Studies* 11(4) (Fall 2009), pp. 74–117.

Shi Cangjin, *Malaixiya huaren shetuan yanjiu* [*A Study of Chinese Associations in Malaysia*] (Beijing: Zhongguo huaqiao chubanshe, 2005).

Shiraishi, Takashi, *An Age in Motion: Popular Radicalism in Java, 1912–1926* (Ithaca, NY: Cornell University Press, 1990).

Smith, Anthony D., *Nationalism and Modernism: A Critical Survey of Recent Theories of Nations and Nationalism* (London: Routledge, 1998).

Smith, Craig A., "China as the Leader of the Small and Weak: The *Ruoxiao* Nations and Guomindang Nationalism," *Cross-Currents* 6(2) (November 2017), pp. 530–557.

Smith, Stephen A., ed., *The Oxford Handbook of the History of Communism* (Oxford: Oxford University Press, 2014).

So, Wai-Chor, *The Kuomintang Left in the National Revolution, 1924–1931: The Leftist Alternative in Republican China* (Oxford: Oxford University Press, 1991).

Shestoi kongress Kominterna: Stenograficheskii otchet. Vyp. 4, Revoliutsionnoe dvizhenie v kolonial'nykh i polukolonial'nykh stranakh [*The Sixth Comintern Congress: Stenographic Report*, vol. 4: *Revolutionary Movement in Colonial and Semi-Colonial Countries*] (Moscow: Gosudarstvennoe izdatel'stvo, 1929).

Stenograficheskii otchet VI kongressa Kominterna, Vypusk 4, 5 [*Stenographic Report of the 6th Congress of the Comintern. Vols. 4, 5*] (Leningrad: Gosudarstvennoe izdatel'stvo, 1929).

Stranahan, Patricia, *Underground: The Shanghai Communist Party and the Politics of Survival, 1927–1937* (Lanham, MD: Rowman & Littlefield Publishers, 1998).

Su Yunfeng, "The Contribution and Sacrifices of the Overseas Chinese in Malaya and Singapore during the War against the Japanese Invasion, 1937–1945," in Ng Lun Ngai-ha and Chang Chak Yan, eds., *Liangci shijie dazhan qijian zai Yazhou zhi haiwai huaren* [Overases Chinese in Asia between the Two World Wars] (Hong Kong: Chinese University of Hong Kong, 1989), pp. 303–324.

Sugihara, Kaoru, "Patterns of Chinese Emigration to Southeast Asia, 1869–1939," in Kaoru Sugihara, ed., *Japan, China, and the Growth of the Asian International Economy, 1850–1949* (Oxford: Oxford University Press, 2005), pp. 244–274.

Sun Jianbin, "Jue bu dang wangguonu: Mianhuai kang Ri xianbei Jiang Qitai, Zeng Shaowu, Lin Boxiang [Don't Become Stateless Slaves: Remembering the Elders of the Anti-Japanese Resistance, Jiang Qitai, Zeng Shaowu, Lin Boxiang]," in Zhongguo renmin xieshang huiyi Fujian sheng Quanzhou shi weiyuanhui wenshi ziliao weiyuanhui, ed., *Quanzhou wenshi ziliao di ershisi ji* [*Literary and Historical Materials of Quanzhou*, vol. 24] (2005), pp. 123–131.

Sun Zhongshan [Sun Yatsen], "Dui Shenhu shanghui yisuo deng tuanti de yanshuo [Address to the Chamber of Commerce and Other Organizations in Kobe] November 28, 1924," in *Sun Zhongshan quanji* [*Collected Works of Sun Yatsen*], 11 vols. (Beijing: Zhonghua shuju, 1986), vol. 11, pp. 401–409.

"Sanminzhuyi [Three People's Principles]," "Minzuzhuyi [Nationalism]," lecture 4. February 17, 1924, in *Sun Zhongshan quanji* [*Collected Works of Sun Yatsen*], 11 vols. (Beijing: Zhonghua shuju, 1986), vol. 9, pp. 220–231.

Suryadinata, Leo, *Peranakan Chinese Politics in Java, 1917–42* (Singapore: Singapore University Press, 1981).

Tai Yuen, *Labour Unrest in Malaya, 1934–1941: The Rise of the Workers' Movement* (Kuala Lumpur: Institute of Postgraduate Studies and Research, University of Malaya, 2000).

Tan Liok Ee, "The Rhetoric of Bangsa and Minzu: Community and Nation in Tension, the Malay Peninsula, 1900–1955." Working Paper (Clayton, Austrlia: Centre of Southeast Asian Studies, Monash University, 1988).

Tan Cheng Lock, Malayan Problems from the Chinese Point of View, ed. C. Q. Lee(Singapore: Tannsco, 1947).

Tan, Pamela, *The Chinese Factor* (Dural Delivery Centre, NSW: Rosenberg Publishing, 2008).

Tarling, Nicholas, *Nationalism in Southeast Asia: If the People Are with Us* (London: Routledge, 2004).

Teiwes, Frederick, *Politics and Purges in China: Rectification and the Decline of Party Norms, 1950–1965* (Armonk, NY: M. E. Sharpe, 1979–1992).

Tertitskii, Konstantin and Anna Belogurova, *Taiwanskoe kommunisticheskoe dvizhenie i Komintern. Issledovanie. Dokumenty (1924–1932)* [*The Taiwanese Communist Movement and the Comintern: A Study. Documents. 1924–1932*] (Moscow: Vostok-Zapad, 2005).

The Three Principles of the People, San Min Chu I. By Dr. Sun Yat-Sen. With Two Supplementary Chapters by Chiang Kai-shek. Translated into English by Frank W. Price. Abridged and edited by the Commission for the Compilation of the History of the Kuomintang (Taipei: China Publishing Company, 1960).

Titarenko, Mikhail L. and Mechthild Leutner, eds., *VKP(b), Komintern i Kitai. Dokumenty. T.III. VKP(b), Komintern i sovetskoe dvizhenie v Kitae, 1927–1931* [*CPSU (Bolshevik), the Comintern, and China. Documents. Volume 3. CPSU (Bolshevik), the Comintern, and the Soviet Movement in China, 1927–1931*] (Moscow: AO Buklet, 1999).

VKP(b), Komintern i Kitai. Dokumenty T.IV. VKP(b), Komintern i Sovetskoie dvizhenie v Kitae, 1931–1937 [*CPSU (Bolshevik), the Comintern, and China. Volume 4. CPSU (Bolshevik), the Comintern, and the Soviet Movement in China, 1931–1937*] (Moscow: ROSSPEN, 2003).

Tolz, Vera, *Russia's Own Orient: The Politics of Identity and Oriental Studies in the Late Imperial and Soviet Periods* (Oxford: Oxford University Press, 2011).

Tregonning, Kennedy Gordon, "Tan Cheng Lock: A Malayan Nationalist," *Journal of Southeast Asian Studies* 10(1) (March 1979), pp. 25–76.

Turnbull, C. M., "Overseas Chinese Attitudes to Nationalism in Malaya between the Two World Wars," in Ng Lun Ngai-ha and Chang Chak Yan, eds.,

Liangci shijie dazhan qijian zai Yazhou zhi haiwai huaren [Overseas Chinese in Asia between the Two World Wars] (Hong Kong: Chinese University of Hong Kong, 1989), pp. 367–374.

van de Ven, Hans, "The Emergence of the Text-Centered Party," in Tony Saich and Hans van de Ven, eds., *New Perspectives on the Chinese Communist Revolution* (Armonk, NY: M. E. Sharpe, 1995), pp. 5–32.

From Friend to Comrade: The Founding of the Chinese Communist Party, 1920–1927 (Berkeley, CA: University of California Press, 1991).

Van Slyke, Lyman P., *Enemies and Friends: The United Front in Chinese Communist History* (Stanford, CA: Stanford University Press, 1967).

Vasil'kov, Iaroslav Vladimirovich and Marina Iur'evna Sorokina, *Liudi i sud'by, Biobibliograficheskii slovar' vostokovedov-zhertv politicheskogo terrora v sovetskii period* [*People and Lives. Bio-Bibliographical Dictionary of Orientalists: Victims of Political Purges during the Soviet Period (1917–1991)*] (St. Petersburg: Peterburgskoe vostokovedenie, 2003).

Vatlin, Alexander and Stephen A. Smith, "The Comintern," in Stephen A. Smith, ed., *The Oxford Handbook of the History of Communism* (Oxford: Oxford University Press, 2014), pp. 187–194.

Wang Gungwu, *The Chinese Overseas: From Earthbound China to the Quest for Autonomy* (Cambridge, MA: Harvard University Press, 2000).

"Chinese Politics in Malaya," *China Quarterly* 43 (1970), pp. 1–30.

"The Limits of Nanyang Chinese Nationalism, 1912–1937," in Charles D. Cowan and Oliver W. Wolters, eds., *Southeast Asian History and Historiography* (Ithaca, NY: Cornell University Press, 1976), pp. 405–423.

"*Tonghua, Guihua*, and History of the Overseas Chinese," in Ng Lun Ngai-ha and Chang Chak Yan, eds., *Liangci shijie dazhan qijian zai Yazhou zhi haiwai huaren* [*Overseas Chinese in Asia between the Two World Wars*] (Hong Kong: Chinese University of Hong Kong, 1989), pp. 11–23.

Wang Naixin et al., eds., *Taiwan shehui yundong shi, 1913–1936* [*History of Taiwan's Social Movements*]. 5 vols. Vol. 3: *Gongchanzhuyi yundong* [*The Communist Movement*] (Taibei: Chuangzao chubanshe, 1989).

Wickberg, Edgar, "The Chinese Mestizo in Philippine History," *Journal of Southeast Asian History* 5(1) (1964), pp. 62–100.

Williams, Raymond, *Keywords: A Vocabulary of Culture and Society* (London: Fontana, 1983).

Winichakul, Thongchai, *Siam Mapped: A History of the Geo-Body of a Nation* (Honolulu, HI: University of Hawaii Press, 1994).

Woodside, Alexander, *Lost Modernities: China, Vietnam, Korea, and the Hazards of World History*. Edwin O. Reischauer Lecture. (Cambridge, MA: Harvard University Press, 2006).

Worley, Matthew, ed., *In Search of Revolution: International Communist Parties in the Third Period* (London: I. B. Tauris, 2004).

Wu Jianjie, "Cong da Yazhouzhuyi zouxiang shijie datongzhuyi: Lilun Sun Zhongshan de guojizhuyi sixiang [From Pan-Asianism to World Great Harmony: Sun Yatsen's Internationalism]," *Jindai shi yanjiu* [*Studies in Modern History*] 3 (1997), pp. 185–288.

Wu, Yin Hua, *Class and Communalism in Malaysia* (London: Zed Books, 1983).

Xie Fei, "Huiyi Zhongguo gongchandang Nanyang linshi weiyuanhui de gong-zuo, 1929–1930 [Remembering the Work of the Nanyang Provisional Committee, 1929–1930]," in *Geming huiyilu: Zengkan 1* [*Revolutionary Reminiscences: Expanded Edition 1*] (Beijing: Renmin chubanshe, 1983), pp. 159–169.

Xu Jie, *Yezi yu liulian: Zhongguo xiandai xiaopin jingdian* [*Coconut and Durian: Little Souvenirs of Contemporary China*] (Shijiazhuang: Hebei jiaoyu chu-banshe, 1994).

Xu Jilin, "Wusi: Shijiezhuyi de aiguo yundong [May 4th: Cosmopolitan Patriotic Movement]," *Zhishi fenzi luncong* [*Compendia of Intellectual Debates*] 9 (2010).

"Xuelan'e Jiaying de xuesheng yundong [The Student Movement in Kajang, Selangor]," in Ershiyi shiji chubanshe bianjibu, ed., *Zhanqian dixia douzheng shiqi. Jiandang chuqi jieduan, Magong wenji, congshu xilie, di yi ji* [*The Prewar Period of the Underground Struggle: The Founding of the Party. Documents of the MCP*, vol. 1] (Kuala Lumpur: Ershiyi shiji chubanshe, 2010), pp. 138–146.

Yamamoto Hiroyuki, Anthony Milner, Midori Kawashima, and Kazuhiko Arai, eds., *Bangsa and Umma: Development of People-Grouping Concepts in Islamized Southeast Asia* (Kyoto: Kyoto University Press, 2011).

Yang Songnian and Wang Kangding, *Dongnanya huaren wenxue yu wenhua* [*Culture and Literature of the Chinese in Southeast Asia*] (Xinjiapo: Yazhou yanjiuhui, 1995).

Yap, Melanie and Dianne Leong Man, *Colour, Confusion, and Concessions: The History of the Chinese in South Africa* (Hong Kong: Hong Kong University Press, 1996).

Ye Zhongling [Yeap Chong Leng], "Chen Jiageng [Tan Kah Kee] dui Magong taidu de zhuanyi: Cong 'ruoji ruoli' dao gongkai chongtu [The Changing Attitudes toward the Malayan CP: From 'Ambiguity' to Open Conflict]," *Yazhou wenhua* [*Asian Culture*] 28 (June 2004), pp. 94–108.

Yeh Wen-hsin, *The Alienated Academy: Culture and Politics in Republican China, 1919–1937* (Cambridge, MA: Harvard University Press, 1990).

Provincial Passages: Culture, Space, and the Origins of Chinese Communism (Berkeley, CA: University of California Press, 1996).

Yen Ching-hwang, "Early Chinese Clan Organizations in Singapore and Malaya, 1819–1911," *Journal of Southeast Asian Studies* 12(1) (March 1981), pp. 62–91.

A Social History of the Chinese in Singapore and Malaya, 1800–1911 (Singapore; New York, NY: Oxford University Press, 1986).

Yeo, Kim Wah, *The Politics of Decentralization: Colonial Controversy in Malaya, 1920–1929* (Kuala Lumpur: Oxford University Press, 1982).

Yeo Song Nian and Ng Siew Ai, "The Japanese Occupation as Reflected in Singapore–Malayan Chinese Literary Works after the Japanese Occupation (1945–49)," in Patricia Pui Huen Lim and Diana Wong, eds., *War and Memory in Malaysia and Singapore* (Singapore: Institute of Southeast Asian Studies, 2000), pp. 106–122.

Ying, Esther Cheo, *Black Country Girl in Red China* (London: Hutchinson, 1980).

Yoji Akashi, "Lai Teck, Secretary General of the Malayan Communist Party, 1939–1947," *Journal of the South Seas Society* 49 (1994), pp. 37–103.

"The Nanyang Chinese Anti-Japanese Boycott Movement, 1908–1928: A Study of Nanyang Chinese Nationalism" (Kuala Lumpur: Department of History, University of Malaya, 1968).

Yong, Ching Fatt, *Origins of Malayan Communism* (Singapore: South Sea Society, 1991).

Yong, Ching Fatt and R. B. McKenna, *The Kuomintang Movement in British Malaya, 1912–1949* (Singapore: Singapore University Press, 1990).

Yu Dafu, "Private Classes and a Modern School," in *Nights of Spring Fever and Other Writings* (Beijing: Panda Books, 1984), pp. 174–180.

Yu Yueting, "Ma Ning yige bei yiwang de liaobuqi de 'zuoyi' zuojia [A Forgotten Extraordinary Left-Wing Writer Ma Ning]," in Zhao Ting, ed., *Shifan qunying guanghui Zhonghua (di ershi juan)* [*Teachers, Heroes, Shining China*, vol. 20] (Xi'an: Shaanxi renmin jiaoyu chubanshe, 1994), pp. 176–185.

Zhang Bao, "Er, sanshi niandai zai Meiguo de Zhongguo gongchandang ren [CCP Members in America in the 1920s and the 1930s]," in *Guoji gongyun shi yanjiu ziliao* [*Research Materials on the History of the International Communist Movement*] 4 (1982), pp. 150–160.

Zhang Jinda, "Mianhuai Zhang Xia xiansheng [Remembering Mr. Zhang Xia]," in Zhongguo renmin zhengzhi xieshang huiyi Fujian sheng Xianyou xian weiyuanhui wenshi weiyuanhui, ed., *Xianyou wenshi ziliao di shiyi ji* [*Literary and Historical Materials of Xianyou County*, vol. 11] (1994), pp. 47–61.

Zhang Weibo, "Datong lixiang yu Zhonggong chuangjian [The Idea of Datong and the Establishment of the CCP]," in Zhonggong yida huizhi jinianguan, ed., *Zhongguo gongchandang chuangjian shi yanjiu* [Studies on the Founding of the CCP] (Shanghai: Renmin chubanshe, 2012), pp. 42–54.

Zhang Xia, "Xianyou xian lü Ma huaqiao yu geming huodong [Immigrants from Xianyou County in Malaya and Revolutionary Activities]," in Zhongguo renmin zhengzhi xieshang huiyi Fujian sheng Xianyou xian weiyuanhui, ed., *Xianyou wenshi ziliao di er ji* [*Literary and Historical Materials of Xianyou County*, vol. 2] (1984), pp. 34–39.

"Xianyou xiandai zhongxue de geming huoguang [The Revolutionary Fire of the Modern Middle Schools in Xianyou County]," in Zhongguo renmin zhengzhi xieshang huiyi Fujian sheng Putian shi weiyuanhui wenshi ziliao yanjiu weiyuanhui, ed., *Putian shi wenshi ziliao di yi ji* [*Literary and Historical Materials of the City of Putian*, vol. 1] (1985), pp. 43–48.

Zhang Yongfu, *Nanyang yu chuangli Minguo* [*Nanyang and the Establishment of the Republic*] (Shanghai: Zhonghua shuju, 1933).

"Zhanqian dixia douzheng shiqi xuesheng yundong de ruogan qingkuang [The Situation in the Student Movement during the Underground Prewar Period]," in Ershiyi shiji chubanshe bianjibu, eds., *Zhanqian dixia douzheng shiqi. Jiandang chuqi jieduan, Magong wenji, congshu xilie, di yi ji* [*The Prewar Period of the Underground Struggle: The Founding of the Party. Documents of the MCP*, vol. 1] (Kuala Lumpur: Ershiyi shiji chubanshe, 2010), pp. 134–138.

Zhao Gang, *The Qing Opening to the Ocean: Chinese Maritime Policies, 1684–1757* (Honolulu, HI: University of Hawaii Press, 2013).

Zheng Chaoling, "Ji Fu Daqing [Remembering Fu Daqing]," *Bainian chao* [*One Hundred Year Tide*] 2 (1998), pp. 61–63.

Zheng Liren, "Overseas Chinese Nationalism in British Malaya 1894–1941" (PhD dissertation, Cornell University, 1997).

Zheng Tingzhi and Li Ruiliang, "Yige jianding de wenhua zhanshi: Chen Junju tongzhi de yisheng [The Life of an Exemplary Cultural Warrior: Chen Junju]," in Zhongguo renmin zhengzhi xieshang huiyi Fujian sheng Putian shi weiyuanhui wenshi ziliao yanjiu wenyuanhui, ed., *Putian shi wenshi ziliao di qi ji* [*Literary and Historical Materials of Putian City*, vol. 7] (1991) pp. 122–128.

Zhonggong zhongyang dangshi yanjiushi diyi yanjiubu, eds., *Li Lisan bainian dancheng jinianji* [*Commemoration on the 100th Anniversary of Li Lisan's Birth: Collection of Writings*] (Beijing: Zhonggong zhongyang dangshi chubanshe, 1999).

"Zhongguo gongchandang diliuci daibiao dahui de jueyi an. Zhengzhi jueyian [The Resolutions of the 6th Congress of the CCP. Political Resolutions]" 9 July 1928, in *Zhonggong dangshi jiaoxue cankao ziliao (1)* [*CCP Teaching Materials*, vol. 1 (Beijing: Renmin chubanshe, 1978).

Zhongguo yu Nanyang. China and Malaysia [*Bulletin of Jinan University*] 1 (1918), in Meng Liqun, ed., *Nanyang shiliao xubian* [*Continuation of the Compilation of Nanyang Historical Materials*] (Beijing: Guojia tushuguan chubanshe, 2010).

Zhonghua renmin gongheguo minzheng bu, ed., *Zhonghua zhuming lieshi di ershisan juan* [*Famous Martyrs of China*, vol. 23] (Beijing: Zhongyang wenxian chubanshe, 2002).

Zhou Min and Rebecca Y. Kim, "Paradox of Ethnicization and Assimilation: The Development of Ethnic Organizations in the Chinese Immigrant Community in the United States," in Khun Eng Kuah-Pearce and Evelyn Hu-Dehart, eds., *Voluntary Organizations in the Chinese Diaspora: Illusions of Open Space in Hong Kong, Tokyo, and Shanghai* (Hong Kong: Hong Kong University Press, 2006).

Zhou Nanjing, *Shijie huaqiao huaren cidian* [*Dictionary of the Overseas Chinese*] (Beijing: Beijing daxue chubanshe, 1993).

Zhu Yihui, "Xu Tianbing," in *Hainan mingren zhuanlüe (xia)* [*Biographical Dictionary of Famous Hainanese (Second Part)*] (Guangzhou: Guangdong lüyou chubanshe, 1995).

Zumoff, Jacob A., *The Communist International and US Communism, 1919–1929* (Leiden; Boston, MA: Brill, 2014).

Index

Academic Research Association for the Study of National and Colonial Problems (NIANKP), 143
A-Fu, 37
Ai Wu, 51
Alien Registration Ordinance, 104–107, 160, 184, 201, 222
All-American Alliance of Chinese Anti-Imperialists, 33
All-American Anti-Imperialist League (AAIL), 19, 33, 44
All-China General Labor Union, 35, 127
Alliance for the Support of the Chinese Workers and Peasants Revolution in America (ASCWPRA), 33, 34
All-Nanyang Colonial Peoples Delegate Congress, 121
anarchism, 6
Annam Committee, 57
Anti-Enemy Backing-Up Society (AEBUS), 180, 187, 204, 215
Anti-Imperialist League (AIL), 34, 38, 64, 66, 87, 90
  in Malaya, 120, 128, 179
Anti-Imperialist League of the East, 119
Anti-Japanese Chinese Residents' Association, 198
Anti-Japanese resistance, 142, 193, 194, 196, 210, 214, 220, 222, 224, 231
Association of Chinese Migrant Workers (Philippines), 73
Association of Vietnamese Revolutionary Youth (Thanh Nien), 24
Australia, 13, 143
Austria, 7

Bandung Conference, 19
Bangkok, 92, 139
Bao Huiseng, 8, 32
Bassa. *See* Zhang Ranhe
Belia Malaya, 66
bin Hashim, Haji Mohamed, 63

bin Prawirodirdjo, Alimin (Alimin), 8, 30, 66, 79, 124, 141, 142
bin Sapi, Salleh, 63
bin Suile, Ahmed Baiki, 63
Bolshevik party, 4, 200, 210, 211, 218, 221
Bolshevization, 5, 12, 25, 83, 94, 128, 150, 218, 220
Borodin, Mikhail, 30
Britain, 22, 45, 48, 103, 143, 190, 204
Browder, Earl, 44
Buddhism, 26
Buddhist organizations, 6
Burma, 26, 52, 58, 121

Cai Mingshan, 179
Canada, 33, 34, 44
Catholic Church, 5, 84
Chen Chengzhi, 186
Chen Duxiu, 20, 30, 62
Chen Gongbo, 158
Chen Hongbin, 179
Chen Jiafei, 146
Chen Junju, 183
Chen Sanhua, 37
Chen Shaochang, 51
Chen Yannian, 30
Chi, C. T. *See* Ji Chaoding
Chile, 33
Chin Peng, 186, 224, 225
China, 120
  ethnic groups, 68
  Japanese occupation, 15, 38
  nationalism, 18
China Salvation Movement
  in Malaya, 185
  in the Philippines, 142
Chinese associations, 73, 85, 86, 89, 90, 93, 113, 141, 227
  non-Chinese members, 38
Chinese Avant-garde, 34
Chinese Communist Party (CCP)
  and the Comintern, 3

257

durian, 3, 15, 69, 230, 236
Dutch East Indies. *See* Indonesia

Eastern International, 159
Eighth Route Army, 3
Emat, 63
Engine, society, 115
Esperanto, 86, 179, 181
Evangelista, Crisanto, 84
extraterritoriality, 99

Federation of the Revolutionary
    Students, 175
France, 45
Freemasons, 5, 84
French Communist Party
    Union Intercoloniale African, 27
Fu Daqing, 30, 37, 51, 53, 123, 130
Fu Hung Chu, 126
Fu Naizhao, 180
Fujian Rebellion, 116

Gandhi, Mohandas Karamchand, 19
Gao Chenglie, 146
Gao Zinong, 73, 75, 76
General Federation of Seamen
    (Singapore), 125
George, Harrison, 84, 145
Germany, 21, 22, 24, 46
globalization, 47
Great Depression, 47, 50, 85, 97, 106
Guangzhou Uprising, 30
guerrilla warfare, 42
Guo Guang, 134
Guomindang (GMD)
    and Chinese overseas, 15, 40, 48, 68, 70,
        76, 89, 157, 159
    anti-colonialism, 46
    Asianism, 39
    break with the CCP, 33
    Central Committee, 4, 22, 23, 178
    educational policy, 26, 160
    in Canada, 33
    in Cuba, 33
    in Malacca, 178
    in Malaya, 99, 184, 217
    in Mexico, 33
    in Singapore, 99
    in Singapore and Malaya, 48, 104
    in the Philippines, 73
    in the USA, 33
    in Xianyou county, 180
    indigenization, 47, 62
    membership, 36
    nationalism, 78

Overseas Bureau, 35
Overseas Chinese Communist Division,
    26
    re-Sinicization policies, 32

Hainanese, 30, 36, 37, 51, 53, 87, 88, 118,
    120, 126, 129, 170, 174, 175,
    180, 199
Hamid, Abdul. *See* Emat
Han Guoxiang, 30
Hands-Off China Society, 21
Ho Chi Minh, 24, 27, 30, 51, 52–53, 62, 65,
    88, 95, 97, 130, 150
Hu Hanmin, 22, 24, 45, 99, 158
Huang Changwei, 168
Huang Ming, 179
Huang Muhan, 126, 128, 131
Huang Shijun, 116
Huang Wenhua, 186
huaqiao, 3, 4, 8, 28, 34, 45, 46, 47, 49, 68,
    69, 70, 71, 85
    in the Americas, 160
    localization of, 160
huiguan. *See* Chinese associations

India, 7, 28, 45, 61, 121, 123
    All-India Communist Party, 131
    revolution, 60
indigenization, 233
    and Bolshevization, 222
    and Chinese organizations, 38
    and communist networks, 62
    and interwar period, 26, 44
    and local conditions, 5, 109
    and Malayan Chinese Association
        (MCA), 229
    and revolution, 43
    and the Comintern, 39
Indochina, 25, 26, 28, 29, 36, 45, 52,
    120, 123
Indo-Chinese Asian Solidarity Society, 19
Indochinese Communist Party (ICP), 52
Indonesia, 3, 6, 14, 28, 37, 45, 52, 58, 63,
    66, 67, 84, 117, 120, 123
    Chinese communists, 177
    Chinese organizations, 110
    nationalism, 20, 79, 80
    pergerakan, 5
Indonesia Raya, 79
intellectuals, 3, 5, 12–14, 47, 51, 65, 69, 70,
    83, 88, 93, 96, 100, 110, 120, 150,
    151, 161, 165, 169, 170, 176
intelligentsia. *See* intellectuals
International Congress of Oppressed
    Peoples, 33

pan-Asianism (cont.)
  Datong, 19, 20
  Great State of the East, 21
  Tianxia, 19
pan-Islamism, 49, 153
pan-Malaysian movement, 145
Pan-Pacific Trade Union, 36, 43
Pang Qinchang, 51
Partai Komunis Indonesia (PKI), 5, 20, 30,
    66, 80
  and Chinese, 112
Partai Nasional Indonesia, 80
Penang, 172
Peng Zemin, 35
Perserikatan Tionghwa Indonesia, 80
Peru, 33
Philippine Revolution, 18, 75, 79, 84
Philippine University, 32, 74
Philippines, 3, 5, 14, 18, 21, 28, 32, 33, 52,
    72, 78, 79, 84
  Chinese immigration, 73, 75, 76
  Chinese mestizos, 18, 75, 76
  Filipinos, 76
  nationalism, 72, 74, 77
Profintern, 42, 117, 120, 123, 133
Proletarian Arts Union, 109
Protestant missions, 6

Qing dynasty, 25
  ethnic groups, 58
  re-Sinicization, 18, 68

Red Aid organization, 90, 98
Rizal, Jose, 75
rubber, 106, 107
Rudnik, Iakov, 128, 131, 134
Ryl'skii, Ignatii, 123

Save the Emperor Society, 19
Selangor, 172
self-criticism, 90, 102, 150, 151
Senghor, Lamine, 27
Shanghai Municipal Police (SMP), 15
Shanghai Student Federation, 35
Shi Huang, 33, 44
Shieng Kien Chu, 126
Siam, 3, 26, 28, 29, 36, 37, 52, 58, 120, 124
Siam Committee, 57
Siam Communist Party (SCP), 140
Singapore
  and the Comintern, 28, 29, 62
  Chinese immigration, 30
  Indian immigration, 29
Siregar, Amir Hamzah, 68
Siregar, Djoeliman, 68

Sneevliet, Hendricus, 8, 20, 27, 28
Song Zhuoming, 134
South Africa
  Boer Wars, 18
Southeast Asia
  Chinese immigration, 17, 48
Soviet Russia, 27
Soviet Union, 21, 60
  Komsomol, 16
  Oktiabriata, 16
  People's Commissariat for Internal
    Affairs (NKVD), 16
Stalin, Joseph, 23
Straits Chinese British Association, 69
Straits Times, 38
strike, 38, 97, 102, 103, 126, 129, 135, 180,
    192, 205, 207
student protests, 109, 161–162, 167,
    174, 175
Students' Society for the Advancement of
    Sun Yatsenism in America, 33
Sukarno, 80
Sultan Idris Training College, 66
Sumatra, 29, 36, 37, 63, 66, 79
Sun Yatsen, 3, 4, 8, 21, 25, 28, 32, 39, 46,
    54, 58, 78, 87, 110, 112
  Asianism, 113
  internationalism, 19
  nationalism, 20

Taiwan, 120
Taiwanese Communist Party, 41, 119,
    128
Tan Cheng Lock, 68, 103
  Malayanization, 107
Tan Kah Kee, 167
Tan Malaka, 8, 27–30, 44, 45, 66, 79
Tan Sin Hoa, 137
teachers, 35, 66, 69, 70, 86, 88, 176, 177
teachers' colleges, 160
Teo Yuanfu. *See* Zhang Ranhe
Thailand. *See* Siam
Three Star Party, 220
Tiandihui, 85
tin, 106, 107
Toiling Children Corps, 109
Tongmenghui, 35
Toynbee, Arnold, 49
Tran How Thanh, 140
translation slippage, 9, 10, 53, 56, 77
Treaty of Versailles, 21, 23

Un Hong Siu, 34, 164
Union of the Oppressed Peoples of the
    East, 24